SUGAR AND THE INDIAN OCEAN WORLD

SUGAR AND THE INDIAN OCEAN WORLD

Trade and Consumption in the Eighteenth-Century Persian Gulf

Norifumi Daito

BLOOMSBURY ACADEMIC
LONDON • NEW YORK • OXFORD • NEW DELHI • SYDNEY

BLOOMSBURY ACADEMIC

Bloomsbury Publishing Plc, 50 Bedford Square, London, WC1B 3DP, UK
Bloomsbury Publishing Inc, 1359 Broadway, New York, NY 10018, USA
Bloomsbury Publishing Ireland, 29 Earlsfort Terrace, Dublin 2, D02 AY28, Ireland

BLOOMSBURY, BLOOMSBURY ACADEMIC and the Diana logo
are trademarks of Bloomsbury Publishing Plc

First published in Great Britain 2024
This paperback edition published 2026

Copyright © Norifumi Daito, 2024

Norifumi Daito has asserted his right under the Copyright,
Designs and Patents Act, 1988, to be identified as Author of this work.

For legal purposes the Acknowledgements on pp. xii–xiii constitute an
extension of this copyright page.

Cover image © 'The Dutch Ambassador (Joan Cunaeus) on his Way to Isfahan.'
Oil on canvas painting by Jan Baptist Weenix (1621–1660), c. 1653–1659.
CPA Media Pte Ltd via Alamy Stock Photo

All rights reserved. No part of this publication may be: i) reproduced or transmitted in
any form, electronic or mechanical, including photocopying, recording or by means of
any information storage or retrieval system without prior permission in writing from the
publishers; or ii) used or reproduced in any way for the training, development or operation
of artificial intelligence (AI) technologies, including generative AI technologies. The rights
holders expressly reserve this publication from the text and data mining exception as per
Article 4(3) of the Digital Single Market Directive (EU) 2019/790.

Bloomsbury Publishing Plc does not have any control over, or responsibility for,
any third-party websites referred to or in this book. All internet addresses given
in this book were correct at the time of going to press. The author and publisher
regret any inconvenience caused if addresses have changed or sites have ceased
to exist, but can accept no responsibility for any such changes.

A catalogue record for this book is available from the British Library.

A catalog record for this book is available for the Library of Congress.

ISBN: HB: 978-1-3503-9921-1
        PB: 978-1-3503-9924-2
        ePDF: 978-1-3503-9922-8
        eBook: 978-1-3503-9923-5

Typeset by Integra Software Services Pvt. Ltd.

For product safety related questions contact productsafety@bloomsbury.com.

To find out more about our authors and books visit www.bloomsbury.com
and sign up for our newsletters.

To my parents and sister

CONTENTS

List of Images	viii
List of Maps	ix
List of Charts	x
Author's Notes	xi
Acknowledgements	xii
INTRODUCTION	1
Chapter 1 SUGAR CONSUMPTION AND THE SUGAR MARKET	17
Chapter 2 ENDURING DEMAND	35
Chapter 3 SUGAR TRADE IN THE PERSIAN GULF: THE VOC	53
Chapter 4 SUGAR TRADE IN THE PERSIAN GULF: THE VOC'S COMPETITORS	69
Chapter 5 ALTERNATIVE SUGAR HUBS: BASRA, BUSHIRE AND KHARG	91
Chapter 6 COMPANY BROKERS	111
Chapter 7 PERSISTENCE OF THE COMMERCIAL MIDDLE GROUND	129
CONCLUSION	149
Notes	152
Bibliography	197
Appendices	210
Index	222

IMAGES

1 Jan Huygen van Linschoten's map of the Indian Ocean   xiv
2 Painting of a Persian banquet   xv
3 Cornelis de Bruyn's painting of a Banian man in Safavid Iran   xv

MAPS

1 Map of the Indian Ocean world   xvi
2 Map of the Persian Gulf and the surrounding world   xvii

CHARTS

2.1	Sugar prices at the Isfahan market, 1737–41	38
2.2	French sugar imports to the Levant, 1750–4 and 1786–9	42
2.3	British sugar imports to Russia, 1764–99	45
3.1	Dutch export of Bengali sugar to Iran	54
3.2	Dutch import of Javanese sugar to Bandar Abbas, 1701–56	55
3.3	Net profits from sugar at Bandar Abbas, 1701–56	56
3.4	Comparative sale value between the two phases 1701–20 and 1721–56	56
3.5	Dutch import of Javanese sugar to Bushire, 1737–48	58
3.6	Dutch import of Javanese sugar to Basra, 1723–51	59
3.7	Sales of castor sugar at Bandar Abbas, Basra, Bushire and Bandar Rig, 1723–52	60
3.8	Sales of candy sugar at Bandar Abbas, Basra, Bushire and Bandar Rig, 1723–52	60
3.9	Five-year average annual imports of castor sugar to Bandar Abbas and Basra, 1723–51	61
3.10	Five-year average annual imports of candy sugar to Bandar Abbas and Basra, 1723–51	61
3.11	Five-year average annual import of castor sugar to the Persian Gulf, 1701–64	62
3.12	Five-year average annual import of candy sugar to the Persian Gulf, 1701–64	63
3.13	Dutch import of Javanese sugar to Kharg Island, 1753–64	65
4.1	Non-VOC sugar suppliers to Bandar Abbas, 1694–1715	72
4.2	Registrations of arrivals at Bandar Abbas, 1694–1715	72
4.3	Origins of English arrivals at Bandar Abbas, 1694–1715	73
4.4	Origins of Muslim arrivals at Bandar Abbas, 1694–1715	74

AUTHOR'S NOTES

Transliteration

The Arabic and Persian transliteration used in this book follows the transliteration system of the third edition of the *Encyclopaedia of Islam*, but without the use of diacritic marks. English spellings of non-Roman place names, such as Bahrain, Basra, Bushire, Bandar Abbas, Kuwait or Muscat, are retained in that form. The spellings of the names of local ruling elites and merchants that appear in the accounts of European observers are not always possible to decipher. These are left in their original spelling and indicated with quotation marks.

Iranian currency

1 *tuman* (unit of account, i.e. ghost coin) = 50 *'abbasi*s
 = 100 *mahmudi*s
 = 200 *shahi*s

ACKNOWLEDGEMENTS

I started this study as an MA student more than a decade ago and have accumulated debts to a wide range of scholars, colleagues and friends. My first debt of gratitude is to my MA supervisor, Hiroyuki Mashita, at Kobe University. His exciting lecture on early modern South Asian history inspired me to explore the vast archives of the Dutch East India Company to conduct a broader study of early modern West Asian history. I also owe special thanks to Yasushi Ogata and Takao Ito, who encouraged me to pursue research in the Netherlands.

Most of the work on this project was completed at the History Department at Leiden University. First and foremost, I would like to thank Jos Gommans, my wonderful PhD supervisor. He welcomed me to the remarkable research centre in 2010 and, two years later, to his stimulating global history research programme, Cosmopolis. It was a great pleasure to work with Jos. He guided my intellectual development by sharing his insights and perspectives. I also owe many thanks to Leonard Blussé, who gave me much support. To Alicia Schrikker, Carolien Stolte and Esther Zwinkels who showed me unfailing hospitality, I owe more than I can say. I also thank Gabrielle van den Berg for her critical but positive comments on my paper at a Cosmopolis workshop in 2015, which was exactly what I needed to develop my study. My sincere gratitude goes to René Wezel, Hugo s'Jacob, Ton Harmsen and Paula Koning, who helped me decipher thousands of complex Dutch texts. Needless to say, any remaining errors are solely my own.

I would also like to express my gratitude to the helpful staff of various archives and libraries that I have visited over the years. These include the Leiden University Libraries, Koninklijke Bibliotheek and Nationaal Archief in The Hague, and the British Library in London.

After I finished my PhD in 2017, many people helped me to carry on this project. Among them I must mention Atsushi Ota, Ghulam Nadri, Miriam Frenkel, Ryuto Shimada, Hiroyuki Mashita, Kazuhiko Tabata, Ikuko Wada, Kazuhiro Shimizu, Hiroyuki Ogasawara, Yukako Goto, Masumi Isogai and Nobuaki Kondo. This would not have happened, however, were it not for generous support from Fuyuko Matsukata, a brilliant historian with a great enterprising spirit. In 2019 she welcomed me to her cutting-edge European inter-archival research project, 'Monsoon Project', at the Historiographical Institute at the University of Tokyo, where I am currently working. Since then she has given me opportunities to speak about my research on various international platforms that she created to support and connect researchers across the world. The feedback I received from professors and students has improved this manuscript enormously. Special thanks to Katsutoshi Kure, Yutaka Horii, Takako Morinaga, Makoto Okamoto, Miki Sakuraba and Ainura Suinova for their insightful comments.

I would like to thank Directors Toru Hoya and Keiko Hongo at the Historiographical Institute, who extended a helping hand whenever I needed it. I feel privileged to have worked with Yoko Matsui, a prominent scholar of early modern Japan–Netherlands relations, before she retired in 2023. Due to her in-depth knowledge of the Dutch East India Company records on Nagasaki, every conversation was a source of inspiration. I am also indebted to Mihoko Oka for her advice and encouragement. In 2022 I was honoured to host Lennart Bes (Leiden University), a stellar archivist and historian of the Dutch East India Company, in Tokyo while I was revising the manuscript. His help was crucial. I am also thankful to Isabel Tanaka-van Daalen for her steadfast support.

I owe debts to Peter Good, who invited me to present this work at the Centre for Medieval and Early Modern Studies at the University of Kent in November 2021; to Anne Gerritsen and Guido van Meersbergen, who arranged for me to give a paper at the Global History and Culture Centre at the University of Warwick in December that same year. I am particularly grateful to Martha Chaiklin, who read key chapters of the manuscript at various times and gave detailed criticisms and suggestions. I have not been able to deal sufficiently with all of their commentary, but their support has broadened my mind and improved the text more than they will probably notice.

Writing and publishing a book is a tough task for scholars, and even more so when you are writing in a foreign language. Hence, I feel blessed to have met Christopher Gerteis, Academic Editor at Institute for Advanced Studies on Asia at the University of Tokyo, in 2020. This project would not have come to fruition without his guidance and support. I also thank Stephen Vlastos for his useful advice. I am deeply grateful to Rebekah Zwanzig, who edited the entire manuscript with amazing skill and clarity. Keiko Kogi prepared the beautiful maps. I thank her warmly. I owe special thanks to two editors at Bloomsbury Publishing, Maddie Holder and Megan Harris, for their expertise and generous support.

Financial support for this study came from Strategic Young Researcher Overseas Visits Program Scholarship (Graduate School of Humanities, Kobe University), Cosmopolis Programme Encompass Scholarship, Student Exchange Support Program (Japan Student Services Organization), Monsoon Project I and II (Joint Usage/Research Center, the Historiographical Institute), Global Activity Support Program for Young Researchers (University of Tokyo), Open Research (A) 'Comparative Study of VOC's "*Hofreis*": Japan, Malabar and Persia' and Open Research (B) 'The Indian Ocean, 1600–1800' (Humanities Center, the University of Tokyo), KAKENHI Grant Numbers JP20K22012, JP21H04355 (Japan Society for the Promotion of Science), and General Research Grant 'Toward a Global History of Inter-State Relations' (Kajima Foundation).

Throughout this project, I was fortunate enough to have the support of numerous colleagues and friends. They have offered me all kinds of help to pursue my research. My special thanks to Murari Kumar Jha, Manjusha Kuruppath, Xiaodong Xu, Sanne Ravensbergen, Ariel Lopez, Pimmanus Wibulsilp, Pojanut Suthipinittharm, Yedda Palemeq, Kate Ekama, Michael Karabinos, Archisman Chaudhuri, Byapti Sur, Mahmood Kooria, Yulianti, Ligia Giay, Neilabh Sinha, Guanmian Xu, Mervyn Richardson, Joshua Batts, Travis Seifman and Aki Tomita.

Image 1 Jan Huygen van Linschoten's map of the Indian Ocean (Alamy).

Image 2 Painting of a Persian banquet (Alamy).

Image 3 Cornelis de Bruyn's painting of a Banian man in Safavid Iran (left).

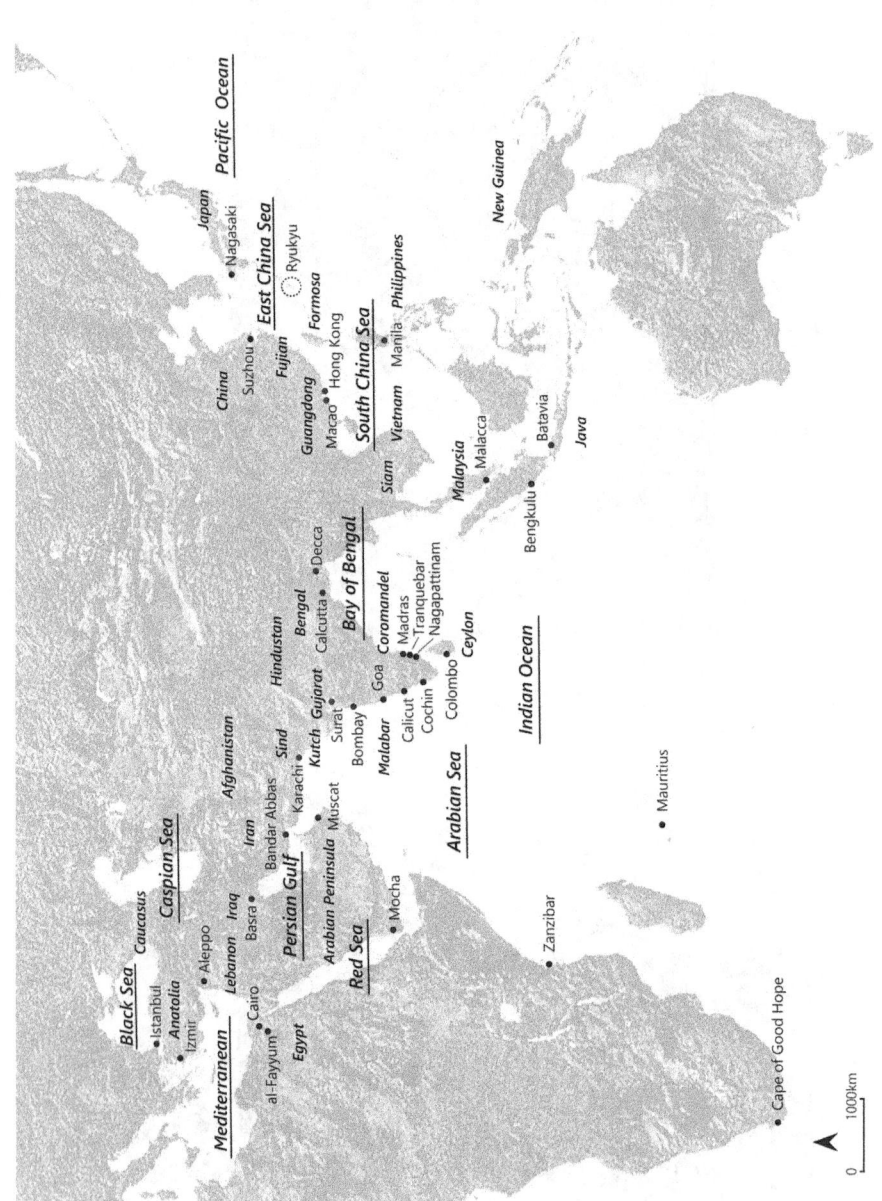

Map 1 Map of the Indian Ocean world.

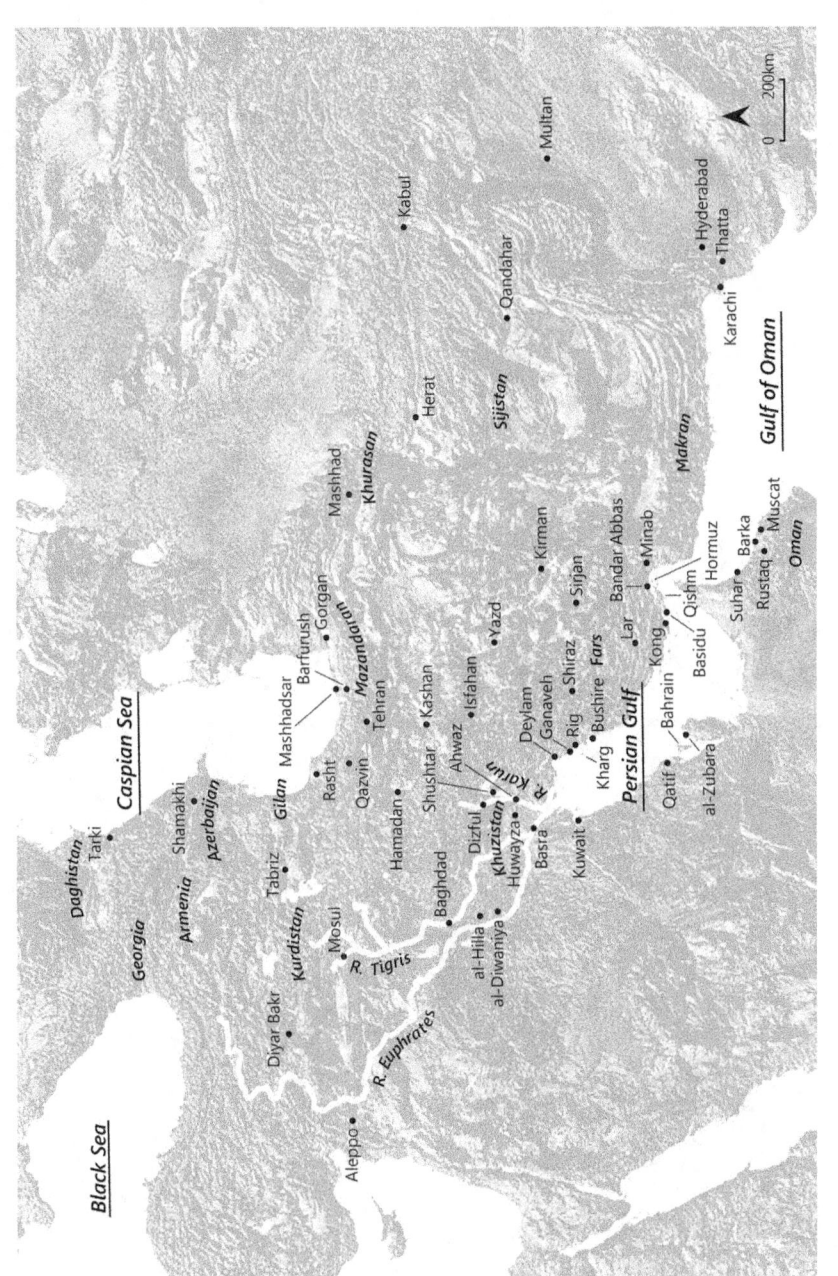

Map 2 Map of the Persian Gulf and the surrounding world.

INTRODUCTION

Iran was a place of wonders for Jean Chardin, a French Huguenot jeweller who visited the country twice between 1655 and 1677, when it was ruled by the Safavid dynasty (1501–1722). Although mesmerized by the exoticism of the region – climate, flora and fauna, minerals, ways of life, science, art, etc. – a certain sense of familiarity arose when he encountered the country's abundant use of cane sugar. It was reminiscent of Europe, where sugar produced in the Caribbean had increased in the market. But Chardin's excitement about his 'discovery' of sugar overshadowed his curiosity. He did not question the Iranian population's lavish consumption of sugar. Nor did he speculate about why the market was currently expanding. Instead, he narrowly focused on whether sugar was originally from the New World. As for sugar, Chardin wrote, there was always some in the East Indies (*Indes*). Even though most authors claimed that sugar was a product of the New World and the Old World used nothing but honey, sugar grew throughout the East Indies easily and in abundance and was not like products brought from remote countries, which never grew well once they were transplanted far from their own soil.[1]

Over the decades, historians have paid much attention to sugar's significant roles in not only changing people's eating habits but also creating types of work that were suited for the Industrial Revolution. Since S. Mintz's pioneering study of the modern history of sugar, *Sweetness and Power* (1985), scholars have tried to portray the dynamic relationship between sugar production and consumption as a prelude to the modern industrial West.[2] Not surprisingly, the majority of scholarship has focused on Europe and its expanding economy across the Atlantic Ocean. However, not only does this narrow focus obscure the important fact that sugar has circulated all over the world for the last four centuries, but it also causes a serious fragmentation and oversimplification of our understanding of the history of its global circulation. This book fills this gap by focusing on the eighteenth-century sugar trade and consumption in the Persian Gulf, a neglected but compelling stage within the history of sugar. Existing historiography of the region still stresses eighteenth-century imperial and economic decline, but I argue that the vitality of the Gulf trade endured, and demonstrate this by illuminating the remarkable developments and changes in the relationship between trade and consumption that occurred in the Indian Ocean.

Nearly four centuries after Chardin's visits, the question of why sugar was so popular in Iran still remains unanswered. What is puzzling is that despite its relatively sparse population, Iran became a major sugar-importing region in the Indian Ocean during the late Safavid period. Prior to this period, Iran had imported sugar from India across land and sea, but in the seventeenth century it began to import substantial quantities from various countries through the Persian Gulf. Iran's population in the early to mid-seventeenth century – the height of the Safavid dynasty – was no more than seven or eight million people, while India boasted between sixty and one hundred million inhabitants during this time, and at the turn of the seventeenth century, there were thirty to thirty-five million in the Ottoman realm. Safavid Iran was an impressive hub for most commodities passing between South and South-East Asia and west Europe. Nevertheless, hardly any of the sugar imported via the Persian Gulf was re-exported. It was destined for major cities in Iran, the Safavid capital of Isfahan in particular.[3]

When discussing trade and the consumption of commodities in the Indian Ocean, the renowned economic historian K.N. Chaudhuri proposed the theory of 'state capitalism'. He argued that the crucial driving force behind the early modern maritime economy was the 'Asian state'. Before the nineteenth-century European technological revolution, he believed that, in the Indian Ocean, the 'Asian state' was 'the single largest financial enterprise with its income and expenditure forming a significant proportion of total production and consumption'.[4]

This concept is applicable to the sugar trade and consumption in Safavid Iran. Muhammad Muhsin, an eyewitness to the last days of the dynasty, blamed the degeneration of the state on the indulgence of the final monarch, Sultan Husayn (r. 1694–1722), and his consumption of food and medicine in his secluded harem, to the degree that it provoked the Afghan conquest in 1722.[5] This claim has been echoed in modern literature on the Safavids.[6] For Marxist historians, the court's penchant for spending was a symptom of the undeveloped state of 'modern capitalism' within the country.[7] In recent decades, scholars have increasingly paid attention to Iran's material culture vis-à-vis its religious and spiritual culture.[8] Some have pointed to the significant development of social life in Safavid Iran, especially in court circles, as being behind the high demand for sugar in the late Safavid period. R. Matthee argues that, on special occasions, honourable receptions for example, specific items, such as skilfully prepared sweetmeats, coffee and the *qalyan* (water pipe), became a social norm.[9] In the same vein, A. Hosseini states that *sharbat* (sherbet, or sugar and fruit water) had a prominent place in the capital's social life.[10] Similarly, T. Morikawa argues that sugar, traditionally a 'medicine', became an indispensable 'condiment' for royal cuisine, surpassing the popularity of indigenous honey.[11]

The situation in the nineteenth century also supports Chaudhuri's hypothesis about the expansion of Western industrial capitalism. While Asian sugar was imported through the Persian Gulf, there was a remarkable rise in supplies of American sugar, which was refined in industrialized European refineries, for markets in northern Iran via the Black Sea. There, sugar from France (especially Marseilles), Great Britain and the Netherlands rivalled for a market share.

Particularly in the latter half of the century, sugar imports increased, and it became readily available to consumers. From the 1860s, French sugar was at the fore in the northern market, but in 1880, cheap beet sugar from Russia started pouring in. Sugar was estimated to represent 24 per cent of total imports in 1910. Coupled with tea drinking, which became popular across Iranian society, sugar became an integral part of the nation's modern diet.[12]

However, the critical question – What was the relationship between the sugar supply and the consumption of sugar in the period from the collapse of the Safavid dynasty to 1800? – remains unanswered. The Afghan conquest triggered serious political disarray that lasted until the establishment of the Qajar dynasty (1796–1925).[13] Although the occasional rise of powerful warlords, including Nadir Shah Afshar (r. 1736–47), Karim Khan Zand (r. 1751–79) and Ahmad Shah Durrani (r. 1747–72), allowed some respite in parts of the country, repeated hostilities forced inhabitants to endure continuous turmoil.[14] So if Chaudhuri's theory of 'state capitalism' is true, there should be a serious decline, if not a rupture, in the relationship between supply and consumption. The prevailing concern in recent literature on the eighteenth-century Gulf is to elucidate how political turmoil severely hindered maritime trade. W. Floor underscores the fact that the Gulf economy depended on the strength of the political entities involved. He argues that the relatively stable rule of the Safavids facilitated Gulf trade by providing security and infrastructure that allowed merchants and commodities to flow smoothly. The disappearance of efficient regional powers after the eclipse of the dynasty, therefore, dealt a crucial blow to trade. This instability led to the decline of Gulf trade.[15] Floor's argument coincides with the traditional view of eighteenth-century Indian Ocean trade: from the early eighteenth century, the Persian Gulf economy, which had until then been an important part of Indian Ocean trade, faced a decline due to political uncertainty and lost considerable trade to Bengal and then China, facilitating an eastward shift in maritime trade. English traders then amassed assets that enabled them to develop imperial interests across the ocean.[16]

Going back to the start

A careful reading of earlier Persian Gulf studies presents a rather contradictory picture. There is a general consensus that during the eighteenth century, numerous ports and regions of the Gulf formed a strikingly resilient regional market for goods travelling to and from countries along the Indian Ocean rim. Since these studies have received inadequate attention, a proper review is due.

Traditionally, the eighteenth century is regarded as a prelude to Britain's predominance in Gulf affairs. After the decline of the Safavid dynasty, increased insecurity permitted the East India Company (EIC), which had survived thanks to the powerful Bombay Marine, to elevate their presence in the Gulf market, thus paving the way for their firm control of the regional economy and politics from the nineteenth century onward.[17] A. Hakima's *History of Eastern Arabia*

(1965) changed this picture. Casting a critical eye on the literature focused on the European companies, he illuminates the rise of maritime Arabs, particularly the 'Utub in Kuwait and Bahrain, in the latter half of the eighteenth century. The increase of 'Utub involvement in commercial shipping and caravan traffic, he argues, allowed Kuwait to developed into a prominent outlet for Indian goods bound for Baghdad, the inner parts of the Arabian Peninsula, Aleppo and Constantinople.[18] Almost a decade later T. Ricks furthered this argument. In an analysis of the eighteenth-century activities of local notables and traders in southern Iran, he revealed that anarchy and chaos were limited to competition for socio-political domination within a group or class of late-Safavid elites. The establishment of the Zand dynasty in Shiraz (1765–94), he argues, restored order in Iran, and the focus of the Gulf trade shifted from south to north. Consequently, Bandar Abbas, the largest market during the Safavid period, went into decline, and Bushire, the outer harbour of Shiraz, developed into a principal centre of trade. He argues that it was not until the turn of the nineteenth century that trade routes with Iran shifted away from the Gulf. Then trade moved further north towards Khurasan and the Caspian regions, where the Qajars, a Turkish clan, established their power base.[19]

In the 1980s, when the Indian Ocean began to draw scholarly attention, A. Das Gupta provided a useful overview of eighteenth-century Indian Ocean trade, including an analysis of the contributions of Hakima and Ricks. He succinctly showed that, although Gulf trade suffered intermittent upheavals after the Safavids, when pressured, it moved to the Upper Gulf. He also showed that the rise of the maritime Arabs of Kuwait and Bahrain improved the situation in the north-western Indian Ocean to some extent.[20] A number of scholars dealing with different areas of the Gulf have corroborated his theories, revealing the remarkable flexibility of the commercial networks of local and regional rulers and merchants in generating alternative trading routes and secondary markets.

S. Grummon scrutinizes the rise of Bushire under the rule of an Arab family, the Madhkurs in the second half of the eighteenth century. He points out that the Madhkurs successfully established effective cooperation with the Zands, a hinterland power: the Madhkurs used their naval power to support the Zands' maritime interests, and the Zands protected the hinterland for the Madhkurs. He claims that as a result, Bushire became a significant 'port-of-call', competing with Bandar Abbas, Basra and Muscat.[21] T. Abdullah reveals that the decline of Bandar Abbas also allowed Basra to become a leading commercial port in the Gulf. From the early 1720s to the mid-1770s, Basra trade developed substantially and began to deal with a wide range of Gulf and foreign actors, such as India, the Red Sea region, southern Iran, Iraq and the Middle East. In the middle of the century, the *Mamluks* in Ottoman Iraq, originally Christian slaves recruited from the Caucasus, founded their own regime in Baghdad. The *Mamluk* rulers encouraged trade, especially towards Baghdad. Although trade at Bandar Abbas remained considerable during the first half of the century, he notes that Bushire rose and competed with Basra, taking larger shares of the Indian trade.[22]

H. Fattah uses the concept of 'free ports' to describe the mid-eighteenth-century emergence of al-Zubara, Kuwait and Bahrain under the control of 'Utub tribesmen. Unlike the Ottoman port of Basra, these ports permitted regional merchants to trade their goods without paying customs tariffs. Thus, they facilitated the transit of trade from Arabia to India, as well as regional trade connecting market towns in the Arabian Peninsula, southern Iraq and Arabistan.[23] Situated in the Gulf of Oman – at the intersection between the Persian Gulf and the Indian Ocean – Muscat formed an integral part of eighteenth-century Gulf trade and shipping. P. Risso deals with the significant growth of Muscat's commerce under the Bu Sa'id dynasty (1749–) in the latter half of the eighteenth century. She ascribes the port's success to three factors: dominating transit trade in Mocha coffee to Basra, the increase of trade with the western coast of India (particularly Javanese sugar to the Dutch settlement of Cochin), and the decline of Bandar Abbas and Basra.[24]

Since the 1990s, Gulf trade has received renewed attention from scholars investigating Eurasia's early modern land commerce.[25] According to many of them, the trans-continental routes and Persian Gulf sea-lanes had a complex relationship. J. Gommans suggests that the eighteenth-century reorganization of Gulf trade coincided with that of Eurasian land trade. Analysing the overland trade routes through Afghanistan under the Durrani dynasty (1747–1973), he claims that, while Gulf trade relocated from the Iranian littoral to the Arabian coast and Basra, caravan trade invigorated the economic centres of India, Iran and Central Asia. On the other hand, the Durrani control of Baluchistan, Makran and Sind created a new link between the Iranian and Central Asian hinterland and the Persian Gulf; many of these regions' outer harbours could easily access Muscat.[26] In *Arabian Seas*, R. Barendse comes into line with this view. He asserts that the Gulf declined as a market for Iran-bound goods when caravan traffic from India to Iran via Afghanistan replaced much of the old maritime trade, but the Gulf continued to play a role as a route connecting the economies of the Mediterranean and South Asia. Therefore, what happened in the Gulf during the eighteenth century was not an overall decline but a shift, and the Gulf was prone to political crises because the financial rewards were enormous.[27]

In sum, these views concur that the idea of an overall catastrophe in the eighteenth century does not carry great weight. Rather this conception of the region bears a noticeable resemblance to the recent reinterpretation of the relationship between merchant and state in eighteenth-century India. That is to say, the fragmentation of the Mughal Empire (1526–1858) seldomly atrophied capital, as was formerly believed. On the contrary, the increased tenacity of merchants, adjusting to political uncertainties, stimulated further commercialization of the so-called successor states.[28]

It appears that during the eighteenth century, sugar trade in the Gulf maintained a considerable level of intensity while also shifting course. In the seventeenth century, Iran imported sugar from China, Taiwan, Oman and Java, as well as from north and west India and Bengal. By 1700, its market became home for Javanese sugar under the management of the Dutch East India Company (*Verenigde Oostindische*

Compagnie [VOC]). The VOC was presumably the single largest supplier of sugar in the late Safavid period. After the fall of the Safavids, however, sales of Javanese sugar dropped sharply. Although the Company tried to maintain business in the rising markets of Basra, Bushire and Kharg Island, their trade did not reach its previous levels, which resulted in their final withdrawal from the Gulf in 1766.[29]

While Floor thinks the downfall of the Company signified a substantial decrease in the population's purchasing power, it is important to note that other suppliers continued to import sugar.[30] After the Afghan conquest, the focus of English private traders, the VOC's biggest competitors, shifted from Bandar Abbas to Basra, and their shipping from Calcutta brought commodities, including sugar, to Basra.[31] In the course of the ensuing century, Omani merchants became very active in the sugar trade. Omani vessels exported Gulf products such as dates and sulphur to Dutch Cochin, and in return they imported Javanese sugar, spices and Malabar pepper. At the turn of the nineteenth century, the Arabs turned their eyes to eastern Indian ports. They sailed to Calcutta to buy cheaper silk and sugar. The Bu Saʿid sultan even sent ships to Batavia annually in order to acquire Javanese sugar and spices at more competitive prices.[32] Floor admits this, pointing out that the VOC permitted Dutch private traders to send the Company's sugar to Muscat between 1777 and 1793.[33]

Sugar trade in the Persian Gulf continued well into the nineteenth century. In the early part of the century, sugar from India filled the Iranian market, although this might have included Javanese sugar the Dutch sold in British-controlled Bombay and Surat. In 1805, goods worth 3.1 million sicca rupees were imported to the Gulf from India; sugar represented 12 per cent. After the Dutch East Indies resumed direct commercial voyages to the Gulf in 1824, Javanese sugar once again edged into markets in southern Iran, while now vying with other varieties from Bengal, Mauritius and Siam.[34]

Sugar and modernity

What made demand for sugar persist during the political instability following the fall of the Safavids, when social life must have been severely diminished? Why did Safavid Iran become a major sugar-importing country? These questions offer us a chance to take a comparative approach to look at Iran. Over the years, many scholars have worked on the question of why particular societies became immensely fond of sugar and regularly consumed it. Mintz opened the debate with his groundbreaking question: 'What really is demand?'

Regarding the phenomenal development of the sugar market in England from the middle of the seventeenth century, Mintz, like many other scholars of the history of consumption, gives consumer preference its due.[35] But he also stresses the important contributions of mercantile and bureaucratic agencies – planters, bankers, slavers, shippers, refiners, grocers and bureaucrats – within the development of the relationship between sugar production and consumption across the Atlantic Ocean. In order to gain more economic and fiscal rewards, he argues, these groups targeted the unexploited potential markets of the lower classes. Through lobbying, they successfully instituted many policies that increased the availability of sugar, molasses and rum in the country, thus bringing the proletariat into the marketplace. According to Mintz, consumers' freedom of choice was therefore 'freedom only within a range of possibilities laid down by forces over which those who were, supposedly, freely choosing exercised no control at all'. Thus, he thinks that in Great Britain, cane sugar, which previously had been enjoyed by a privileged minority, became quite common around 1650, and it found its way into the diet of every working household by 1900.[36]

The picture that Mintz portrays – the evolution of a system of industrial capitalism across the Atlantic Ocean that would allegedly spread throughout the rest of the world – has since offered a useful framework for historians writing about the history of sugar.[37] His grand narrative has been supported by E. Wallerstein's prominent theory about modern world-systems.[38] However, it has also opened up debates about how the substantial growth of the sugar market came about. J. de Vries conceives the change of consumer behaviour in the households of England and the Low Countries in the seventeenth century as behind the expansion of the market. Proposing an 'industrious revolution', he argues that, over the course of the century, households in north-west Europe became eager to acquire more manufactured goods and luxuries, including sugar, coffee and tea, so they worked longer to earn more wages. Thus, the 'industrious revolution' preceded the Industrial Revolution.[39] Instead of crediting north-west Europe for this change, E. Stols has suggested a long-term much earlier expansion of the sugar market in west Europe. While analysing the spread of sugar preserves and the scope of sugar trade and refining, he points out that sugar was already commonplace in cities throughout Portugal, Spain, Italy, France, Flanders and the Netherlands around the mid-sixteenth century, possibly even earlier. He ascribes mass consumption to 'a marked urbanization and modernization' of European society between 1500 and 1650 rather than the depression of prices from the mid-seventeenth century.[40] Important works by scholars such as Maxine Berg have further explored the boundaries of European consumer demand, arguing that Europeans' tastes and their relentless pursuit of Asian luxury goods in the early modern period were crucial driving forces behind the development of a global economy.[41]

In contrast to this somewhat Eurocentric inquiry into the 'demand' for sugar, other scholars have called attention to the parallel development of sugar markets in China and Japan.[42] This review of the scholarship has shown that sugar consumption in East Asia developed over a long period of time, and this facilitated comparable regional modernization and industrialization.

Opinions vary regarding the origin of the cultivation of sugarcane, but it is likely that started in New Guinea and then spread to Indonesia, Malaysia, India and south China over time. A primitive method for transforming the cane (*Saccharum officinarum*) into sugar crystals appeared in north India sometime after the first century CE.[43] And sugarcane technology travelled both eastwards and westwards. Towards the east it is thought to have been introduced into Tang China (618–907), and during the Song (960–1279) and Yuan dynasties (1271–1368), vibrant urban consumption sparked the commercial production of sugar (from *Saccharum officinarum* or another plant variety, *Saccharum sinense*) in the southern provinces of China, such as Zhejiang, Fujian, Guangdong and Jiangxi, and in the interior province of Sichuan. In his analysis of the traditional Chinese sugar industry, C. Daniels has shown that during the Ming period (1368–1644), agricultural methods, as well as sugarcane crushing, clarification and claying techniques, profoundly improved in Fujian, the leading producer, and new technologies spread to Guangdong and other neighbouring provinces from the late sixteenth century through the steady migration of entrepreneurs, artisans and peasants from Fujian. Expertly refined sugar attained wide popularity and invigorated trans-regional coastal trade between north and south China, as well as inland commercial traffic along the mid- and upper reaches of the Yangzi River. Sugar production mastery spread overseas to countries in East and South-East Asia, including Taiwan, the Philippines, Vietnam, Java and Siam, and the Chinese home market received supplies from many of these overseas sugar colonies. Learning of the Chinese innovations in the sugar industry and its economic potential, the ruling elite in Ryukyu and Japan also strove to bring advanced sugarcane cultivation and sugar-making skills to their own lands.[44]

G. Souza applies the concept of 'commodity chains', previously used to describe the global circulation of Latin American products, particularly in the nineteenth and twentieth centuries, to the trans-regional flow of Chinese sugar in 'early modern Asia'. By examining the economic considerations involved in the stages of its circulation (production, transportation, exchange and consumption), he illustrates how sugar produced in Guangdong, Fujian and Taiwan became one of Qing China's primary exports to Tokugawa Japan during the eighteenth century.[45] G. Xu points out the remarkable development of sugar markets in the Lower Yangzi in the late seventeenth and early eighteenth centuries. Drawing from a wealth of historical sources, he shows that sugar production in Taiwan increased significantly in the 1720s; the island annually exported about 54,240 metric tons, outnumbering any other sugar-producing island in the Caribbean. He argues that the product was mainly destined for market towns in the Lower Yangzi, especially Suzhou. This region witnessed the rise of a bustling urban sweet culture. Wudingsheng, a local confectionery chain, served a wide variety of tea cakes and other dishes. Many of these Suzhou-style confections are still enjoyed today.[46] In his analysis of the consumption of grain and consumer goods, including sugar and tea, K. Pomeranz claims there is a notable resemblance in the living standards of west Europe and East Asia, particularly the Lower Yangzi, up to the end of the eighteenth century. Therefore, he argues, the European economy was not exceptional, as there were similar economic and social conditions in European and East Asian economic centres during this period. According to him, this parity began to decline after Europeans crossed the Atlantic Ocean to exploit the New World's enormous resources.[47] K. Yao depicts Japan's transition from *kinsei* to *kindai* (Japanese historiographical periodization terminology more or less corresponding to 'early modernity' and 'modernity', respectively) by highlighting the sweet culture that developed in northern Kyushu, a region where sugar was readily available during the Edo period (1603–1867) due to its proximity to the international trading port of Nagasaki. Not only were there large supplies from 'Chinese junks' (coming from south China and South-East Asia), VOC ships docked at Nagasaki with considerable quantities of Taiwanese sugar, and later Javanese sugar, on a regular basis. Some confectionery brands gained wide popularity, and this went hand in hand with the rise of the region's coal industry in the early twentieth century; they provided coalminers with indispensable nutrition.[48] Today UNESCO has marked the region as a site of Japan's Meiji Industrial Revolution.

The persistent consumption power of Japanese and Chinese societies is part of Japanese revisionist scholars' conception of the Asian economy in the period after 'the Great Divergence', when, as Pomeranz claims, Europe hit a burst of industrialization and left Asia behind. K. Sugihara, a leading scholar on this subject, maintains that in the latter half of the nineteenth century and the first half of the twentieth, vigorous intra-Asian trade revolved around regional industrialization in East Asia, South-East Asia and South Asia, where consumer taste preferences dictated the parameters of market exchange. Therefore, contrary to previous beliefs, the Asian economy could accommodate 'Western impact'.[49] The nineteenth-century Dutch industrial production of cane sugar in Java supports this view. Their sugar industry was initially designed in response to the growing European need for sugar due to soil exhaustion in the West Indies and the abolishment of the slave trade. However, by 1900 Java catered to major Asian sugar markets, such as China, India and Japan.[50] This strong demand for sugar also allowed British entrepreneurs such as Jardin, Matheson & Co. and John Swire & Sons to set up modern refineries in Hong Kong. In the early twentieth century, the Taiwanese sugar industry took off under the auspices of Imperial Japan, rivalling Java and Hong Kong, while the frontier of sugar cultivation was expanding across the Pacific Ocean.[51]

While this line of inquiry has provided many clues for tracing the development of sugar consumption in Europe, it has only paid attention to other regions where sugar played a role in passing. T. Sato's posthumous publication, *Sugar in the Social Life of Medieval Islam*, explores this oversight. Gleaning evidence from the economy of production, trade, medicine, cooking, festivity and gift-giving in Abbasid Iraq, and Fatimid to Mamluk Egypt, he argues that Islamic civilization played a pivotal role in the history of sugar. As mentioned earlier, the basic processes associated with making sugar appeared in north India and then spread to the west. While waves of migrants from Fujian were instrumental in the eastward expansion of sugar production, Arab Muslims played a similar role in its westward journey. The Arabs expanded their geographical conquests soon after the death of the Prophet Muhammad in 632. In a single century they conquered North Africa, pursued authority over major parts of the Iberian Peninsula, and founded the Abbasid caliphate in Baghdad (749–1258). Growing cane for sugar fabrication, which in Iran possibly dated back to the Sassanid period (226–651), expanded after the Arab conquest. The conquerors recognized the fabulous properties of cane sugar – culinary and pharmaceutical as well as commercial and fiscal – and nurtured its production in the southern provinces of Iran, including Khuzistan,

Fars and Sijistan, and in the Tigris-Euphrates delta in Iraq. Sugarcane cultivation travelled further west: to Lower Egypt by the ninth century and to Lebanon and its adjoining areas by about the tenth century. Sato reveals that from the twelfth to thirteenth centuries, production sites blossomed in Upper Egypt, such as in al-Fayyum, which made Mamluk Egypt (1250–1517) the principal producer of sugar in the eastern Mediterranean. Islamic sugarcane technology involved tremendous capital investments and administrative efforts to organize and apply a series of agricultural practices, milling, and sugar-making methods. This last process featured engineering techniques using cone-shaped earthenware moulds called *ubluj*, the secret to extracting sugar and molasses separately from the cane juice. This method, together with the use of milk, helped to yield pure white sugar. In line with Daniels and others, Sato thinks that the Islamic art of refining sugar with *ubluj*s was carried from Egypt to Yuan China in the second half of the thirteenth century.[52] An increased demand for sugar in foreign markets in Europe (especially Italy) and other Islamic counties corresponded to this technological development, and bustling international trade passed through Egypt. However, Sato indicates another important factor: in Egypt (Cairo), the consumption of domestic raw sugar (*qand*) and molasses ('*asal*) began to expand from the wealthy to the common (*haqir*) people – quite surprisingly from as early as the eleventh century. Thus, he suggests that an embryonic form of mass consumption appeared in Egypt long before it did in west Europe.[53] Though protracted, the westward expansion of sugarcane cultivation continued to advance. The Arabs gradually brought sugar cane and sugar production to Mediterranean islands such as Cyprus, Crete and Sicily. After the mid-eleventh-century Arabic references to sugar making appear in the Maghreb (especially Morocco) and southern Spain. Its arrival in Iberia marked a turning point in Islamic technological achievement. Sato stresses that in the fifteenth century, the Portuguese and Spaniards, who were by then well versed in it, introduced sugar production to the Atlantic Islands under their rule (e.g. Madeira and the Canary Islands), and hence into the Caribbean and Brazil in the ensuing century. Notably, he questions the popular belief that the New World sugar industry's use of slavery – the organized and ruthless exploitation of (African) agricultural labourers – was also utilized by the Arabs in their Mediterranean production.[54]

Sato's claim about Islam's central role in the history of sugar awaits further examination because his research does not extend past the fifteenth century. It remains uncertain what became of the Muslim sugar industry, especially after the seventeenth century, when colonial sugar from the New World arrived in markets in the eastern Mediterranean basin. Nevertheless, it is quite telling that the global spread of sugar consumption over the last four centuries may have had different origins and routes from Europe and East Asia, and that those routes might be uneven and often intersecting, generating a relentless desire for the product as well as a modern mindset. It is clear that predominately associating the role of sugar with Europe's technological modernity ultimately distracts our attention from many sugar-consuming countries where, arguably, neither an 'industrial' nor 'industrious' revolution happened. On the other hand, Sato's view of Islam as a geographical framework is worth reconsidering. As he points out, Jewish merchants, who were known to be refinery managers or retailers from the eleventh to thirteenth centuries, were deeply involved in the Egyptian sugar business.[55] One additional blind spot in his Egypt-centric perspective is Iran, another major sugar-consuming region in what Sato calls 'the Islamic world'. The Iranian history of sugar appears to follow a different trajectory than the westbound narrative described above. Floor says that local Iranian sugar production dwindled after the Mongol invasion in the thirteenth century, when it began to receive supplies from the ancient heartland of sugar production, India.[56] Regardless, in the seventeenth century, Iran became an enticing destination for sugar suppliers from various regions along the Indian Ocean and the China Seas.

Sugar for bullion and copper

What approach should we take to understand the case of eighteenth-century Iran? Although his perspective has received much criticism, Mintz's concept of an 'invisible' agency tracking down 'demand' remains inspiring; it gives us an opportunity to think about the broader economic settings that activated consumers. In Iran, too, the sugar use unmistakably thrived at a time when increased consumption was assured by the merchant world and flows of capital. The Safavids established Bandar Abbas in the early 1620s as their gateway to the Indian Ocean, and it rapidly developed into an active hub for a wide range of entrepreneurs – planters, suppliers, shippers, brokers, wholesalers, hawkers, bankers, transporters, retailers, refiners, drug dealers, confectioners, sherbet makers, etc. – thus forming the crucial instruments for 'demand'.

Yet, two questions remain. First, how did the commercial agency as a whole function in the Safavid period? Second, how did this machinery change the economic environment in the following period? One crucial point to consider is that in the seventeenth and eighteenth centuries, sugar, being lucrative ballast, not only facilitated the flow of commodities in Asian waters but also functioned as an effective means for acquiring precious metals and copper. Since the early 1640s the VOC had tried to trade sugar for bullion and copper in Japan. Japan supplied silver and gold, and later principally copper. Iran played a similar role. In the late Safavid period it supplied the Dutch with bullion, and later also copper. These items were indispensable for the VOC and allowed them to orchestrate various circuits of international trade, notably procuring highly profitable cotton textiles in Coromandel and Bengal.[57] In the course of the eighteenth century, the VOC also promoted sugar sales at Surat and in return acquired silver specie to pay for spices in Ceylon and textiles in Bengal.[58] China's state and private traders similarly tried to exploit Chinese sugar as a ballast good for outward junk navigation to Japan so that they could obtain the Japanese copper needed for the manufacture of small denomination coins, as dictated by Qing monetary policies.[59] As far as Iran's place in the bullion flow is concerned, the gold and silver coins that passed through the country came all the way from America via Europe. Hence, sugar shipments to Iran helped stimulate global monetary flows. This fact helps us reconsider the historiography of sugar, which focuses on the dichotomy between Europe and (East) Asia.

However, few studies have been done on the exact process through which sugar imported to the Persian Gulf was turned into exported bullion. We know that in the late Safavid period, this was not achieved through 'bartering'. In order to gain specie for export, it was necessary for a maritime trader to sell his sugar at Bandar Abbas and then transfer the proceeds of the year's sales to the principal bullion market of Isfahan. He had to arrange bills of exchange for remittances, which required expert knowledge of monetary transaction and rich knowledge of the regional economy. Not surprisingly, such processes were a tall order for the VOC and other European traders. Moreover, foreign traders always had substantial difficulties overcoming linguistic barriers and adapting to unfamiliar local conventions.[60] In order to handle these issues, they needed to use local merchants as their brokers and interpreters.

We have very limited knowledge about the relationship between local merchants and the VOC, since scholars have tended to view this relationship in terms of competition. About forty years ago, the Danish historian N. Steensgaard argued that 'early Asian Trade' was made up of numerous itinerant traders, none of whom were powerful enough to control either individual markets or individual commodities. The unpredictability of the market and the arbitrariness of protection made rational calculations difficult for the 'pedlars'. But the VOC and the EIC, as 'Companies', could stabilize price fluctuations by controlling supply and internalized protection costs using their own resources. As a result, they successfully directed a significant proportion of the Asia–Europe trade to the Cape route, thus reducing the trans-continental caravan trade.[61] Studies of Indian merchants and the Julfa Armenians in Safavid Iran have since responded with sharp criticisms of the Companies' supposed structural superiority. They contend that these communities developed sophisticated information networks and legal and financial devices, such as *commenda* (a medieval form of limited partnership contract) based on family or extended family ties. The 'family firms' overcame the market's lack of transparency and diversified their trans-regional commerce vis-à-vis the Companies.[62] While admitting some collaboration between Julfa Armenians and the EIC, E. Herzig states that it was not as successful as the collaboration in India, and the parties were mostly in direct competition.[63] Floor emphasizes that even the VOC, probably the most powerful commercial organization in Safavid Iran, did not have much leeway in the regional market. Revisiting the 'peddler market' model, he argues that there was 'fierce competition between merchants from different nations and purchasing power, while no single competitor had the means to dictate the market price, which was determined by supply and demand'.[64]

There is another reason for the lack of attention paid to the relationship between the VOC and local intermediaries. Since the 1970s, scholars have criticized the colonial literature that dwells on the Indian commercial sector's susceptibility to the rapacious nature of the political elite.[65] Culling evidence from merchants in various South Asian regions, they have revealed a spectrum of relations between the merchant and the state, ranging from fundamental separation to structural interdependency.⁶⁶ Since the 1990s, historiographical works on Safavid Iran have been cropping up. Scholars such as R. Klein, Matthee and Floor have described the complex relations between merchants and the military and bureaucratic elites.⁶⁷ In an analysis of Safavid involvement in the Iranian raw silk trade, Matthee argues that the political–military elite coexisted and actively interacted with local and foreign merchants, particularly Julfa Armenians. But he also thinks that there was a social distinction between rulers and merchants. This is unlike the notion of an 'early modern' (south) Indian mercantile sphere, where so-called 'portfolio capitalists' actively entered into a wide range of domains, including trade, politics, agriculture and the military.⁶⁸ From a close examination of the Safavid administration of Bandar Abbas, Floor maintains that there were essential differences of interest between the authorities and 'foreign merchants'; the Safavid elite sought 'political rather than economic efficiency' while the 'European and Asian merchants' were concerned with 'economic efficiency'.⁶⁹ These works suggest a relatively high degree of unity among the merchants as they faced the Safavid authorities. On the other hand, such a delineation functions as a trick to divert our attention from the diversity of commercial interests and directions *among* individual merchants. We know little about the way different economic considerations attuned to one another. Moreover, how, if at all, did the state affect the process?

In fact, we do not know who acted as business intermediaries at Bandar Abbas. Matthee indicates that most of the European company brokers in Safavid Iran were Banians, or Gujarati Hindus, and tended to practise their profession on a familial basis. In general Banians acted as moneychangers (*sarraf*s) and brokers (*dallal*s) and began to dominate as moneylenders after the mid-seventeenth century, having replaced the Jews.⁷⁰ Concerning the origin of the brokers, A. Qaisar also points out that most of the brokers who worked at Bandar Abbas, Basra and Bandar Rig in the first half of the seventeenth century were Hindu Banians. He thinks that these Banians might have been connected to well-established families who served the EIC as brokers in Agra, Gujarat, Sind, etc.⁷¹ Conversely S. Dale argues that most merchants from Mughal India who conducted business in Iran, Turan or Russia came from Multan in today's Pakistan. Among those who carried the *nisba* (a name often indicating a person's place of origin) 'Multani' in those countries, nearly all the Hindus were Punjabis from the Khatri caste and most Muslims were Afghans or Pashtuns. Moreover, he assumes that the 'Banias' or 'Banians' recorded by contemporary Europeans might also have been Multani merchants.⁷² Mainly following his line of thought, Floor notes that most 'Indians' active in Safavid Iran were indeed of Multani origin and that besides their own business, they also acted as brokers and moneylenders for foreign merchants, including the VOC and the EIC.⁷³ J. Onley also thinks that the largest group of Indians in the Gulf region during the Safavid period were Multani Khatris. But he claims that after the decline of the Khatris following the fall of the Safavid dynasty, the Bhatia and Bhaiband Lohanas, other Hindu merchant groups from Sind, Kutch and western Gujarat, became the major Indian groups in the Gulf.⁷⁴ As for interpreters, M. Haneda illustrates that some Armenian merchants who served the VOC and the

EIC as interpreters at Bandar Abbas in the Afghan interregnum (1722–9) acted as mediators between the port government and the Companies.[75] These studies imply that Banians and Armenians played important roles in the process in question. However, they tell us little about the individuals involved.

For the period following the Afghan conquest, the available information is even more limited. The VOC was in severe decline. But if this is true, how did other suppliers survive? Who in the country could afford to purchase the imported sugar in troubled times? More importantly, how were merchants' interests co-ordinated so that particular commodities, like sugar and bullion, could be in continuous circulation? In his recent book, *The East India Company in Persia*, P. Good points out that the EIC formed impressive collaborations with various local business intermediaries, especially Armenian and Iranian merchants at Kirman, to obtain Kirman wool and copper for export, as well as to sell English woollen cloth.[76] We will examine this development through the lens of the VOC's sugar trade.

Understanding the sources

The traditional idea of a serious setback in the eighteenth century may be critically misinformed because of its flawed initial premise that the VOC, which had so far been a key component in Gulf trade, faced a total decline in trade due to political uncertainty. Dutch reports from the Gulf after the Safavid period include a multitude of complaints about increasing difficulty maintaining their commerce in the region. As Floor has argued, this might appear to form a 'dismal record' of the 'Persian' economy.[77] However, a careful and detailed examination of the VOC archives reveals the curious fact that most of these concerns were not really about frequent shifts of the political climate but about the reorganization of the Indian Ocean sugar trade caused by these shifts. They explain how the news of approaching armies prevented inland merchants from coming to the Dutch factory for trade, and other places in the Gulf and neighbouring countries took advantage of their misfortune and offered alternative markets. English arrivals sailed from one port to another, offering sugar to the local merchants at incredibly cheap prices. The Banian brokers who had traded imported goods for the VOC became bankrupt and were no longer reliable; therefore, the Company had to rely on the brokers' servants to continue their trade. Because no regular accounts were left by other merchants who engaged in sugar trade in the Gulf, these records form a treasure-trove of information for understanding the remarkable changes in the region's political economy during the eighteenth century.

However, the VOC reports were made for the scrutiny of superior officers in home offices, as well as in Batavia, who kept an inquisitive eye on their employees' performance and looked for any sign of corruption, especially in their failures. Hence, it is quite possible that when there were bad sales of Javanese sugar Dutch officials were desperate to justify their position and conveyed every detail, regardless of whether it was true or not. Moreover, quantitative data on

Dutch trade is not readily available. Another difficulty faced when utilizing VOC sources is that most were written on the coasts and thus their authors were rather unfamiliar with inland events, including the flows of commodities, markets and consumption, even though this disadvantage was to some extent compensated for by the broad information networks of their local staff, who provided valuable news on a regular basis.

For a closer examination of the changing relationship between the sugar trade and consumption during the eighteenth century, I scrutinize Dutch records in conjunction with other source materials. While local records in Arabic and Persian are silent about the workings of sugar circulation, we can still learn much from the anecdotal descriptions of sugar consumption left by 'outsiders'. Iran and bordering countries were visited by many Europeans in the seventeenth and eighteenth centuries. In addition to officials deployed by the European trading companies, there were also merchants, diplomats, military people, missionaries, scholars and explorers. An obvious disadvantage is that their accounts are less informed by tested knowledge about local society and often lack any profound understanding of people's words, attitude and motives. Yet it is important to note that in these countries, Europeans were not just observers but active participants in social and economic life, giving presents and providing hospitality, and sugar played a key role. In this regard their accounts approximate a record with the dual perspective of both locals and Europeans.[78]

The VOC archives likewise present a wealth of detailed information on the history of the multi-layered interactions between Europe and countries surrounding the Indian Ocean and the China Seas. Recently, VOC historians have written about the Company's vigorous participation in local ceremonial rites and gift-giving in Asia, especially Japan, Thailand, India and Yemen. These were 'Dutch' efforts to adjust to 'local' conventions, and the society was one of overlapping, if not shared, identities that coincided with the development of the global circulation of objects in the early modern period.[79] I supplement this argument by looking at Dutch encounters with the Iranian court and show that Dutch attempts at diplomacy factored in the socio-cultural practices of the region and the Indian Ocean economy, contributing to the development of such a society.

Organization

In Chapter 1 I examine the 'demand' (i.e. the relationship between sugar trade, especially imports of sugar in the Persian Gulf, and its consumption in the late Safavid period) in terms of the places where sugar was consumed. I consider the various socioeconomic arenas in which sugar played a role, such as medicine, nutrition, festivities, gifts and treats, and as an economic resource. In Chapter 2, I argue that there was remarkable flexibility and continuity in the sugar consumption market during the eighteenth century, as opposed to the altered commercial settings which will be discussed in subsequent chapters.

It is claimed that the VOC sales of Javanese sugar in the Gulf substantially decreased after the Afghan conquest, causing their final retreat from the region in 1766. This traditional description is, I think, inadequate. The focus on the decline overshadows another important fact, that they sold sugar in new marketplaces, like Basra, Bushire, Bandar Rig, Kharg, Muscat and Sind. Therefore, in Chapter 3 I conduct a quantitative analysis of the sales in those places to examine the extent to which the Company successfully adjusted to the transformation of the Gulf market.

The VOC's decline also reflected increasing threats from other sugar suppliers. This development probably began in the late Safavid period despite the successful sales the Company recorded during that time. In Chapter 4, I discuss other suppliers shipping to Bandar Abbas and their flexibility in utilizing alternative markets in the Gulf from the end of the seventeenth century to the fall of the Safavids. Thereafter, I look at the sugar trade of the VOC's competitors at Bandar Abbas after the Safavids. My aim is twofold. First, to show how these traders adjusted to the changing economic settings so quickly, such as changes of regime, emergent alternative channels of trade and increased cash scarcity, and grabbed the market share from the Company. And second, to show that sugar traffic maintained a considerable level of vigour in the southern Gulf.

In Chapter 5, I focus on the competition the VOC encountered at Basra, Bushire, and Kharg. I believe that the breakdown of Dutch trade was not so much a failure of the relationship between trade and consumption as a sign of an unsettled time, one out of which, as Das Gupta suggests, 'the more peaceable formations of the next century emerged'.[80] I hope to show the influx of export bullion into the Upper Gulf regions, the increased demand for copper, the active itinerant wholesale merchants, and the brisk local shipping and caravan traffic as part of such formations. This leads to a discussion of the important link between sugar and precious metals.

In Chapter 6, I deal with the relationships between the VOC and local merchants who engaged in this particular economy as the Company's brokers. I illuminate various aspects related to these business intermediaries – family ties, ethnic backgrounds, places of origin, types of merchant and relations with the Company and the ruling elite – and the way the cooperation functioned not only as Javanese sugar's main entrance to Iran but also as conduits through which bullion found its way to overseas markets. Finally, in Chapter 7, I argue that the local agency was transformed after the Safavids, and that brokers and intermediaries from various ethnic backgrounds continued to be crucial maritime mediators, who sustained local consumer demand and the transregional circulation of minerals during that period.

Chapter 1

SUGAR CONSUMPTION AND THE SUGAR MARKET

Chaudhuri counters David Ricardo's theory and asserts that pre-modern Indian Ocean trade was not necessarily a matter of comparative price differences but that 'consumer tastes' and 'social conventions' played an important role in shaping the demand for luxury goods.[1] Is Chaudhuri's theory of the Indian Ocean's cultural commerce supported by Safavid Iran's sugar trade and sugar consumption? Apart from the Dutch East India Company's (*Verenigde Oostindische Compagnie* [VOC]) commercial records, the most important sources we can utilize to answer this question are contemporaneous accounts by Europeans who visited Iran and its bordering countries. These accounts contain many references to encounters with sugar. As is often the case, the writers were not familiar with local society, and their interests were highly diverse due to their ulterior motives. Nevertheless, collecting fragmentary anecdotes makes it possible to show how the population's socio-cultural practices actively formed and altered vast trading networks of sugar suppliers in the Indian Ocean during the late Safavid period.

The contexts of Iranian sugar consumption

The Safavids came from Turkish-speaking areas of eastern Anatolia and at the outset were a Muslim mystical order based in the north-western Iranian town of Ardabil. They became a powerful polity led by Isma'il (1487–1524). Rallying Turkmen semi-nomadic warriors known as *Qizilbash*, Isma'il took western Iran from the Aq Quyunlu dynasty (*c.* late fourteenth century to 1508) and proclaimed himself shah in Tabriz in 1501. In 1510 he wrested Khurasan from the Shaibanid dynasty (1500–99) while clashing with the Ottoman Empire in Mesopotamia. He utilized *Tajik*s (urban Iranians proficient in Persian) for the civil and judicial administration of these acquired lands. Isma'il also proclaimed that Twelver Shi'ism was the faith of his realm and invited many prominent scholars from Iraq, Lebanon and Bahrain to give their authoritative guidance. During the reign of his successor, Tahmasb (r. 1524–76), the Safavids intensified their interactions with bordering provinces. Although increased threats from the Ottomans forced Tahmasb to move his capital to Qazvin, a city located further east, he made forays into the Caucasus and successfully extended his authority over Georgia. Thereafter, the Caucasus regions, including Georgia, Armenia and Circassia, provided the Safavids with *Ghulams*. As 'royal slaves', the *Ghulams* were recruited and employed in the military and civil administration. Those assigned to special regiments of the army were more trustworthy than the *Qizilbash*, whose loyalty was often questionable. Many women from the Caucasus, especially from Georgia, also served in the royal harem, where through their proximity to the king they exerted considerable influence over court politics.

Under 'Abbas I (r. 1588–1629) the *Ghulams* were integrated into the royal armed forces and upheld Safavid imperial interests. At the turn of the seventeenth century 'Abbas I secured most of Khurasan from the Shaibanids, as well as Georgia, Armenia and Azerbaijan from the Ottomans. In 1624, his armies advanced into Ottoman territories and took some parts of Iraq and eastern Anatolia. Shah 'Abbas was the first Safavid ruler to gain control over the Iranian Persian Gulf littoral and take part in Indian Ocean trade. In 1622, Imam Quli Khan, a Georgian *Ghulam* and governor-general of Fars (*beglerbeg*), expelled the Portuguese from Hormuz Island, a trading centre in the Lower Gulf, with the help of the East India Company's (EIC) naval support, and drew trade from Hormuz towards a newly established port on the mainland named after the shah, Bandar Abbas. The port was under Imam Quli Khan's jurisdiction. After its establishment, three European East India Companies set up trading posts in Bandar Abbas: the EIC (*c.* 1623), the VOC (1623) and the French (in the late seventeenth century). In return for their naval assistance, the EIC was entitled to half the customs duty for goods that landed at the port.[2]

In the early seventeenth century, Safavid inroads into the Persian Gulf reflected diplomatic and commercial concerns that were influenced by their ongoing struggle with the Ottoman Empire. In order to seek allies against the Ottomans, Shah 'Abbas actively sent envoys to Europe and Russia. In Isfahan, his new capital, he hosted various Christian monastic orders, including Augustinians, Carmelites, Capuchins and Jesuits, who also acted as diplomats, representing Christian countries such as Spain, France and the Vatican. By 1619, in order to enhance royal revenues, Shah 'Abbas consolidated a monopoly over the export of raw silk produced in the northern provinces of Gilan and Mazandaran. Since large quantities of silk were exported to Europe through Ottoman territories, the shah welcomed the English and Dutch Companies, who sought Caspian silk to ship by way of the Cape of Good Hope, thereby circumventing Ottoman involvement in trans-regional trade.

Shah 'Abbas facilitated the flow of people and commodities through his empire. During his reign, he established secure roads for both local and foreign travellers. Many caravanserais, the remains of which can still be found in present-day Iran, endure as a legacy of his glorious rule. These circumstances encouraged the EIC and VOC to conduct trade inland, in cities such as Shiraz, Isfahan and Kirman. In order to utilize Armenian commercial prowess, the shah relocated numerous Armenians from Julfa in Azerbaijan to a suburb of Isfahan called New Julfa (hereafter Julfa), and gave them many commercial privileges, especially relating to the export of silk.

Shah 'Abbas's successors defended the Safavid territories, except for Iraq, which Safi (r. 1629–42) yielded to the Ottomans. 'Abbas II (r. 1642–66) retook Qandahar – a key travel route in Afghanistan that Safi had lost – from the Mughals. Trans-regional trade continued and established ever stronger connections to Indian Ocean trade. The royal port of Bandar Abbas linked many points along the Indian Ocean with Iran's major cities, such as Shiraz, Isfahan, Kirman and Yazd, and functioned as a major node of trans-regional trade in the Persian Gulf. Bandar Abbas was home to multiple ethnic groups, most of whom engaged in trade; Indians – 'Banians' and 'Multanis' – were perhaps the most numerous. Around 1670 the population of Bandar Abbas was estimated at about 9,000 people, of which one third were said to be Indians. Other ethnic groups included Iranians, Armenians, Jews, Arabs, Europeans and others.[3] The Portuguese, who established an agreement with the Safavids in 1630, set up a trading base in Bandar Kong, a port close to Bandar Abbas.[4] While Kong played a similar role to Bandar Abbas in Indian Ocean trade, it was primarily linked to Muscat; Kong imported Sindi textiles and South-East Asian spices over Muscat, as well as extending trade to Basra. Kong also developed as an important market for pearls from Bahrain, the chief pearling centre in the Gulf. Gulf pearls had a moderate share of the Indian market.[5] Kong's population was also made up of diverse ethnic groups, and it might have been somewhat larger than Bandar Abbas.[6]

After the brutal execution of Imam Quli Khan in 1632, Safi transformed the entire province of Fars, to which the ports had belonged until then, into a crown demesnes (*khassa*).[7] Bandar Abbas was ruled by a governor (*hakim/sultan/khan*) and a customs-master (*shahbandar*), and Kong's chief officials were a *darugha* (chief or superintendent) and *shahbandar*.[8] In the mid-seventeenth century, the Safavids attempted to establish a unified, effective customs administration in Bandar Abbas, Kong and other Gulf ports to secure the royal customs income, but they were ultimately unsuccessful. At the beginning of the reign of Sulayman (r. 1666–94), the government adopted an innovative approach to this problem. The role of *shahbandar* of all Persian Gulf ports, including Bandar Abbas and Kong, was given to the highest bidder. This policy continued until the collapse of the Safavid dynasty in 1722.[9]

During the reign of Sultan Husayn (r. 1694–1722), Bandar Abbas and Kong were growing insecure due to mounting tensions between the Safavids and the Ya'rubi Imamate (1624 or 1625–c. 1720) in Oman. Omani Arabs raided Kong in 1695 and later captured Bahrain and other islands in the Gulf. In addition, Bandar Abbas was raided by Baluchi tribesmen who drove deep into southern Iran from Baluchistan.[10] These offenses negatively impacted commercial life at the royal ports, which both continued to function as important hubs for Indian Ocean trade until Isfahan fell to Afghan invaders in 1722.

Despite these facts, V. Minorsky and L. Lockhart have argued that the Safavid dynasty saw a decline in its ability to rule after the death of 'Abbas I, and this continued until the Afghan conquest. During the reigns of Sulayman and Sultan Husayn in particular, so they claim, there was serious moral decline among the ruling classes. In their view, Sultan Husayn was utterly ignorant of state affairs during the dynasty's final years. Brought up in the harem, he spent most of his time in the inner palace, conversing with Shi'i clergy, *sayyids* (descendants of Prophet Muhammad), eunuchs, etc. while eating and drinking indulgently. The king also lavishly presented religious authorities with valuable objects and land. Neither his ministers nor military leaders had full control of the government; they were preoccupied with endless power struggles. This power vacuum allowed the arbitrary intervention of a 'shadow government', formed by the queen mother and eunuchs.[11]

The picture Minorsky and Lockhart drew is supported by eyewitness accounts. However, their stance articulates an undeniable Orientalist (and maybe also Puritanical) bias against the Safavid court's extravagant expenditures on food. Extravagant consumption in royal courts' inner circles was just as common in Europe at the time, which has generated lively debate among scholars of consumption history about the origin of mass consumption in Western society. Regarding sugar consumption, Mintz argued that European courts played a crucial role in displaying the use of sugar to the lower social strata. De Vries proposed that mass consumption evolved more or less independently through reformations of the urban household.[12] In contrast, many scholars claim that Safavid Iran developed a saga of spectacular ethical decay that led to the weakening of the dynasty. Only recently have some historians shunned this long-held concept of Iranian moral and imperial decline. A.J. Newman, looking at the production and procurement of court paintings during the reign of Sultan Husayn, pointed out that the ruling elite's purchasing power remained strong. Newman also made a case for a similar vitality among non-elite actors in Safavid Iran when looking at lustre ware, enamel work and steel products.[13] Matthee concisely remarks: 'Royal debauchery is of all time: emperors and kings in East and West have always whiled away much time in their private quarters and dissipated treasure on lavish banquets and costly hunting practices'. Therefore, one should be careful not to use the term decline as an overarching category that overshadows all possible countervailing forces that may occur within a particular system; and instead, the specific thing that is declining needs to be identified.[14]

What does sugar consumption in late Safavid Iran tell us about continuity and change in that society? The lingering concern is how, despite many unfavourable economic conditions, Safavid Iran became a major sugar-importing region in the Indian Ocean. The Safavid realm and the Iranian Plateau overlapped considerably. The plateau is an oblong-like basin rimmed by the Zagros and Alborz Mountains in the west and north and by uninhabitable barren lands, such as the Lut Desert, in the south and east. Composed of vast spreads of arid and semi-arid areas, the heartland of the dynasty had very little arable land, even though great rivers like the Zayanda Rud and Karun, both starting in the Zagros range, were exploited for cereal production and in some regions to irrigate agriculture using underground water. These harsh geographic conditions resulted in a relatively sparse population. Out of the total population of around seven or eight million, about one third were nomads and the rest lived in scattered villages and towns.[15] By contrast, the northern borderlands that lay between the Caspian Sea and the

Alborz range were blessed with ample precipitation and a mild climate, and hence were highly productive agricultural regions. The lush Caspian provinces of Gilan and Mazandaran developed lucrative sericulture. Most of the raw silk was exported to European markets by way of the Levant or Russia, thereby generating flows of gold and silver coinage back into the region. Aside from silk, however, Safavid Iran exported few other products that could generate substantial foreign demand. As a consequence, Iran underwent a serious cash drain. The trade imbalance with the Indian subcontinent was especially severe, from which it received many consumer goods, such as pepper, sugar and textiles, in return for bullion. Re-exporting imported goods generated inflows of much-needed metals during this time, but coinage was scarce in general.[16] Furthermore, the rugged Zagros range impeded the movement of people and goods between the Iranian Plateau and the Persian Gulf. During the late Safavid period, a major trading route passed from Bandar Abbas, through Lar and Shiraz, to Isfahan, and this Zagros trek took one month to complete, if the caravan hurried.[17] Because of the scorching hot and humid climate, Iran's low coastlands were known as *Garmsir* (hot country); most of the terrain was desolate and infertile. The Safavid port towns of Bandar Abbas and Kong were unique to this area. Like other Gulf regions, *Garmsir* was settled by a number of autonomous Arab tribes. The geographical isolation and adverse physical environment made it nearly impossible for any pre-modern hinterland power, with the exception of the Safavids, to establish lasting rule over the low country.

The thorny question of Safavid Iran's sugar consumption still needs to be scrutinized in detail, but I argue that, even if Iran's economy – production and consumption – was rather modest and scattered, sugar trade influenced much of it, changing and connecting existing elements. Importantly, in Safavid Iran, sugar supplies imported through the Gulf by no means diminished the use of local sweeteners, such as honey, dates, grapes and manna. Almost all travellers who visited Iran during the Safavid period commented on the abundance of fruit in the country and how important they were to the population's daily diet. John Fryer, an Englishman who stayed in Iran between 1676 and 1677, stated that the primary diet of the Iranians was fruit, and that no country was more taken with sweetmeats, not even the Lusitanians (Portuguese).[18] One secret to sugar's popularity was that it could be combined with this fruit-eating culture. In Safavid Iran, sherbets were made from various fruit juices, such as pomegranate or citron, and adding sugar to them led to more varieties.[19] In the late seventeenth century Safavid Iran developed a tradition for entertaining honoured guests with decorative sweetmeats, called a 'sugar banquet', alongside coffee and a water pipe.[20] Earlier, according to European eyewitnesses, 'conserves' had a prominent place in customary feasting. Jan Smidt, an ambassador of the States-General and the VOC who visited Iran near the end of ʿAbbas I's reign, described the 'Persian banquets' he encountered:

> The time of their [Persian] gathering is around 10 o'clock in the morning. The sitting places are all on the ground, which is covered with carpets and excellent tapestries. They sit in the manner of tailors in our country because people have

no idea about tables here. This manner of sitting is quite difficult for those who are not accustomed to it. Firstly, as we know, people enter the square room. In the place where the guests will sit, fruits, and (after the harvest season) some bottles of wine, are placed. From beginning to end [wine] is usually passed around, since serving [wine to each] is unusual, and even if that happens, [wine] is passed around. After having sat in the [same] manner for a while, around noon a breakfast (*ontbijt*) chiefly consisting of conserves (*confituren*) and sweetmeats (*zoetigheid*) is dished out. Half an hour would pass this way, and people again sit for a while. Around 2 to 3 o'clock the meal (*maaltijd*) is laid out. The banquets are indeed very luxurious but not beautiful, with few variations of food, for they cook all their food with rice. ... The plates on which [food] is served are generally as big as the bottom of a barrel. At the table where the ambassador [Smidt] sat, forty gold dishes of this size were placed side by side in which food was served for more than 200 people, so their luxuriousness mainly comes from the quantity of food. The food is later served to each of the guests' servants according to his status, because the Persians are very liberal in treating the servants of their guests. After having sat for about one to one and a half hours as before, the tables are removed and the guests are given warm water to wash their hands well, because everything is very messy during the meal, for [they] tear food by hand and do not use spoons or knives much. After the food has been cleared away, they may stay for another two to three hours, when some dancers are called into the middle of the room. The Persians enjoyed their dancing and singing very much while continuously drinking.[21]

Presumably, not all 'conserves' were prepared with cane sugar, since people knew how to make them without using sugar and were skilled at processing sweeteners from other substances, such as grapes and dates.[22] However, as in contemporary west Europe, it seems reasonable that the social role of 'conserves' was influenced by the geo-spatial role of sugar. Smidt experienced this during his travels from Bandar Abbas through Shiraz and then to the capital city of Isfahan, and Pietro Della Valle, an Italian noble who came from Baghdad to Isfahan in 1617, witnessed a similar ceremonial meal. When he arrived at Hamadan, a western access point to Safavid Iran, he described a service of fruit, wine, conserves (if one was a guest of the shah and other dignitaries), pilaf, etc. at a Persian banquet. He noted that was fit for all the powerful, inlcuding the shah.[23] Adam Olearius, a German secretary for the Holstein mission, which travelled to Safavid Iran through the northern frontier zone of the Caspian coastlands during the late 1630s, also commented that the governor of Shamakhi invited the mission to a banquet, where he offered them all kinds of preserves (*Konfect*).[24]

The Safavid court was responsible for a large portion of the country's sugar consumption. In 1660 VOC officials noted that the shah spent almost a year in his retreat at Ashraf in Mazandaran 'with an unbelievably large following, including most of the grandees, who all are wont to indulge in a rather dissolute life, and who account for the largest part of sugar consumption'. During this period, market prices in Isfahan dropped, as there was not much demand, but once the court returned to the city, the price of sugar promptly rose.²⁵ In 1703, Dutch painter Cornelis de Bruyn noted that, in return for royal silk, the VOC sent the court 1.8 million Dutch pounds of sugar every year, which was all consumed in Isfahan.²⁶ The noble's travelling 'tent' was akin to a mobile centre of consumption. Fryer stated that when any 'magistrate' returned from hunting or entered or left a major town or city, all classes of people marked the occasion with the liberal consumption of tobacco, tea, coffee, rosewater and sugar candy.²⁷

While sugar was in demand in cities along the major sugar supply line stretching from Bandar Abbas and Kong to Isfahan, these cities, especially Isfahan, also functioned as distribution centres for Iran and beyond. The scarcity of available information renders it difficult to identify precisely how much sugar was redistributed from the capital to any particular destination, but in the late Safavid period, some of the imported sugar was meant for northern and eastern cities. Traders from Qazvin and Tabriz usually bought sugar to the Isfahan market.²⁸ In Shamakhi in the early 1680s the German doctor Engelbert Kaempfer was served fruits, sugar-coated almonds, brandy and tea.²⁹ De Bruyn saw sugar sellers (*suikerverkopers*) in the Kashan bazaar.³⁰ In the eastern part of Safavid Iran, sugar and coffee were imported from Isfahan to Mashhad during the last part of the seventeenth century.³¹

Iraq might also have imported sugar from Isfahan, if not from Basra. It was well known as a sugar-consuming region since the Abbasid period. A tenth-century cook book dedicated to the Abbasid caliph and other notables contains more than 200 recipes, many of them using various forms of sugar, such as rock sugar (*sukkar tabarzad*) and pounded white sugar (*sukkar abyad madquq*).³² However, some of the sugar imported from the Safavid capital might have been re-exported to Ottoman markets in the Middle East and Anatolia, since in the early seventeenth century the VOC reported that the Turks were also seeking sugar, while the Arabs consumed little.³³

In the late Safavid period Bandar Abbas and Kong were the principal supply lines for importing sugar into Iran, there were also some alternative channels in the Persian Gulf. The most important was Basra, a port city located close to the northernmost part of the Gulf. It is situated at a major intersection between Indian Ocean shipping lines and the caravan routes through the Syrian Desert, making it a traditional link between the economies of the Indian Ocean and the Middle East. Access to the Tigris and Euphrates to the north and the Karun River to the east directly connected Basra to regional economic centres like Baghdad, Mosul, Shiraz and Isfahan. Trade thrived, especially in the first half of the seventeenth century, when the city and its surrounding areas formed a stable, semi-autonomous state ruled by a local clan, the Afrasiyab, who nominally acknowledged Ottoman authority. In the 1640s, when political and commercial conditions in Safavid Iran became unfavourable, both the EIC and VOC entered the Basra market to utilize the port as an alternative sea route to neighbouring Iran. EIC correspondence indicated that they could sell sugar there. After the 1660s, however, Basra underwent a period of prolonged unrest, punctuated by internal feuds, Ottoman and Safavid interventions and aggressions by local Arabs, as well as epidemics. Consequently, trade slowed, and the VOC only occasionally used the port for trade.[34]

Muscat was another viable alternative to Bandar Abbas and Kong. Lying at the mouth of the Persian Gulf, the natural harbour formed an important hub for Indian Ocean shipping, as well as local and regional navigation. Muscat transit trade developed significantly under the rule of the Ya'rubi Imamate in the second half of the seventeenth and early eighteenth centuries.[35] The Ya'rubi imams, who followed Ibadi principles, led a tribal confederation from the interior of Oman and expanded their rule over the Omani littoral, expelling the Portuguese from the country in 1650, a process similar to the Safavid expansion across the Iranian littoral.[36] Muscat was administered by a governor (*wali*) appointed by the Ya'rubi imam, who lived in Rustaq, around 75 miles inland from the port.[37] Between 1672 and 1675, the VOC had a trading station in Muscat to tap the commercial potential of Muscat trade. According to Georg Wilmson, a Dutch official in charge of the trading station, Muscat imported 'black sugar' (*zwarte suiker*) from the western coast of India.[38] More importantly, locally produced sugar was exported from Muscat to Iran, a subject to which I shall return later.

The Safavid shah and his grandees were an important factor in Iranian sugar consumption, but women in the home also played a significant role. In 1682 the VOC resident Reynier Casembroot reported that 'the principal treat Persians use to offer at all respectable meals and invitations, both before and after midday, consists of sugar confectionery and costly candied sweets; besides, many sweets are consumed in private homes, especially by women'.[39] Domestic servants in upper-class houses also accounted for a substantial portion of the country's 'luxury'.[40] Later, the Muscovy Company merchant Jonas Hanway lamented that his guests partook little of the sweetmeats that he had served and gave the remainder to their servants. There were often so many servants that a treat of this kind would cost 10 or 12 crowns, and this custom, absurd and expensive in his view, had 'something of the air of hospitality in the person entertaining'.[41]

There appears to have been no ethnic barrier to sugar consumption in Safavid Iran, unlike, at least to some extent, with liquor and wine. The inhabitants of Safavid Iran were ethnically very diverse. The largest ethnic group was the Iranians, which might have also included Kurds. There were also large numbers of Turks, who together with Iranians formed the core ethnicity under Safavid rule. As the dynasty expanded, it also incorporated Georgians, Armenians, Circassians, Baluchis, Afghans, Arabs, Indians, Zoroastrians, Europeans, etc.[42] The customary 'Iranian' treat of sweetmeats was also common among 'foreign' residents, such as Julfa Armenians and Banians.[43]

As in many other sugar-consuming countries, gluttony was a concern. *Qalandars* (ascetics) reprimanded the lavishness of cooks, bakers, *qannadis* (confectioners), etc. in the mid-seventeenth century. It is unclear whether they suffered due to these admonitions, but the reprimand itself illustrates the intensity of urban consumption.[44] Isfahan's size is relevant here. Estimates given by various European visitors ranged widely, from 200,000 to 500,000 people. If the latter was true, about 9 per cent of total settlers might have been clustered in the capital.[45] The rural population, however, was quite unfamiliar with sugar until the mid-nineteenth century. By this time, increasing supplies of sugar, from Java, France and later Russia, gradually put it within reach of the lower classes.[46] However, some specific uses might have been common among the lower classes. The wide popularity of sherbet in Safavid Iran provides a good illustration. In the *Tadhkirat al-muluk*, an early-eighteenth-century Persian manual of Safavid administrative practices, the sherbet house (*sharbat-khana*) is described as one of the royal workshops, and the chief officer (*sahib-jam'*) took care of the department's belongings: vessels of gold, silver, china, glass and copper; crystal sugar (*shikar*), candy sugar (*qand*), medicinal herbs, coffee, tobacco; as well as lemon juice, rosewater, spirits, etc.[47] But Kaempfer noted that sherbet was popular both 'in huts and palaces' (*in aulis et caulis*).[48] Its proximity to major trading routes compensated for sugar's relatively high price to some extent. A VOC report said that one poor toll collector (*rahdar*) in charge of an almost neglected village relied on gifts of spices, pepper and candy sugar from caravans passing through his village.[49]

Sugar varieties

Iran had long been a sugar-producing country, cultivating sugar cane since at least the Sassanid period. In the Islamic period, sugar cane was grown in south-western, southern and south-eastern Iran, especially in Khuzistan, Fars, Sijistan and Makran. However, after the destruction of the irrigation system in Khuzistan during the Mongol invasion, the country imported most of its sugar from India, both over land and by sea, even though domestic sugar continued to be available.[50] During the Safavid period, various sugar-producing regions, including Punjab, Gujarat, Bengal, south China, Taiwan, Oman and Java, catered to Iranian consumers.[51] After the establishment of Safavid rule in the Iranian littoral of the Persian Gulf in the 1620s, those countries sent various types of sugar, including castor or powdered sugar and candy sugar, to the Gulf, mostly to the royal port of Bandar Abbas. Due to the scarcity of available information, it is difficult to know how these different varieties of sugar functioned in the market, but the complex trading networks and the commercial value of sugars exported to Safavid Iran amply document the importance of the Indian Ocean sugar trade for the early modern global mercantile economy.

In an analysis of the wholesale prices of powdered and candy sugars from Hindustan, Bengal, Batavia and China (including Taiwan) at Bandar Abbas in the seventeenth century, Klein suggests that the eventual price of sale was determined by the total supply, and that all varieties competed with one another for a market share.[52] He admits, however, that the character and quality of sugar varied considerably depending on the source. Such differences, combined with taste preferences, created an intriguing situation in which some varieties were almost exclusively employed for specific purposes. In other words, all varieties were not always in outright competition with each other. After the establishment of their trading station in Bandar Abbas in 1623, the VOC began to import sugar from north and west India, Bengal and China, and they significantly increased the sales of Taiwanese sugar, an import they controlled until they lost Taiwan to Zheng Chenggong's forces in 1662.[53] Towards the mid-seventeenth century, other suppliers also actively traded Bengali sugar. The principal areas of sugar production in Bengal were Sirpur, near Sonargaon in Decca, and Chandrakona, in Bardwan (now in Midnapore).[54] Muslim and Hindu merchants and officials of the Golconda dynasty (1512–1687) sent shipments of sugar to Iran.[55] According to the Dutch, however, the increased trade in Bengali sugar was not necessarily harmful to their trade in Taiwanese sugar. In 1650 they wrote that Taiwanese sugar could be used for all purposes for which Bengali sugar was not suitable.[56]

Taiwanese sugar was used to prepare sherbet and competed with Omani loaf sugar for this market share. Soon after the Dutch were expelled from Taiwan, the status of Omani variety grew significantly in the Iranian market. In Oman, sugar cane was cultivated in the oases surrounding interior settlements such as Bahla, Manah and Nizwa. By the mid-1670s manufacturing loaf sugar for export came under the strict control of the Ya'rubi imam.[57] Large portions of the Omani output were destined for Iran via Muscat or other harbours in the country. The Dutch factors wrote that Omani loaf sugar was used to make refreshing drinks such as sherbet, while Bengali sugars (with the except of the Sirpur variety) were employed for candied sweets. Omani sugar was also sent to other areas in the Gulf, such as Bahrain and Basra, and even to Mocha.[58] Under these circumstances, the VOC turned to Bengali sugar.

In the 1680s the VOC gradually shifted the core of their sugar trade towards Javanese sugar produced in the environs (*ommelanden*) of Batavia. Although Floor asserts that Javanese sugar came to dominate the Iranian sugar market by 1680, and this continued until the end of the eighteenth century, relations between Javanese sugar and other varieties were complex.[59] The Dutch usually imported two types of Javanese sugar to Iran: *poedersuiker* (castor sugar), and *kandijsuiker* (candy sugar). Dutch candy sugar was in direct competition with Muscat loaf sugar (*Masquetse broodsuiker*). Muscat sugar, which was melted and refined into loaves and candy sugar (*brood- en kandijsuiker*) in Isfahan and used for the preparation of sherbets and other drinks, was more suitable for these processes than the Javanese variety, because it did not lose much weight after refinement, as if it 'has some sugar in itself' (*in zichzelfs enige zoetigheid*).[60] Moreover, the Iranians had been 'imitating' (*namaken*) Javanese candy sugar since the turn of the eighteenth century.[61]

However, Dutch castor sugar succeeded in developing its own market. In 1695, when the VOC decided to give up the still-lucrative trade in Bengali sugar in Iran in order to enhance sales of Javanese sugar, the Company's brokers in Bandar Abbas advised them to continue to import Bengali (castor) sugar. Importing Javanese sugar would not hinder the Bengali sugar trade, they claimed, because in the Safavid realm, Bengali sugar was consumed in a different manner than Batavian castor sugar. In fact, although the VOC had not imported Bengali sugar for a number of years, as they were importing large amounts of Javanese castor sugar, Bengali sugar shipments remained active, and English, Armenian, Muslim and other local merchants sold even more of the Bengali variety, and for good prices.[62]

One year later, VOC officials reported that Bengali and Javanese sugars were used for different processes when preparing sugar banquets (*ieder tot een bijzonder gebruik bij de suikerbanquet verarbeid worden*). Quoting a Dutch proverb, 'The abundance of rye makes the price of wheat drop' (*de overvloed van rogge de prijs der tarwe doet dalen*), they said that large imports of Bengali sugar could reduce the price of Javanese castor sugar but could not decrease its sales.[63]

Javanese castor sugar generally fetched higher prices than Bengali sugar, which probably motived the VOC decision to switch to the Javanese variety. The Company sent small quantities of Bengali sugar as ballast goods in the financial years 1706–7 and 1707–8.[64] According to Dutch annual sales statements (*rendementen*), Bandar Abbas sold Bengali castor sugar at 2¼ *mahmudi*s per *man*, while they sold Javanese castor sugar at 2¾ *mahmudi*s per *man*. For 1707–8, Bengali castor sugar yielded only 42 per cent net profit, while Javanese castor sugar netted 103 per cent profit.[65] In other words, Dutch castor sugar developed its own market despite its relatively high price.

However, sales of Bengali and other cheap sugars in Bandar Abbas had a tendency to pull the wholesale price of VOC castor sugar down, making it more difficult for the Company to meet projected sales targets for Javanese sugar.[66] Therefore, the Dutch tried to sell their 'fancy' sugar quickly before the other sugars drove the price down. The trade at Bandar Abbas in the 1705–6 financial year provides an illuminating example of this. In July 1706, the Dutch factors wrote that for the last two years they had not sold many goods because the English had cornered the market. In order to stop these other traders from winning the market, they made the decision to sell their principal weighed goods (*pondgoederen*), such as castor sugar, candy sugar, pepper and tin, immediately after they were unloaded from the ships that reached Iran in October and December 1705. In response to this sudden move, the English also had to sell their well-refined and white Chinese sugar quickly, and they managed to fetch a price of 2¾ *mahmudi*s per *man*. Four English ships that arrived from Bengal and China sometime later were obliged to sell imported Bengali and Chinese sugars mixed together at a lower price of 2 *mahmudi*s per *man*. Furthermore, a Danish ship that docked with both their own goods and freight goods from Bengal in May 1706 also had to dispose of Bengali sugar at 2 *mahmudi*s per *man*. The English could not sell all their sugar and other goods at Bandar Abbas, and they began to send some to Isfahan by caravan. As the Dutch officers noted, the price of the Chinese sugar was ¼ *mahmudi* cheaper than the VOC price, and the price for which the English and the Danish sold their sugars was 1 *maumudi* cheaper (i.e. the VOC sold their castor sugar at 3 *mahmudi*s per *man*).[67]

Javanese castor sugar was well-refined and thus in high demand in Iran, and the Company tried to maintain a steady supply of quality castor sugar for the Iranian market so that its appeal would not waver. In 1694 it was recorded that in Bandar Abbas the quality of sugar sent from Batavia had become gradually worse since 1688, when the Dutch ship *de Grote Visserij* had imported excellently refined and very white castor sugar. If they had received such a quality product, they claimed, they would have been sure to sell 5,000 to 6,000 chests of it every year, but if the quality continued to deteriorate, they might not be able to sell 3,000 chests of castor sugar or to maintain its current price.[68] Wholesale merchants in Iran expected the VOC to bring well-processed sugar to the market. At the beginning of the eighteenth century, the Company tried offering unrefined muscovado sugar (*muscovade suiker*) alongside castor sugar, and they managed to sell it at 1.5 *mahmudi*s per *man-i Tabriz* (equivalent to 6 Dutch pounds), half the price of castor sugar. However, a Dutch report stated that the merchants disliked the raw sugar, saying this was the last time they would buy unrefined sugar from the Dutch.[69] The merchants who traded with the VOC primarily aimed to procure Javanese castor sugar from the Company. In 1717, the Dutch ambassador Joan Josua Ketelaar instructed Bandar Abbas factors to dispose of the remaining spices that were low in demand and add sugar, especially castor sugar, because the item was in high demand in Iran.[70]

Klein points out that towards the mid-1680s, Iran's growing cash shortage reduced the import of ocean-transported sugar; consumers turned to cheaper local fructose, produced from grapes and dates.[71] Even so, seafaring merchants who continued trading with the Gulf in the 1690s did not suffer greatly in the sale of well-processed sugar. The Dutch project to provide the market with their castor sugar spurred other merchants to import different refined varieties. In March 1694, Dutch officials in Bandar Abbas complained that the castor sugar they had received from Batavia remained unsold because of its low quality, and they requested that Batavia send them very white and well-dried sugar. They also reported that, in addition to the Muslims and Armenians who were importing sugar from Bengal, the latest arrivals from Surat had imported a reasonable quantity of Manila sugar. The sugar, which was 'exceptionally pure and as white as the first snow' (*uitnemend schoon en zo wit als de eerste gevallene sneeuw*), was brought from Manila on ships owned by a renowned Bohra merchant in Surat named 'Abd al-Ghafur. His agents had purchased the sugar for 2 to 2.5 *rijksdaalder*s per picol; and once it was brought to Surat it was sold for 3.5 rupees for 36¼ Dutch pounds. The Dutch officials concluded that, if this was correct, the variety yielded a good profit and would encourage 'Abd al-Ghafur and other merchants to ship more sugar from Manila, which would cause great problems for the Company's trade. In fact, the Manila variety, due to its whiteness and purity, attracted merchants from upcountry, and it fetched a price of 3 17/20 *mahmudi*s per *man*. The ships that imported Manila sugar from Surat into Bandar Abbas that year included an Armenian ship, *St. Thomas*. This ship came from Bengal on 28 January 1694 with freight, mostly weighed goods, including large amounts of Manila sugar and various varieties of Bengali sugar. Soon afterwards another ship also brought various kinds of sugar, including Manila sugar. According to the VOC, this ship, recorded as an English private vessel from Bengal, had procured the Manila sugar at Madras on its way to Bandar Abbas. At Bandar Abbas the sugar fetched a price of 3 7/10 *mahmudi*s per *man*.[72]

Furthermore, English private traders were busy importing well-processed Chinese sugar into Bandar Abbas.[73] In the competitive year of 1705–6 the Dutch officials mentioned the enormous import of refined sugar by the Company and by English traders that year. They quote wholesale merchants who said there was far too much to dispose of in the next two years.[74] What was a greater menace to the Dutch, however, was the fact that the Chinese castor sugar the English imported that year was outstandingly pure and 'as white as the first snow'.[75]

It should be noted that while the VOC was trying to overtake other sugar suppliers, fierce competition among the Company's competitors contributed to the declining price of sugar in Safavid Iran. On 10 April 1706, an English ship, *The Loyal Cook*, came from Bengal to Bandar Abbas with 2,000 sacks of Bengali sugar. According to the ship's crew, they would be followed by many other competitors, including two more English ships, a Danish ship, two Muslim vessels from Bengal and a few ships from China and Coromandel. This news evoked a surprisingly positive response from the Dutch. They believed that the increased competition might reduce their rivals' profits. Ultimately, they hoped the traders would have to give up shipping to Bandar Abbas the following season, and then the VOC could dominate sugar imports into Iran.[76] Soon afterwards four other non-Dutch ships appeared with sugar cargoes. Three were English vessels, two from Bengal and one from China; the other was a Danish ship from Bengal. A Dutch report recorded the arrival of the above-mentioned English vessel, '*de Wettelijke Kok*' (*the Legal Cook*), laden with only 1,000 sacks of castor sugar, which was followed by *The Loyal Cook* from Bengal one month later, whose cargo presumably included Bengali sugar.[77]

Sugar in Safavid Iranian society

The varieties of sugar imported to Safavid Iran and the increase in demand invites examination of how sugar consumption was imbricated in the social, cultural, fiscal and diplomatic practices of the Safavid dynasty, including medicine, diet, festivities, gifts and treats, overseas trade and the consequent outflow of specie.

Medieval Arabic medicine held sugar in high regard and claimed it contained valuable pharmaceutical properties. Following the traditional Galenic theory of Greek medicine, Arabic pharmacology classified sugar as 'hot' and 'moist' (and old sugar as 'hot' and 'dry') and believed it was effective against colic, eye disease, cough, asthma and urinary retention, as well as useful for the kidneys and liver.[78] In Safavid Iran the most popular medicinal use of sugar was probably sherbet. It was in great demand among urban populations and was used to relieve sore throats caused by the hot, dry climate.[79]

Sherbet was valued as an appropriate gift for the elite as much as it was valued for its medicinal qualities. During his stay in Isfahan, Chardin sometimes received generous treats of conserves, sherbets and the like from the sister of ʿAbbas II, the late shah.[80] At elite receptions and meals, sherbet was customarily served as a refreshment.[81] Raphaël du Mans, the head of the French Capuchin mission, noted that on such occasions sherbet, pomegranate or lemon juice with sugar and ice added to it, was served as a refreshing drink.[82] The shah's sherbet house functioned as a sort of guest house, where foreign ambassadors were offered sherbet while awaiting a royal audience.[83]

During the Safavid period, the powerful and wealthy valued sugar as a condiment and sweetener.[84] While the use of this still-luxurious 'food item' had increased, many European visitors to Safavid Iran observed the frugality of the Iranian diet. Chardin commented that Asians in general, and Iranians in particular, ate much less food than Europeans. He wrote that Iranians only had two meals per day. The first was eaten between 10 am and noon, consisting of fruit, such as melons and grapes, cheese, milk and conserves. The second, their main meal, was eaten around 7 pm and consisted of soups prepared from fruit and herbs, roasted meat, eggs, vegetables and pilaf (*pilo*).[85] Fruit undoubtedly provided many needed calories. Jean de Thévenot, a French traveller who visited Iran in the mid-1660s, described how the Iranians were especially immoderate in the amount of fruit they ate. Fryer quoted French inhabitants of Isfahan who said that more melons, cucumbers and other fruit were consumed there in one month than in Italy, France and Spain in half a year.[86]

Sugar was a consistent element in this fruit-centred diet. The wealthy consumed conserves and sherbets in private, not just at formal receptions and when entertaining. Sugar was stored in their houses along with conserves and sherbets. They enjoyed confections made with musk, amber and some sort of conserves before and after their meals.[87] The increased intake of calories from sugar went hand in hand with urbanization. The most extravagant aspect of this, in Fryer's view, was the public baths (*hammam*s). They were found in every city and were open to everyone, and both sexes, for a small price. When visitors of an elevated status retired from a bath and went to put on their clothes, they would find a collection of fruits, sweetmeats and various perfumes, such as rosewater, awaiting them. The attendants and waiters also prepared coffee (*coho*), tea, tobacco or brandy for them.[88] We could say that sugar had become a 'necessity' among Isfahan's lower classes by 1670. In the early 1670s, the confectioners and pastry cooks in the capital requested that the grand vizier (*i'timad al-dawla*) introduce a fixed price for sugar. If the government failed to prevent the merchants who bought sugar products to Bandar Abbas from selling it at unreasonable prices in Isfahan, they claimed that food riots would occur due to a prolonged shortage of supplies.[89]

As in many other sugar-consuming countries, sugar was deemed to be a symbol of prosperity and blessing in Safavid Iran. Dishes prepared with sugar were lavishly consumed during festivals such as Nowruz.[90] At the enthronement of 'Abbas III, a puppet shah, in Isfahan in September 1732, his regent, known as Tahmasb Quli Khan (later Nadir Shah), envisioned the restoration of Safavid power by distributing a 'royal sugar banquet' (*koninklijke suikerbanquet*).[91] The consumption of sweetmeats at special family events, such as a marriage, was also an important social norm in the Safavid period.[92]

The custom of presenting sugar was widespread among upper classes during the Safavid period. During his stay in Isfahan between 1618 and 1621, Della Valle saw 'Abbas I receive large tributes from the governor of Shiraz, *Ghulam* Imam Quli Khan, who was trying to establish Safavid rule in the Iranian littoral of the

Persian Gulf. Included in this tribute were two lumps of loaf sugar, which were so large they needed to be transported in a separate wagon. Interestingly, Della Valle thought the gigantic loaves of sugar reflected the material inferiority that the Iranians felt towards India. He said that the shah had ordered the governor to make them that big in order to demonstrate to the Indian ambassador, who was known to boast about his country's sugar, that Iran was also overflowing with it.[93]

Because of the reciprocal nature of gift-giving in Iran, the presentation of sugar was a sign of mutual social recognition; it provided an opportunity to recognize each actor's place and rank within the Safavid dynasty.[94] Foreign agents in Safavid Iran, from European Companies in particular, complained about the costly custom of offering presents, including sugar, to the shah and high-ranking individuals in order to gain favour and receive benefits. Joan Cunaeus, a Dutch envoy to the court of ʿAbbas II, therefore rejoiced when he received seven big dishes of sweetmeats (*gebakken suiker*) from the court, which had been prepared for the shah at the royal banquet that evening, since this was deemed a great honour.[95]

As Smidt and Della Valle observed, an early-seventeenth-century Iranian banquet was chiefly comprised of a serving of fruits, wine, conserves and pilaf. Further research is required to know when the 'sugar banquet', coffee and tobacco appeared in the ceremonial diet and how they transformed it over time. What we can say with certainty is that this lavish style of eating had become quite common among the upper classes by the fall of the Safavid dynasty. During his court visit in 1717–18, around five years before the Afghan conquest of Iran, Ketelaar recorded that a sugar banquet, coffee, warm rosewater and tobacco were a common Iranian treat (*het gewone traktement van suikerbanquet, cauwa en warm rosewater als ook een caljoen*).[96]

This strong appetite for sugar turned the elites' attention to the economic and financial rewards that sugar offered. In the 1670s, various local officials in ports and provinces, such as the governors of Bandar Abbas, Lar and Shiraz and the customs master of Bandar Abbas, were all involved in the sugar trade.[97] The governors of Lar and Shiraz would earn income from offering travellers provisions, including sweetmeats. Fryer stated that while travelling from Bandar Abbas to Isfahan in 1676, as he approached great cities or populous towns, the governors would send out their deputies to welcome and guide him to his lodgings. They would bring provisions for his party, serving not only dried and fresh sweetmeats but also mutton, barley, rice, etc. Upon their departure, the party was offered horses, but could not leave until they had paid for all these items. He said, 'So soon their humanity is turned to avarice; for how can that be esteemed a gift, which is bestowed with an intent to gain?'[98] In 1706, Sultan Husayn honoured a *sayyid*, Mirza Murtada, with the title of 'the king's merchant' (*koningshandelaar*) and issued an edict ordering his treasurer to give him 4,000 *tuman*s so that he could buy sugar and other bulk goods from the Dutch and English at Bandar Abbas and sell it to other merchants. He was expected to earn a profit, for the edict stipulated that Mirza Murtada had to use two thirds of it to reimburse the court officials (perhaps shared sponsors) and was entitled to the rest.[99] According to Hajji Nabi, one of the VOC's leading trading partners in Shiraz, the court officials included the *nazir-i buyutat* (the superintendent of the royal household).[100]

The court's high demand for sugar was also reflected in the diplomatic practices of the late Safavid period. A change in the commercial relationship between the Safavids and the VOC during the reign of Sultan Husayn reveals this. Silk contracts defined their relationship during the seventeenth century: the VOC bought a given amount of Iranian raw silk from the court for a contracted price, either in cash or goods, every year, and the court in turn gave the Company various commercial privileges, such as trading goods with no inspection and exemption from customs and tolls. For instance, their agreement in 1695, at the beginning of Sultan Husayn's reign, stipulated that the VOC would buy 300 *cargas* of silk at 44 *tumans* per *carga* (200 kg), and the court in turn guaranteed the Company free trade and exemption from customs duties (up to an annual import and export of 20,000 *tumans*) and road tolls (*rahdaris*).[101]

Towards the end of the seventeenth century, however, the higher cost of silk made the court reluctant to deliver the contracted amount, prompting them to look for an alternative financial arrangement.[102] In July 1699, the court suggested that the silk trade be discontinued and offered to confirm the Dutch's usual rights on the condition that the VOC deliver an annual tribute (*recognitie*) of cash, some rarities and goods.[103] The VOC declined to accept this unfavourable change to their treaty. Lengthy negotiations ensued until the court and Dutch ambassador Jacob Hoogkamer finally reached an agreement in November 1701. The new protocol stated that the shah would promise to continue to supply 100 *cargas* of silk at 44 *tumans* every year and allow the VOC exemption from import, export and other duties (*in-, uitvoer en andere gerechtigheden*) up to the amount of 20,000 *tumans* as before. What is noteworthy is that the VOC had to submit goods to the royal workshops (*konigsgebruikhuizen*) as tribute (*schenkagiegoederen*) in order to conclude a silk contract. The Company did not have to send these goods if the shah failed to deliver the contracted amount of silk, but the Company was obliged to send it whenever the shah delivered silk, even if it did not want to accept the goods.[104] The *konigsgebruikhuizen* without a doubt referred to the royal sherbet houses; in 1707 the VOC submitted the treaty goods to the workshops (*serbethuizen*) in return for 40 *cargas* of silk.[105] The new treaty specified the items to be submitted, consisting mostly of castor sugar (83 per cent) with some candy sugar (9 per cent), amounting to 32.2 tons in total (as below).[106]

10,000 *man-i Tabriz* (ca. 2.9 kg) castor sugar
1,120 *man-i Tabriz* candy sugar
144 *man-i Tabriz* cardamom
144 *man-i Tabriz* cloves
284 *man-i Tabriz* cinnamon
284 *man-i Tabriz* pepper
1,000 *mithqal* (4.608 g) nutmeg
130 *man-i Tabriz* mace
650 *mithqal* agarwood
4 *man-i Tabriz* benzoin
24 *man-i Tabriz* white sandalwood

2,000 *mithqal* radix china
8 *man-i Tabriz* nutmeg preserves (*geconfijte*)
4 *man-i Tabriz* preserves of cloves

It was not unusual for the Safavid court to ask for goods, especially sugar, in return for silk, but this arrangement would be further modified after a conflict between the Safavids and the VOC in the 1710s. Early in the decade, their agreement became virtually invalid when it was disclosed that the VOC was 'smuggling' specie out of the country for other merchants, thus exploiting their right of free transport.[107] In June 1715, the shah wanted to expel the Dutch from his country to make it 'all the more prosperous', but the grand vizier, Shah Quli Khan Zangana, asked him to be patient, saying, 'if the Europeans left the country, the prices of sugar and spices would rise'.[108] Instead, the court demanded that the VOC send the specified goods twice a year.[109] The prominent mercantile-cum-political mindset of the Kurdish grand vizier is reminiscent of India's 'portfolio capitalists'.[110] The diplomatic issue was finally settled in August 1717. Sultan Husayn reconfirmed the previous silk contract and stipulated that the VOC be exempt from tolls, road tolls and 'one per cent' (*een pro cent*) of the tariff on their annual imports and exports, up to a limit of 20,000 *tuman*s, with the proviso that they did not smuggle other merchants' goods under the Company's name. However, now it was no longer the silk trade but sugar that secured the Company their usual rights. The royal edict stated that whether the court supplied silk or not, the VOC's commercial privileges would be confirmed only when they submitted the prescribed goods.[111]

In late Safavid Iran, sugar entered existing social and economic contexts and became imbued with a variety of cultural values. Iran's rich fruit diet led to large amounts of cane sugar being imported during the Safavid period. Once associated with conserves and sherbets, sugar became an integral part of the Iranian diet. Iran was considered an important part of 'the Islamic world', but there was no religious or ethnic boundary to sugar consumption in Safavid society, only the issue of affordability (and, to a lesser extent, morality). As Chaudhuri argues, people's diverse tastes profoundly influenced which variety of sugar was used for what purpose, thus generating complex trading networks of suppliers in the Indian Ocean. Although sugar was destined for many different markets in Iran, and probably overseas, the Safavid court was by far the largest consumer. Sugar was in great demand in court circles and was used for medicine, diet, festivities, gifts and treats, and as a fiscal tool. The VOC played a role in all these uses. The shift of focus from silk to sugar in the Dutch-Iranian commercial agreement during the reign of Sultan Husayn illustrates the importance of Dutch diplomatic practices in the Iranian sugar market. It is noteworthy that urban sugar consumption was also commonplace in Safavid Iran. As in Europe and East Asia, although still a 'luxury', by the turn of the eighteenth century sugar had moved closer to becoming a 'necessity' imbued with rich social and economic value, even for the lower urban classes.

Chapter 2

ENDURING DEMAND

The chaos and turmoil in Iran after the fall of the Safavids has led scholars like Floor to stress the imperial and economic decline of this period.[1] On the other hand, Abdullah, Barendse, Fattah, Gommans, Grummon, Hakima, Ricks and Risso have claimed that alternative channels of commerce, away from the turbulent centre of Isfahan, banded together and formed functional political entities. They note that in the second half of the century, the hub of Persian Gulf trade shifted away from Bandar Abbas to the northern ports of Bushire and Basra, as the Zands in Shiraz and the *Mamluk*s in Baghdad encouraged trade through their territories. And Durrani rule in Afghanistan facilitated caravan commerce from Gujarat and Sind to Iran. At the turn of the nineteenth century, the Qajars in Tehran further stimulated these land routes to northern Iran. In the meantime, the rise of the ʿUtub in Kuwait and Bahrain and the Bu Saʿids in Muscat increasingly redirected Indian Ocean shipping to Iran away from the Iranian littoral to East Arabia, while developing a new link with the Iranian hinterland through Sind.[2] Available historical records on sugar flows in Iran and bordering countries largely substantiate these views.

Restructuring the sugar market

The Afghan conquest of Isfahan triggered a prolonged power struggle among regional and local elites in Iran. The Afghans conquered Shiraz, but the Ottomans capitalized on the ensuing political disarray to penetrate into Georgia and Iraq, and under Peter the Great (r. 1682–1725) the Russians invaded the Caspian provinces. Among the many pretenders to the crown of Iran who appeared in this time, Tahmasb, one of Sultan Husayn's sons, became a serious contender thanks to his capable regent, Tahmasb Quli Khan (later Nadir Shah). Born to a branch of the Afshar Turkmen in Khurasan, Nadir joined Tahmasb's camp in 1726 and soon proved to be an intrepid military leader. In September 1729, Nadir delivered a crucial blow to Afghan forces in Mihmandust, near Damghan. The Afghans were routed and left Isfahan after looting it, fearing a popular pro-Safavid uprising. Later that year Tahmasb was enthroned in Isfahan, but Nadir ruled behind the scenes. Nadir's army forced the Ottomans back to their borders and recaptured some parts of the Caucasus. Nadir then deposed Tahmasb and placed his infant son on the throne, only to dethrone the child in 1736 and crown himself as Nadir Shah.

Nadir spent most of his reign in military camps. He marched to Qandahar, then to Delhi and Bukhara, and further campaigns took place in the Caucasus and Iraq. He was also known as the founder of Iran's first navy in the Persian Gulf. He sought to subdue the coastal Arabs as well as the principal ports of Basra and Muscat. However, his incessant military activities meant Iran's population was overburdened with taxes. His capricious rule and aggressiveness generated great terror among his subordinates. In 1747, Nadir was murdered by a band of conspirators led by his nephew, 'Ali Quli Khan, who then assumed the throne as 'Adil Shah (r. 1747–8). However, this did not bring lasting order to Iran but renewed the civil war around the country.

In eastern Iran, Ahmad Khan, chief of the Abdalis Afghans, gained power soon after Nadir's death. Elected by a council of Afghan clan leaders, Ahmad Khan became Ahmad Shah. Crowning himself *Durr-i Durran* (Pearl of Pearls), he established the Durrani dynasty, with his capital at Qandahar. During Ahmad's reign, the Durrani authority extended from Amu Darya (Oxus) to the Gulf of Oman, and from the Ganges plain to Khurasan. After his death in 1772, his son, Timur Shah (r. 1772–93), struggled to maintain his father's polity. He lost effective control of some areas, including Sind, while facing the disintegration of Afghan tribal support, which caused the capital to be moved from Qandahar to Kabul.

In central and western Iran, many competed for supremacy, but Karim Khan, leader of the Zands, a pastoral group of Lurs living in the west, gradually ascended to power. In 1750, he took Isfahan from the Afsharids and formed an alliance with 'Ali Mardan Khan Bakhtiyari in the name of a nominal Safavid shah, and then removed his former ally. After years of warring, Karim Khan defeated his rivals one after the other – including Muhammad Hasan Khan Qajar of Astrabad in 1759 and Fath 'Ali Khan Afshar of Urmia in 1763 – and finally gained rule over all Iran, with the exception of Khurasan, which was a tributary to the Durranis. Unlike Nadir Shah, Karim did not declare himself shah but assumed the title of '*Wakil al-Ra'aya*' (Deputy of the People) in his capital city, Shiraz. However, Karim did have a similar expansionist policy in the Persian Gulf: exerting his influence on Bushire, the outer harbour of Shiraz, he also made efforts to control Basra and Muscat.

The death of Karim Khan in 1779 ushered in a new phase and power struggle, but Agha Muhammad Khan Qajar, a son of Muhammad Hasan Khan, rapidly rose to power. Agha Muhammad, who was Karim's hostage, fled to his native land on the Caspian and launched tireless, aggressive campaigns until he conquered all of Iran. In 1796, he ascended the throne in Tehran, thus founding the Qajar dynasty. In the same year, the new Iranian shah eliminated remnant Afshar elements in Khurasan and thus ended a century of debilitating uncertainty.

Isfahan and Tehran

Isfahan was the largest sugar market during the Safavid period. Understanding the mechanisms of sugar consumption in this city is a good starting point for understanding sugar consumption in general under the Safavids. The Afghan siege of Isfahan, leading to the surrender of Shah Sultan Husayn on 21 October 1722, caused a serious food shortage in the city. It is intriguing that sugar remained a valued source of nutrition during the siege. Prices of staple food goods in the city rose due to the siege, and then, remarkably, the population, rich and poor alike, began to demand sugar. The Dutch East India Company's (*Veregnigde Oostindische Compagnie* [VOC]) Isfahan diary states:

> At present one sees the poor stamping horses' and camels' bones into pieces and then eating them. We have not learnt that the rich show any pity for them by helping them. Meanwhile sugar, which is sold now in the shops instead of bread, because of lack of life's necessities, costs 40 *mahmudi*s or Dfl. 17 for powdered sugar and 44 *mahmudi*s or Dfl. 18.14 per *man* for lump sugar. This commodity sold well, both to the commoners and to the nobles.[3]

In order to quell the population's frustration, a supervisor of comestibles at Isfahan punished some confectioners and allowed the poor to plunder their shops. By taking this measure, the Dutch said, 'it was hoped that the other sellers of life's necessities would be so frightened that they also would sell at lower prices. However, the result was rather the reverse of what had been expected, for all the shops were now closed and one sees only some horse and donkey meat hanging here and there in the bazar'.[4] The demand for sugar during the Afghan siege was so high that, even after the Safavid regime was restored in the early 1730s, the grand vizier kept accusing the East India Company (EIC) of overcharging for sugar during the siege.[5] The VOC was also accused of this. According to English Muscovy Company agent James Spilman, 'the Dutch, during the siege, before the Afghans took the city, got prodigious riches by the sale of a quantity of sugar for money and jewels, for which Shah Mahomed [the Afghan leader Mahmud] imprisoned and fined them very extraordinarily. Yet they made a considerable figure, tho' they pretended to be poor'.[6]

It is likely that the availability of sugar in Isfahan decreased over the course of Nadir's rule. Available lists of the prices of commodities sold at the Isfahan market suggest that the price of sugar began to rise around 1740 (Chart 2.1).

There is little information about the Isfahan market after Nadir's reign. The ongoing power struggle among the Afshars, Karim Khan and ʿAli Mardan Khan in central Iran notwithstanding, in 1750 VOC officials in Bandar Abbas reported that, because of the extraordinarily high price of foodstuffs in the upper regions (*extra duurte der levensmiddelen in de bovenlanden*), the merchants wanted to spend their money to get sugar and fine textiles.[7] This remark is interesting because it reveals that wholesale merchants continued to consider sugar a worthwhile investment, but it is not clear whether the upper regions mentioned here included the area around Isfahan. In any case, the market had become a mere shadow of its former self by 1785. According to Louis-François de Ferrières-Sauveboeuf, a French traveller who stayed in Isfahan between 1784 and 1785, two-thirds of the city was in ruins, and a large number of Iranian inhabitants, and also many Armenians, the principal mercantile community in the city, took refuge in Baghdad and Basra.[8]

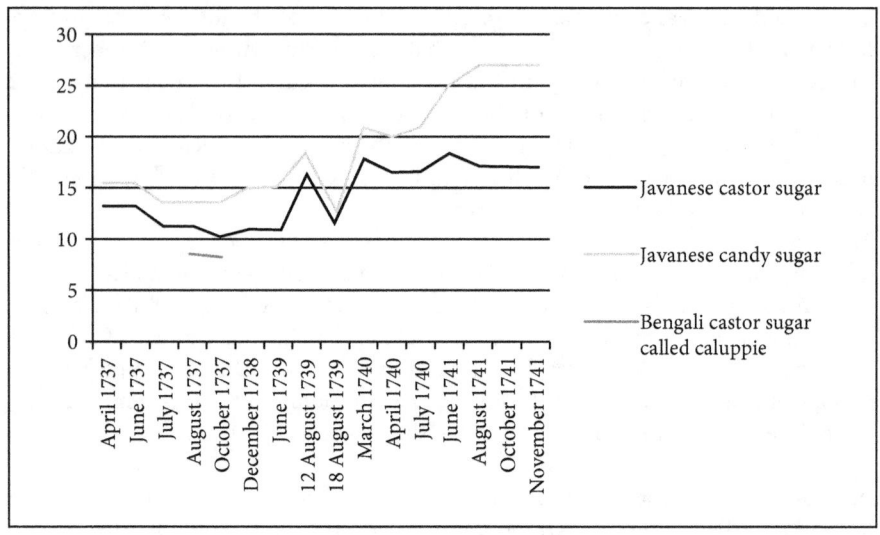

Chart 2.1 Sugar prices at the Isfahan market, 1737–41 (*mahmudi*s per *man-i shahi*).
Source: See Appendix 1.

We know little about Isfahan and its market in the last two decades of the eighteenth century, but urban sugar consumption might have picked up towards the turn of the century. Guillaume-Antoine Olivier, a French entomologist who visited Kirmanshah, Tehran and Isfahan in 1796, commented that the Iranians loved all kinds of sweets (*sucreries*), conserves and candies (*bonbons*).[9] Iran not only imported candy sugar (*sucre candi*) from Bengal and Batavia but also exported fruit preserved in various substances, such as vinegar, grape-jam, and honey, as well as sugar to Hindustan.[10] However, the establishment of the Qajar capital in Tehran attracted more sugar to the new capital. In September 1796, at a caravanserai in Tehran, a resident of Isfahan held a feast for six compatriots who had just come back from Khurasan with the royal army. After music and dramatic performances, he served a supper of cooked rice and meat, sweets (*friandises*), conserves, many fruits and a little wine to around twenty guests.[11] There were many similarities between the Safavid and Qajar courts' consumption of sugar. Sugar was an integral part of political, social and diplomatic life at the Qajar court and was used in cultural practices such as gift-giving and entertaining. Therefore, Justin Perkins, an American missionary who visited early Qajar Iran, remarked that 'the noblemen will have it, be the price exorbitant'. Sugar also featured as a valuable condiment in Qajar cuisine.[12]

Kirman, Yazd and Khurasan

The old commercial highway from Bandar Abbas, through Lar and Shiraz, to Isfahan steadily declined and an alternative avenue from Bandar Abbas – the trading route to northern cities such as Kirman and Yazd – developed significantly.

In the late 1720s, merchants bought sugar from the VOC at Bandar Abbas to send to Kirman.[13] Moreover, merchants from Kirman, Khurasan and Multan became the principal buyers of Dutch sugar at the port, while merchants from Lar, Shiraz and Isfahan faded away.[14]

At first the northern route functioned as an alternative passage to Isfahan. For example, in 1737 a Dutch caravan sent from Bandar Abbas reached Isfahan fifty-one days later, after travelling through Sirjan and Yazd; this was about twenty days longer than the Lar-Shiraz route. After travelling for one month along an unfamiliar mountain pass through Sirjan, the Dutch party was welcomed by the chief toll collector (*rahdar-bashi*) of Yazd. He guided them to an impressively pleasant rest place in a suburb inhabited mostly by Zoroastrians (*Gebbren*). At that time the city was ruled by Muhammad Sharif Beg (Mahmet Sherreeff Beecq). Four days later, the Dutch set out for Isfahan after sending the governor, his secretary and the toll collector the customary gifts, including candy sugar and pepper.[15] During this journey, the caravan encountered six merchants who were also on their way to Isfahan: four Banians, one Armenian and one Khurasani Muslim.[16]

In 1747 Kirman was in utter chaos. Nadir Shah launched a punitive campaign against the city for withholding their tax allocation, which he needed to sustain his relentless military activity. The marauding armies executed a merciless campaign that brutalized the citizens, sacked the city and decimated the population.[17] However, after this dreadful devastation, trans-regional trade resumed. Thereafter, Kirman and Yazd were closely linked with the trade in Khurasan and other locations in the Durrani realm. In 1762, EIC officials in Bandar Abbas noted that all goods traded at Khurasan, Qandahar, Mashhad, etc. headed to Kirman first, and the only alternative passage was via the Sirjan–Yazd route.[18]

Meanwhile, both local and foreign merchants were steadily bypassing Bandar Abbas. As a result, northbound caravan traffic changed course to Minab, an eastern settlement near Bandar Abbas. The EIC noted that caravans laden with various Indian goods left for Kirman and other places in the interior from this town.[19] These goods undoubtedly included sugar from Muscat, then under Bu Saʻid rule, since in those days merchants crossed the Gulf from Minab to Muscat to get it for more competitive prices.[20]

Gujarat and Sind

Barendse argues that sugar supplies to Iran shifted from using sea lanes to a land route. He said that in the latter half of the century, caravan commerce from India to Iran via Herat, a Durrani stronghold, developed to such a degree that it replaced much of the old maritime Gulf trade.[21] In this regard, it is useful to note that during the period following the decline of the Safavids, maritime traders increasingly explored sugar markets in west India, especially Gujarat. From the late 1740s, Surat, a leading trading port in Gujarat, experienced an influx of sugar. Dutch sales of Javanese castor sugar tripled, from 27.1 million pounds between 1702 and 1744 to 81.2 million pounds between 1746 and 1791.[22] The English and Portuguese also imported sugar from Bengal, Batavia, Malacca and China, while the French did the same from Mauritius in the last quarter of the century.[23] Moreover, by 1790 indigenous cane sugar also contributed to a competitive market.[24]

Why did sugar accumulate in Surat in the latter half of the eighteenth century? G. Nadri suggests that sugar consumption in Gujarat grew substantially in the eighteenth century. Although part of the sugar imported to Surat moved on to Deccan, Kutch, Sind, Multan and even Tibet, he claims that a large part of it was consumed in Gujarat, because 'a large cluster of relatively prosperous intermediate and subaltern groups' in the region increased their sugar consumption during that period.[25]

One may safely assume two additional reasons for the enormous flow of sugar into Surat. First, those who received sugar from Surat also promoted sugar consumption in their own towns. Second, under the Durranis Sind developed as a significant redistribution centre for sugar to Khurasan. The VOC's trial marketing in Sind in 1757 is a case in point. In the seventeenth century, the Dutch, as well as the Portuguese and English, regarded Sind as an important textile-producing country. The articles manufactured there yielded good profits in Iran, but more importantly in Basra. In order to promote this trade, the VOC built a factory in Sind in the 1650s.[26] One century later, however, the possibility of selling Javanese sugar there appealed to the VOC. During their expedition, the Dutch described Javanese castor sugar as a principal commodity, 'without which, it is impossible for that nation [the population of Sind] to survive'.[27] It was commonplace for town rulers to treat guests to various items, such as sweetmeats and rosewater.[28] They also wrote that two Afghan merchants (*Aguaanse kooplieden*) named 'Gopieramme' and 'Radjarimal' bought their sugar.[29] These Afghan merchants might have only conducted local trade, but in the late eighteenth century, Sind was a site for transit trade. In 1790 the EIC wrote:

> The southern parts of Khurasan are supplied with such foreign articles as are in demand there from Muscat by means of the Indus. And the northern traits of this province are sometimes supplied from the same place, when impediments occur to its communication with Ispan [Isfahan] or the northern and eastern parts of Hindostan [Hindustan].[30]

This comment shows that even if Durrani authority over the region wavered, Sind received supplies of sugar from Muscat, and from there it was carried up the Indus River to the southern parts of Khurasan; and when the province was cut off from supplies from Isfahan and Hindustan it headed further north.

Basra and Iraq

Recently, historians of early modern Iran have focused on continuity and change in Iranian society during the period spanning from the fall of the Safavids to the rise of the Qajars.[31] The development of Sind as an alternative route for sugar circulation, however, invites analysis of situations in a context beyond Iran's geographical boundaries. Iraq was another important site for trade.

In response to the Ottoman invasion of western Iran, Nadir Shah sent troops to Iraq in 1733 and besieged Baghdad in 1737. Ahmad Pasha, the formidable governor (*wali*) of the Ottoman province of Baghdad (r. 1723/24–47), successfully repelled him with his *Mamluk* corps. Like *Ghulam*s in Safavid Iran, *Mamluk*s were recruited from the Caucasus, especially from Georgia. It is said that Ahmad's father, the former governor of Baghdad, Hasan Pasha (r. 1704–23/24), initiated their recruitment. The *Mamluk*s served as an integral part of the Ottoman army and administration in Iraq. In 1743 Nadir's troops once again invaded Iraq, but Ahmad repelled them once again.[32]

In the meantime, Basra developed as a prominent hub for trans-regional sugar trade across the Persian Gulf. The EIC and VOC re-entered the market by 1725. Some of the imported sugar was re-exported to Iran. In 1737 VOC residents in Isfahan reported that some '*Gorguaanse kooplieden*' (either Gorgan or Georgian merchants) came over from Basra and sold castor sugar.[33] According to Abdullah, Basra was initially a semi-autonomous entity but came under the jurisdiction of the Ottoman province of Baghdad in 1733. Ahmad Pasha died in 1747, and his *Mamluk* son-in-law Sulayman Pasha succeeded him. He gained virtual independence from the Sublime Porte, thus beginning the *Mamluk* dynasty (1749–1831). After 1750 Basra was firmly under *Mamluk* control. The city was administered by a governor (*mutasallim*) appointed by the governor of Baghdad, a commander of the fleet (*qapudan pasha*), a customs master (*shahbandar*), and other officials.[34]

In 1753, the VOC left Basra and established a new commercial base on Kharg Island in order to create their own hub for sugar trading in the Upper Gulf. In 1759 the Company also left Bandar Abbas to concentrate on Kharg trade. The Dutch project on the island continued with some successes until 1766, but this does not mean trade in Basra was in decline. Rather, relatively stable *Mamluk* rule facilitated trade. During his stay at Basra in the latter half of 1765, the German traveller Carsten Niebuhr saw many Armenians establish factories in the city after turmoil broke out in Iran. He acknowledged Sulayman Pasha's contribution to increased security in the region. Sulayman's rule (1749–62) met with so much approval that, 'upon his death, the Arabs made lamentations, which one still often hears in the coffee houses and on the street in Baghdad. Never have the Arabs been controlled as well as in his reign and that of his father-in-law'. The Arab nomads held him in awe, calling him *Abu Layla* (Father of Night), because he usually made night raids, giving them no chance of escape. As a result, Niebuhr noted, the trade from India that used to pass through Bandar Abbas and Isfahan now passed through Basra and Baghdad.[35] This is an interesting clue about the Caucasians' role in further shaping Indian Ocean sugar trade in the early modern period. Former *Ghulam*s, such as Imam Quli Khan, opened up a major sugar supply channel into Iran, and now the *Mamluk*s had diverted it to Iraq.

While Basra functioned as a centre for redistributing sugar to Iran, we should not overlook the fact that Iraq was also a significant sugar-consuming country. Part of the sugar imported to Basra after the Safavid period was meant for regional consumption. Julius Griffiths, an Englishman travelling from Aleppo to Basra in 1786, noted that the Coromandel Coast and Bengal supplied rice, sugar, muslins

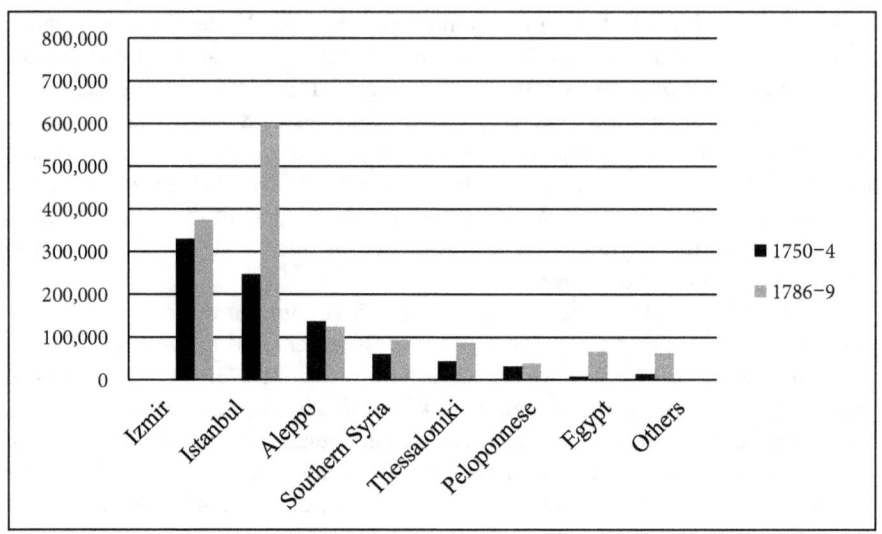

Chart 2.2 French sugar imports to the Levant, 1750–4 and 1786–9 (*livres tournois*).

Source: R. Paris, *De 1600 à 1789. Le Levant*, vol. 5 of *Histoire du commerce de Marseille* (Paris: Librairie Plon, 1957), 558.

and a vast quantity of white and blue cloths for common use.[36] What is even more remarkable, however, is that American sugar entered markets in Iraq in the latter half of the eighteenth century. Atlantic Ocean sugar, refined in Marseilles and reshipped to the Levant, was increasingly sold in major Ottoman markets, such as Izmir, Istanbul and Aleppo (Chart 2.2).[37]

Some of the French sugar sent to Aleppo was probably re-exported further eastwards, though still in limited quantities. English naval surgeon Edward Ives, passing through Mosul in 1758, said that European lump and powder sugar was very scarce and expensive there, while candy sugar was more readily available, and at rather reasonable prices.[38] Since American sugar was superior to Indian sugar, Olivier commented, it was always preferred, unless the price was very dear. Yet, significant amounts of sugar also came from Batavia and Bengal through Basra for consumption in Baghdad and Arabia, and some of this was also destined for Iran.[39]

Bushire and Shiraz

While the Iraqi route under *Mamluk* rule became a prominent supply line to Iran, on the northern Iranian littoral new waterways emerged alongside the rise of regional powers. The port of Bushire is located at the northern end of a low-lying peninsula projecting from the northern Iranian littoral. Although it was known as a port of some local importance by the seventeenth century, it remained a small port on the Gulf, little more than a fishing village.[40] It was not until the late 1720s, when increased insecurity made travel from Bandar Abbas to Shiraz difficult for merchants, that Bushire began to develop as a major port of entry to Shiraz.[41] In the mid-1730s, the town gained prominence in the region after Nadir Shah selected it as the base for his naval campaigns against Basra (1735), Bahrain (1736), Oman (1737–9, 1742–4), and Makran (1739).[42] The VOC set up a trading post at the port in 1737.

We do not know much about the bureaucratic structure of the port during the eighteenth century, but the main administrators seem to have been a governor (*sultan*) and a customs master (*shahbandar*). Towards the middle of the century, the Madhkurs, a local Arab family, supposedly of Omani origin, consolidated uncontested authority over the port, and members of the family retained both positions for the rest of the century.[43] Following Nadir's death, Bushire was mired in local power struggles, which made the VOC retreat from the port in 1753. However, neighbouring ports such as Bandar Rig, Bandar Deylam and Bandar Ganaveh emerged in its place, and they continued to receive Dutch goods, especially sugar from Kharg, for inland cities such as Shiraz and Isfahan.[44]

After Karim Khan Zand assumed sole power in Iran in the first half of the 1760s, trade prospered around his capital, Shiraz. Archaeological evidence shows that located at the foot of the Zagros Mountains, Shiraz was well connected to Gulf ports, including Bushire, Bandar Rig, Bandar Deylam, and Bandar Ganaveh, by a refined network of caravanserais; some sites in the province of Fars can be dated back to Karim's rule.[45] Vibrant regional commerce also attracted the EIC to Bushire. In 1763 the EIC abandoned their Bandar Abbas factory, and as a consequence, their chief establishment shifted to Basra, and Bushire was a secondary trading station. They soon withdrew, but returned to the port in 1776.

Karim followed in Nadir's footsteps and attempted to control Gulf trade. Demanding a tribute from the Bu Sa'id imam Ahmad b. Sa'id (r. 1749–83), he aspired to extend his authority over Muscat. In 1775 he turned his eyes towards Basra, sending his troops to take the port from the *Mamluks*. During the subsequent siege, the Bu Sa'ids, who had considerable business interests in Basra, sent vessels with provisions for the besieged, but the city fell to the Zands, who occupied it until 1778.[46] The tripartite power struggle among the Zands, *Mamluks* and Bu Sa'ids is indicative of the enormous economic rewards that Gulf trade offered regional ruling elites.

The arrival of sugar suppliers on the northern Iranian littoral generated consumers in Zand Shiraz. William Francklin, an EIC servant who stayed in Shiraz between 1786 and 1787, was favourably impressed by the sumptuous bathhouses there. He wrote:

> During the spring, the bath in Persia are decorated in great finery, a custom distinguished by the natives under the name of Gul Reàzee [*gul-rizi*] (or the scattering of roses), from the vast quantity of those flowers strewed in the apartments; this ceremony continues a week or ten days, during which time the guests are entertained with music, dancing, coffee, sherbet, &c. and the dressing apartment is decked out with paintings, looking-glasses, streamers and other ornaments at the expence [*sic*] of the master of the humaùm [*hammam*],

who compliments his customers on the occasion, though a small present is generally made by them to the musicians. The baths are used alternatively by men and women every other day, but each sex generally use them once a week, or in every ten days at farthest.[47]

It is probable that in the vicinity of Shiraz, even the lower classes, such as farmers, were familiar with sugar, not just cheap local sweeteners like grapes and manna.[48] In 1802 an EIC merchant, Scott Waring, wrote that an antidote against animal poisons called '*dum*' (*dam*, i.e. breath) was well known there. People believed that the power to withstand animal toxins occurred in a person as a reward for fasting and meditation, and this immunity could be passed on to someone, the beneficiary deemed deserving of the blessing. Many people visited a man with such gifts at the time of the wheat harvest, and he extended his favours by breathing onto a piece of sugar (or something else) that they were then ordered to swallow.[49]

The Caspian provinces

It is clear that Iran continued to import sugar through various channels after the fall of the Safavids. Not only did the immediate hinterland of the Persian Gulf, including Shiraz, import sugar, but also remote parts such as Tehran and Khurasan. Further north, Gilan and Mazandaran were also major destinations for sugar. Gilan and Mazandaran were an important economic centre in Safavid Iran because of the raw silk produced there, one of the few local products that could generate substantial foreign demand. Probably due to its rich natural resources, after the dynasty fell, there were territorial tussles between the Russians and the Iranians near Iran's northern borders, as well as repeated hostilities among regional ruling powers. There is little doubt that the Caspian economy was seriously affected by these incursions, but quite surprisingly, available sources tell us that sugar markets in the Caspian provinces were very active in the late eighteenth century because of consumption patterns. In the early 1770s, German botanist Samuel Gottlieb Gmelin noted that Iranians living in the Caspian regions had exceptional sweet tooths. There were all kinds of sugar-coated fruits and various jams on their plates, in which 'they indulge in a very wasteful manner, because they uncommonly love sweetmeats'.[50]

Where did the sugar come from? George Forster, an Englishman travelling from India overland via the Caspian to England in 1783–4, said that despite the demand for sugar in the southern territories of Russia, one would expect the Mazandaran region to 'derive extensive benefits from such a possession, especially through its navigable vicinity to the southern territories of Russia, where a large quantity is consumed, at an advanced price'. Forster concluded, however, that due to 'an ignorance in the methods of preparing and refining it, this valuable product yields but a limited utility'.[51] Much in the same vein, Gmelin stated that, because of its unrefined form, Mazandaran sugar was hard to dissolve in tea, had an unpleasant rancid taste, and looked blackish-yellow.[52] Sugar suitable for further processing was brought in from the Persian Gulf. Gmelin noticed that Isfahan

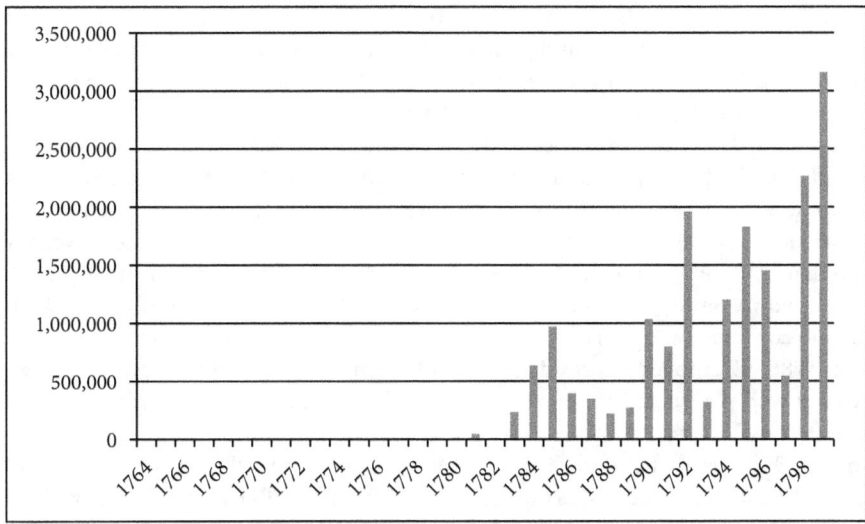

Chart 2.3 British sugar imports to Russia, 1764–99 (British pounds).

Source: A. Kahan, *The Plow, the Hammer and the Knout: An Economic History of Eighteenth-Century Russia* (Chicago: University of Chicago Press, 1985), 222–5 (table 4.63).

supplied sugar and cotton manufactured goods to Mazandaran.[53] Considering that Iran was relatively well connected to Gulf trade under Karim's rule, it is likely that sugar carried in from Isfahan came via Bushire. The EIC in Bushire wrote that sugar was one of the articles most in demand in the Gilan market.[54]

As in Iraq, the Caspian countries had also begun to import American sugar from Russia, presumably in the latter half of the eighteenth century, and Russia increasingly imported refined sugar from Great Britain over the North and the Baltic Seas towards the end of the century (Chart 2.3).

Sugar became a prized delicacy among the Russian gentry, but some of the sugar sent to Russia was destined for northern Iran.[55] Gmelin mentioned that Shamakhi and Rasht imported various goods, including sugar, from Russia.[56] According to Forster, the sugar sent from Russia was American sugar. He stated that the sugar he bought at Mashhadsar in Mazandaran was 'the produce of West Indies, manufactured in England, and imported at Petersburgh [St. Petersburg], whence it came into Persia by the tract of Astracan [Astrakhan]'.[57]

Muscat

The flexibility of the sugar trade in the Persian Gulf and the adjoining countries after the Safavid period illustrates Muscat's importance as a principal hub for Indian Ocean sugar trade. After the death of the Yaʿrubi imam Sultan b. Sayf in 1718, a war of succession broke out, and hostilities rapidly spread throughout the interior. However, Muscat transit trade carried on. In 1725 the VOC explored the possibility of trading sugar there for the money they needed.[58] The transit trade became connected to India's Malabar Coast in the 1730s. From 1730, numerous merchants from Cambay, Sind, Kutch, Muscat, etc. who formerly traded in the Persian Gulf, began to visit the Dutch trading station at Cochin to buy sugar and other commodities for their home countries.[59]

From 1737 until 1747, the political situation in Oman became more fluid because of Nadir Shah's military intervention. During this period, he used his navy to nominally support Sayf b. Sultan, a contender for the imamate, but more likely to subjugate the country. Iranian intruders were contained by the Ya'rubi governor of Suhar, Ahmad b. Sa'id, and he founded the Bu Sa'id dynasty after his success.[60]

Ahmad b. Sa'id and his successors firmly controlled Muscat and were able to pursue commercial opportunities thanks to Indian Ocean trade. Hamad b. Sa'id (r. c. 1786–92) moved his residence from the inland capital of Rustaq to Muscat. Sugar trade played an important part in this commerce. Batavia sent sugar to Muscat on Company ships in 1756 and 1757, and on private ones between 1777 and 1793. Towards the end of the century the Bu Sa'id sultan Sultan b. Ahmad (r. 1792–1804) engaged in this lucrative trade, and he regularly sent ships to Batavia to purchase sugar.[61] As a result, Muscat rose as the major sugar depository for West Asian markets. In 1790 the EIC reported that the import of sugar to Muscat was very large and sufficient 'for the supply in that indispensably necessary article of the countries of Persia, Arabia Deserta, Mesopotamia, Coordistan [Kurdistan], Armenia, Georgia and Natolia [Anatolia]'.[62]

War and the persistence of urban sugar consumption

The remarkable continuity of the sugar trade in the Persian Gulf during the eighteenth century poses the question: who consumed the imported sugar? In Iran, the ruling classes retained a strong demand for sugar. VOC archival documents containing material from Iran after the Safavid period, particularly during Nadir Shah's rule, include numerous accounts of the goods that the Company presented to the shah and state officials. Many of these presents included castor and candy sugar.[63]

Rising local powers also actively participated in the economy of gift-giving and entertaining. Sometime after his arrival in Bushire in August 1737, Dutch agent Jacob van Schoonderwoerd was informed that a leading figure of Bushire, Shaykh Madhkur (*Scheeg Maskoer*), the head of the Arab Madhkur family, had given presents, including two horses and a large quantity of candy and castor sugar, to the *sardar* (commander-in-chief) of Nadir Shah's troops, Mirza Mahdi, who was then in charge of suppressing the Gulf Arabs. The Dutch were therefore obliged to promise to prepare commensurate presents as soon as possible.[64] At the feast of '*Id al-Fitr*, the shaykh visited the Dutch lodge with a great retinue. Schoonderwoerd had to serve all of them coffee, rosewater and sugar 'according to the local custom' (*na 'slands gebruykt*).[65]

Another important group of consumers were the servants of rulers. A Muscovy Company agent, Hanway, travelling in the Caspian region in the early 1740s, said that the practice of entertaining was vital for the powerful to sustain a relationship with their subordinates. When he realized that the sweetmeats he served to his guests were mostly taken away by their servants, he said:

> ... is it not absurd, in fine, that a strange corruption of manners should induce almost every master to contract with his servant that the greatest part of his wages shall be paid him by his neighbours, though his own expenses are by this means not only increased, but also rendered impatient and vexatious, whilst servants, on the other hand, become extravagant, in consequence of these preposterous revenues, and their morals spoiled by the folly of their masters?[66]

The ruling elite's incessant demand for sugar was an annoying factor that increased operating costs, but in post-Safavid Iran, it is likely that offering or receiving sugar as a hospitable treat acted as an important element of polity-making. In his comment on Iranian conventional regaling, Francklin stated that Iranian hospitality had lost some of its former art because of the protracted civil war, but it played a new role in displaying subordination and mastery in uncertain times.

> A practice of the hospitality is with them [Iranians] so grand a point that a man thinks himself highly honoured if you will enter his house and partake of what the family affords, whereas going out of a house without smoking a *caleàn* [*qalyan*], or taking any refreshment, is deemed affront; that they say that every meal a stranger partakes with them brings a blessing upon the house. To account for this, we must understand it as a pledge of faith and protection, when consider that the continual wars, in which this country has been involved, with very little cessation, since the extinction of the Sefi family [the Safavids], has greatly tended to a universal depravity of disposition, and a perpetual inclination to acts of hostility. This has lessened that softness and urbanity of manners for which this nation has been at all former times so famous, and has at the same time too much extinguished all sentiments of honour and humanity amongst those of higher rank.[67]

As discussed in the previous chapter, urban sugar consumption grew substantially during the late Safavid period. In the period that followed, sugar continued to be consumed in cities and towns, especially when there was relatively stable rule and order. A scarcity of contemporary accounts about Kirman, Yazd and Khurasan makes it difficult to ascertain the precise details of sugar consumption there. It seems, however, that Kirman and Yazd's development as great commercial nodes after the Safavid period led to an increased use of sugar as gifts to authorities, as well as at caravan stations located along the trading routes to these cities.[68]

The inhabitants of Zand Shiraz were accustomed to consuming sugar on special family occasions. A proposal for marriage would involve the father or mother of the prospective bridegroom (or sometimes his sister), along with his friends, going to the house of the intended bride. If the woman's father accepted the proposal, he would immediately order sweetmeats to be brought out as an unambiguous sign of agreement. A few days after a child was born, the friends and relatives of the mother would assemble at her house to enjoy music and dancing girls. After this amusement, a learned Muslim (*mulla*) would be introduced. He would take the baby in his arms and ask the mother what name she had chosen for the child. Then, the *mulla* would begin to pray, reciting the name into the infant's ear three times so the baby would remember it, and tell the child to be obedient to his/her parents and to venerate the Quran and the Prophet Muhammad. Having repeated the profession of faith (*shahada*), the *mulla* would return the child to the mother. Then the company would be entertained with sweetmeats, some of which the female attendants would take away in their pocket since they believed it was an 'infallible means' of having babies themselves.[69]

The practice of giving a sugar treat also had an important place in urban life along the Caspian coast. Peter Henry Bruce, an English military man who joined the Russian campaign to the western and southern coasts of the Caspian Sea in 1722, happened to meet one of the principal inhabitants of Tarki (Tirku), Daghistan on the street. Although he did not have an appointment, the man welcomed Bruce and several officers to his residence, where he entertained them with coffee, fruit and sweetmeats.[70] Another English military man, John Elton, also experienced this customary hospitality. When he dropped by a town called 'Languaon' (possibly Langarud) east of Rasht, in 1739, the vizier of the place treated him to coffee, tea and sweetmeats.[71] The people of the town liked to consume sweetmeats when drinking. During his visit to an admiral in the Persian navy, Muhammad Khan, at Barfurush (Balfrufh), Hanway was entertained with a supper, as well as with dance and music. After dinner, the admiral invited him to drink brandy. When he declined, Muhammad Khan expressed much amusement that Hanway, 'being an European and Christian, did not delight in spirituous liquors'. It was common, Hanway commented, 'for each person to set a plate of sweet-meats before him, and drink their liquor in tea-cups till they are drunk, which is generally affected in a very short time'.[72]

Generally speaking, the daily diet of the powerful and wealthy was the same as during the Safavid period. Just like Europeans who visited late Safavid Iran, at the turn of the nineteenth century, Olivier was amazed at the population's taste for conserves, cakes and sherbets, which was a stark contrast to their meagre diet:

> People perfectly know how to preserve a great number of fruits well all the year around, but it is conserves, candies and cakes (*gâteaux*) in which the Persians excel. Nowhere else have I seen so much of them nor tasted them as pleasant. They preserve a large number of products of the country in sugar. They import much of it from India. They make candies and cakes in all forms and colours with some rice flour and wheat flour, together with eggs, honey, almonds, pistachios, pignolias, sesame, grape-jam, sugar and particularly manna ... They preserve in sugar a great number of flowers and fruits, in which they put all the essences and perfumes of the Orient. The sherbets or beverages which they consumed around the clock are equally varied, equally good, and equally flavoured.[73]

The rise of the Iraqi sugar market in the eighteenth century reflected a bustling social life in communal meeting places, notably coffee houses. Periodic conflicts and epidemics notwithstanding, residents of the inhabited areas dotted along major trading routes in Iraq had active social lives during the eighteenth century. Baghdad played an important role. In October 1774, Abraham Parsons, an English merchant, witnessed the scars left behind by a plague that hit Baghdad one year earlier. He wrote that the disease had reduced the population – of around 500,000 before the plague – to less than 100,000. On the other hand, he also witnessed a strong recovery taking place. He calculated that since the plague had abated in July 1773, it had grown to 200,000 inhabitants.[74] Consequently, a bustling urban life returned. What excited Parson's curiosity was the popularity of coffee houses. According to his investigations, there were 955 coffee houses on the Persian side of the Tigris, of which more than half had been leased within the last six months. It was usual to see anywhere from 200 to 300 people at a time in these venues, some playing chess and others smoking, drinking coffee, or engaging in similar leisure activities.[75] People also enjoyed sherbet in the coffee houses.[76]

Around the same time, al-Hilla became known as 'Little Baghdad' because the town and its buildings looked so much like those in Baghdad. Straddling the Euphrates, the town also had many licensed coffee houses. Parsons estimated the population to be upwards of 30,000.[77] In spite of Nadir Shah's siege in 1743, Mosul remained active. Niebuhr, who travelled from Basra to Aleppo via Baghdad in 1766, wrote that Mosul seemed to have developed recently. He estimated it to have a population of 20,000–24,000 and described the city as reasonably handsome. All public coffee houses, baths and bazars belonged to the ruling family of 'Abd al-Jalil.[78]

The remarkable vigour of urban life in Iraq during the eighteenth century can be attributed to the gradual migration of people away from Iran to major Iraqi cities. Many Armenians moved to Basra after the Afghan conquest. Samuel Eversfield, an EIC agent who visited Baghdad in 1779, wrote that the city was large and populous, enjoying the considerable commercial advantage of the Tigris. There were nearly 80,000 houses in the city, and the inhabitants consisted mainly of Iranians, Armenians, Turks and Jews.[79] On his way back from Isfahan in 1785, Ferrières-Sauveboeuf was also impressed by the grandeur of the city. He attributed it to three things: immigration from Iran, urbanization resulting from the inflow of Arabs who were 'fed up with life in tents', and the city's location, which was suited to commerce. In connection to the first point, he said that 'a great number of Iranians had come over with their families, while the Armenians, refugees from Julfa [at Isfahan], had brought their resources and industry'.[80] About ten years later, Mosul was very prosperous. Olivier noted that the population of the province of Mosul was 200,000, and that, since the city was one of the great markets in the Orient, merchants who sought shelter from regional conflicts ran to this growing entrepôt and engaged in commerce freely.[81] In Olivier's view, Baghdad was more an Iranian city than a Turkish one, because there were a large number of bazars devoted to merchants and workers. He stated that since Sulayman (*Abu Layla* or the Great,

r. 1780–1802) became governor of Baghdad, the population had increased by 30,000–40,000, of whom 12,000–15,000 were Iranians who had escaped the troubles and civil wars to which their homeland had been subjected for more than half a century. Jews and Armenians had also settled in the city in order to expand their commercial enterprises to Turkey and India.[82]

Iraqi upper classes, like their Iranian counterparts, valued the use of sugar. Ives experienced this at the provincial court of al-Diwaniya, a town on the highway between Basra and Baghdad. After his arrival from Basra on 10 May 1758, he and his English companions had an audience with the governor of al-Diwaniya, 'Ali Agha, who was 'a native of Persia' and 'the most important [official] of any in this part of the world, the Basha of Baghdad excepted'. He commanded a vast region extending from al-Qurna, where the power of the governor of Basra ended, and up the river as far as al-Hilla.[83] During the reception, 'Cojee Pagoose', an Armenian merchant from Basra who was staying in al-Diwaniya, and a man called 'Hemet' served as interpreters for the English party.[84] According to Ives, Hemet was of French origin. He had served the EIC at Isfahan as an interpreter for many years, but because of the civil war he had left Iran. He joined Ives at Basra and was now on his way to Baghdad, 'where his family resided, and he proposed carrying them from thence to Venice, his wife's native [place]'.[85] 'Ali Agha talked to the English party through the intermediaries of Cojee Pagoose and Hemet; Pagoose spoke to Hemet in Persian and then Hemet translated this into French, and sometimes into 'broken' English, to the party. Meanwhile, the party was served a saucer of sweetmeats. Some members tasted four or five very small spoonfuls and obviously intended to finish the whole saucerful. Hemet stopped them, however, because tasting just one spoonful would have been more polite, whispering 'for dat one spoonful only, was de more polite'. Then a small cup of coffee was brought, and after a short interval, a small basin of warm sweet water scented with roses. Lastly, their handkerchiefs were dampened with rosewater, and their noses were refreshed with ambergris and agarwood smoke.[86] In November 1774, travelling from al-Hilla for five days, Parsons arrived at 'a very large Arab town on the Chaldean side' of the Euphrates called 'Arjar'. The town, consisting of tents, was governed by 'an *emir* (an Arabian prince)'. After offering some presents, Parsons invited the Arab governor to his cabin to drink coffee and smoke a pipe. When the governor came to the ship, sweetmeats were served. Parsons wrote that, on this occasion, the governor not only ate the sweetmeats but also filled his pocket with them, and his followers, more than ten in total, followed their master's example.[87]

It was also a sign of respect to serve sherbet and conserves. On 20 July 1730, when Dames Heij and Carel Koenad, the VOC residents at Basra, visited the governor, they were treated to coffee and sherbet according to local custom.[88] Upon his arrival in Mosul in June 1743, Jean Otter, a French envoy to Nadir Shah's court, had an audience with Husayn Pasha (Huseïn Pacha), the governor of the city, at his residence (*seraï*). After exchanging the usual Turkish greetings, Otter and the governor conversed with each other in Persian and Arabic. Meanwhile, the governor entertained him with conserves and coffee. The audience lasted one hour and then sherbet and perfume were brought in, and after that Otter took his leave. About one week after he left Mosul Otter had another reception with a Kurd chief (*buluk bashi*), 'Abd al-Rahman Agha. The chief invited Otter to his tent – his companions were invited to other tents – and was civilly treated to dinner. In return for this warm reception Otter sent him several pounds of tobacco and Mocha coffee, a box of sherbet (ingredients?), and dozens of coffee (beans?).[89]

A question that has yet to be answered is how these individuals developed their purchasing power. Recently, R. Kazemi and G. Sood have suggested that there was significant commerce in Iran and Iraq during the eighteenth century. They argue that people in these countries, especially those outside governmental purview, increased their business activities over the course of the century.[90] Another consideration to point out is that after the Safavid period, copper became an important alternative export to gold and silver. Gold and silver came from Europe, but copper was produced in Anatolia, Kirman and Khurasan. It is likely that this relatively easy access relieved the population of some of the chronic financial hardships that plagued them. I shall return to this subject in Chapters 4 and 5.

After the demise of the Safavid court, which had been the main market for sugar, many other markets developed throughout Iran and neighbouring countries. While the distribution route changed, the trade continued. Accordingly, sugar supplies followed different channels. These changes coincided with the rise of efficient regional governments: the Durranis in Afghanistan, the *Mamluks* in Baghdad, the Qajars in Tehran, the Zands in Shiraz, and the Bu Sa'ids in Muscat. As a result, the Bandar Abbas-Yazd-Kirman route, the Basra-Baghdad route, and the Bushire-Shiraz route became the main supply lines from the Gulf, while Muscat rose significantly as a major distribution centre of sugar for West Asian markets. A lively consumption of sugar continued in regional courts and towns after the fall of the Safavids. In Iran, the regional and local elites demanded large amounts of sugar in their power struggles because it was a source and symbol of power. Therefore, even after the Safavids were removed, the ruling classes were still the primary sugar consumers. However, what is more remarkable is the persistent demand for it in West Asian urban life. Sugar featured as an indispensable social tool in urban arenas, particularly in the Caspian regions and Iraq. These regions began to import American sugar from Russia and the Mediterranean. This process of the globalization of the West Asian market would develop further in the following century, but we should not overlook the fact that it concurred with vigorous regional realignment. The growth of the Iraqi sugar market in the eighteenth century may well owe much to a gradual migration from Iran to Iraq after the Safavid period. Through this process, Iraq increasingly shared a socio-cultural setting with Iran, where sugar enjoyed a privileged dietary status.

Thus, the flexibility and endurance apparent in the eighteenth-century consumption of sugar in West Asia underlies the resilient nature of the circulation of sugar in the Persian Gulf during that period. Outlets for sugar in the Gulf corresponded to shifting political and commercial magnets in the interior. This gives rise to questions. Who was involved in transporting the flexible supplies of sugar into the Gulf? What enabled them to adjust rapidly to the changing conditions of trade? In order to answer these questions, in subsequent chapters we shall investigate data from the eighteenth-century Gulf sugar suppliers.

Chapter 3

SUGAR TRADE IN THE PERSIAN GULF: THE VOC

The revamping of the West Asian sugar market beyond Iran after the decline of the Safavid dynasty promoted the development of many ports of trade in the Persian Gulf. To show how sugar suppliers adjusted to the new environment, this chapter will present an overview of eighteenth-century Dutch East India Company (*Verenigde Oostindische Compagnie* [VOC]) sales of sugar in the Gulf. During this period and up to their final withdrawal from the Gulf in 1766, the Company traded in Javanese sugar at multiple locations in the Gulf, including Bandar Abbas (1722–59), Basra (1724–53), Bushire (1737–53) and Kharg Island (1753–66). Although Nadri analyses this particular trade using many of the so-called *rendementen* (the VOC's annual sales statements) recorded at these places, he deals with the sugar sales of different trading posts collectively as 'Persia'.[1] In order to get a clearer picture of the extent to which the Company adjusted to the reorganization of the Gulf market, this chapter will examine sugar sales at each station using the Company's *rendementen*.

Bandar Abbas

The VOC was a joint-stock company run by a board of seventeen directors known as the '*Heren Zeventieen*' or '*Heren XVII*', who were based in Amsterdam. The *Heren XVII* entrusted the management of operations in Asia to the High Government of Batavia, the Governor-General and Council of the Indies (*Gouverneur-Generaal en Raden van Indië*). Within the VOC operation in Asia, 'Persia' formed a directorate, or an area with a director (*directeur*) as its head officer; the director was based in Bandar Abbas for most of the time. In 1713 the Dutch factory in Bandar Abbas was manned by twenty-nine people, twenty-four of whom were administrative personnel. This number remained almost the same until 1722, when Batavia sent reinforcements due to increased insecurity along Iran's southern coast: 150 soldiers, five officers, nine sergeants and twelve corporals. The VOC had a branch office in Isfahan (1623–1746). The Isfahan factory played an important role with the Company's export of items for overseas markets, such as Iranian raw silk and precious metals. The VOC also had a trading post in Kirman for procuring goat wool, as well as an operational base in Shiraz for making exportable wine.

The Persian directorate included not only Iran but also Basra and Muscat when the need arose. The VOC's Asian operation had a formal hierarchy. The director held the status of senior merchant (*opperkoopman*). Under him, in descending order of rank, were a merchant (*koopman*), a junior merchant (*onderkoopman*), a bookkeeper (*boekhouder*) and finally, an assistant (*assistent*).[2]

Although raw silk brought the VOC to Safavid Iran, they promptly noticed that Iran could provide gold and silver for export. Since these precious metals were essential for financing their intra-Asian trade, the VOC increasingly participated in the marketplace, where Taiwanese sugar initially played a key role.[3] In 1651 Bandar Abbas imported 306,762 pounds of castor sugar and 301,404 pounds of candy sugar from Taiwan and also sold 571,424 pounds of Bengali castor sugar. After the Dutch were expelled from Taiwan in 1662, the Persian director Henrik van Wijck lamented the loss of the Taiwanese sugar trade: 'Formosa sugar was formerly the flower of the Persian trade, which also yielded the highest profit. This will be less now, so that we are less able to help Coromandel. If we would have had Formosa sugar as before our profits would have been 33⅓ per cent higher.'[4]

After this, the VOC pivoted their sugar trade towards Bengali sugar. In 1662–3 there was a sharp increase in the Dutch export of Bengali sugar to Iran; it reached 1.17 million Dutch pounds. The VOC also exported sugar from Java, but the Javanese sugar sent to Iran that year amounted to only 90,000 pounds. The gross profits from these varieties were different: 172 per cent and 159 per cent, respectively (Chart 3.1).[5]

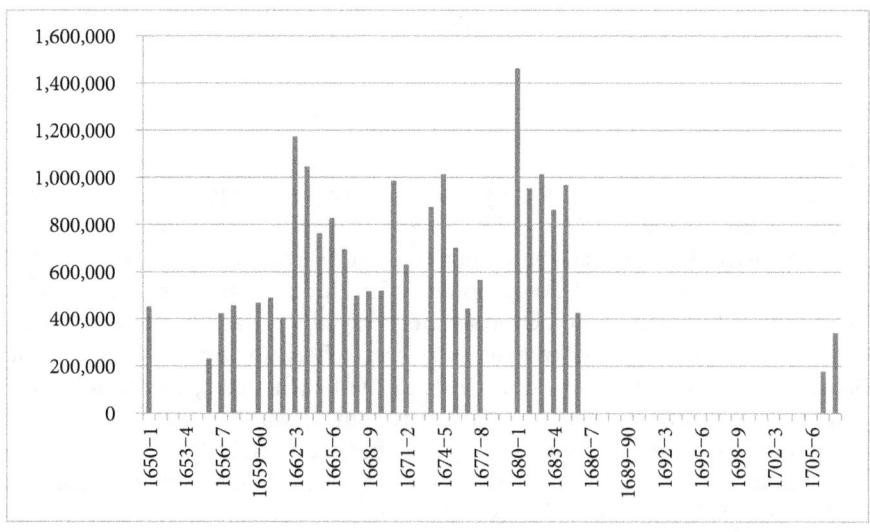

Chart 3.1 Dutch export of Bengali sugar to Iran (Dutch pounds).
Note: Data for 1652–3, 1653–4, 1678–9, 1680–1 and 1686–7 to 1705–6 are not available.
Source: Prakash, *The Dutch East India Company*, 174–5.

The export of Bengali sugar to Iran peaked in 1680–1 at 1.46 million pounds and produced 186 per cent profit in Iran. During this time the High Government encouraged sugar production in the *ommelanden* of Batavia for overseas markets.[6] Even though Bengali sugar yielded a higher net profit than Javanese sugar in the 1680s, Batavia had put an end to this lucrative trade by 1700. The small quantities of Bengali sugar exported to Iran in the years 1706–7 and 1707–8 served simply as ballast on the ships sailing to Iran.[7]

According to Dutch annual sales statements between 1701 and 1720, on average the VOC imported an annual weight of about 1.2 million pounds of castor sugar (*poedersuiker*) into Bandar Abbas. This shows that Batavia's switch from Bengali sugar to Javanese sugar was a success. On the other hand, their candy sugar (*kandijsuiker*) had a relatively small share of the market, averaging around 241,000 pounds annually (Chart 3.2).

After spices, Javanese sugar was the VOC's most profitable trade item in the Gulf.[8] The annual net profits accrued from castor sugar and candy sugar during 1701–20 averaged 168 per cent and 116 per cent, respectively. In the successful year 1703–4 castor sugar yielded a profit of 264 per cent (Chart 3.3). Thanks to its high profitability, sugar accounted for nearly one third of the total sale of imports to Bandar Abbas during this same period (Chart 3.4). There is little doubt that such favourable results boosted the development of the Dutch sugar industry in Java. During the first two decades of the century, 20 per cent of Dutch sugar shipments from Batavia headed for Iran, whereas those headed for the Netherlands comprised 36 per cent, and those for Japan 19 per cent.[9]

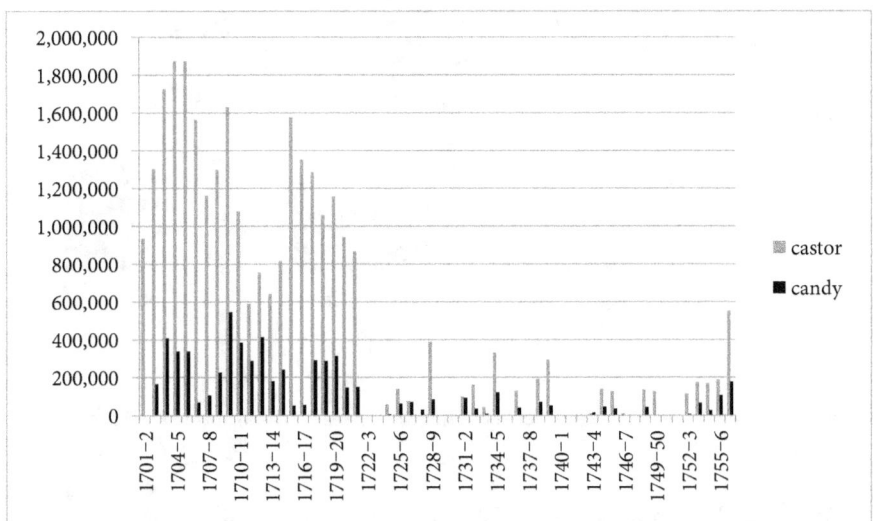

Chart 3.2 Dutch import of Javanese sugar to Bandar Abbas, 1701–56 (Dutch pounds).
Note: Data for 1722–3, 1723–4, 1730–1, 1735–6, 1737–8, 1740–1 and 1751–2 are not available.
Source: See Appendix 2.

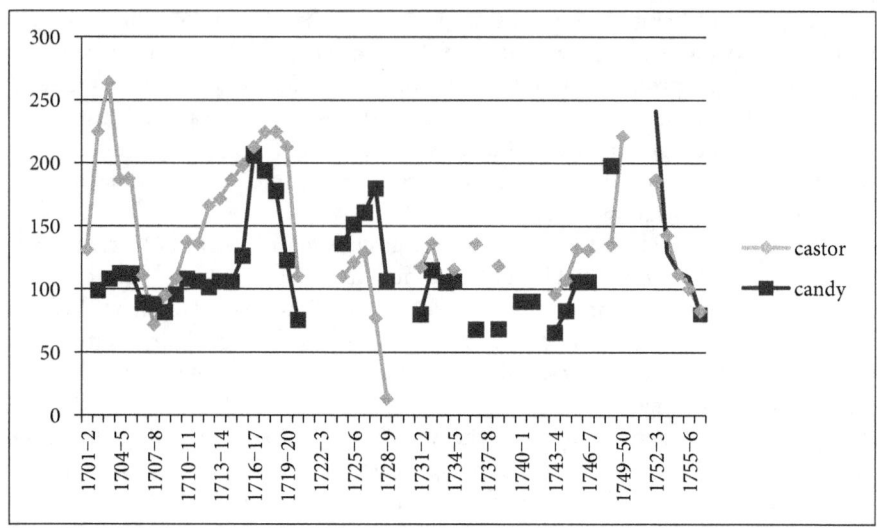

Chart 3.3 Net profits from sugar at Bandar Abbas, 1701–56 (per cent).
Source: See Chart 3.2.

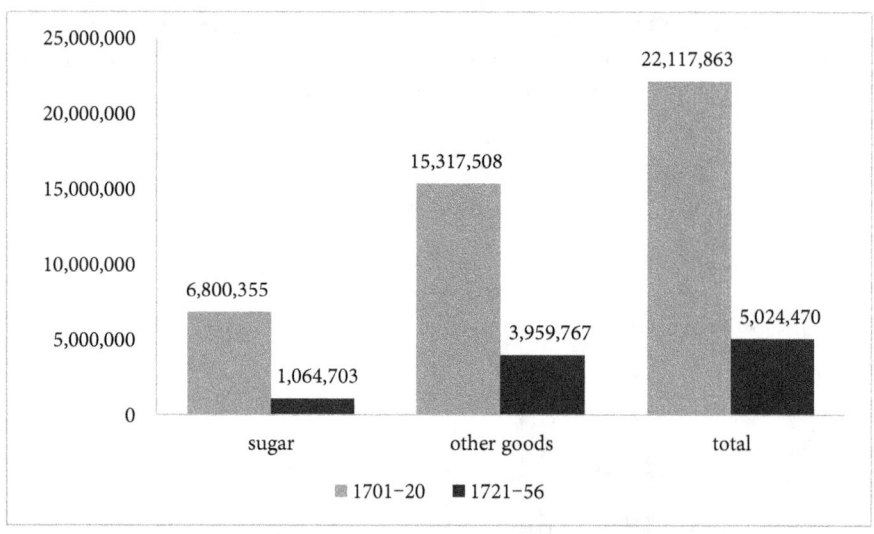

Chart 3.4 Comparative sale value between the two phases 1701–20 and 1721–56 (guilders).
Source: See Chart 3.2.

After the Afghan conquest of Isfahan in 1722, the VOC sugar trade was a disaster. During the Afghan interregnum (1722–9), Dutch sugar trade at Bandar Abbas almost came to a complete standstill. Even after order was restored in the early 1730s, trade did not recover to its former levels. Between 1721 and 1756 annual imports did not even reach half a million pounds, except in 1756–7, when the market for Dutch Javanese sugar in the Gulf was temporarily revived (Chart 3.2). The troubles in Batavia's *ommelanden*, which led to the massacre of Chinese sugar plantation workers in 1740, caused a shortage of sugar supplies to the Gulf in the early 1740s, thus dealing an additional blow to this ailing trade.[10] Consequently, the value of Dutch sales of sugar severely decreased, falling from 6.8 million guilders between 1701 and 1720 to one million guilders between 1721 and 1756. There was a significant correlation between this particular trade and the VOC's total sales at Bandar Abbas. The overall sale value of goods sold by the VOC between 1721 and 1756 fell by 74 per cent in comparison to the period between 1701 and 1720, as the sale value of Javanese sugar dropped by 85 per cent (Chart 3.4). The VOC retreated from Bandar Abbas in 1751, but returned the next year, they finally abandoned the port in 1759.[11]

It is also worth mentioning that, from the late 1730s to the mid-1740s, the VOC occasionally sold Javanese sugar at Isfahan. Bandar Abbas supplied the necessary cash for running the Isfahan business, transferring the proceeds of the year's sales through local financial agents. After the Afghan conquest, however, the local banking network was damaged so severely that, instead of transferring earned money, Bandar Abbas had to send cash crops to Isfahan by caravan.[12] The remaining *rendementen* suggest that the transported goods included sugar in limited amounts. In the financial year 1737–8 the Isfahan factory sold 16,618 pounds of castor sugar and 2,117 pounds of candy sugar. Yet the profit was rather low: castor sugar yielded 59 per cent and candy sugar 36 per cent. In 1741–2, the total sales of sugar amounted to no more than 2,463 pounds. Even so, the profits from the two varieties were extraordinarily high: castor sugar yielded 668 per cent and candy sugar 424 per cent. The sharp rise of the price of sugar in the early 1740s might be the cause: in 1737–8 castor sugar and candy sugar fetched 10.5 *mahmudi*s and 13 *mahmudi*s (per *man-i shahi*) respectively, but in 1741–2 it fetched 20.5 *mahmudi*s and 26 *mahmudi*s.[13]

Bushire and Bandar Rig

After the establishment of their factory in Bushire in 1737 the Company imported goods for Iranian cities such as Shiraz and Isfahan, from which Bandar Abbas was often cut off. However, there are few existing *rendementen*, so it is difficult to ascertain the trends of Dutch sales of Javanese sugar at Bushire during the period between 1737 and 1753. Looking at the scattered evidence, however, it is probable that the total sales of sugar at Bushire during that period was very low, much lower than at Bandar Abbas (Chart 3.5).

In 1747, the VOC removed the Basra factory from under the Persian directorate and placed Bushire under the head of the Basra factory.[14] The principal reason for this was Basra's prominent status as a major emporium for goods to Iran. There seemed to be much confusion when Dutch residents in Basra wrote about the Company's sales at Bushire, stating that although a considerable amount of the goods they had sold at Basra had been transported to Iran through Bushire,

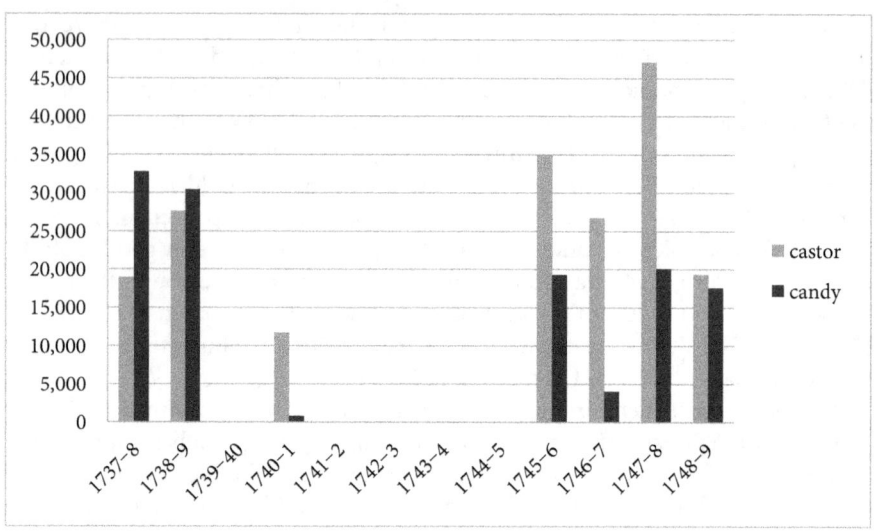

Chart 3.5 Dutch import of Javanese sugar to Bushire, 1737–48 (Dutch pounds).
Note: Data for 1739–40, 1743–4 and 1744–5 are not available.
Source: See Appendix 3.

those same goods attracted no buyers at Bushire. They therefore suggested that the VOC dismiss the Dutch officer in Bushire and leave only a local broker there to keep them informed of the arrival of caravans and markets and to enable Basra to supply the goods required in Bushire in a more effective manner. This point will be discussed further in Chapter 5.[15]

Traders habitually circumventing Bushire was in part due to the rise of Bandar Rig, a neighbouring port, in the early 1750s. When they noticed this, the VOC sent a commission around 1752 to utilize the new channel. According to an existing *rendement*, at that time the VOC imported 12,869 pounds of castor sugar and 13,646 pounds of candy sugar, and they were satisfied with their profits from these varieties: 166 per cent and 137 per cent respectively. Sugar represented 17 per cent of the total value of the sale of goods during the commission.[16] However, this was also when the Dutch retreated from the Iranian littoral to concentrate on their commerce at Kharg Island.

Basra

Basra began to thrive in the early 1720s, and the VOC entered this growing market in 1724. Dutch sugar trade at Basra had relatively favourable years in the late 1740s (Chart 3.6).

Basra compensated for Dutch sugar trade sales at Bandar Abbas. The Company transported sugar to Basra when they found it difficult to dispose of at Bandar

3. Sugar Trade in the Persian Gulf: The VOC

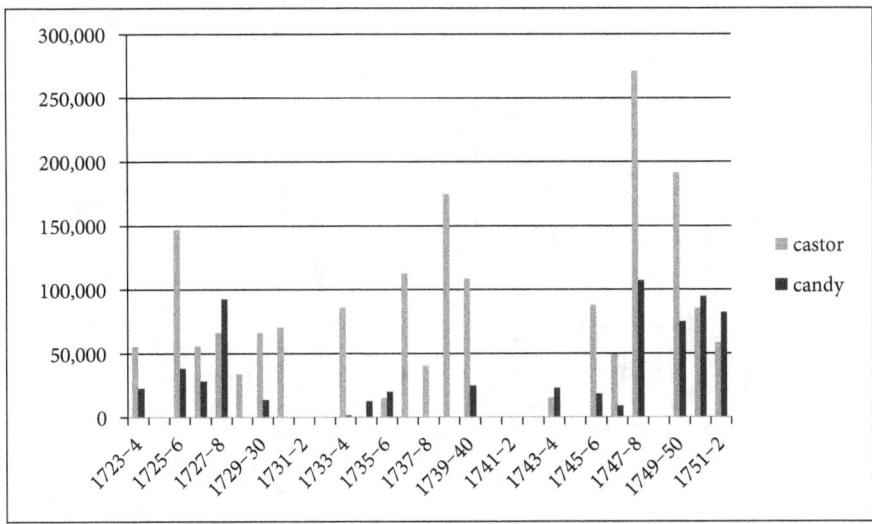

Chart 3.6 Dutch import of Javanese sugar to Basra, 1723–51 (Dutch pounds).
Note: Data for 1732–3 and 1744–5 are not available.
Source: See Appendix 4.

Abbas. In the 1720s, inland merchants hardly ever went to Bandar Abbas, and the VOC counted on the Basra market. However, it was less successful, for at Basra, during the period 1723–7, annual imports averaged about 65,000 pounds of castor sugar and 36,000 pounds of candy sugar, while at Bandar Abbas it averaged about 68,000 pounds of castor sugar and 42,000 pounds of candy sugar. In the early 1730s trade at Bandar Abbas showed signs of improving. The war between the Ottomans and Nadir in Iraq probably meant Bandar Abbas stopped sending goods to Basra.[17] However, in 1734 Basra complained that their trade could have been more successful if they had been provided with goods over the last three years. Instead, the English and French gleaned the remaining sales, despite not having obtained much profit the previous year due to the war.[18] However, it was not long before the VOC realized that Bandar Abbas's trade fell far short of their expectations. From the late 1730s onwards, the Company paid closer attention to the markets at Basra and Bushire. In 1737, the VOC reported that both castor sugar and candy sugar could fetch the highest price at Basra, followed by Bushire.[19] After 1743, when Batavia resumed sugar shipments to the Gulf, Basra became the most important destination in terms of sales. Average annual sales of castor sugar in Basra between 1743 and 1747 were about 106,000 pounds; this far exceeded those in Bandar Abbas during the same period, where they were only about 57,000 pounds (Charts 3.7, 3.8, 3.9 and 3.10).

Sugar yielded acceptable profits in Basra. There was some fluctuation, but the average annual profits from castor sugar and candy sugar between 1723 and 1751 were 103 per cent and 118 per cent respectively. Sugar represented 16 per cent

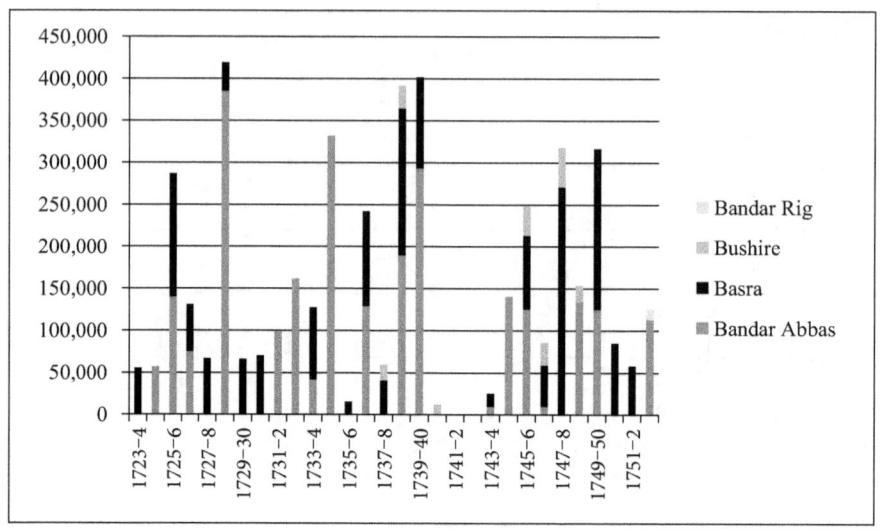

Chart 3.7 Sales of castor sugar at Bandar Abbas, Basra, Bushire and Bandar Rig, 1723–52 (Dutch pounds).

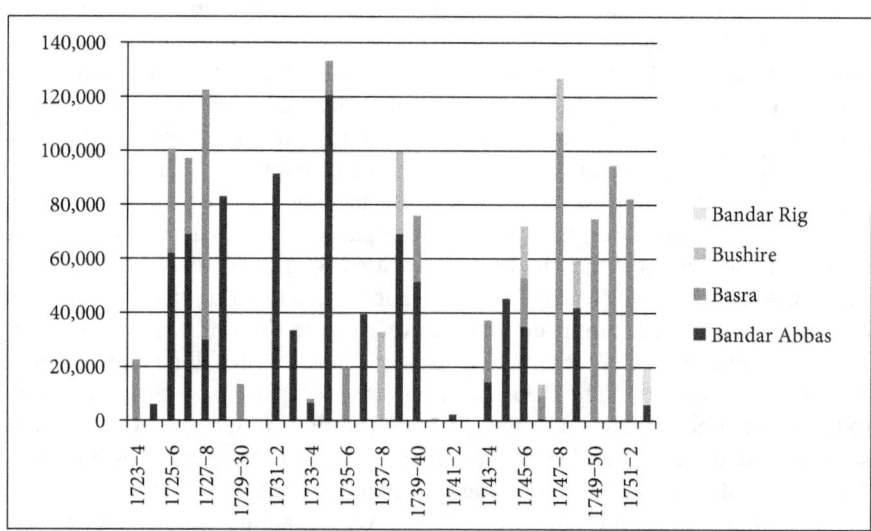

Chart 3.8 Sales of candy sugar at Bandar Abbas, Basra, Bushire and Bandar Rig, 1723–52 (Dutch pounds).

Sources: See Appendices 2, 3 and 4; NL-HaNA, VOC, 1.04.02, inv.nr. 2863, p. 46.

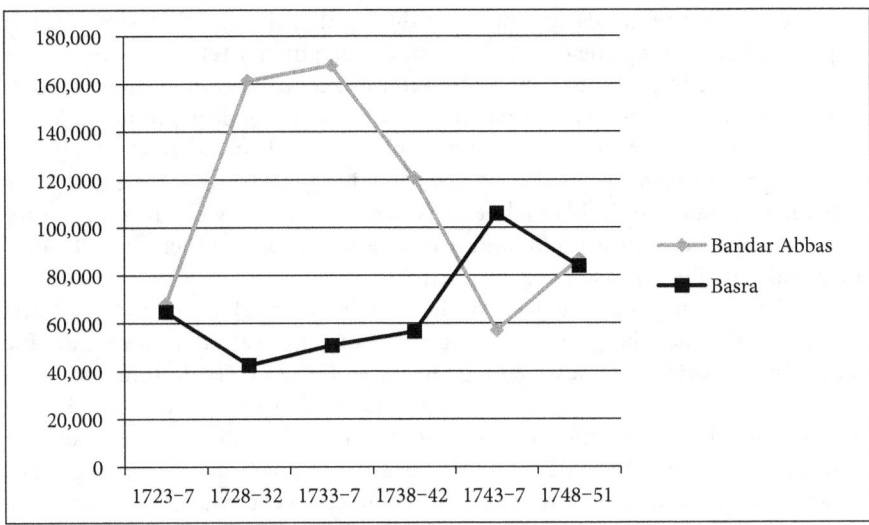

Chart 3.9 Five-year average annual imports of castor sugar to Bandar Abbas and Basra, 1723–51 (Dutch pounds).

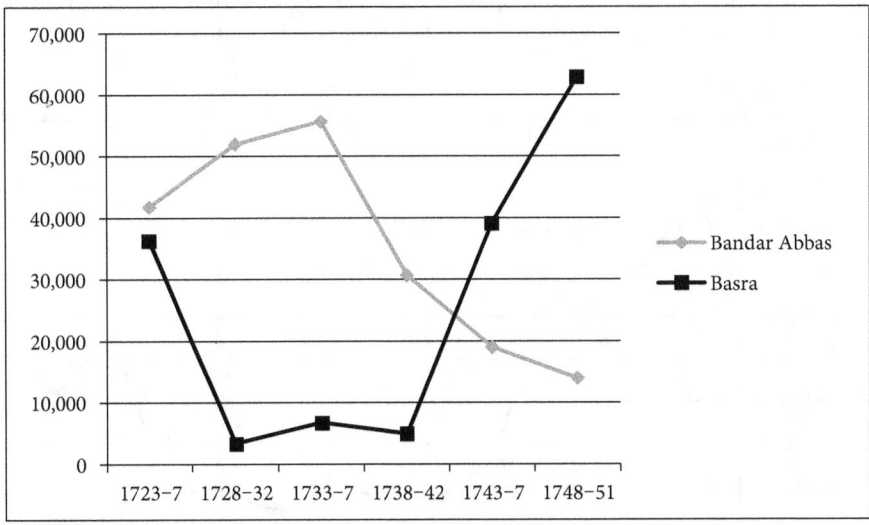

Chart 3.10 Five-year average annual imports of candy sugar to Bandar Abbas and Basra, 1723–51 (Dutch pounds).

Sources: See Appendices 2 and 4.

of the total value of goods sold at Basra during that time, with castor sugar at 10 per cent and candy sugar at 6 per cent (Appendix 4). Yet sugar might have been even more important to the VOC's commerce in Basra than these records suggest. Basra residents wrote that the Basra factory was less profitable in the financial year 1751–2 because they had not received an adequate supply of weighed goods (*pondgoederen*), which included sugar, but were instead dealing with a large number of individual items (*stukgoederen*). They claimed that castor sugar generated the most profit, and it was very difficult for them to sell candy sugar without offering castor sugar as well.[20]

Despite such an optimistic view of the Javanese (castor) sugar trade at Basra, it is fair to say that the projects at Basra and Bushire were not successful. The sales at the factories were never enough to stave off the VOC's declining fortunes in the Gulf. The five-year average annual import of castor sugar to the Persian Gulf fluctuated between 1.54 million pounds and 0.87 million pounds between 1701 and 1720, but between 1721 and 1755 it barely reached 0.2 million pounds (Chart 3.11). Such a serious recession also applied to candy sugar (Chart 3.12). These data suggest a severe decline in the demand for VOC Javanese sugar in the Gulf market after the fall of the Safavids.

In 1753 the VOC became embroiled in a conflict with the Turkish authorities at Basra, which eventually forced the Dutch staff to clandestinely retreat from the port.[21] Because of these circumstances, the Company was attracted to setting up trade at Kharg Island, which appeared to have escaped much of the political disorder that currently plagued the northern shore of the Gulf.

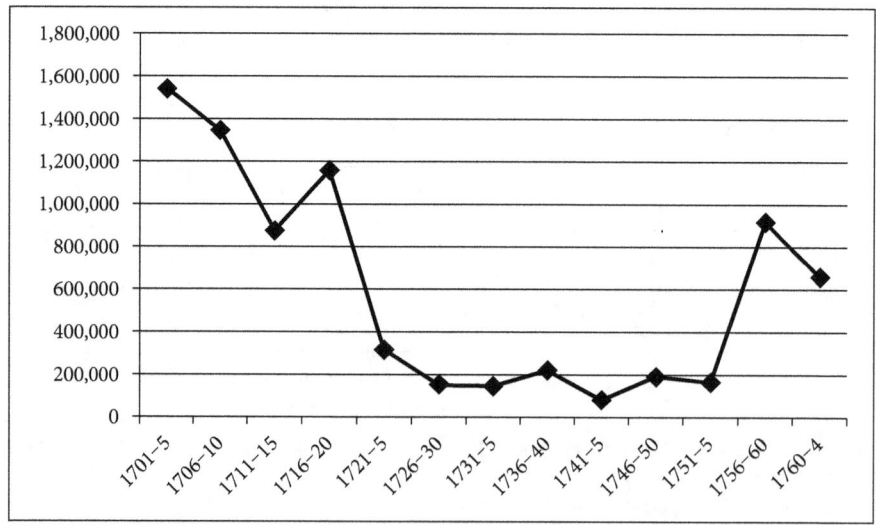

Chart 3.11 Five-year average annual import of castor sugar to the Persian Gulf (Bandar Abbas, Basra, Bushire, Bandar Rig, Kharg, Muscat and Sind), 1701–64 (Dutch pounds).

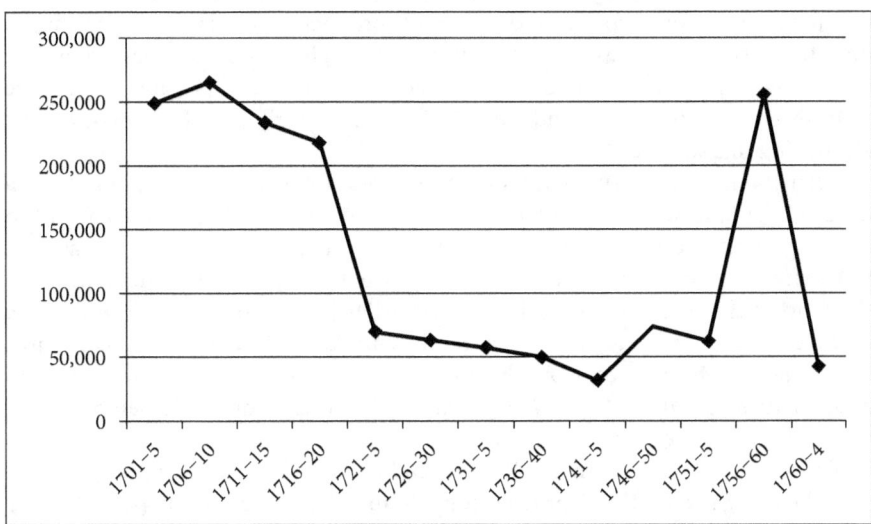

Chart 3.12 Five-year average annual import of candy sugar to the Persian Gulf (Bandar Abbas, Basra, Bushire, Bandar Rig, Kharg, Muscat and Sind), 1701–64 (Dutch pounds).

Sources: See Appendices 2, 3, 4 and 5; NL-HaNA, VOC, 1.04.02, inv.nr. 2863, p. 46; VOC, 1.04.02, inv.nr. 2885 1, p. 53; VOC, 1.04.02, inv.nr. 2937, pp.45–5, p. 85.

Kharg Island, Muscat and Sind

Although the VOC Javanese sugar trade in the Gulf was in severe decline from the time of the fall of the Safavids until their simultaneous withdrawal from Basra and Bushire in 1753, it is intriguing that it improved impressively after the VOC set up their final trading station in the Gulf on Kharg Island in 1753. Not many *rendementen* are available, so we do not know the exact results of the Dutch sugar trade there. But we do know that Kharg sold an average of 60,000 pounds of castor sugar and some 200,000 pounds of lump sugar during the 1750s.[22] Trade at Kharg was in full force after the Company closed down the Bandar Abbas factory in 1759.

In the meantime, the VOC actively explored the possibility of developing two other western Indian Ocean markets for their Javanese sugar, namely Muscat and Sind. The High Government was intent on disposing of surplus stocks of sugar in Batavia as much as possible, and this led to three commercial voyages to Muscat. The first shipment took place in January 1756: Schoonderwoerd sailed from Bandar Abbas to Muscat on his way to Batavia to assess the feasibility of selling goods there.[23] He sold only 24,200 pounds of iron and 100,121 pounds of castor sugar. His net profit from the castor sugar was 85 per cent.[24] Although it was a poor result, Schoonderwoerd thought it was due to the scarcity of money at Muscat during his limited stay, and he could have sold most of his cargo if he had stayed for an additional three to four months. He therefore suggested that the Company send a medium-sized ship to Muscat every year, and the ship should stay for three to four months and sell goods on one-month credit. According to him, the best trading season at Muscat was the beginning of October, when 'the Mocha monsoon' (*de Mochase mousson*) started. It was also possible to procure Spanish reals, *rijksdaalders* and Venetian ducats, as well as coffee, Socotra aloe, etc. during this season.[25]

After the first shipment, a second voyage soon followed. In July 1756, Batavia ordered Captain de Nijsz of *de Marienbosch* and Captain Brahé of *'t Pasgeld* to sail to Muscat and try to sell their goods there, sugar in particular. In case the Muscat market proved difficult, Brahé was instructed to proceed to Sind and assess the market there. Both ships left Batavia on 19 July 1756, but *de Marienbosch* reached Muscat first, on 27 August 1756. The market was slow. It took six months to sell all the goods except one bale of Ceylonese cinnamon and five cases of manufactured goods. When *'t Pasgeld* arrived at Muscat on 19 September 1756, she left for Sind one month later (26 October).[26]

Brahé arrived at Karachi on 8(?) November 1756.[27] After selling some sugar there he navigated up the river from Karachi to search for better markets. During the voyage he succeeded in selling most of the sugar on board, though at the same price as at Karachi.[28] The *rendement* recorded on this voyage tells us that the VOC sold 638,747 pounds of castor sugar and obtained 74 per cent profit. Castor sugar represented 71 per cent of the total value of goods sold during that venture.[29]

The profit from sugar had not been as high as expected. Nevertheless, Brahé and another senior mariner, Mahué, were very positive about the potential for Dutch sugar on the Sind market. They wrote that it was impossible for the people of Sind to survive without castor sugar. They attributed the poor profit to their unfamiliarity with the local language and commercial traditions and the unexpected expenses incurred when moving from one trading post to another. They proposed that Batavia send a big ship with merchandise to Muscat and Sind every year, and the ship should visit Sind first, at the end of October or the beginning of November, to unload most of its sugar shipment and spices that could be sold there over three to four months. The ship could then proceed to Muscat with some sugar and a considerable amount of spices, iron, tin, lead and zinc.[30]

The third voyage to Muscat turned out to be more successful than the previous two. Soon after de Nijsz's expedition, the High Government sent another ship, *de Barbara Theodra*, to Muscat to dispose of excessive sugar stocks from Batavia. Rood, the captain of the ship, arrived at Muscat on 21 September 1757 and stayed there until 7 December 1757.[31] According to the existing *rendement*, in this period the Company sold a great amount of castor sugar, 794,568 pounds and 33,810 pounds of candy sugar, resulting in net profits of 118 per cent and 58 per cent, respectively.[32] In his report, Rood noted that his expedition showed a profit of 107,612 guilders 4 stivers. This amounted to 101 per cent profit, 30 per cent more than the last voyage, all because of successful castor sugar sales.[33]

Batavia was satisfied with the *de Barbara Theodra*'s profit, but the Dutch factory at Kharg Island was very apprehensive. Any regular sugar shipments to Muscat

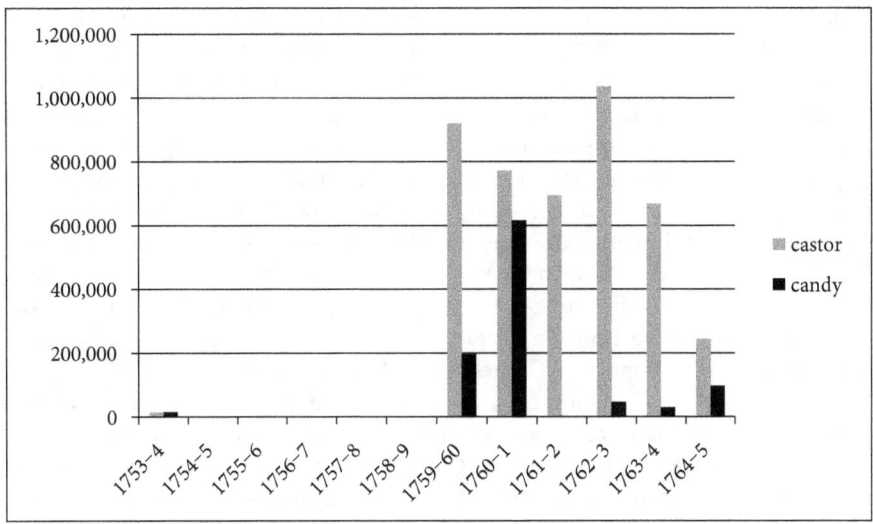

Chart 3.13 Dutch import of Javanese sugar to Kharg Island, 1753–64 (Dutch pounds).
Note: Data for 1754–5, 1755–6, 1756–7, 1757–8 and 1758–9 are not available.
Source: Appendix 5.

might hinder their Javanese sugar trade at Kharg. Therefore, they appealed, claiming that if Batavia sent ships to Muscat or Mocha, Kharg would be deprived of profits. This would also hold true for any goods brought to Sind, which might also reduce profits from the VOC trade at Surat and Malabar.[34] They eventually convinced the High Government to discontinue all voyages to Muscat and Sind.[35]

Thus, VOC trade in sugar in the Gulf concentrated on Kharg Island towards the end of the 1750s. Chart 3.13 shows that, during the period between 1759 and 1764, the Company imported substantial amounts of Javanese sugar into Kharg.

In successful years (1759–60, 1760–1 and 1762–3), the Company imported more than one million pounds of Javanese sugar. The slight decline of sugar sales in 1763–4 was to a certain degree due to a shortfall in the sugar supply caused by the shipwreck of *de Amstelveen* off the Omani coast on 5 August 1763.[36] The average annual net profits from castor sugar and candy sugar at Kharg between 1759 and 1764 were 104 per cent and 48 per cent, respectively (Appendix 5). Floor argues that the remarkable improvement of sugar sales in the early 1760s gave Batavia 'unrealistic' expectations about the Gulf market's capacity for absorbing Dutch sugar, and this obsession delayed their decision to withdraw from Gulf trade altogether.[37] Between 1759 and 1763, for the first time since the Safavid era, the average annual import of Dutch sugar into the Gulf had almost reached one million pounds. It would have been quite natural for VOC officials on the ground to take this fact as a positive sign.

During the period following the fall of the Safavids, merchants from Cambay, Porbandar, Kutch, Sind and Muscat visited Malabar, especially Dutch Cochin, by '*bombara*' (a type of ship used along the western coast of India) to buy sugar and other items. According to Das Gupta, the first *bombara*s arrived at Cochin in 1730 and their trade continued well into the 1780s.[38] As a result, Batavia exported sugar to Malabar during this time. E. Jacobs claims that annual sales in Malabar had increased to about 1.5 million pounds, even though Nadri suggests the actual import might be lower or that there were high fluctuations.[39] The Malabar market also whetted the interests of non-VOC sugar suppliers. From the 1740s the VOC opened up part of the Company's sugar trade in the South and West Asian markets to Dutch private sectors, such as VOC officials, free-burghers and indigenous persons.[40] Consequently, there were frequent clashes of interest between the Company and private trade in Malabar.[41] The Portuguese also participated in the vibrant market, importing Chinese sugar from Macao.[42]

Because of these developments, there was competition between Kharg and Cochin to enhance sales of Javanese castor sugar. Trade in 1760 is a case in point. Since merchants who came over to Kharg Island wanted to buy mainly castor sugar, the Kharg factory usually urged them to buy a little candy sugar together with castor sugar at an approximate ratio of 8:1 or 10:1; otherwise, they threatened to not sell any castor sugar.[43] In May 1760, however, a Dutch ship called *'t Slot van Cappelle* imported more candy sugar than usual, producing a ratio of 1:1 for castor sugar to candy sugar in their warehouses. As a result, in spite of the Dutch residents' great efforts, four to five hundred canisters (*canasser*) of candy sugar ended up unsold. Kharg claimed that this unexpected surplus of candy sugar was caused by the Cochin factory. When the ship docked there on its way to Kharg it unloaded 460 canisters of castor sugar (sugar that could have reached Kharg) and only 98 canisters of candy sugar.[44] Castor sugar was their principal stock, and Kharg ordered more of it, claiming that otherwise the merchants would easily abandon the rest. So they requested that, when Batavia sent a ship via Malabar to Kharg with sugar, the High Government must forbid Cochin to unload castor sugar from the ship because it would damage Kharg's trade, as was the case with *'t Slot van Cappelle*.[45]

Any prospect for a full recovery of the VOC sugar trade in the Gulf quickly grew dim. In spite of the VOC policy to 'Make trade not war', the Company once again got involved in a power struggle among notables in Bandar Rig, Bushire and Shiraz towards the mid-1760s, which resulted in a conflict with the ruler of Bandar Rig, Mir Muhanna. The tension culminated when Mir Muhanna conquered Dutch Kharg in January 1766. The destruction of the Kharg factory not only crushed the Company's remaining hope of any further improvement of their trade there but also ended their commerce in the Gulf. All remaining Dutch staff left the Gulf in July 1766.[46]

This chapter has presented the details of the 'overall' decline of the eighteenth-century VOC import of Javanese sugar in the Gulf by analysing their sales at particular places that developed as alternative markets after the Safavid period. Taking all the evidence into account, it is clear that the sales at Basra, Bushire and Bandar Rig were never enough to compensate for their decline at Bandar Abbas. Such a serious decline suggests a breakdown in the Gulf market for Javanese sugar, so it is all the more interesting to see that the VOC trade picked up in the following years. Batavia actively sent sugar shipments to Muscat and Sind in 1756 and 1757, with some agreeable results. The improvement of sales of sugar at Kharg in the last part of the 1750s is remarkable. The VOC's import of Javanese sugar between 1759 and 1763 averaged almost one million pounds per year – sales not seen since the Safavid period.

The fact that the Gulf market for the VOC's Javanese sugar was so active from the late 1750s to the early 1760s also allows us to rethink the idea that intermittent political dislocations deprived Iran's population of their purchasing power. Conversely, it raises the question of why this happened during this particular time. Why not earlier? It is important to note that VOC officials who were deployed to Gulf stations after the Safavids continuously reported that, apart from increasing expenses to cope with socioeconomic disorder, their 'competitors' were hindering their sugar trade. Who were these 'competitors'? How did they carry on their business in rapidly changing trading conditions? How different was their trade from that of the VOC? What insights into the reorganization of the Gulf market can their activities provide? These questions will be answered in the next two chapters.

Chapter 4

SUGAR TRADE IN THE PERSIAN GULF: THE VOC'S COMPETITORS

Sugar was highly profitable in Safavid Iran, and this encouraged many traders, European and Asian alike, to import sugar into the Persian Gulf. It comes as no surprise then that some of them were cut-throat competitors. The Dutch East India Company (*Verenigde Oostindische Compagnie* [VOC]) entered this promising venture soon after they set up a trading station at Bandar Abbas, and they had to face the challenge of other suppliers importing sugar. While adequate scholarly attention has been paid to seventeenth-century competition, little is known about it during the eighteenth century, especially after the fall of the Safavids, when the Gulf market witnessed a significant re-shuffling. This chapter will examine the competition at Bandar Abbas from the close of the seventeenth century up to the VOC's departure in 1759. Few documents have survived from the VOC's 'competitors', so it is difficult to accurately ascertain who the 'competitors' were and how they profited from their speculative enterprises. But the detailed Dutch accounts monitoring other traders provide valuable insights into the ways in which their rivals became involved in commerce at Bandar Abbas.

Non-VOC sugar shipments in the late Safavid period

As explained in the previous chapter, the VOC initially obtained substantial profits importing Taiwanese sugar into Iran; a trade they monopolized until 1662. Then Bengali sugar offered the Company an opportunity to resume commerce. However, this triggered intense competition from other suppliers. By the early 1680s, competitors entering this lucrative trade included Surat merchants such as the Chelebi family, Golconda notables, and Orissa and Bengali officials. In the late 1660s Dutch private trade from Bengal was an obstacle to the VOC. In 1668-9, when the Dutch ship *Duinvliet* docked at Colombo in Ceylon, it uncovered 374 bags of illegitimate private sugar.[1] The greatest threats to the VOC, however, were English private traders. Large amounts of English goods were being imported to Iran and bought by merchants from Isfahan. So in 1672, VOC officials at Bandar Abbas tried to dissuade these merchants from trading with the English by under-pricing the English sugar at the Isfahan market. This strategy seems to have been effective because, a few years later, many Isfahan merchants refused to buy sugar from English ships that arrived in Iran before Dutch ships.[2] The competition never ceased. According to Barendse, by 1687 English private trade from Bengal to Bandar Abbas exceeded that of the East India Company (EIC).[3] In the early 1680s the EIC agent in Bengal, Matthew Vincent, was known as one of the VOC's main competitors for Bengali sugar in the Iranian market.[4] The EIC engaged in this venture in the 1680s, though on a smaller scale.[5]

Previous studies have highlighted the VOC struggle to import Bengali sugar into Bandar Abbas in the second half of the seventeenth century, but have failed to look at the more critical phase that followed. From the 1690s onwards, the VOC concentrated on the sale of Javanese sugar produced in Batavia's *ommelanden*. Dutch officials' regular correspondence provides many references to the activities of other traders shipping sugar across the Indian Ocean to Bandar Abbas, but the details are rather fragmentary and sporadic. The most important Dutch records are the so-called 'shipping lists'. The EIC factory at Bandar Abbas compiled similar lists, but they are not as detailed as the Dutch ones.[6] The Dutch records contain lists of non-VOC ships arriving at and departing from Bandar Abbas between 1694 and 1715, though with minor gaps. The lists provide valuable information about trans-oceanic shipping, including the names of the ships, their registration, dates of arrival and departure, origins and destinations, and occasionally their sizes, owners, cargoes, etc. These data are a treasure trove of information about sugar imports to Bandar Abbas by non-Dutch vessels during this period, but historians have not made full use of them.

There are four main difficulties when looking at the lists of non-VOC arrivals and departures. Like many other trading centres along the Indian Ocean, Bandar Abbas was a terminal for long-distance shipping and a node for local and regional shipping, connecting numerous secondary ports in the Gulf with their neighbours. Local shipping usually involved numerous smaller-sized craft, mostly referred to as *trankies* in the Company records. They were essential to invigorating trade at Bandar Abbas. However, the Dutch lists ignore these crafts and primarily focus on large ocean-going ships, for their imports were the ones that represented a major threat to the Company's annual profits in Iran. We have noted that there were no local shipments of Omani sugar to Bandar Abbas via Muscat or other Omani harbours on the list, even though a significant part of those shipments was destined for other marketplaces along the Gulf, such as Bahrain, al-Hasa and Basra and even Mocha.[7]

The second difficulty with utilizing the Dutch lists is that they register foreign vessels only by nationality: English (*Engels*), sometimes distinguishing EIC (*Engelse Compagnie*) vessels from English private (*Engelse particulier*) ones; Danish (*Deens*); French (*Frans*); Muslim (*Moors*); Armenian (*Armeens*); and others. The ships' registrations did not always record the names of the traders who organized the ocean trade. A Danish vessel, *Princess Sophia Hedwig*, which imported sugar from Bengal to Bandar Abbas on 14 June 1709, had in fact been hired by English traders.[8] It is also important to remember that many ships not only carried goods for the community noted in the registry but also carried a considerable amount of freight for other merchants. The freight packages brought by a Muslim ship, *'Ali Shahidi*, on 15 May 1701 included conserves (*confituren*) and sugar from Bengal, though we do not know who placed those commodities onto the ship.[9]

Thirdly, the lists note the origin of the sugar suppliers and sometimes the ports the ships visited on their way to Bandar Abbas, but it is not certain where the sugar was actually loaded. Ships from Bengal and China, most of which conveyed sugar, might have procured the sugar from local sugar-producing areas in those regions, but we cannot identify any sugar and conserves in their cargo from other places. For example, it is often unclear whether sugar sent from Surat was from north and west India or somewhere else. This is demonstrated in a list for a Muslim ship from Surat called *Ilahi Shahidi*. This ship imported 355 sacks of Bengali sugar to Bandar Abbas on 25 January 1697.[10] But conserves frequently occur on the cargo lists from Surat, which suggests they were manufactured locally for export.[11]

The fourth limitation of the lists is that they note the amount of cargo arriving in container units, such as canisters (*canasser*), sacks (*zak*) and bags (*blaas*), with no indication of their weight. Even so, we can speculate the total sugar import by non-Dutch ships for certain years. The total foreign import of sugar in the competitive year 1705–6, as seen in Chapter 1, was 8,200 sacks and 6,000 'small canisters' (*kleine canassers*).[12] Assuming that a sack weighed 300 Dutch pounds and a 'small canister' 145 Dutch pounds (with a large canister about 290 pounds), the grand total would amount to about 3.33 million pounds.[13] But this figure is somewhat unrealistic. The English ship *Leijer Sester*, for instance, arrived from Bengal on 9 May 1706 with 3,000 sacks, or 900,000 pounds, of sugar. But the tonnage of this ship is listed as 200 *lasten*, or about 600,000 pounds.[14] Therefore, we should reduce the provisionally calculated grand total, but it is still high, since the VOC's total import of sugar that year was about 2.2 million pounds.[15]

These limitations notwithstanding, it is possible to get an overall picture of non-VOC shipping to Bandar Abbas and the sugar imported. The shipping lists record 256 arrivals at Bandar Abbas during the period between 1694 and 1715, of which ninety-four vessels unloaded sugar at the port. The average annual number of arrivals during this period is twelve ships, with an average of four shipping sugar during that period (Chart 4.1).

Chart 4.2 clearly shows that English shipping accounted for the majority of ocean traffic. Between 1694 and 1715, 136 English vessels (EIC and private combined) arrived at Bandar Abbas, representing 53 per cent of the total shipping. Muslim shipping took second place, with a total number of seventy-six (30 per cent) during the same period. Local ships, presumably Persian (*inlands*) and Arab vessels (*Arabisch*), made significant contributions to regional shipping. Other European vessels, Portuguese, French and Danish, regularly appear in the lists of arrivals.

Since both EIC and English private traders participated in shipping at Bandar Abbas, the records are limited because they describe them both as 'English'. This may be because at Bandar Abbas it was hard to distinguish EIC vessels from private English ones. In 1693 the VOC noted that English private traders were abusing the EIC's exemption from customs and tolls and selling their goods at Isfahan at a quarter of the price of other merchants.

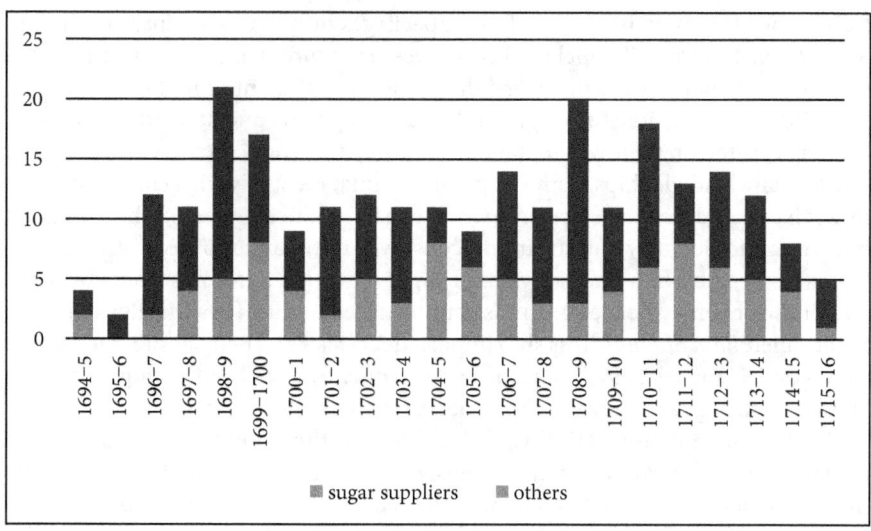

Chart 4.1 Non-VOC sugar suppliers to Bandar Abbas, 1694–1715 (number).

Note: The VOC's financial year begins on 1 September and ends on 31 August in the following year. This roughly corresponded to the trading season in Bandar Abbas. In the years 1694–5 and 1695–6, the VOC covers only the period from 28 June 1695 to 31 October 1695, after which no record is available till 1 November 1696. The document for foreign shipping is almost unbroken from 1697 to 1715. In 1716, the list ends on 15 February. Sugar suppliers shown in the figure include those who conveyed cargoes of conserves.

Source: See Appendix 6.

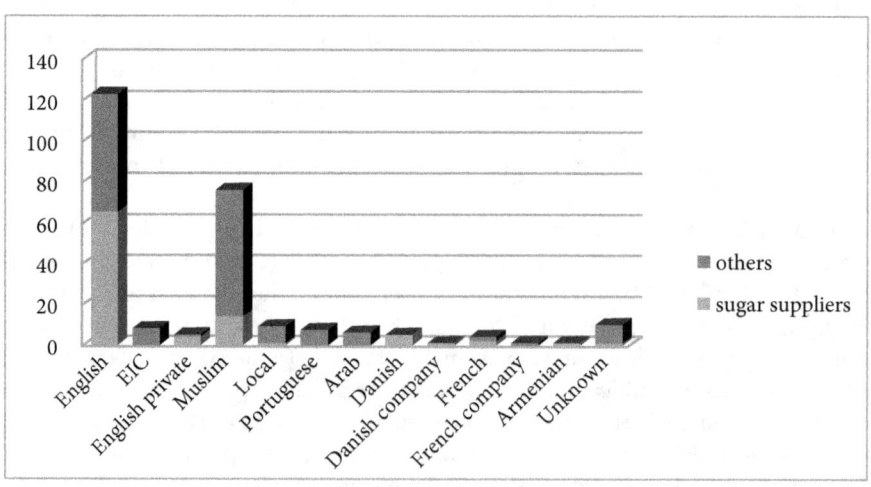

Chart 4.2 Registrations of arrivals at Bandar Abbas, 1694–1715 (number).

Note: Sugar suppliers shown in the figure include those who conveyed cargoes of conserves.
Source: See Appendix 7.

The Dutch wrote that most of the goods imported by the EIC, or under its name, did not belong to the Company but to English private traders. Private traders often sold their goods to EIC officials at Bandar Abbas so they could circumvent paying customs at the port and tolls (*rahdari*) on their way to Isfahan. The only thing they needed to know was what percentage of the brokerage to pay to the EIC brokers.[16] English private trade in the Persian Gulf flourished towards the turn of the eighteenth century, as many English and private ships with merchandise arrived at Bandar Abbas and the nearby port of Bandar Kong (Congo).[17]

The amount calculated above also shows that, during the period between 1694 and 1715, the English posed the greatest threat to VOC sugar imported to Bandar Abbas. During this period, sixty-nine English vessels imported sugar (73 per cent). Muslim import was active too; cargoes of sugar were listed on fourteen Muslim ships (15 per cent). It is noteworthy that all six Danish ships (both the Company and private) that reached Bandar Abbas during that period carried sugar. The lists give the impression that the English were deeply involved in Danish shipping, and the French and Armenians were also engaged in lucrative commerce.

Where did the English ships come from? Chart 4.3 indicates that many of the ships came from, or at the least passed through, South Asia, where the EIC had set up trading stations, including Bengal, Bombay and Surat. Bengali shipping was of particular importance. Between 1694 and 1715, fifty-four ships came from Bengal, or 40 per cent of all English shipping.

Not surprisingly most of the English arrivals from Bengal traded in sugar. Sugar, chiefly Bengali but sometimes Chinese, was transported by forty-five of

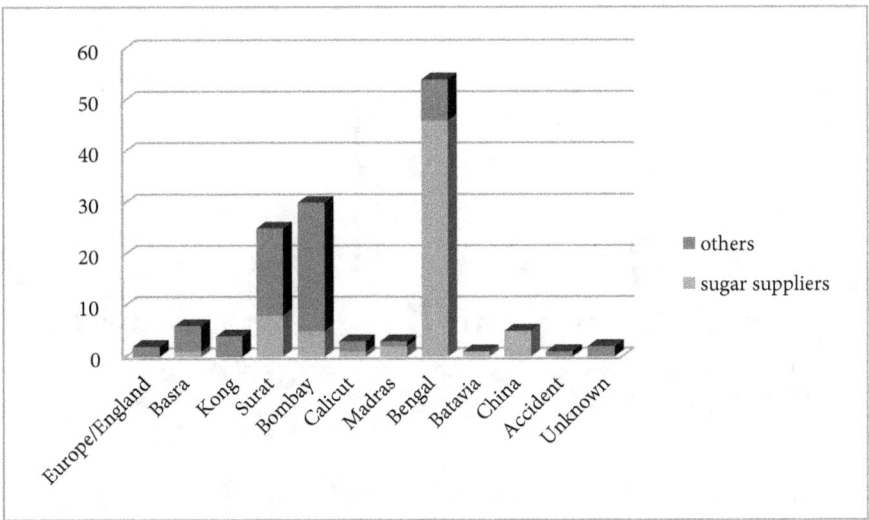

Chart 4.3 Origins of English arrivals at Bandar Abbas, 1694–1715 (number).

Note: Sugar suppliers shown in the figure include those who conveyed cargoes of conserves.

Source: See Appendix 8.

these ships.[18] Chinese sugar also featured in English sugar shipping to Bandar Abbas. Between 1694 and 1715, five English ships arrived from China, and all of them brought Chinese sugar. It is remarkable that, while the VOC endeavoured to cultivate a market for 'their' Javanese sugar in Iran, English traders also tried to benefit from this growing trade. An English ship called *King*, which arrived at Bandar Abbas from China on 25 April 1705, imported 700 canisters of Javanese sugar (*Batavise suiker*) and 500 canisters of Chinese sugar.[19] The English also brought sugar from Surat, Bombay, Calicut and Madras. But, as mentioned above, it is difficult to know the precise origins of the sugar sent from these countries. It seems likely that Bombay and Calicut functioned as transit hubs for sending Bengali and Chinese sugar on to Bandar Abbas.[20] One entry about sugar imported from Basra refers to a cargo of Bengali sugar that had been carried back, probably since the Basra market was inactive when it arrived.[21]

While the English ships dominated shipping from Bengal, Muslim ships were actively engaged in sailing from Gujarat, particularly from Surat (Chart 4.4).

Thirty-nine Muslim ships arrived from Surat between 1694 and 1715 (51 per cent). The accumulated arrivals from other places in Gujarat, such as Ghogha, Patan and Bharuch, mean that Gujarati navigation constituted about 60 per cent of the total Muslim shipping to Bandar Abbas. Surat's important position in Muslim shipping is also evident because vessels coming from Kong were usually laden with freight for Surat.[22] During the same period twelve Muslim ships imported sugar from Surat. Of these, ten came with various kinds of conserves, and the rest brought Bengali sugar and 'black sugar' (*zwarte suiker*).[23] Another two Muslim ships brought Bengali sugar from Bengal.

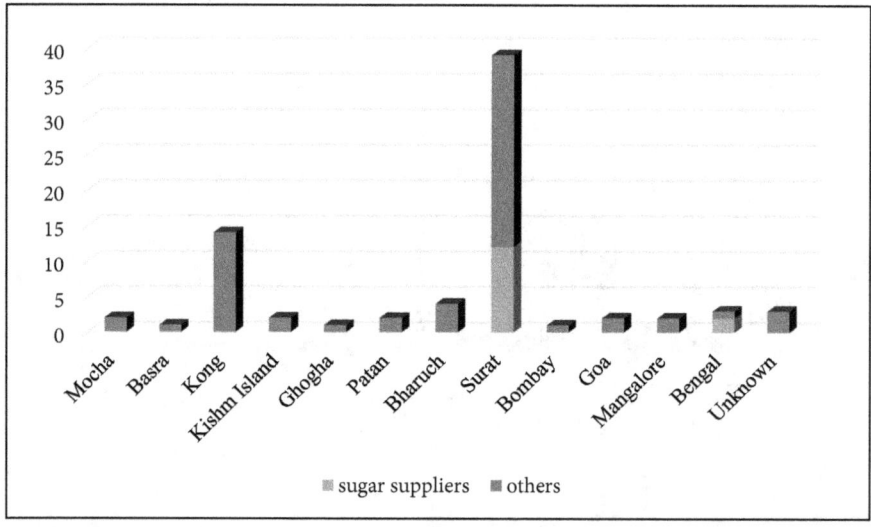

Chart 4.4 Origins of Muslim arrivals at Bandar Abbas, 1694–1715 (number).

Note: Sugar suppliers shown in the figure include those who conveyed cargoes of conserves.

Source: See Appendix 9.

It is unfortunate that the shipping lists at Bandar Abbas give us few clues as to the identities of the owners of non-VOC vessels carrying sugar. There is, however, another type of Dutch list that describes eighteenth-century non-VOC shipping at Surat, and some of them list several shipowners. The Dutch factors in Bandar Abbas noted that a Muslim ship called '*Triadoulet* [*Darya Dawla*]', importing sugar from Bengal on 25 April 1704, belonged to a Muslim merchant named 'Miersa Mamet Jaet'.[24] This vessel seems to be identical to the one called '*Derria Dolled*', which appears in a Dutch list of non-VOC vessels anchoring at Surat in June 1701. According to the record, the ship belonged to Mirza Muhammad Shahid Bengali, a powerful merchant and shipowner residing in Surat.[25] Sometime after the sugar shipment to Bandar Abbas, ownership of the vessel apparently passed to his sons, Hajji Muhammad Taqi and Hajji Muhammad Baqir.[26] Another craft that can be traced is the *Isfahan Merchant*, a Muslim vessel arriving on 3 January 1715 with conserves.[27] This vessel regularly shows up in lists of Dutch passports (*pas*) issued for non-VOC vessels at Surat. In the early 1710s, the ship was known to belong to a Muslim shipowner from Surat named Agha Habib, but it was rented to a Parsi merchant named Nanabhai Ratanji. A pass was issued for the latter's voyage from Surat to the declared destinations of Calicut and Mangalore.[28] In later references, Parsi merchants from Surat, including the above-mentioned Ratanji, appear as shipowners. The Dutch authorized their navigation from Surat to Mangalore, Cannanore, Persia and Malacca.[29] This suggests that Muslim and Parsi merchants and shipowners based in Surat were involved in 'Muslim' sugar shipping to Bandar Abbas in the early eighteenth century.

The lists of non-Dutch shipping at Bandar Abbas do not always note what cargoes sugar-importing ships were loaded with on their return voyages, but the evidence we do have clearly shows that whatever communities a vessel belonged to, it was loaded with Iranian items, such as madder (*ruinas*), rosewater, almonds, fruits, wine and tobacco. All this was for export, either for their own account or for that of other merchants.[30] Dutch lists also record that many departing ships carried precious metals away from cash-strapped Iran. They give the impression that European vessels (English, Danish and French) actively exported bullion in large sums, but that vessels from other communities did not necessarily engage in this export.

Whether or not this inference is justified, it is noteworthy that in the late Safavid period, Bandar Abbas was a main transit port for bullion and Iranian products headed to South Asian countries bordering the Indian Ocean, particularly to Surat.[31] Any merchant at the port exporting goods procured in the upper countries could find both Asian and European freighters on hand to ship his goods abroad. Some late-seventeenth-century and early-eighteenth-century lists of freight goods loaded into the VOC vessels at Bandar Abbas show that many Armenian, Banian and Muslim merchants entrusted the VOC to transport gold and silver specie, such as ducats and '*abbasi*s, pearls and other Iranian products, to their business associates in Surat.[32] Early-eighteenth-century Dutch documentation of freight business at Bandar Abbas contains many accounts of fierce competition among India-bound ships for larger shares of Asian freight. The freight businesses of

Armenian merchants are a case in point. In 1705, the Dutch ship *de Lek* transported gold and silver specie, etc. from Bandar Abbas to Tuticorin (on the Coromandel Coast) for some Armenian merchants, thereby earning 2,455 guilders.[33] This was a cause for concern for the factors at Bandar Abbas: facilitating trade among Armenian and other local merchants between the Persian Gulf and some Indian regions might create a disadvantage for the Company's maritime commerce. They faced a dilemma. If the Company denied the merchants the use of their ships, other shipowners would benefit. They wrote that since many of the Armenian merchants possessed vessels, those who did not possess vessels could utilize those Armenian vessels. English ships, and sometimes Danish vessels, were also available for dispatching cash and goods.[34]

Gulf market flexibility

Although Bandar Abbas received large amounts of sugar in the late Safavid period, other ports in the Persian Gulf also offered trading opportunities for sugar suppliers. Alongside Bandar Abbas, Kong also functioned as a main terminal for Indian Ocean shipping in the Gulf. In 1694 Dutch officials in Bandar Abbas noted that they had to sell their goods hastily, because after the arrival of the Company's ship, many English, Armenian, Muslim and Banian ships arrived at Bandar Abbas and Kong from various Indian countries with large amounts of all sorts of goods.[35] The active non-VOC shipping to Kong reflects maritime traders' intention to circumvent paying customs at Bandar Abbas. According to the VOC, throughout the night, and even in bad weather, the subordinates of the *shahbandar* of Bandar Abbas would be watching for what they viewed as 'smuggling' along the Iranian littoral. In December 1705, after hearing about the arrival of two ships at Kong with freight from Surat, the *shahbandar* left Bandar Abbas for Kong to collect customs and discourage 'smuggling' (*sluikerijen*).[36]

Muscat's role as a terminal for Indian Ocean shipping is also remarkable. It was an alternative to Bandar Abbas and Kong towards the turn of the eighteenth century. In 1694, the Dutch factors in Bandar Abbas recorded that, since goods brought to Muscat were transported on to Bandar Abbas, Kong, and up the Gulf in local barks, the Company had to sell their weighed goods quickly before local shipments filled the market.[37] At that time the Arabs of Muscat increased hostilities, not only against their arch-enemies the Portuguese, whom they drove out of Oman in 1650 and whose commercial base was now at Kong, but also against the Safavids and those they regarded as their allies, such as the Armenians.[38] In 1695, despite ongoing political tensions, local crafts (*inlandse vaartuigen*) from Muscat and the Arab coast continued sailing to the Iranian littoral 'as freely as ever'.[39] Active transit trade continued in the early eighteenth century. In 1713, the VOC officials in Bandar Abbas commented that few English ships arrived without stopping in Muscat.[40]

Although it was not until the fall of the Safavids and the onset of lingering turmoil in Iran that Basra became a serious contender for principal port for sugar trade in the Gulf, this development began in the early eighteenth century.[41] The conflict between Arabs and Iranians increased in the southern Gulf, and so some ships forwarded their merchandise from Bandar Abbas to Basra. The extent to which this move affected trade at Bandar Abbas is evident in the *shahbandar*'s 1705 complaint: European ships were coming to Bandar Abbas with freight goods, and often reshipped goods to Basra, thus depriving the shah of customs revenue. The VOC, however, claimed this was not done by their ships but by English and local vessels.[42] By 1720, it became common for sugar suppliers, particularly the English, to use Basra as an alternative port for sugar.[43] It is likely that much of the sugar imported to Basra in the early eighteenth century was then exported to Iran. A Dutch report written about one decade later states that trade at both Basra and Bandar Abbas could not flourish unless they were at peace. When 'it rained' (their terminology) in Basra, Bandar Abbas flourished, and vice versa. If Basra re-exported imported goods to the Iranian borders, the Iranian market would become saturated and suppliers would be stuck with unsold merchandise.[44]

It is noteworthy that in the early eighteenth century, Mocha, a key port of trade at the entrance to the Red Sea, acted as a distribution centre for sugar bound for the Persian Gulf. The VOC also engaged in Javanese sugar trade at Mocha and Jeddah in the first half of the eighteenth century. Dutch imports across the Red Sea during that period were quite meagre, with an annual average of slightly over 350,000.[45] The Dutch officials in Bandar Abbas initially thought that trade at Mocha was probably directed to a different market, not the Persian Gulf. They said that the Company's import of principally weighed goods, such as pepper, castor sugar and candy sugar, to Mocha would not negatively affect those coming into Bandar Abbas.[46] Towards the end of the decade, however, it seems that both markets became increasingly intertwined and regional shipping from Mocha entered the Persian Gulf. In February 1716, Bandar Abbas reported that wholesale merchants at the port did not rush to make a deal but waited for Muslim and other vessels to bring cheaper sugar from Mocha, where castor sugar and candy sugar were sold for unprecedentedly low prices.[47]

Relocation and new connections: Afghan interregnum (1722–9)

Towards the close of the Safavid period, Bandar Abbas's position in the sugar trade began to change, as non-Dutch suppliers used alternative venues to the southern Iranian littoral. This change was accelerated by the commotion that plagued Iran after the Afghan conquest. Basidu is a prime example of these alternative venues. Located on the west of Kishm Island, in the 1720s merchants viewed this port as a commercial shelter. The powerful Arab ruler of Basidu, Shaykh Rashid, seized this opportunity to make a profit. Claiming to be the *shahbandar* of Bandar Abbas, he announced that he would collect customs at Basidu instead of at Bandar Abbas and thereby attracted ocean-going ships into his port in the latter half of the 1720s.[48] His ambition was thwarted by the EIC, who, also interested in the Bandar Abbas customs revenue, deployed their naval forces against the shaykh several times in

1727. Basidu clearly acted as an alternative market to Bandar Abbas around the mid-1720s.[49] In 1725 gold ducats were available at Basidu at a slightly higher price than at Bandar Abbas. On the other hand, the Basidu market for Javanese castor sugar was more favourable: sugar was sold at 4 *mahmudi*s per *man* (equivalent to 6 Dutch pounds), one *mahmudi* more than at Bandar Abbas.[50]

Oman, whose loaf sugar occupied a notable position in the Iranian market in the late Safavid period, also witnessed the outbreak of civil war. It rapidly engulfed the entire country, causing fierce territorial conflicts among local tribes, and the production of cane sugar in the interior declined significantly, if not entirely.[51] Floor argues that Muscat's position in Gulf trade also plummeted when it faced a serious crisis. In addition to political disorder, he claims that a severe hurricane hit the port city in 1723 and turned Muscat into 'a spent power', both militarily and commercially, for the rest of the decade.[52] Conversely, Dutch documents from this time give the impression that, despite these misfortunes, Muscat's role as an alternative trading port continued to develop. In 1724 Dutch factors at Bandar Abbas reported that the merchants in the lower countries were still fearful that local governors would deprive them of their money, and the merchants tried to stay under the radar, so many of them had already taken refuge in Surat, Basra and Muscat, etc.[53] In 1725, the VOC was able to sell small amounts of castor sugar at Bandar Abbas, but with enormous difficulty, and it was known that it had recently fetched much higher prices at Muscat.[54]

Meanwhile, 'Ottumsjent' and 'Issourdas', the VOC brokers at Bandar Abbas, were bankrupt. After the Afghan invasion of Iran, most of the Company's direct debtors, and the indirect ones for whom Ottumsjent and Issourdas stood surety, were killed, ruined or forced to run away. All the unsettled debts then fell on the brokers' shoulders.[55] In order to improve the brokers' liquidity, the Bandar Abbas factory transported 117,543 pounds of the brokers' own sugar alongside 288,853 pounds of VOC sugar to the Muscat market on the Company's account.[56] However, at the Arab port the Dutch official in charge, Bartholomeus Lispensier, accompanied by Issourdas, sold only 49,149 pounds of the castor sugar to petty Banian merchants. Lispensier ascribed the poor sales to the arrival of an English vessel called *Cadogan*, which sold its sugar at very high prices, siphoning cash away from the market.[57]

In the early 1720s Mocha also functioned as an alternative to Bandar Abbas. In 1722, when the Afghan invasion unsettled Iran, a large number of ships – twenty-one Muslim, fifteen English, one French and one from Ostend – sailed to Mocha with merchandise. The VOC commented that, since the suppliers sold their goods, which primarily consisted of sugar, pepper and textiles, at low prices at Mocha, merchants who reshipped those goods to Basra, Kong, Muscat and other places in the Gulf were able to obtain larger profits.[58]

While the relocation of sugar market was taking place, what remained of it at Bandar Abbas began to connect to the growing markets of Basra and Kirman. The Afghan invasion of Iran disrupted the large market for bullion at Isfahan. Soon afterwards Basra became a dependable substitute. Gold and silver coins found their way to the Basra market, a subject to which I will return in the next chapter.

As a result, cash flows from Basra were essential for trans-oceanic commerce in the southern Gulf in the latter half of the 1720s. The VOC reported that Armenian and Banian merchants in Basra who had specie on hand tried to capitalize on this. Through their business correspondents in Bandar Abbas or Basidu, they said, the Basra merchants urged even petty merchants to accept precious metals, such as gold ducats, at high prices, although this practice pushed seafaring traders to resort to bartering.[59]

It is remarkable that powerful wholesale merchants in Lar, Shiraz and Isfahan, who had virtually monopolized trade with the VOC at Bandar Abbas in late Safavid times, seldom appear in routine Dutch subsequent correspondence. Instead, merchants who traded with Kirman became important buyers of the Company's goods, including sugar, from the mid-1720s onwards. As far as we know, such trade began in the financial year 1726-7. In March 1727 the VOC negotiated with some merchants who intended to load their caravan with Javanese sugar and transport it to Kirman. Eventually they agreed to sell them castor sugar and candy sugar at 2 17/20 *mahmudi*s per *man* and 6 *mahmudi*s per *man*, respectively.[60]

Resilience of the English trade

The EIC factors in Iran irritatedly reported the socioeconomic crisis they underwent during the Afghan occupation. But, in the eyes of the Dutch, their activities appeared quite successful. A Dutch report in early 1727 relates that English commerce had been improving remarkably for some time and that locals' trust in this nation had increased. Apart from the fact that the EIC had repaid their debts, the Dutch felt that the EIC policy of 'Do as the Romans do' (*in Rome met de Romeinen moeten leven*) lay behind their success; they had been flexible and adjusted to the changing situations. The Dutch noted that the EIC used the money they had spent when dealing with the government of Kirman to procure 256 bales (weighing 23,040 Dutch pounds) of Kirman wool. Furthermore, the English had sent their goods from Bandar Abbas to Kirman and carried back various items for export, such as shawls, madder and various fruits, on their own account.[61]

While developing their commercial network with Kirman, the English attempted to make in-roads in Shiraz and enter the market at Bushire. Regarding the English success in the Kirman wool trade, the VOC bitterly wrote that the English boasted about themselves everywhere as if they were king. According to the VOC, their remarkable progress was initiated by the EIC chief Thomas Waters (1726-8), who the Bombay Presidency vested with enormous authority and received the timely assistance of local consultants, and who took all measures necessary to survive the troubling times. By placating local authorities with presents sized according to the importance of the matter at hand, so the Dutch factors wrote, the English established their commerce so solidly that the Company could not compete with them. In spite of a shortfall of cash, the English could still exchange their goods for money. They sent it by small craft to Bushire and then by land to Shiraz using an Afghan escort. At Shiraz, they acquired wine, rosewater, etc. and travelled back to Bandar Abbas. When the English requested support from local regents at Lar, Kirman or elsewhere, they were not refused. The English seem to have been held in higher esteem than some local leaders.⁶²

Because the VOC usually referred to the EIC and English private traders as 'English', it is uncertain who exactly engaged in these new trade methods. However, there is no doubt that, as in late Safavid times, the interests of the Company and private traders, particularly EIC factors in Iran, were deeply entangled. The EIC's contact with Bushire in 1729 provides a striking example. On 10 February 1729 an EIC officer named William May asked other council members of the Bandar Abbas factory to let him go to Bushire to conduct his own business. According to him, he was trading a large quantity of goods at Bushire, but he sold a part of it in November, and since then, he had not received any notice of the sales of the remainder from the person to whom he had consigned his goods. He wondered if the *shahbandar* of Bushire was interrupting trade. The council not only granted his petition but also tried to make use of this occasion to set up 'English' trade on firm footing in this rising market.⁶³ During the Afghan occupation, the EIC struggled to maintain their old right of exemption from customs duties and tolls in Iran. Therefore, the council members suspected that the *shahbandar* was charging customs on English goods.⁶⁴ On 14 February, the factory sent May to Bushire on the Company's ship *Success* with instructions to demand satisfaction from the *shahbandar* for the money that he had charged on goods belonging to servants of the EIC's interpreter at Bandar Abbas. However, when May arrived in Bushire, the man in question was no longer the *shahbandar* and the present officeholder was out of town and staying in Shiraz.⁶⁵ The Bandar Abbas factory ordered the English resident in Isfahan to lobby the Afghan court to discharge the *shahbandar* of Bushire with the charge that he was hindering merchants from buying English goods at his port.⁶⁶

Change in competition patterns: The 1730s

During the 1730s more and more Indian shipping to the Persian Gulf headed for Basra instead of Bandar Abbas. English and French vessels from India, which presumably constituted the main part of non-Dutch shipping to the Gulf after the Safavid period, headed to Basra without stopping at Bandar Abbas. We shall explore this in the next chapter, but here it is important to note that during this period Bandar Abbas trade was still lucrative enough for competitors to continue to challenge the VOC's trade.

From the perspective of the VOC, EIC commerce in Iran experienced a serious downturn in the mid-1730s. In 1734 the Dutch noted that, while actively drawing bills of exchange to procure export goods at Kirman, the English were failing to liquidate those bills on time; they could not reach satisfactory agreements, even though they tried to settle mostly in goods. Because of increased debt, their creditors were now saying that there would be only delays and disgust if they continued to tolerate the English.⁶⁷ The situation worsened the next year. In April

1735, the EIC fell into disfavour with the new ruler of Iran, Tahmasb Quli Khan (later Nadir Shah). His naval campaign against Basra had been humiliated by two English warships that lent naval assistance to the port's Turkish government. The growing tension jeopardized the safety of EIC staff in Iran, leading to the temporary withdrawal of most personnel to Bombay.[68]

The EIC's unexpected retreat gave the VOC hopes of reinvigorating their trade, which had been negatively affected by the English throughout the previous decade. Yet their hopes were dashed in the years that followed. In December 1736 the Dutch factors wrote that the English and French had badly hampered the Company's trade. Wholesale merchants were willing to trade with the English whenever, in whatever goods they could, and by paying however much, while they would not spend money on the Dutch unless the Company dropped the prices of their goods, specifically that of sugar.[69]

Amidst the protracted unease in Iran during Nadir Shah's rule, it is worth mentioning that many Dutch reports refer to the mounting threat of French shipping and trade from India. Dutch officers frequently complained that it was not just the English but also the French who were trying to attract wholesale merchants suffering from Iran's shortage of cash. They were permitting them to trade using long-term credits. However, this rise in French activity could weaken the English menace. The credit the French were extending to local merchants, the Dutch wrote, was unrealistic and might result in the disruption of their trade. In addition, it was reckless for the French to adopt such 'brusque' behaviour with the local governors. But if French trade went into decline, the English would take over their merchants and be able to trade everywhere in the Gulf with ease.[70]

The competition between the VOC and other sugar suppliers at Bandar Abbas from the 1730s onwards is evident in the four main measures, which the VOC partook in hesitantly, to handle the increasing scarcity of cash in the market: price adjustments, credit sales, acceptance of copper and utilization of the Kirman market. As argued in the first chapter, despite its relatively high price, the market for the Javanese castor sugar the VOC imported to Bandar Abbas grew substantially in the late Safavid period. It seems that this 'fancy' sugar retained a certain level of appeal. A Dutch letter, written in August 1735, states that, because of its superior quality, the Company still managed to sell Javanese castor sugar at a price of 3½ *mahmudi*s per *man* at the port, despite the English selling Bengali sugar for less.[71] However, there is little doubt that wholesale merchants thought Dutch sugar was too expensive, and as we have seen above, they preferred to trade with the English, unless the Dutch reduced the price of their sugar.[72] Nevertheless, the VOC did not compromise. In 1739 Dutch officers repeated the idea that, while Batavia provided them with quality Javanese sugar, they could turn better profits than those supplied with other varieties of sugar.[73]

In the constricting financial environment of the late Safavid period, it was important for wholesale merchants in Iran to obtain maritime goods on credit. The High Government of Batavia therefore permitted the factors in Bandar Abbas to sell the Company's goods on three-month credit. Bandar Abbas allowed Hajji 'Abd al-Rida, a wealthy wholesale merchant from Shiraz who dominated trade with the VOC at the port, to be given five-month credit.[74] After the Safavid period they became alarmed that many merchants were becoming insolvent, and Batavia suspended the policy and ordered Bandar Abbas not to sell any goods on credit, only for direct cash payments.[75] This measure turned out to be a fatal mistake. It enabled other sugar suppliers, particularly the English and French, to attract more attention from penurious local merchants by offering them even longer terms of credit. The VOC pointed out these developments in reference to the arrival of numerous non-VOC vessels at Bandar Abbas during the financial year 1734–5. Twenty-eight ships had arrived, as well as five big boats (*grote vaartuigen*). Seventeen of them belonged to the English. If no money was available in Bandar Abbas, the Muslim traders would sail to Basra or somewhere else, and the captains (*nakhuda*s) of the boats would likewise not unload their goods. But the English and French would sell their goods on a long six-month credit. There were also some 'smugglers' (*lorrendraaiers*) who imported their goods under the EIC name to avoid paying customs at Bandar Abbas and this seriously undercut VOC trade.[76]

The Dutch officers in Bandar Abbas saw the total breakdown of the Company as inevitable unless they were once more allowed to sell their goods on credit for three or three and a half months, even though the English and French usually allowed much more competitive terms of five to six months.[77] To make matters worse, the officers said, the English and French were not charging interest on their credit sales. The wholesale merchants were unwilling to pay interest because, in these turbulent times, they carried the risk of transporting purchased goods all the way to Kirman, Isfahan and other places where they had agents to sell the goods for profit. The English and French only contracted them to procure goods for return in those places, a manner of trade they still considered profitable.[78] In late 1736, the Dutch factors expressed their impatience. In a rather self-justifying remark they said that, despite their utmost efforts, the French import of castor sugar, candy sugar and textiles had diminished the Company's prospect.[79] The next year Batavia eventually acquiesced to Bandar Abbas's request for credit sales.[80] However, for the most part, the VOC sugar trade in Bandar Abbas continued to reflect Batavia's aversion to credit sales. In 1755, four years before the Company's withdrawal, Schoonderwoerd, the Dutch director in Bandar Abbas, reminded his successor, Gerrit Aansorg, that Bandar Abbas had to trade the Company's goods for cash or exchange them for return goods as required, without allowing credit.[81]

In their pioneering study of the Iranian monetary system *The Monetary History of Iran*, Matthee, Floor and P. Clawson call the period from the fall of the Safavids to the rise of the Qajars 'The Age of Copper' and argue that the Iranian monetary system became effectively trimetallic, with gold, silver and copper circulating freely. Copper coins were traditionally small denominations and used for local transactions, and bartering was also widely practised as an alternative or supplementary means of exchange. However, gold and silver specie were extremely scarce in the Iranian market after 1730, and copper coins known as *paysa* or *qazbegi* became an important currency in regional trade as well. More importantly, merchants became very interested in procuring copper money for export, which made copper an alternative payment medium for trans-regional trade. The increased importance of copper led Tahmasb Quli Khan to integrate copper money into Iran's traditional monetary system, which was based on gold and silver, by introducing official exchange rates between gold, silver and copper coins.[82]

The English also showed far more flexibility than the VOC when it came to copper. In the early 1730s the English mainly targeted *paysa* coins for export, while the Dutch gleaned what remained of any gold and silver at Bandar Abbas and Basidu. Since copper was prone to smaller losses than gold and silver, according to the Dutch, the English exchanged all their imports for copper money and exported it to Surat, Madras and Bengal.[83]

Over the course of the decade, many maritime traders resorted to copper coins and, when these were almost used up, to whatever copper ware they could find, in spite of repeated official bans on the export of copper starting in 1737.[84] In these circumstances, local wholesale merchants who came to Bandar Abbas for trade began to only bring copper coins (*koper munt*).[85] We do not know much about the origins of the copper, but there seems to have been multiple supply channels to Bandar Abbas. According to the VOC, copper that the English purchased at the port in the mid-1730s came from three places: the town of Niriz near Shiraz; Qazvin; and a village called Sirhindi (Zerendi). Sirhindi was a two-day journey from Kirman, where copper was mined.[86] At the port, the English minted the copper they acquired into smaller coins (*kleinder muntspecie*), copper 'cakes' (*koeken*), or other shapes for export.[87]

When they saw their rivals' bustling trade in copper, in 1732, if not earlier, the VOC engaged in *paysa* export, though in limited numbers.[88] In the latter half of the 1730s the Company began to export copper in some form as well. However, Batavia ordered clean and refined (i.e. intact and unused) copper, the material from which *paysas* were made, and copper of such a quality was hard to obtain in the market. The Dutch factors in Bandar Abbas had to clean (*met fenken en kloppen zuiveren*) the oxidized copper material (*koperwerken*) they procured in Bandar Abbas and Bushire, although such procedures cost money.[89] Copper export from Iran was not very profitable for the VOC. Dismayed at the soaring market price of copper ware due to English and French trading, in 1736 Dutch officers had no idea how their rivals could make a living from it. In their view, the English and French were not concerned about the quality of the return goods they bought. These traders exchanged their imports for insignificant products which the Dutch were prohibited from trading. But they also accepted any sort of copper as means of payment.[90] The principal reason why the VOC persisted in what was for them an unfavourable enterprise was to prevent the English and the French from dominating the market. Though procuring profitable copper cakes was not easy, the officers said it would be unreasonable to back out of the trade, because even if their competitors pretended copper yielded small profits compared to other return goods, they would be the winners, since local merchants who had copper would be more inclined to trade with them.[91]

From the mid-1720s, it became usual for the VOC to trade with merchants whose trade was directed towards Kirman. This was also the case with the

EIC. Recently Good has shown that in the post-Safavid period the EIC actively participated in the Kirman market to trade English woollen goods – the Company's principal import item from Europe – for Kirman wool and copper.[92] This line of trade began in the late 1730s, when they did not receive a proper offer at Bandar Abbas. At the close of 1736, due to the scarcity of old copper and copper money (black money), wholesale merchants trading EIC woollen goods asked the factory to allow them credit of at least nine months.[93] Although regular buyers, such as Khurasani merchants, still visited Bandar Abbas, the EIC sent a trial load to Kirman the following year and instructed their resident there to procure copper and copper coins in return.[94]

Dutch letters provide new insights: the transit of goods from Bandar Abbas to Kirman was also linked to the private interests of EIC officials, and those goods included sugar. In 1736, William Cockell, then agent of the English factory (1733–8), forwarded a considerable amount of goods, worth 9,000 *tumans* or 382,500 guilders, to Kirman.[95] The French took advantage of the English caravan traffic and managed to transport their goods to Kirman as well.[96] As much as the Iranian authorities extorted money from impoverished local merchants, the Dutch complained the English continued to dispatch massive caravans to Kirman with woollen goods (*lakenen*) and shawls (*sjaals*), as well as with the same kinds of goods the VOC traded at Bandar Abbas, including candy sugar and pepper. Meanwhile, the impoverished merchants at the port offered to buy VOC goods up to the value of 2,000 *tumans* on a four-month credit, but the Dutch factory could not accept those terms without permission for credit sales from Batavia.[97]

Further relocation: The 1740s

The 1740s has been viewed as a critical phase in the history of Bandar Abbas. Floor argues that, after the disruption of trade in the Afghan interregnum, Nadir Shah failed to re-establish conditions that would have enabled trade at the port to recover to its former level. Instead, his protracted power struggle with Arab notables on both shores of the southern Gulf forced local labour, foodstuff and essential supplies to be diverted into royal service. This in turn gave Nadir and the administrators involved opportunities to satisfy their greed by extorting exorbitant terms for loaning ships and for extracting money and presents from the merchants. As a consequence, trade at Bandar Abbas was no longer profitable and the port rapidly degenerated and was restricted to local distribution.[98]

Conversely, Ricks contends that despite this upheaval caravan trade in southern Iran and maritime trade in the Persian Gulf continued. Trans-oceanic shipping proceeded as before into India and the Red Sea, and both the EIC and the VOC prospered. In this regard, he puts particular stress on the rise of Kirman as a grand hub for goods coming from Bandar Abbas to Mashhad and from Bandar Abbas to Isfahan and Shiraz. Although Kirman experienced an economic recession in the mid-1740s, Ricks claims that its market revived under the aegis of a strong local notable named Shahrukh Khan Afshar by 1750; the major trading routes to Mashhad and Isfahan reopened. Kirman continued to be a major distribution centre in southern Iran until the early 1760s, when it was replaced by Shiraz, which was supported by the Zand rulership.[99]

Dutch records of sugar trade at Bandar Abbas give the impression that Bandar Abbas continued to be an important destination for sugar traders when the economic climate permitted, but the relocation to other regional markets, such as Kirman and Bushire, steadily advanced.

In the early 1740s, sugar was still in demand at Bandar Abbas. Dutch officers were deeply depressed about the commotion in Batavia's *ommelanden* in 1740 and the interruption to sugar supplies it caused at Bandar Abbas. In 1742 they noted that, if the troubles in Batavia ended and sugar mills resumed their sugar supplies to Bandar Abbas, they could obtain much profit, because the turmoil had also reduced the sugar trade of their 'competitors' (*medecompetiteuren*) sugar supplies, and Iranians were suffering from a shortage.[100] The term *medecompetiteuren* might refer to English and French traders, given the fact that one year later, the officers requested Batavia to provide them with goods as soon as possible before the English and French private traders filled the market.[101] This request indicates that other traders posed a substantial threat to the Dutch monopoly on Javanese sugar in the Iranian market, as happened in the Surat market in the mid-1760s. We know that the Dutch factory at Surat was receiving only the most meagre supplies of Javanese sugar, and it was the worst sort of sugar. But the English and local (Gujarati) ships were the largest importers of the best sorts, which were being 'smuggled' in from Java by small craft through the Strait of Malacca or Bengkulu in Malaysia to Bombay and Surat.[102]

The scarcer copper became, the more acute the competition for the metal. In 1742, copper ware and *paysa*s completely disappeared from Bandar Abbas.[103] When copper was brought in later, prices were inflated due to the fast trading of the English and French.[104] The Dutch factors were baffled that merchants were offering them 2,600 pounds of copper cakes at as high as 15½ *mahmudi*s per *man*, and the factors would not accept it; they thought they would lose on a deal in Coromandel, where the item was being exported.[105] The enormous amount of gold and silver that Nadir Shah brought as booty from Hindustan in the last part of the 1730s somewhat made up for the scarcity of copper. In 1742, Bandar Abbas trade was carried out using silver coins called *nadiri*s, which Nadir struck to be used alongside Thatta, Delhi and Agra rupees. However, the Dutch said the English and French were also amassing these coins and exporting them all over India.[106]

Trade came to a halt after 1743, when an uprising carried out by Muhammad Taqi Khan Shirazi, one of Nadir's generals who was then in charge of the Iranian flotilla in the Gulf, threatened safe passage to Bandar Abbas. Writing in July 1746 the Dutch factors explained that trade at Bandar Abbas was currently at a complete standstill and merchants neither came to trade nor maintained their houses at the port. They therefore requested Batavia to allow them to transport goods to Isfahan, Kirman or somewhere else, where they could sell them for cash (*contanten*) and obtain copper ware and other profitable export items in return.[107] The displacement of merchants in the port city is illustrated by the departure of two merchant communities: the 'Multani Banians' (Multannee Banyans) and the 'Banksallee caste'. In May 1747, after suffering all kinds of difficulties at the hands of the authorities, the 'Multani Banians', along with many members of the 'Banksallee caste', left the port and took shelter in Barka (Birka), a coastal town in Oman. As a result, few people remained in town except those associated with the EIC and the VOC.[108] Many of them probably never returned, as soon afterwards the Banians in Bandar Abbas received business updates from their correspondents in Sind and Kutch via Barka.[109]

According to the VOC, in 1747–8 there were four reasons why inland merchants did not come down to Bandar Abbas for trade, even in peaceful times. First, the merchants had to pay more than twice as much tax (*gerechtigheden*) at Bandar Abbas as at Bushire or any other place in the empire (*rijk*). Second, travel expenses and freight fees from Isfahan and Shiraz to Bandar Abbas cost more than those to Bushire, etc. Third, the climate was extremely unhealthy throughout the empire. Fourth, and most significantly, the English sent all of their woollen goods, and even most of their other goods, from Bandar Abbas to Kirman themselves. For other merchants it was easier and less risky to assign their goods to English caravans because the roads were not safe, even in good times. Moreover, pack animals were not always available at the port.[110]

The EIC also reference this first point as a crucial factor for the waning of the Bandar Abbas market. The ways merchants circumvented Bandar Abbas at the turn of the 1750s is vividly penned in the following English letter dated 6 March 1752:

> For many years past the upcountry merchants complained greatly of the distress they are in from the oppressions of the g[overn]ment [of Bandar Abbas], which convinces us most of their families would remain under the Ho[nourable] Company's [the EIC's] protection, while themselves ventured with goods from any of the sea ports where the roads adjacent were free from robbers, and as there would be a considerable advantage accruing to any of the petty governours [sic] where they landed the goods bought of us, it would soon occasion great emulation among them, as everyone would be in hopes of accumulating all the profit to himself by a civil behaviour to passengers. On the contrary, were the merchants to attempt shipping their goods from this place, or land from other ports, what duties imposed by these people [the authorities of Bandar Abbas] would eat up all profits, as there is no settled prcentage [sic] but everything at the will of the custom house writers, and we are well informed fifteen, sixteen and se[ven]teen prcent [sic] is often exacted. Under us this grievance would be remedied and by their embarking from Minnoe [Minab], Cong [Kong] or any place where no showbunder [*shahbandar*] resides, have little more than boat hire to pay. The great difference of [-] would establish the centre of all trade in the Gulph between Muscat and Bussorah [Basra] at our settlement.[111]

This letter shows that, in order to avoid the imposition of a high tariff from the Bandar Abbas customs house, inland merchants 'smuggled' their goods by boat from neighbouring places where no *shahbandar* resided, such as Minab and Kong. They secured the 'protection' of the EIC, who continued to enjoy customs exemption at Bandar Abbas. In these circumstances the 'petty governours', or governors of small ports in the Gulf vied with each other to attract traders.

The second and third reasons the VOC pointed out for the decline of Bandar Abbas are not as convincing today. These geographical and climatic disadvantages did not always prevent merchants from coming to Bandar Abbas during the late Safavid period. The fourth point, however, requires special attention in light of the devastation that befell Kirman after Nadir Shah's punitive campaign in 1747. The EIC records also tell us that this destruction was a temporary setback. The English diary states that on 24 May 1748 a large caravan left for Kirman, mainly with sugar, sugar candy, pepper, a small quantity of woollen goods and a few other trifling articles.[112] At the close of the 1740s the stagnation engulfing Bandar Abbas was somewhat relieved when caravan traffic from inland markets, particularly from Kirman, began to return.[113] It seems, though, that some English officials continued the Kirman enterprise on their own account. In 1752, EIC chief Danvers Graves traded his private goods in Kirman through a son of the Company's interpreter in Bandar Abbas, who was resident of Kirman at the time.[114]

Muscat-Minab-Kirman: The 1750s

In the 1750s, non-VOC suppliers of sugar remained interested in the Bandar Abbas market. Existing lists of non-VOC shipments to Bandar Abbas for the periods from 1 September 1753 to 20 December 1754 and 21 November 1757 to 4 February 1759 record twenty-seven arrivals, of which six carried sugar. Four of the sugar suppliers came from Bengal, one from Bombay and one from Coromandel.[115] Yet, some of these sugar shipments were likely destined for markets in the Upper Gulf. For instance, while a Dutch letter relates that on 4 December 1754 an English vessel called the *Queen of India* came from Bombay with a large amount of sugar, pepper, tin, etc., the EIC diary notes that this ship (they called it the *Indian Queen*) left for Bushire on 12 December after unloading woollen goods.[116]

Whatever the situation might have been, the VOC was not free to sell sugar at the port. At the port inland merchants were preoccupied with whether to invest their limited fortunes in VOC sugar or EIC woollen goods. In April 1757 the EIC realized that, if merchants saw it was more profitable to buy sugar and other goods from the VOC, they would not trade for EIC goods. The English factors therefore reduced the price of their woollen goods and thereby managed to dispose of 80,000 rupees worth.[117]

Fierce rivalry and a lack of flexibility in their approach to cash shortages continued to shackle the VOC sugar trade. It was almost inevitable that the Bandar Abbas factory would agree to sell the Company's goods on credit against the wishes of Batavia. The local merchants had been demanding credit for months on end, pretending that the English allowed them credit for up to 1,000 or 2,000 rupees a time. Nonetheless, the Dutch only acceded to the requests of Multani merchants, whom they believed were 'rather wealthy' (*tamelijk gegoed*).[118] Besides, it was normal for the VOC to blame this on other traders, who placed extravagant bids for copper. In 1753, while accusing the English and other traders of not following the market principles, Schoonderwoerd compromised on an inflated price of 17 stivers per Dutch pound. If he had not he would have lost all his buyers.[119]

An overall cash shortage in the eighteenth century led merchants to resort to barter more and more when trading. But Batavia had a strong preference to trade for cash, and this was another disadvantage for the Company's sugar trade at Bandar Abbas. In September 1756, the factors claimed that, if the Company, like their competitors, dared to barter their goods (*bij ruiling voor negotiegoederen*), the current year's sales would increase.[120] The English were particularly good at this style of trade. While it was profitable for the English to barter for local products, such as madder and asafetida, Schoonderwoerd commented that the same might not be true for the Dutch, given that the English were able to get up-to-date price lists from Bombay any time they needed them and therefore knew the actual rates for those goods at their main destination in India.[121]

The Dutch struggle to sell sugar at Bandar Abbas was also reflected in Muscat's sugar market. From the 1740s Dutch private sectors started to actively participate in the sugar trade, and it soon became clear that a potential threat loomed for all VOC factories that conducted sugar trade in the regions.[122] In 1753 the Dutch factory in Bandar Abbas was obsessed with a suspicion that a Dutch arrival called *Fortuin* had been clandestinely carrying a larger amount of private sugar than was permitted and had imported much of it to Muscat on its way to Bandar Abbas.[123] Although further investigation did not support the hypothesis, the factors remained concerned about any negative effects resulting from private sugar shipments to Muscat. One year later they requested that Batavia forbid the captains (*overheden*) of Dutch ships from visiting Muscat on their voyage to Bandar Abbas, except in the case of a serious emergency.[124]

What is more noteworthy is that over the decade, Muscat became increasingly connected to Minab due to local shipping. It is recorded that the governor of Bandar Abbas, Mulla 'Ali Shah, and his customs officials were inclined to be rapacious, so many local merchants went to Minab to find boats (*vaartuigen*) and cross over to Muscat. At the time it was very easy to barter their goods for sugar.[125] This development of a new commercial line between Muscat and Minab made sugar trade at Bandar Abbas more difficult for the VOC. Immediately after the arrival of the Dutch ship *Stralen* on 28 April 1757, the VOC sent for Multani merchants. None who came had any interest in imported sugar, whatever offer the Dutch made. The factors had no option but to forward the ship's cargo to Muscat. The governor of Bandar Abbas interfered once the shipment embarked, and he sent the *shahbandar* and those merchants to the Dutch factory, requesting the Company store the cargo in Bandar Abbas as usual. But the shipping formalities were already in progress, so the Dutch made a rather outrageous condition, insisting that the merchants agree to promise to buy the entire cargo of sugar, or at least a large part of it. The *shahbandar* did not let them go. At his urgent request the merchants eventually came to an agreement that they would take the sugar in two months time, and they would pay within the same period. It turned out that they were disinclined to keep their word.[126]

In the 1760s the Muscat-Minab trade was closely linked with Kirman. In 1761 the EIC record states:

> There has been no trade carried on here [Bandar Abbas] for some time past, no merchant boats as usual coming and going to this port, [and] such as formerly came here now carry on their business to and from Minoe [Minab], from whence we learn caffilas [*qafilas*] with different sorts of India goods go to Carmenia [Kirman] and other places inland. In short this place seems near at an end and nothing can recover it but a change of government and good management in a governour [*sic*].[127]

This description of the situation indicates that at the turn of the 1760s, the channel for inland commerce in the southern Iranian littoral had diverted from Bandar Abbas to Minab, thus making Minab the new hub for maritime trade and caravan commerce between Muscat and Kirman and other inland market towns in eastern Iran and beyond.

This chapter has examined the ways non-VOC sugar suppliers tried to adjust to changing trade conditions at Bandar Abbas after the Safavid period. From the evidence we have obtained, it is certain that, while protracted political instability after the Afghan conquest in the southern Iranian littoral steadily made importing sugar to Bandar Abbas burdensome for the suppliers, competition continued. The English and French attracted more local merchants than the VOC, because they offered cash-strapped merchants cheaper sugar and longer terms of credit. The greater use of copper for domestic trade and the rise of copper's role as an alternative export item to gold and silver specie are key factors in this development. These suppliers were also more flexible in their willingness to accept copper money and copper ware, both in payment and as return goods.

We have also seen how swiftly non-VOC sugar suppliers headed for other regional markets, especially Kirman and Muscat. Their active rechannelling of trade caused a steady decline of the Bandar Abbas market, thus exasperating the Dutch. But this also sustained a vigorous sugar trade in the Lower Gulf. This leads us to believe that the sugar trade was more intense in the Upper Gulf, where it is likely that more suppliers sought alternative channels of trade. How did they carry out sugar imports there? How did their activities reflect the restructuring of the Gulf market? We will deal with these questions in the next chapter.

Chapter 5

ALTERNATIVE SUGAR HUBS: BASRA, BUSHIRE AND KHARG

In Chapter 3 we saw how the Dutch East India Company (*Verenigde Oostindische Compagnie* [VOC]) continued to try sell Javanese sugar at Basra and Bushire, and later at Kharg Island, until their final withdrawal from the Gulf in 1766. This chapter analyses another aspect of the Company's struggle: they faced renewed competition from other sugar suppliers in the Upper Gulf. Through an examination of the increased activities of rival suppliers with whom the VOC had to contend in Basra, Bushire and Kharg, this chapter will highlight the flexibility of the sugar trade in the Upper Gulf and the interplay between the forces that formed and characterized this flexibility.

The rise of Basra in the Indian Ocean sugar trade

In his study of the English documentation concerning Basra shipping, Abdullah described the period between 1724 and 1756 as a phase of relative growth for trade. Despite repeated conflicts between the Ottoman Empire and Nadir Shah in the early 1730s and early 1740s, as well as the plagues that occasionally hit the country seriously impacted trade at Basra, Abdullah claims that such disruptions were temporary setbacks. During this period the average number of large vessels arriving at Basra was about eleven.[1] The Dutch documentation of non-VOC shipping and trade at Basra during the same period supports Abdullah's argument.

Replacing Bandar Abbas: The 1720s

In the 1720s the bulk of trade that had formerly passed through Bandar Abbas was redirected to Basra. According to the VOC, who had a factory at Basra in 1724, the total number of foreign arrivals in the financial year 1727–8 was fifteen: five English vessels and one French vessel from Bengal, two English private ships from Bombay, three Surat Muslim ships, one East India Company (EIC) ship, two Muslim crafts from Mocha, and one private French ship.[2]

By 1730 Basra had become English private traders' main trading station in the Gulf. In 1731 the Dutch noted that the English traders maintained a 'domicile' for their trade in the city, and the EIC re-established a residence there in 1727; perhaps this referred to the appointment of the new English resident, Martin French. The VOC did not send much merchandise to Basra early on, and between 1726 and 1729 English trade made sales at Basra extremely difficult for the Company.[3] In fact, some English privateers residing in Basra actively imported sugar to the port. On 6 April 1725, the English ship *Meridon* came through Bandar Abbas from Bengal with 300 packs (*pakken*) of cloths (*kleden*), Chinese candy sugar, Bengali castor sugar, pepper, etc. The ship belonged to an Englishman named George Petty who was staying at the port, and he instantly sold his Chinese candy sugar at 27 *mahmudis* per *man* (equivalent to 25 Dutch pounds in Basra).[4] The *Dean*, an English frigate that arrived from Bengal on 22 May 1725, was owned by another Englishman, James Neville. It carried 700 packs of cloths, textiles (*lijwaten*), Bengali sugar, pepper, etc. both for himself and on the behalf of others, including some Armenian merchants.[5] The Bombay Presidency quickly recognized the increase in private trade at Basra and tried to benefit from it by introducing various duties, such as consulage. Consulage was a 2 per cent duty on the value of all private goods sold at Bandar Abbas and Basra. The EIC collected the duty from English private traders as part of the Company's 'consul' service.[6] But their consulage duty at Basra provoked a flood of complaints from private traders, including Petty and Neville.[7]

In the 1720s much of the Surat Muslim shipping that had provided Bandar Abbas with sugar regularly in the late Safavid period also turned its attention to Basra. On 10 August 1725, the vessel *Fayd Rasani* arrived at Basra from Surat. It was registered as belonging to Muhammad 'Ali, the grandson and successor of the celebrated Bohra merchant from Surat, 'Abd al-Ghafur, who had been involved in the Manila sugar trade at Bandar Abbas in the late seventeenth century. This ship carried a variety of Surat textiles and Bengali sugar.[8] There was also another Muslim arrival (*Moors schip*) from Surat, the *Fath-i Dawla*, which suggests that other mercantile communities in Surat were involved in 'Muslim' sugar shipping to Basra, as during the Safavid period. The *Fath-i Dawla* arrived four days after the *Fayd Rasani*, with numerous packs of textiles, Bengali sugar and rice for the Muslim merchants living in Basra.[9] This ship bore the same name as one that received a Dutch passport at Surat for a voyage to Hormuz, Kong, Basra, Mocha and Jeddah on 23 March 1725. It may have been the same ship, although the issue date was rather late in the season for navigation to the Persian Gulf. The ship's owner was known to be a 'heathen' (*heidens*, i.e. a non-Muslim) called 'Sammeltje Herridas', who was a resident of Surat.[10]

The French sugar trade also found its way to Basra. On 27 May 1729, *St. Joseph*, a French East India Company ship, arrived at Basra from Bengal laden with 500 packs of coarse textiles and certain amounts of pepper, rice, cardamom, sugar, etc.[11] The VOC grew concerned about the French trade at Basra when, according to the Dutch, they (and perhaps the English too) had to pay 5 to 6 per cent (and often more) import duty on both individual items and weighed goods, but the

French were allowed to pay 3 per cent duty on individual items and 4½ per cent on weighed goods, thanks to the splendid gifts they presented to the port authorities.[12] We still need to gather further evidence before we can assess the port's eighteenth-century customs administration. What is known is that the VOC were constantly attempting to get better treatment, but it took them more than a decade to achieve a 3 per cent duty. The EIC apparently only obtained 5 per cent.[13]

After the Afghan conquest disrupted the bullion market at Isfahan, Basra developed as an important alternative, and many seafaring traders participated in this rising commercial arena. Every year the bullion trade at Basra began with the arrival of numerous 'galleys' and boats from Baghdad that carried substantial amounts of bullion.[14] The VOC also started procuring bullion specie for export, gold ducats and silver reals in particular, but supplies were never sufficient to meet the merchants' demands.[15] Competition was fierce and drove up prices excessively.[16] The result was the same as in Iranian markets: copper rapidly became an alternative export item. Copper dominated the market by 1730. In July 1729, the Dutch factors wrote that it was unclear why the 'Bengali traders' (*Bengaalse kooplieden*) procured copper (*roodkoper*) so vigorously that year, but perhaps it was because exporting copper produced less of a loss than other poor-quality currencies, and since these traders had been so eager for copper, merchants from the upper countries had brought large amounts into Basra.[17] The 'Bengali traders' might have included English privateers who supplied sugar from Bengal for the Basra market. An Englishman named Durley is a case in point. His ship, the *Edward*, arrived at Basra from Bengal on 21 February 1729, importing textiles, castor sugar, etc. Two months later it sailed away with a full cargo of old copper and Iranian copper coins (*paysas*) worth 297,500 guilders.[18]

From then on copper continued to be transported to Basra. The inland merchants occasionally carried the metal to Huwayza (Hawise), a mint town in Khuzistan in south-western Iran, for distribution to Basra and Bushire. Much of the copper transferred to Huwayza might have originated from Iran, even though, according to the Dutch, by 1740 Iran's mining industry had significantly diminished due to overexploitation.[19] Another possible source of copper was Russia. According to Barendse, in the eighteenth century Russian copper mines in the Urals grew substantially, producing large volumes of coins called *kopeks*. Some were sent to the markets at Shamakhi, Isfahan and Mashhad, facilitating Russian trade with Asia, and some may possibly have reached the Upper Gulf.[20] The most stable source, however, was Anatolia. During the eighteenth century, copper mined around Diyar Bakr was transported by river and caravan to Mosul in Iraq, where it was smelted and moulded into 'cakes'. From there, the cakes were transported by boat, first to Baghdad and then on to Basra for export to India. It was subjected to customs duties in all these cities. Nevertheless, Anatolian copper exports continued throughout the eighteenth century.[21] At the end of the century, Olivier observed that the interior of Turkey was providing Baghdad and Basra with very few commodities, with the exception of large volumes of old copper (*vieux cuivre*). Copper from Syria, Mesopotamia, Anatolia, Armenia and Kurdistan all passed through Mosul on its way to Baghdad and Basra.[22]

Boom: The 1730s

Using data from the EIC archives Abdullah argues that Basra experienced a serious recession between 1733 and 1736 due to the Iranian invasion of Iraq; trade recovered later in the decade.[23] The Dutch records, however, provide a more positive view of the Basra market during that time, specifically for sugar. As mentioned in Chapter 3, during the first half of the 1730s, the Dutch factory at Basra received limited supplies of sugar. However, other suppliers, especially the English and French, continued to serve the market. According to a Dutch list of English and French shipping at Basra between 1 January 1733 and 30 April 1734, seven English vessels and two French ships appeared in the harbour. Three of the English arrivals came from Surat (one carrying sugar), and two from Bengal (both laden with sugar). The other two were importing coffee from Mocha. One of the French ships came from Bengal and the other from Mocha, the first bearing castor sugar and candy sugar. The list records the total import of sugar from these vessels as 5,500 sacks and 150 canisters.[24] If we assume that a sack weighed 300 Dutch pounds and a canister 290 pounds, this would amount to about 1.7 million pounds. Even in its most successful year, 1747–8, the Dutch factory sold less than 400,000 pounds of Javanese sugar, and these other nations certainly tried to trade as much sugar as they could at Basra.[25] Similar large quantities continued in the years that followed. The Dutch noted that eleven non-VOC ships reached the port between 1 May 1734 and 25 May 1735, and four of them, all registered as English vessels, imported sugar from Bengal and elsewhere. The total volume of their sugar cargoes was recorded as 3,600 sacks and fifty canisters, or about 1.1 million pounds.[26] The Dutch factors had been feeling neglected for some time, and they expressed their chagrin to Batavia in June 1736, saying that they had not received a single shipment, even during the past few years' great opportunities for trade. Instead, English, French and Armenian merchants, among others, had visited the port with at least twenty-three ships, both big and small, as well as a large number of boats (*vaartuigen*), and they had profited from most of the trade.[27]

From the 1730s onwards, Portuguese and English private traders actively exported Chinese sugar to Indian markets. Spurred on by Guangdong Province's growth in its sugar cane cultivation in the late 1730s, the Portuguese in Macao embarked on a project to sell it on the Malabar Coast, and in return they obtained pepper for the Chinese market. For the rest of the century, the Portuguese and English regularly conveyed Chinese sugar to major outlets on the western coast of India, including Surat and Cochin, places where the VOC found it difficult to sell Javanese sugar.[28] Likewise, on the Coromandel Coast, a major transit site for Chinese and Javanese sugar going further west, annual shipments of Chinese sugar from Macao impeded VOC trade.[29] As Souza suggests, some of the sugar sent to the Indian markets was in fact destined for the Persian Gulf. In 1740 the Basra factors wrote that English and Muslim merchants sometimes brought small boxes of 'snowy-white' (*hagelwit*) candy sugar to Basra from Madras and Surat, indicating Basra's demand for well-refined sugar. These merchants reportedly carried those cargoes on their own ships, while most of the time the English and

French imported normal (i.e. not quite as white) candy sugar and well-refined castor sugar from the Malabar Coast and Madras.[30]

Who purchased sugar at Basra? Merchants from Iraq and elsewhere in the Middle East were important buyers. One chronic headache for the VOC was that, as soon as well-loaded English and French vessels reached the port, the merchants who came from Baghdad, Mosul, Aleppo, etc. spent their money on their imported merchandise, and thus deprived the Company of opportunities to obtain ready cash and old copper ware for export.[31] In the late 1730s itinerant merchants from Baghdad, Aleppo and Greece visited Basra every year and strengthened its market by spending a considerable amount of money.[32] Some merchants who lived in Basra also took part in the sugar trade. In 1738 the VOC entered into a contract with a certain Basra merchant to sell him Javanese castor sugar at 13 *mahmudi*s per *man*. When the factory was about to hand over the sugar to the merchant, however, he fell seriously ill and died, so the sales contract lapsed. The VOC comforted themselves, saying it was a good thing they had not made the delivery; it would have been very difficult to collect the payment, because the merchant was insolvent. It is likely that he would have distributed any proceeds from his sales to his creditors, despite his contract to pay the Company first.[33] Last but not least, merchants from Iran and further north featured greatly in this burgeoning trade. In 1737, some Gorgan or Georgian merchants from Basra appeared in Isfahan and sold castor sugar at 9½ *mahmudi*s per *man* (equivalent to 12 Dutch pounds in Isfahan).[34] More than a decade later, Iranian merchants came to Basra from various other regional trade hubs carrying ready cash from Bandar Rig and copper ware from Shushtar and Dizful.[35] Furthermore, some sugar imported to Basra was re-exported by local craft to another developing sugar outlet at Bushire. From there it went overland to Shiraz, as I shall explain below.

Like pirates disposing of their booty

At both Bandar Abbas and Basra, non-VOC sugar suppliers showed striking flexibility when adjusting to the eighteenth-century's chronic shortage of cash. For them, negotiating the price was a way to draw the attention of cash-strapped wholesale merchants. In 1736–7 the Basra factory were reasonably optimistic about their ability to dispose of their commodities in Basra quickly. But they thought that castor sugar and candy sugar would be more difficult to trade. They said the Company would have to wait for the English to sell all their sugar because their prices were cheaper, and purchasers would prioritize dealing with the English.[36] One year later some of the castor sugar sent from Batavia turned out to be wet and syrupy, and the officers found it even more difficult to find buyers. The English and French, even with their better quality sugar, daringly reduced their prices further. The Dutch said they sold castor sugar (origin unspecified) at 8½ to 9 *mahmudi*s per *man*; their Chinese candy sugar 'as white as glass' fetched 24 *mahmudi*s on credit for three to six months. They were like pirates (*buithaalders*) disposing of their booty.[37] In fact, the VOC were selling their castor sugar at much higher prices, 13¼ and 14 *mahmudi*s per *man*, but they recorded no sales of candy sugar.[38]

Because the VOC were reluctant to sell their goods on credit this gave their rivals a competitive edge in the marketplace at Basra. EIC officers at Basra who privately engaged in the sugar trade offered buyers a long credit of between seven and nine months, or even as much as a year.[39] In addition, when cash was hard to find in the market and credit was quite risky, the English and French would barter for local export items, such as gum, mastic and madder, to avoid the risk of defaulting on sale and interest payments. They could then set out on a return voyage immediately. Every year English and French sugar shipments reached Basra earlier than those of the VOC, and this gave them an advantage. The Dutch factors were annoyed to report that other traders had made deals with most of the wholesale merchants before their own vessels reached port.[40]

The underlying question is why the VOC insisted on cash payments. According to Abdullah, the EIC did the same at Basra, which suggests that these Companies felt more of a need to do this than other sugar suppliers.[41] If this is true, the simple answer is that the Companies, who had to manage permanent stations and workforces at Basra, could not afford to continue without immediate settlement. However, perhaps a more important factor is that the VOC carried their shipping and trade from as far as Batavia, while their competitors came mainly from Indian ports. It is quite probable that this geographical disadvantage made it difficult for the Company to adjust quickly to the capricious Persian Gulf market. But it is still not clear how rival suppliers could employ such a risky business method. In an analysis of eighteenth-century British private trade in the western Indian Ocean, T. Davies points out that in the late 1720s and early 1730s the EIC governor of Bombay, Robert Cowan, gained profits from trade to the Gulf despite hazardous conditions, but he earned even more profit from trade with China and Bengal. He also accrued a substantial income by offering loans and the like.[42] Whether this was also the case with English privateers is unclear. However, considering the significant rise of the English economic presence throughout India and the increase in their seaborne trade towards South-East Asia and China during the century, it is reasonable to assume that these traders could to some extent balance the risk of failure in the Gulf against more reliable and profitable markets in the east.[43]

As mentioned earlier, in the late 1720s copper became an alternative export to gold and silver coins. Non-VOC sugar suppliers also excelled in this export. Whereas the VOC always exported gold and silver, including gold coins called *sjalotte*s (an Ottoman name for a coin derived from the Polish *zloty*), other suppliers had been laboriously collecting old copper ware and sending it to Bengal and other markets in India.[44] The VOC started doing this as well in the early 1730s but soon found it difficult to gain a profit, as their competitors had scraped up all the copper – copper ware, cakes of copper and *paysa*s – available in Basra. The Dutch were able to procure the metal from Nagasaki in Japan in return for Javanese sugar, and this made them hesitant to venture into the highly competitive business. Recent studies on the VOC Japanese copper trade reveal that the Company's copper sales in Coromandel, Bengal and Gujarat, the major producers of world-famous Indian cotton textiles, remained high until the 1760s. After that, other European companies and merchants greatly increased their imports of English and Swedish copper into the regions, thus undermining the VOC's commercial position in the subcontinent.[45] Increasingly marginalized in the Persian Gulf market, the Company's main objective became to hinder their rivals from dominating the copper trade as much as they could, just as at Bandar Abbas.[46]

Crisis and resilience in the trading network from the 1740s on

Between 1743 and 1750, Basra experienced a series of political disturbances. In 1743 Nadir Shah's armies once again crossed the border and marched to Mosul. Basra also suffered a three-month siege, and this negative impact on trade lingered until the middle of the decade.[47] Basra had enjoyed relative stability until 1748.[48] Towards the close of the decade Sulayman Pasha, the first *Mamluk* governor of Basra and Baghdad, increased his control over the port and adjacent areas. However, this was not a straightforward process. He faced serious military opposition from local notables, such as Mustafa Pasha, his deputy and *qapudan pasha* who led a popular rebellion in 1750 – in part due to his harsh financial exploitation of Basra's population.[49] During this time many inhabitants left the city, including Armenian merchants, who took refuge in Bandar Rig.[50]

The turmoil reduced non-VOC shipping to Basra in 1748–9. According to a Dutch memorandum, from April 1748 to June 1749 there were only four non-VOC arrivals (two Dutch private vessels and two English ships). Most of their imports consisted of textiles.[51] Such a reduction, which likely reflected a general decline in shipping to the Gulf, continued until the end of 1749.[52] Yet trade returned to its former levels in 1750. Despite the *qapudan pasha*'s rebellion, merchant ships began to appear in Basra from Baghdad. Upon the arrival of the first group of merchants from Baghdad, the VOC sold goods to the value of 60,003 guilders and 12 stivers. However, the Dutch factors noted that the Company would have garnered more profit if the English ship *Bonito* had not reached Basra from Bombay some days before the Company's vessel. The English ship, which came by way of Surat, imported a cargo of Javanese sugar by freight as well as loads of their own goods.[53] In the following financial year, 1750–1, the VOC faced an enormous supply of Bengali sugar from four English ships and a French vessel.[54] The English and the French remained active in the years that followed. From June to August 1752, five English ships – three from Bengal, one from Madras and one from Bombay and Surat – and two French ships, one of which came from Bengal, arrived, as well as the Dutch private vessel *de Hoop*. These suppliers imported more goods than ever before. The Dutch stated that wholesale merchants were making very low bids, which brought trade to a near standstill.[55]

Competition for bullion for export also picked up. The 1750s saw silver rupees flowing into the Basra market.[56] In 1752, however, the coins totally vanished from the market because the ships from Bengal, Coromandel and Surat that came to Basra that year had taken them away.[57] Under these circumstances, Dutch personnel in Basra were increasingly interested in the freight business. In the late Safavid period, the VOC conducted their own trade in Iran, while engaging in the transport of gold and silver specie, pearls and other Iranian products to Indian ports for other merchants. But now, it seems, the Dutch factors considered it more beneficial for the Company to discontinue the excessively competitive bullion trade and instead transport freight between Basra and Surat. They became aware that Armenian and Muslim merchants had been earning profits from bringing trade from Surat to Basra, despite taking on the risks of bottomry contracts (*bodemerij*),[58] freight fees (*vracht*) and customs duties (*tollen*). The officers were convinced that if the Company sent a ship from Surat to Basra every year, like the English and French, to transport goods and money for these merchants, their profits would be greater, for they believed the merchants preferred to use Dutch vessels.[59]

Basra credited much of its prosperity from trade to the port having close connections with interior markets, and the persistence of non-VOC shipping to Basra in the early 1750s reflects the flexibility of inland commercial traffic. Though they were occasionally blocked, the roads between Basra and Baghdad continued to serve as the principal commercial network in the region.[60] The situation improved during Sulayman Pasha's rule; his efforts to ensure road security worked to their advantage.[61] The same is true for caravan traffic with Iran. The civil war that followed Nadir Shah's assassination often impeded the flow of goods across the border, but never precipitated a total catastrophe. In February 1751 the Dutch factors were optimistic about sales for that year since 'the road from Baghdad and [that] over Shushtar and Dizful to Persia' were still open. In fact, the VOC had obtained 92,000 pounds of old copper ware from a large caravan that arrived from Iran.[62] The Dutch reference to Shushtar's crucial location within regional traffic supports Ricks's argument that ongoing rivalries among the leading families of Khuzistan over the governorship of Shushtar was not the cause of an overall regional economic crisis but a rational consequence of its continuous development.[63] The route from Basra to Shiraz and Isfahan also continued to operate, but with temporary halts.[64]

However, this was also a time when there was growing concern among merchants about the efficiency of trade at Basra. Going over the VOC's recent poor sales, Tido von Kniphausen, a leading officer in the Gulf, noticed with some vexation that, even though the Iranian merchants came to Basra from Bandar Rig, Shushtar and Dizful with cash and copper ware to buy the Company's goods, they had to pay a heavy customs duty (7 per cent) on both import and export. On top of this, Turkish government officials at the port extorted them and treated them badly. Arab merchants who traded with Basra also suffered the same kind of abuse. These merchants preferred not to go to Basra if there was some other place close by where they could obtain the same goods. As a result, von Kniphausen argues, Basra became nothing more than a transit port (*interpost*) where Dutch goods were re-exported. About half of the goods sent to Basra were destined for Persia (*Perzië*), about 25 per cent for Arabia (*Arabië*) and another 25 per cent for Turkey (*Turkije*). Transport to Turkey, though, was almost impossible, because Sulayman Pasha prevented caravans from taking the desert route to Aleppo and instead forced them to use the Euphrates route through Baghdad. The land route took twenty-five days and was toll-free, but by river it took over three months and was subject to various heavy taxes imposed by the pasha.⁶⁵

Von Kniphausen did not identify where the goods were transferred to, but the 'Utub ports of Kuwait and al-Zubara on the Arabian coast undoubtedly benefited from this development.⁶⁶ The situation along the Iranian coast was much more complex. While Bushire maintained a high profile in regional trade, several ports in the north, such as Bandar Rig, Bandar Deylam and Bandar Ganaveh, rose impressively and threaten Bushire's position.

A new Iranian waterway

According to May, who visited Bushire in February 1729 on behalf of the EIC, some traders had been born and grew up there. May tried to convince them to return to Bandar Abbas for trade, but the merchants contended that they were happier in Bushire. They viewed Bandar Abbas as the last place to go because of marauding Baluchis and an oppressive Afghan government. May wrote that the port annually imported both weighed and itemized goods to a value of more than 5,000–6,000 *tumans* from Bengal by way of Basra, as well as many more products from Surat, Ghogha (Gogo), Gujarat (Guzzerat), Sind (Duil), etc. Yet serious trade could be carried out for immediate payment only, chiefly with copper coins called 'goz', since gold and silver coins (white money) or bills of exchange were very costly there.⁶⁷ There is little doubt that the imported goods included sugar.

The emerging trade of Bushire was composed of various groups, including Iranians, Arabs, Armenians, Jews and Banians, and was anchored on the idea of family, clan and ethnicity.⁶⁸ Leading members of the ruling Madhkur family were also important merchants. Schoonderwoerd, the first Dutch resident in Bushire, landed on 18 August 1737 and described Shaykh Madhkur, the head of his family, as 'a kind of chief merchant, who is engaged in commerce on a daily basis and who has good credit'.⁶⁹

However, as discussed in Chapter 3, in the Upper Gulf, Basra was the principal market for sugar being exported to Iran; the Bushire market was of secondary importance. It is likely that Nadir Shah's navy continuing deployment in the region – who tended to conscript the local workforce and any financial resources into the royal service indiscriminately – made directly shipping sugar to Bushire precarious for sugar suppliers in general. Shortly after his arrival, Schoonderwoerd was confronted with the fact that the region's economy had born serious financial burdens to support the naval activities. The interventionist practices of the port authorities further increased the Company's difficulties conducting business.⁷⁰ On the other hand, Schoonderwoerd could also see that Bushire was receiving regular supplies of commodities, sugar in particular, through Basra and Muscat. According to his journal, the total number of ships that arrived in the port between 18 August 1737 and 10 April 1738 was twenty-seven. Most were local transport vessels (*vaartuig/tranki*). Nine of them brought sugar to Bushire. In addition to the VOC ship *Antonia*, another two possibly brought their sugar from outside the Gulf.

A Malabar vessel that arrived from Muscat on 17 September 1737 was carrying canisters of Javanese sugar (*Bataviase suiker*), pepper and ginger; it is possible that the ship had acquired the sugar at Muscat during its voyage. About one month later a Muslim ship came from Mocha with castor sugar (origin unspecified) and coffee beans. The others were all local transport craft – five from Basra and one from Muscat. The route to Basra was particularly important. One of the Basra craft, registered as a big *tranki* (*grote torank*), was carrying 300 big canisters (*grote canasser*) of Javanese castor sugar, which amounted to 87,000 Dutch pounds.[71] This figure is striking when linked with the fact that even in their best year the VOC's annual sales of Javanese castor sugar in Bushire did not reach 50,000 pounds.[72]

Although Bushire presented itself as a modest sugar market during Nadir Shah's reign, the port contributed substantially to the regional market for export bullion. During his reign, the Bushire market occasionally provided gold and silver for export to India. According to the VOC, in 1742–3 English and other private traders accepted gold ducats for a high price of 21 *mahmudi*s per *man* (equivalent to 6¾ Dutch pounds in Bushire), proposing to sell them in India for 21¼ *mahmudi*s.[73] We are not certain where this metal came from, but since Bushire enjoyed close commercial links to Shiraz and Isfahan, it is possible that much of it came from there. However, it is interesting that some traders tried to import silver coins into Bushire from overseas. In October 1742 the Dutch factors reported that Spanish reals (*Spaanse matten*) and *rijksdaalder*s had not been brought in by merchants from the inland countries but were imported via Muscat and Mocha, principally by other European traders. The merchants would not let go of their coins easily unless they could exchange them for profitable export items. Eventually they gave up the idea of trading their silver coins and instead reshipped them to India.[74]

However, as in the Basra market, copper held the prominent position in the Bushire market. Bushire was relatively well stocked with copper, probably on account of its proximity to Huwayza, where local merchants could bring the metal for minting. Indeed the main reason why the VOC tapped into the market was to procure copper and copper coins (*paysas*).[75] Though some other maritime traders' commitment to the Bushire market may have differed from that of the VOC, they shared the same purpose. The Dutch noted that on 10 March 1740 the English ship *Martha*, after selling most of its cargo at Muscat, came to Bushire with Banian merchants aboard in order to acquire copper.[76]

Not surprisingly, here too, the VOC faced daunting challenges posed by their English and French rivals. In 1741 the Dutch officers in Bandar Abbas became embittered by reports about the poor results of the Company's copper trade in Bushire. They remarked disapprovingly that, despite copper's exorbitant prices, the English and French were eager to obtain it. In late 1740 copper *paysa*s were rare, and one had to pay between 11 and 13½ *mahmudi*s per *man* for copper. The officers regretted that they had been forced to acquiesce in order to not lose the entire market to their competitors.[77] In the midst of this, compounded by difficulties dealing with the port authorities, Carel Koenad, the Dutch head of Bandar Abbas, proposed closing the Bushire factory.[78]

Trade at Basra was uncertain in the late 1740s, and it is conceivable that Bushire could have achieved the prime position in the Gulf market at this time. Yet according to von Kniphausen, Bushire did not benefit from the uncertainty. Bushire's situation was as bad as Basra's, he said, because merchants could not buy goods valued at more than 100 rupees without the governor's permission. When some Company goods were imported, the governor prevented the merchants from buying them, and even from entering the Dutch lodge. Then the governor or his agent checked the goods and forced the Company to sell them for the prices he set. He distributed a quarter to a third of the purchased goods among the Iranian and Armenian merchants for the same prices he had paid. The rest would go to other merchants, to whom he sold the goods for at least a 20 or 30 per cent profit. Von Kniphausen claimed that Bushire was nothing more than a transit channel for the Company's goods.[79] This dim prospect illuminates another important aspect of the Bushire trade: the favoured position of Iranians and Armenians. This suggests that these merchants, along with the governor, were main purchasers of sugar.

In early 1753 Mir Nasir (d. 1754), the Arab ruler of Bandar Rig, took advantage of this situation and invited the VOC to settle on Kharg Island, situated northwest of Bushire. His proposal was sensible, offering a place to trade, away from the coast's volatile politics and away from direct challenges from other sugar suppliers. His invitation was attractive enough for the Dutch officers to believe that the Company would have more leeway for trade on the island. Under the leadership of von Kniphausen the VOC established their factory on Kharg in November 1753 and embarked on their last venture in the Gulf.[80]

'A very favourable location'

It is clear that in the mid-eighteenth century, VOC officers felt that it was increasingly difficult to accurately guess how trading channels would shift and all factors that might influence them. By 1750 they noticed that Basra and Muscat had become prominent sugar markets, but there were many alternatives in the Persian Gulf, such as Bandar Abbas, Kong and Bushire. Outside the Gulf, Mocha in the Red Sea and Cochin in Malabar also functioned as reliable substitutes. On the other hand, the officers were reaching the conclusion that one of the major factors in the Gulf market's flexibility was the busy local shipping to and from every point in the Gulf. On the Gulf coastlands many Arab and Iranian inhabitants depended on shipping and fishing. If a regular market was obstructed for some reason, their transports helped find an alternative avenue of trade for the merchandise. The VOC project to turn Kharg Island into a large market was supported by their observation that the island could also benefit from this. Now that Basra was in a recession, von Kniphausen stated:

> The above-mentioned island [Kharg Island] has a very favourable location regarding that it is situated 10 miles distant from the river of Basra, 5 miles equally away from Bushire and Bandar Rig, 12 miles from Green [Kuwait] on

the Arabian Coast (from which place the great caravan leaves for Aleppo), and about 20 miles from Qatif and Bahrain where the robust pearling is going on.[81]

Noting the merits of its fine anchoring near the shore, he was convinced that Kharg was the best place in the Gulf to set up a factory and supply Persia, Arabia and Turkey with goods.[82] Moreover, Kharg was inhabited by a group of skilled sailors. During the eighteenth century they were known as the best pilots for European ships sailing to Basra, where the channel was difficult to navigate.[83] In the winter of 1753–4, soon after moving to Kharg, the VOC began to construct a fortress (named *Mosselsteyn* after Jacob Mossel, the Governor General of Batavia) in the north-eastern corner of the island in order to improve safety and which would be convenient for local ships (*inlandse vaartuigen*) stopping for loading and unloading.[84]

Development of local shipping

The VOC enterprise in Kharg immediately impacted the economic environment on the northern Iranian coast, where the Company would send a large portion of its goods. The ports at Bandar Rig, Bandar Deylam and Bandar Ganaveh, as well as Bushire, all became important destinations for shipments from Kharg. Bandar Rig, which had been a small trading port in the seventeenth century, began to attract more trade at the close of the Safavid period. By 1720 it was known as an active site for inland trade with Shiraz.[85] It had a crucial position in regional trade in the mid-eighteenth century. As we have seen, around 1752 the Dutch factors at Basra sensed the growth of trade at Bandar Rig, and they transferred some goods, including sugar, to that market.[86] They also entrusted some Armenian merchants from Bandar Rig to procure copper ware for export.[87] Because of the deterioration of trading conditions in Isfahan after the Afghan conquest, a number of Armenians from Julfa took shelter in Bandar Rig. In February 1753, some of these Armenians requested the VOC allow them to trade under the Company's protection.[88] Around this time Bandar Deylam also rose in significance. By 1755 the Dutch trade at Kharg came to rely on caravans regularly arriving from inland and heading to Bushire, Bandar Rig and Bandar Deylam.[89]

Even though in Bushire there were more Iranian merchants running lively caravan trade with markets in the interior, Bardar Rig, Bandar Deylam and Bandar Ganaveh were perhaps even better situated than Bushire to send goods upcountry. The remarkable rise of these ports in the middle of the century owed much to their rulers' efforts to connect goods shipped from Kharg with inland traffic. Mir Nasir once bought goods worth 30,024 guilders and 15 stivers from the VOC with the intention of transporting them to Shiraz on his own account.[90] According to the VOC, around mid-1755, while the ruler of Bushire charged merchants who imported goods from Kharg a 10 per cent duty, the rulers of Bandar Rig, Bandar Deylam and Bandar Ganaveh advertised an appealing rate of no more than 3 per cent.[91]

Bandar Rig, Bandar Deylam and Bandar Ganaveh were also in direct competition with each other. After Mir Nasir was murdered by his son Mir Muhanna in July 1754, Bandar Rig was in turmoil. In 1756, Bushire saw increased hostilities with Bandar Rig. The VOC noted that Bandar Deylam and Bandar Ganaveh began to rise by capitalizing on this situation. Their rulers employed every means to attract merchants and caravans and be on good terms with the Company. At the time, some Dutch service deserters had fled Kharg to the territories of Bandar Deylam and Bandar Ganaveh. When the Company asked for them to be extradited, the ruler of Bandar Deylam agreed to hand over one he had caught on condition that he would not be punished. The ruler of Bandar Ganaveh handed over the deserters without any conditions.[92]

Sugar was also regularly shipped from Kharg to Basra. Surprisingly, the Dutch records contain few references to this, but the English documentation on the Dutch Kharg includes an intriguing note.

> The Dutch at Carrack [Kharg] keep three stout gallivats [a kind of warship] by means of which none dare to insult them. They have no dispute with any one besides the shaik of Bunderick [the shaykh of Bandar Rig] and this is owing to the[ir] refusing paying the annual sum they at first agreed for the island. Their gallivats they sent to diffs. [different] ports to give convoy to such merchants as want to come and purchase goods. Carrack produces nothing but onions and was it not for its contiguous situation to Busshire [Bushire] and Bussas. [Basra], the Dutch would not be able to subsist. There are only two people on the island who may be call'd merchants, the one a Jew and the other a Persian. The former monopolizes all the sugar and spice for Bussa [Basra] market, and the latter most of what goes into Persia. There are about one hundred European soldiers and forty seamen with some coffres [coffers].[93]

This description suggests that VOC sugar was usually shipped to the Basra market through a Jewish merchant who resided in Kharg. Much of the sugar sent to Basra might have been destined for Baghdad given the growth of Jewish commerce along the Basra-Baghdad route in the eighteenth century.[94]

In the latter half of the 1750s, Kharg also shipped sugar to Mocha. Dutch officers in Kharg complained to Batavia about two Dutch ships – *de Marienbosch*, which tapped into the Muscat's market in 1756, and *'t Pasgeld*, which sailed to Sind for trade in the same year. They pointed out that if either of these ships had provided Kharg with sugar, iron and tin, etc., they could have increased their sales and profits. They continued:

> In this regard, it is necessary for us to inform Your Honour that the shipping in this Gulf and the Red Sea (*de Mochase Golf*) is so actively carried out, and the costs of freight fees (*vracht*) are so small that, no matter where the Company's weighed goods are brought in, it makes little or no consequence on the sales. Namely, the merchants who continuously go back and forth by their craft

(*tranquies*) appear wherever the goods are available, and transport them to various places where they expect to trade. This appears evident from the sugar and iron unloaded from *de Marienbosch* at Muscat, then transferred to Mocha. Besides, the merchants of Mocha (*Mochase kooplieden*), after making sales of their coffee at Basra, take sugar, iron, tin and spices here [at Kharg] on their way back, after a month, and export them to Mocha. For this purpose some of them have stored a little sugar here. Therefore, if Your Honour sends ships to Muscat or Mocha, the greatest part of the profits obtained there would wind up as a loss to our factory. The loss of the same kind will be proved by the goods imported into Sind (*Deviel en de Cust van Diewel Sindie*) to the sales at Surat and Malabar.[95]

However, active local shipping enabled sugar suppliers to unload their sugar virtually everywhere in the Gulf. This always posed a potential threat to the VOC, who intended to develop Kharg as the premier centre for shipping and trade. On 5 August 1756 the Dutch factors reported that English and French ships appeared with large amounts of commodities that year, flooding the whole Gulf market. They traded their goods on the cheap for precious stones, copper, wheat and all kinds of drugs. If this practice continued, the Company feared they would not be able to sell anything but spices.[96] According to existing Dutch shipping lists, between 8 December 1755 and 4 August 1756 Kharg saw twelve non-VOC ships arrive at or pass by the island; five with sugar. This merits attention because those ships were engaged in the sugar trade in different places in the Gulf. The English vessel *Prince George*, bound to Basra from Bengal, had sold sugar in Bandar Abbas before it arrived at Kharg on 8 December 1755. *La Moore*, a French arrival from Bengal on 26 December 1755, carryed 600 sacks of sugar. The English ship *Ganges* passed the island on 24 June 1756 and headed for Basra with 600 sacks of well-refined sugar (*witte suiker*). The ship was followed by *Elizabeth*, another English vessel, which had sold part of its sugar cargo at Bandar Abbas and Muscat along the way. The French *Tegenepatnam* reached Kharg on 1 July 1757 with 700 packs of sugar, perhaps meant for Basra.[97]

Later, Kharg became more of a transit site in the Upper Gulf. In 1764 the Dutch head Wilhelm Johannes Buschman lamented that no trade was conducted on Kharg Island itself. Because all merchandise that came there was certain to be reshipped, the Company's toll incomes were scant. Goods that should have been unloaded there were actually transported from one boat to another 'a little off shore, in the roadstead' (*op de buiten rede*), and then transported to wherever the buyer or owner of the goods wanted them to go.[98]

Conflicts and flexibility of traffic

In the late 1750s and 1760s rivalries increased between the ruling elite of the Upper Gulf regions. The VOC and EIC became embroiled in them, which sometimes resulted in attacks on shipping lanes. Historians, such as Abdullah, Floor, Grummon, Ricks and Qasimi, have identified two Arab shaykhs, Mir

Muhanna the ruler of Bandar Rig, and Shaykh Salman (d. 1767), the leader of the Banu Ka'b, Khuzistan, as the main players.

The basic information is as follows. After consolidating his power in Bandar Rig in 1758, Mir Muhanna began to attack the shipping bound for Bushire and Basra and harass caravan traffic from Bushire to Shiraz. In the middle of the 1760s, when the Zands of Shiraz, under the strong leadership of Karim Khan, launched a military expedition against him, he had to abandon Bandar Rig, but soon afterwards he expelled the VOC from Kharg in order to settle there. From this new base, he continued to hinder Basra shipping until 1769, when he was overthrown by his subordinates, arrested near Basra and executed by the *mutasallim*. Around the same time the Ka'b, under Shaykh Salman, who was in control of the Dawraq plains, developed into a powerful Gulf maritime power. Taking advantage of the inaccessible marshy areas from Dawraq, a town about 80 km south of Ahwaz, to the coast, and by pitting the Ottomans against the Zands, the Ka'b formed a politically semi-independent entity. Their ships also repeatedly attacked shipping lanes to Basra. This did not abate until the late 1760s, when the EIC, at the request of the *mutasallim*, intervened with their navy to check the Ka'b, as well as to secure the safety of ships to Basra from Mir Muhanna's attacks.

Recently Floor has argued that, after Nadir Shah's reign, the centralizing states in Iran and Iraq, such as the Zands and the Ottomans (the *Mamluk* regime), were unable to subdue the costal Arab shaykhdoms and allowed them to rise in power. The surge of Arab principalities on both sides of the Gulf led to hostilities and piracy and contributed to growing insecurity across the Gulf. As a consequence, Gulf trade fell into decline.[99] This characterization is reminiscent of the 'myth' of Arab piracy echoed in British colonial literature on the Persian Gulf.[100] But the rise of the Gulf Arabs mostly reflects the swiftly developing Gulf trade during the eighteenth century, rather than its breakdown – earlier scholarship supports this idea. Grummon argued that Bushire's incontrovertible status as the principal trading port of the region after the recession of Bandar Rig may have driven Mir Muhanna to engage in his 'piracy' operations; this was the only feasible economic occupation left to him.[101] Ricks perceived that the steady growth of trade from Basra to Bandar Shapur, close to Dawraq, and then to Shiraz and Isfahan between 1753 and 1763 was behind the emergence of Shaykh Salman and the Ka'b.[102] According to Abdullah, the war between the Ka'b and the government of Basra was fuelled in part by Basra's shipping boom between 1766 and 1774.[103]

During the eighteenth century the rivalries among many independent Arab shaykhdoms on both shores of the Gulf often impaired Gulf shipping. However, it is not unlikely that, when two or more entities fell into an outright conflict, there were other seafaring groups who, not aligned with either side, used their rivals' struggle to gain more profit. The situation in 1760–1 is a case in point. Shaykh Salman, in an alliance with the 'Utub tribesmen of Kuwait, fought the shaykh of Bushire, Shaykh Sa'dun, for control of Bahrain. This war involved Basra and the Huwala Arabs (*Houlaase Arabiers*, a group of powerful Arabs of the Lower Gulf); the former aligned themselves with Bushire, and the latter split into two factions. As a consequence, almost all local shipping (*kleine vaart*) was prevented.

Nevertheless, craft belonging to the inhabitants of Kharg Island remained in operation. They freely sailed back and forth in the Gulf since both parties let them pass without harassment due to the neutral position the VOC adopted.[104] The busy Kharg traffic was probably one of the main reasons for the Dutch's successful sugar sales at the beginning of the 1760s (see Chapter 3).

There was also a similar adaptability in the land traffic taking merchandise to and from the Gulf. Buschman noted that the inland military operations on the Iranian side would not have impacted trade at Kharg as greatly as at Bushire and Bandar Rig, for the Iranian kingdom was so 'vast' (*wijdluftige uitgebreidheid*) that not all roads towards it could be stopped or barred at once.[105] The alternative passages for the VOC sugar he had in mind might well have included Iraqi routes. Some time later he wrote that, although there was still confusion in the neighbouring provinces, the roads to Basra, Baghdad, and through them to Iran, reopened.[106]

Even more remarkably, there was unfaltering demand for sugar inland. In early 1763 the Euphrates route was blocked by local Arabs; commercial traffic from Basra to Baghdad, Shushtar and elsewhere ceased altogether. This was due to the war between the governor of Baghdad and Basra, Ali Pasha and the desert Arabs. On top of that, trade in the Gulf down to Muscat was at a complete standstill. Despite all this Buschman was still confident of seeing improvement in the Company's trade. He was informed that sugar had already become extremely scarce in the upper countries, and hardly anyone could obtain it, even if they had the money.[107]

Meanwhile, Mir Muhanna's increased aggression against the Bushire-Shiraz caravan routes fostered an alliance between the Madhkurs and Karim Khan. The peace that the alliance ensured encouraged traffic from Bushire to Shiraz.[108] In the early 1760s trade further developed as Karim extended his mastery over most of Iran's interior, and this facilitated merchants and goods moving through the country. Bushire was well connected from Shiraz to Isfahan and even to Russia, especially after February 1763, when Karim defeated his arch-rival Fath 'Ali Khan Afshar in Azerbaijan.[109]

The vibrant Bushire market attracted the EIC, which was looking for a new outlet for English woollen manufactures on the Iranian littoral after their departure from Bandar Abbas in February or March 1763. The EIC set up a trading post in April 1763.[110] In May 1763 the Dutch at Kharg expressed growing concern about the English, who had carried out a 'crafty scheme' (*finesse*) to import not just woollen goods but also weighed goods, such as lead, tin and notably a batch of Batavia, Cochin and Chinese castor sugar. The Dutch were concerned that the newly established English factory and trade would get a firm footing and deter trade at Kharg once the roads became a little safer.[111] In the last days of the VOC Kharg venture the Company faced vigorous English shipping to the Upper Gulf, as well as complications due to the conflicting interests of the local and regional elites. According to a Dutch memorandum, in the financial year 1763–4, twelve English ships came to Basra and Bushire from Bengal, Bombay and Surat, as well as two Muslim vessels and two Dutch private sloops.[112] A Dutch shipping list for the same period lists six non-VOC ships that appeared in Kharg with sugar. According to the document they all belonged to the English – two EIC and four private – and their shiploads of sugar, which consisted of Bengali, Javanese and Chinese varieties, were probably destined for Basra and Bushire.[113]

Buschman ascribed the vigour of English sugar imports to the shipwreck of the VOC ship *Amstelveen* in August 1763, which resulted in a shortage of Javanese sugar. When they heard of the disaster, he wrote, the English brought in a considerable amount of Bengali and Javanese castor sugar, as well as Cochin and Chinese candy sugar. However, the unsecure roads meant they only managed to sell part of it before another VOC ship, the *Lapienenburg*, arrived on 14 August 1764. Soon afterwards, many caravans came to Bushire, and the English began to trade their sugar for fruits (*fruitage*), kapok and rosewater for export to Bengal. In order to attract the attention of inland merchants back to Kharg – merchants who knew that sugar was available in Bushire and Basra would not think it profitable to risk crossing the water – the Dutch reduced their rate for castor sugar to 20 guilders per *pikol* (equivalent to about 120 Dutch pounds), 2 guilders lower than the projected price. According to Buschman, this measure was so successful that every day merchants came over to take the Company's sugar, while the English were at a loss for what to do with theirs.[114]

Like in Kirman, the English merchants showed flexibility when pushing their way into the interior market of Shiraz. By September 1764 the English had their commissioning agent (*commissie*) in position in Shiraz, which caused a 'noticeable drawback of the merchants going out and coming to Bushire and its inhabitants in general'. The Dutch wrote that if the English could not sell their goods at Bushire, as they wanted, they would send the articles to their agent by caravan on their own account, as they had done with their import of castor sugar and Cochin and Chinese candy sugar.[115] This English agent was possibly a man called Edward Hercules. According to an EIC officer, without the permission of either Basra or Bombay, Hercules acted as the EIC ambassador in Karim's court and conducted private trade in co-operation with Benjamin Jervis, the EIC resident at Bushire.[116]

After the VOC's withdrawal

I will briefly trace the trajectory of sugar shipping and trade in the region in the period after the VOC's final departure from the Gulf in 1766. It is likely that from 1766 to 1774 Basra was the principal sugar outlet in the Upper Gulf. Abdullah shows that shipping at the port prospered during this period – except in 1773, when a terrible plague hit Basra. Before this period, annual arrivals barely surpassed fifteen, but between 1766 and 1772 more ships arrived each year. In 1773 the number dropped to less than five, but was back to seventeen the next year.[117] He credits this to increased security: the threat from Ka'b had diminished, Iran was suffering internal fragmentation, and the EIC navy was increasingly involved in policing the sea lanes.[118] We need to further study the details of shipping to Basra between 1766 and 1774, but its surge must be related to the disappearance of the VOC and its sugar trade from the Persian Gulf.

The remarkable growth of Basra shipping, which deprived Bushire of trade, incited intense rivalry from the Zands in Shiraz. In 1769 Karim Khan appointed Mir Husayn (among those who had ousted Mir Muhanna from Kharg) as admiral of the Gulf and allowed him to take over all Mir Muhanna's vessels. This enabled him to begin attacking the shipping lanes to Basra. On 22 June 1771 the fleet captured *Britannia*, an English ship from Bombay laden with goods, including sugar, iron and spices belonging to the English captain William Show. They also took a country ketch flying the English flag and a craft from Muscat. They proceeded to Bahrain and sold half the goods there, as well as at other places, on the way back to Kharg.[119] Karim's ambition to control the sea lanes culminated in the siege and occupation of Basra from 1775 to 1778. After that, Basra trade significantly declined. Before this, the customs house of Basra had raised three to four thousand *tumans* annually from European ships alone, but in 1785, the amount fell to barely more than 500 *tumans*. Abdullah claims that the commercial stagnation in Basra dragged on well into the nineteenth century.[120]

The town that benefited the most from the confusion in the Upper Gulf and the resulting Basra market recession was Muscat.[121] According to a 1790 English report by Samuel Manesty and Harford Jones, two EIC officers in Basra, Basra began to decline after the 1773 plague, even though it still attracted foreign and local vessels – English, Surat Muslim, Muscat Arab, etc. – and many wealthy inland merchants.[122] After the death of Karim Khan in 1779, Bushire also stagnated. Its trade was affected by the war of succession that ensued, but then it recovered a little under the rule of Ja'far Khan (r. 1785–9).[123] Muscat by contrast was thriving. The report says, 'Commerce is [a] never falling source of wealth and it has rendered Muscat a more rich and more flourishing sea port than any other bordering on the Persian Gulf'.[124] Whereas trade languished and the bullion specie scarcity increased in Turkey and Persia, the merchants of Muscat conducted capital commercial enterprises and their sales and purchases were generally transacted for ready money.[125] They exported copper and large sums of gold and silver coins, including German crowns and Venetian sequins, to Surat, Bombay, the Malabar Coast and Calcutta every year.[126]

Richly provided with copper and gold and silver specie, Muscat attracted suppliers of two principal West Asian consumables – coffee and sugar:

> The wealth derived to them [the merchants of Muscat] from the valuable importations annually made at Muscat of coffee from the ports of Hedeeda [al-Hudayda] and Mocha in the Red Sea, and of sugar from Batavia are alone sufficient to render them rich and respectable. The importations of coffee amount to near one half of the quantity annually produced in Yemen and is sufficient for the full consumption thereof in the countries of Persia, Arabia Deserta, Mesopotamia, Coordistan [Kurdistan], Armenia, Georgia and Natolia [Anatolia] and in part to satisfy the demand for that article of luxury in Syria, Turkey in Europe, Germany, Poland, Russia and other northern kingdoms. The importations of sugar are very large, and are sufficient for the supply in

5. Alternative Sugar Hubs: Basra, Bushire and Kharg 109

that indispensably necessary article of the countries of Persia, Arabia Deserta, Mesopotamia, Coordistan, Armenia, Georgia and Natolia.[127]

The report relates that ships belonging to European nations, specifically to the Dutch and French, were important sugar suppliers.[128] More to the point, however, is the lively Arab shipping which passed through Muscat to many other trade routes in surrounding countries. Goods were sent in dhows, dinghys and square-rigged vessels belonging to the Arabs.[129] Every year the Arabs of Muscat sailed to al-Hudayda and Mocha with a variety of goods, including candy sugar, and they brought back rich cargoes of coffee and considerable quantities of Venetian sequins and German crowns.[130] As mentioned in Chapter 2, sugar was also exported from Muscat to Sind, and then along the Indus to the southern parts of Khurasan.[131] Bushire, where the EIC kept their factory, could count on sugar supplies from English shipping, and it also received regular shipments of sugar from Muscat: '[t]he commercial intercourse which subsists between Bushire and Muscat by boats affords large importations to the latter of sugar, sugar candy, spices of various sorts, coffee, metals of different sort[s] and a variety of different petty articles'.[132] Last but not least, the 'Utub tribesmen of Kuwait and al-Zubara, who had by then expanded their control to Bahrain, conducted freight trade between Muscat and ports on the Arabian Peninsula. Their vessels and boats carried sugar from Muscat to the area's major commercial nodes, such as Kuwait, Bahrain, al-Zubara and Qatif.[133]

Dutch and French shipping decreased in the late 1790s because of the Anglo-French war (1793–1802). In 1796 the EIC forced the Bu Sa'ids to agree to deny the French, as well as the Dutch, their ally, access to the port. Yet the recession was offset by Muscat merchants, especially the Bu Sa'id sultan, engaging in ocean-going shipping, sailing as far away as Calcutta and Batavia.[134] In 1800 John Malcolm, an EIC officer at Bushire, noted that India's trade to Arabia (Basra, Bahrain, etc.) was much more considerable than to Persia. India's exports, including sugar, came via Muscat and were traded for dates from Basra, pearls from the Arabian shores, European gold, silver lace from Aleppo, and copper from Diyar Bakr. Most of these items also passed through Muscat to India.[135]

Evidence regarding the continuing trade of non-VOC sugar suppliers, as documented by the Dutch in Basra, Bushire and Kharg, marks the epilogue to the end of the Company's commercial history in the Persian Gulf. However, the narrative appears similar to the captivating saga of the continuity and realignment of trans-regional trade through the Gulf. As in the Lower Gulf, after the Safavid period the competition for sugar imports in the Upper Gulf reveals the notable endurance and flexibility of non-VOC suppliers' trade, particularly the English. But it also reflects local Arab shipping's commitment to the sugar trade, notably in the 1750s and 1760s. Contrary to traditional beliefs about Arab piracy, the suppliers and the Arabs were not always in conflict but needed each other to cater to the unflagging demand for sugar coming from urban populations in West Asia. A temporary revival of VOC's trade also illuminates this point. At the turn of the 1760s, when serious power struggles among Arab notables hindered shipping, Kharg attracted more local sugar traffic because the VOC took a neutral position on this issue. However, the relationships between the suppliers, distributors and consumers of sugar were not merely governed by the law of supply and demand but were defined by a spectrum of forces that created broader economic constraints. We have noted India's strong demand for gold, silver and above all Anatolian copper, which was a catalyst for eighteenth-century commerce from West Asia to South Asia.

This trade relied on local merchants who worked on behalf of maritime traders. They were a crucial link between regional and global economies, trading imported sugar for profitable goods for the return voyage, principally precious metals and copper. Who were these merchants? How did they become involved in the sugar trade? How did the successful ones involve themselves in these changing trading situations? We will deal with these questions in the following chapters.

Chapter 6

COMPANY BROKERS

The endurance displayed by eighteenth-century sugar suppliers and distributors in the Persian Gulf mirrored both West Asia's persistent demand for sugar and India's status as a magnet for precious metals and copper. For a better understanding of sugar's crucial role in this, this chapter will discuss local merchants who acted as the Dutch East India Company's (*Verenigde Oostindische Compagnie* [VOC]) brokers and traded the VOC's Javanese sugar for gold and silver specie. Despite their important role, little research has been conducted on the collaboration between the Company and these merchants. In the 1970s Steensgaard proposed the concept of Asian 'pedlars' as the counter to the modernized European 'companies'.[1] Since then, scholars who have tried to redeem the characterization of the Asian merchants and scholars who have criticized the European companies' structural advantages have agreed that in Safavid Iran, the relationship between the companies and other merchants was one of competition.[2] They have paid attention to their interactions only in passing. By bringing the relationship between the VOC and their brokers to the fore, as well as the various factors that cemented or jeopardized this relationship, this chapter aims to describe the broker's socioeconomic arena, and how Javanese sugar flowed into it from the late seventeenth century until the Afghan conquest of Isfahan.

The VOC's brokers

Throughout their enterprise in Safavid Iran, the VOC utilized many locals as brokers (*makelaar*), interpreters (*tolk*), Persian secretaries (*Persiaanse schrijver*), wine makers (*wijnmaker*), wool collectors (*wolinzaamler*), messengers (*loper*) and other capacities. The Company maintained two brokers, one principal (*eerste makelaar*), another secondary (*tweede/co-makelaar*), at Bandar Abbas on a fairly consistent basis. They also had two interpreters, one at Bandar Abbas and another at Isfahan, where they had another broker.[3] They stationed a wine maker at Shiraz and wool collectors at Kirman to procure wine and wool for export. In the late Safavid period, it was primarily the brokers at Bandar Abbas and Isfahan who were in charge of selling the Company's sugar and securing specie.

The Rauwel family

It is well known that in the Safavid period, Iran's mercantile sector comprised – as in many other parts of the world – many merchant groups who conducted business as 'family firms', or through family or extended family ties. The merchants/brokers who served the VOC at Bandar Abbas in the late seventeenth century belonged to one particular family: the 'Rauwel' family. 'Toquidas', the head of the Rauwel family at Bandar Abbas and who was in the Company's service starting in the 1670s, acted as the VOC's principal broker, and his younger brother 'Coridas Rauwel' was co-broker (Appendix 10).[4]

We still need to study the early history of this particular family further, but their involvement in VOC commerce might have begun in the 1630s. According to a 1632 Dutch memorandum, a Banian named 'Rawel' did business with the Company; and another in February 1638, 'Rauwel', presumably the same man, was known as the Company's broker.[5] In 1652, the VOC once again called 'Rauwel' their broker. Dutch linguist H. Kern associates 'Rauwel' with the Indian names 'Rāhil' and 'Rāhoel', and also with abbreviated forms of 'Rawidatta' and 'Rawigoepta'.[6]

After the death of Coridas on 19 January 1702, his sole son and heir, 28-year-old 'Kissendas', succeeded to his father's position. The VOC described Toquidas and Kissendas as solvent enough to carry out the requirements of brokership.[7] According to the Company, Toquidas was indispensable to their commerce. Five years later, on 26 February 1707, Kissendas died leaving no son, and Toquidas made a request for his brother 'Bonidas' to replace his late nephew as second broker. The Dutch factors granted his request readily since they were afraid Toquidas would not be happy if they refused. Toquidas held this prominent status until his death on 30 June 1712. Then his eldest son, 22-year-old 'Nata', took over his post. Around four months later Bonidas also died; his eldest son 'Darmdas', who was over forty, replaced him.[8]

Because of the lack of historical sources from the merchant family it has not been possible to ascertain their ethnic identity. The VOC usually referred to their brokers at Bandar Abbas and Isfahan as 'Banians' (*Benjaan*).[9] The significance of the VOC's terminology is not certain. According to *Hobson-Jobson*, in European accounts the term Banians refers to Hindu traders, specifically from the province of Gujarat, but was often applied to Hindus in general.[10] Matthee thinks the Banians in Safavid Iran were Gujarati Hindus, and that most of the European companies' brokers were Banians.[11] Qaisar claims that the majority of Banians in Bandar Abbas came from Sind. He states that the brokers who worked in Bandar Abbas, Basra and Bandar Rig in the first half of the seventeenth century were mostly Hindus, and many of them were connected to powerful merchant families who served the East India Company (EIC) as brokers in Agra, Gujarat, Sind, etc.[12] But Dale suggests that the Banians recorded in contemporary documents might have been 'Multani' merchants. According to him most merchants from India who ran businesses in Safavid Iran came from Multan, and consisted largely of Punjabi Hindus of the Khatri caste and Afghan or Pashtun Muslims.[13] Floor seems to agree with this idea when he says that 'Indians' in Safavid Iran, roughly 10,000 to 20,000 people, were mainly from Multan and that besides attending to their own businesses, they acted as brokers and moneylenders for foreign merchants, including the VOC and EIC. But he also says that the Dutch used the term Banian to refer to Hindu merchants from India, especially from Gujarat.[14] Onley thinks that the Indian population in the Gulf region during the Safavid period was made up of Multani Khatris.[15]

The VOC once described their brokers from the Rauwel family as 'the Company's Khatris or heathen brokers' ('s Comp[agnie]s Ketteris, of heidense makelaars).[16] However, I believe, at least as far as the Dutch wording is concerned, that both 'Banians' and 'Khatris' are generic terms applicable to any merchant with economic, social or religious ties to India and adjoining regions. The Company more generally referred to their Isfahan broker as 'the Company's [East] Indian broker' ('s Comp[agnie]s Indiaanse makelaar).[17]

A Dutch report from 2 August 1693 offers valuable insight into the origin of the Rauwel family. It says that in July of that year the Dutch factory had trouble with the governor of Bandar Abbas, who was pressing them for money. He went as far as to demand tributes from 'every group of Banians' (ieder soort of kaste van de Benjanen). First of all, the governor referenced a caste called 'Bangsalties', the one the Dutch considered their brokers to be from. The brokers were rather prominent in the community, so the governor pressed one of them, Coridas, to make his caste assent to whatever was demanded of them. But Coridas refused, claiming that he was a Company servant and therefore free from any such obligation. This reply made the governor so angry that he beat him with a stick several times and then arrested him. The Dutch immediately sent their interpreter to the governor to petition for the broker's release and compensation for the harassment.[18] This record highlights two facts: first, the broker's family belonged to one of Bandar Abbas's 'Banian' castes, the 'Bangsalties'; and second, the brokers were leading figures in the community.

There is a paucity of information on the word 'Bangsalties'. After comparing the VOC and EIC records on Bandar Abbas, I think the EIC called this same group of people 'Banksallee caste'.[19] This English form suggests that it is connected to the Anglo-Indian word 'bankshall' (a warehouse or the harbour master's office).[20] A Hindu commercial caste from Kutch, Kathiawar and Sind called Bhansali offers another linguistic clue. The early history of this community is obscure, but at the turn of the twentieth century the Bhansali were known as a caste of husbandmen, shopkeepers and traders.[21] An 1901 ethnographic survey by the Bombay Presidency of British India states that the Bhansali (also called Vegus) had 15,774 members – 8,112 men and 7,662 women – principally inhabiting Kutch, Kathiawar and Sind. The report notes that they were generally labourers.[22]

Away from their homeland, these foreign brokers must have felt inclined to return from time to time. On 14 August 1700 the Safavid authorities once again arrested Coridas, this time claiming that he had poisoned a 'heathen woman' (heidense vrouwmens). Despite strong protests from the VOC, his detention continued till 18 August, when he promised the court he would pay a large sum of money. When he returned to the factory, Coridas complained that if he was robbed like this every year he would love to return to his country.[23] This attachment to home is reminiscent of C. Markovits's concept of a 'circulation society', which arose from his historical inquiry into the global networks of Hindu traders from Shikarpur and Hyderabad. Questioning the feasibility of broadly applying the category of 'diaspora', which connotes a real or imaginary physical separation from one's homeland, he argues that the Sindi merchants, while geographically dispersed from the eighteenth century onwards, formed resilient networks, connecting their hometowns with many places of business abroad. Through these networks, personnel, credit, information and goods were in regular circulation, which ensured that those involved maintained a socioeconomic unity.[24]

In light of this Bandar Abbas can be described as a 'home' for the brokers. While merchants from Shikarpur, and to a lesser extent from Hyderabad, were either unmarried or had wives and children that they left back home, it was not unusual for the Rauwels in Bandar Abbas to bring their wives with them.[25] In April 1737 Ottumsjent, the principal broker at Bandar Abbas, took leave to go to Bombay to collect (*afhalen*) his fiancée. This turned out to be a tragic decision; he died in Bombay later that year.[26] In May 1747 when many of the Banksallee in Bandar Abbas took refuge in Barka, they also brought most of their wives with them.[27] Apparently many, if not most, of the Dutch brokers had grown up in Bandar Abbas. When the Dutch appointed Nata and Darmdas as their brokers, they noted that they had known both of them since their childhood.[28]

Nata, the principal broker, died on 25 April 1713, less than a year after his appointment. Reflecting on the valuable service that Nata's father Toquidas had rendered the Company, the Dutch factors intended to find a successor among his sons. But the oldest candidate was only fifteen years old. They therefore decided to ask 'Bouwendas' to support his brother Darmdas as co-broker. His appointment was slightly delayed because of the fact that Nata had died so suddenly. There was a rumour circulating in town that he must have been poisoned, and the port government wanted to investigate.[29] This may also imply that some family members were disputing the appointment of the Dutch brokership.

However, the brothers Darmdas and Bouwendas did not live up to expectations. In January 1719 the VOC factors wrote that the brokers had been somewhat careless and had not observed their instructions well. Therefore, they had to turn to Ottumsjent and Issourdas, Toquidas's sons, for the sales of textiles and cloths; the VOC described Toquidas's sons as 'active young men' (*wakkere jongelingen*).[30]

More importantly, for most of the 1710s the Isfahan broker 'Kiemtsjant Matouradas' stayed at Bandar Abbas and played a crucial role in the Company's trade. In May 1712 Dutch officials wrote that thanks to his involvement the sale of the Company goods had doubled. They therefore asked Batavia for permission to bestow a costly robe of honour (*eer kleed*, i.e. a *khil'a*) on Kiemtsjant and also to bestow robes on the brokers and the interpreter at Bandar Abbas.[31] Five years later, the Dutch ambassador Ketelaar also recommended that the factory have Kiemtsjant assist Darmdas and Bouwendas. He wrote that other brokers had often advanced money to the Company, but Darmdas and Bouwendas were heavily indebted to them (197,694 guilders 5 stivers 8 pennies, as of 8 March 1717). Therefore, in addition to these two 'very languid' (*zeer lusteloos*) fellows, the factory should employ Kiemtsjant, a 'reasonable and diligent man' (*redelijke en ijverige man*) who was known to possess immense capital and was therefore trustworthy. Ketelaar added that Darmdas and Bouwendas would not oppose his employment because Kiemtsjant was not an 'outsider' (*vreemdeling*) but one of the Company's many local servants.[32]

Despite causing the Company to doubt his financial reliability, Darmdas was a prominent figure in Bandar Abbas's mercantile community. In May 1719 the VOC stated that port authorities were disregarding the royal edict that the Company-affiliated 'Banians' (*Banjaanse natie*) in Bandar Abbas and Kong were exempt from the capitation tax (*jizya*). Instead they tried to impose it on Darmdas and 'the other heads of the Banian castes' (*de andere hoofden van de Benjaanse kastes*) by force.[33] This statement suggests that at the time, Darmdas was the head of his caste.

On 12 March 1719 Bouwendas died. Darmdas requested that someone close to him – either Ottumsjent or Issourdas, the sons of Toquidas, or his brother 'Bilbilderdas' – should be appointed to support him in his duties. The VOC selected the 'vigilant young men' (*vigilante jongelingen*) Ottumsjent and Issourdas as co-brokers. This appointment seems to have helped the line of Toquidas regain some of its former clout. Although Ottumsjent and Issourdas were of age, the Dutch knew that Toquidas's estate was still under Darmdas's supervision. In spite of the Company's repeated orders, he had not transferred a penny of it. Yet the new brokers would be able to square accounts with Darmdas soon, for both sides had agreed to co-ordinate their capital into one fund so that it would be more convenient for the Company.[34] Darmdas passed away on 3 April 1721 on the eve of the Afghan conquest of Iran.[35]

The Kiemtsjant family

For the last two decades of the Safavid period, the VOC used Kiemtsjant Matouradas as their broker at Isfahan. He was appointed around 1701 and held the office until his death on 17 August 1723.[36] Like the Rauwel family in Bandar Abbas, the Kiemtsjant family inherited the Dutch brokership in Isfahan.

While the Isfahan brokers principally stayed in the capital to prop up the Company's commerce there, Bandar Abbas was also 'home'. In late 1710, Kiemtsjant asked the Company's permission to leave Isfahan for a while in order to travel to Bandar Abbas and get married. The Dutch noted that he wanted to do this to maintain his high esteem among 'his people' (*zijn natie*).[37] His clerks (*bedienden*) in Isfahan acted as his deputies while he was away.[38] When Kiemtsjant died (possibly in Bandar Abbas), his post was passed on to 'Heemraadje Jedmelanie', his brother's son who lived in Isfahan. The VOC appointed co-successors, Heemraadje and 'Wissendas Jedmelanie', another of Kiemtsjant's nephews who at the time lived in Bandar Abbas, and they assumed responsibility for his debt to the Company.[39]

The Isfahan brokers were usually called 'Banians', but this tells us nothing about their actual ethnicity or native country. Our preliminary research suggests that they also had close socioeconomic ties with Sind. The career of a Banian clerk in Kiemtsjant named 'Nagha Natta' is a case in point. According to a Dutch letter dated 18 May 1737, Natta used to serve Kiemtsjant in Isfahan. Afterwards he stayed in Bandar Abbas for about twelve years and then moved to Sind (Diuel). He was, at the time of the letter, back in Bandar Abbas staying with Heemraadje Jedmelanie. This implies that the Kiemtsjant family of brokers formed part of a highly mobile mercantile society that had branches in Isfahan, Bandar Abbas and Sind.[40]

Brokers as individual merchants

Safavid Iran was an Islamic society that banned its Muslim subjects from engaging in usury. But exchanging currency and providing credit was crucial for trade, so this tended to be consigned to religious minorities. The Banian merchants were adept at accounting and handling coinage and held an esteemed position in this particular sector of the economy, acting as money changers (*sarraf*), simple bankers, or brokers (*dallal*).[41] In Dutch records the Rauwels and the Kiemtsjant family also primarily appear as merchants proficient in brokering and transferring and changing money, a subject to which I shall return later.

It is important to remember that there were many other Banian merchants in Safavid Iran, as well as Company brokers who traded regular commodities for their own account, functioning as wholesalers (*tajir*).[42] There is scattered evidence indicating the Rauwel family brokers sold sugar for the Company and also engaged in trade on their own behalf. As described in Chapter 4, the brokers Ottumsjent and Issourdas went bankrupt after the Afghan invasion of Iran. As a consequence of their ruined financial network in Iran, they could not repay the huge amount of money the Company had entrusted to them. In order to support the brokers, in July 1725 the Dutch factory in Bandar Abbas shipped the brokers' own sugar alongside the Company's to Muscat for trade. Issourdas participated in this project, together with his 'Banian secretary' (*Benjaanse schrijver*) 'Kaliaan' and another servant (*dienaar*).[43] Around the same time the VOC utilized the Basra market for the same purpose. The goods remaining in the Basra factory in the financial year 1724–5 included some belonging to the brokers – 65,132 pounds of castor sugar and 24,999 pounds of zinc (*spialter*) – which had been sent from Bandar Abbas.[44]

The Isfahan broker Kiemtsjant was an important VOC merchandise wholesaler. In 1700–1 Kiemtsjant, who was in Isfahan at the time and using his '*vaquel*' (*wakil*, i.e. agent) in Bandar Abbas named 'Natawaskan', placed an order with the Company for 10,000 *tumans* worth of goods. Since he knew the Dutch would not sell wholesale merchants any desirable items unless they also took ones in low demand, he agreed to the condition, but requested that the factors add the least popular goods to his quota on a proportional basis, like they did for 'other major merchants' (*andere zware kooplui*). He also requested that his first payment should be deferred for seven months, and then he would settle his account, unless the Company happened to receive raw silk from the Safavid court. If they did, his debt would be cleared, as he would cover the cost of receiving the royal silk, debiting the sum to the Company's account. Kiemtsjant was particularly interested in buying cloth (*kleden*) in these circumstances.⁴⁵

Our knowledge of the brokers' commitment to overseas trade is very limited. We can assume that the Rauwel brokers were land-based merchants who mainly engaged in buying goods imported by the VOC in Bandar Abbas. In 1696 Adriaan Verdonk, the Dutch director of Bandar Abbas, stressed the credibility of the brokers Toquidas and Coridas:

> For the Company's brokers are so wealthy and established that one does not have to be afraid of bankruptcy or loss, all the more because they conduct no foreign or overseas business (*geen buitenlandse of overzeese negotie*). They even advanced money to the Company many times as may be seen in the accounting books.⁴⁶

He thereby suggests that maritime trade had high risks but probably offered the chance of high profits.

We should also consider the possibility that Kiemtsjant was involved in exporting bullion from Iran. His prolonged stay in Bandar Abbas provides a useful clue. At the turn of the 1710s he became embroiled in a dispute between the VOC director in Bandar Abbas, Willem Backer Jacobsz and the head of Isfahan, Pieter Macaré, who was his deputy. This internal feud seems to have been related to the officers' private trade and developed into a serious diplomatic conflict between the VOC and the Safavids. Macaré, who had been unseated by his colleague Adriaan van Biesum, resorted to the desperate measure of appealing to the court for support. In order to have this matter taken seriously, Macaré informed the government that the Company was engaged in exporting goods, especially gold ducats, without paying the required customs duty, using their right to free transport to export goods for other merchants.⁴⁷ Sultan Husayn immediately prohibited the VOC from exporting from Isfahan without inspections and charged a toll of 3/5 *mahmudi* per ducat.⁴⁸ The authorities, with the aid of Macaré, also detained the VOC's local staff – Kiemtsjant's agents and the interpreters – to investigate whether they had been exploiting the Dutch right for their own trade.⁴⁹ Kiemtsjant was a top suspect, but he stayed on in Bandar Abbas, waiting for the uproar in the capital to subside. According to the VOC's inquiry in 1717-18, Kiemtsjant was blameless, at least according to an inspection of his accounts. Yet there remained some lingering concern on the part of the Dutch. Ketelaar, who had supervised the enquiry, recognized that Kiemtsjant could not have survived without conducting some trade in addition to his brokerage services, so he strongly recommended him not to take advantage of the Company's privileges and to avoid any more complaints coming from the court; he reminded him to 'Render unto Caesar the things that are Caesar's' (*de keizer geven, dat keizers is*).⁵⁰

Kiemtsjant probably neither owned nor rented ships for trade on the high seas. No reference to such involvement can be found in the Dutch lists of non-VOC shipping at Bandar Abbas during the late Safavid period. But people with no claim to a ship had plenty of opportunities to find a suitable freighter in port whenever they wanted.⁵¹ This suggests that 'non-investment' in ocean-going ships was a general practice among the merchants of Bandar Abbas. Given the fact that Bandar Abbas was one of the principal hubs of Indian Ocean shipping, some merchants might have possessed or hired ships for maritime trade. In the Dutch documents, however, it is uncommon to find evidence of this type of engagement. However, there is abundant evidence that the Arabs in the neighbouring port of Bandar Kong were actively running sailing enterprises. The Dutch shipping records covering the first two decades of the eighteenth century at Bandar Abbas and Surat regularly mention vessels sailing between Bandar Kong and Surat, and many of them are registered as assets of Arab merchants from Bandar Kong, including ʿAbd al-Shaykh and his agent ʿAli b. Sultan.⁵²

In this respect Bandar Abbas stands in stark contrast to Surat, where a great number of local ship-owners, especially Muslim entrepreneurs, orchestrated long-distance maritime trade, as well as coastal shipping. The brokers in Surat offer a case in point. According to Nadri, almost all the brokers who served English and Dutch Companies in Surat during the seventeenth and eighteenth centuries were rich local merchants who mainly conducted large-scale inland trade, similar to the Rauwels and Kiemtsjant. Furthermore, they expanded their business along the Indian Ocean rim, and some of them invested their capital in ships. Kishandas, a Banian merchant who acted as the VOC's broker between 1659 and 1686, and whose family retained the post until the end of the Company's operation in Surat, ran his maritime trade with his own ships. Mancherji Khurshedji, a Parsi VOC broker, was known for his shipping prowess in the second half of the eighteenth century, a time of relative decline for Muslim shipping. His trading vessels regularly sailed to Siam and Batavia.⁵³

The Company and the family firm

Around four decades ago, Steensgaard described Asian merchants as 'pedlars'. Emphasizing the crucial importance of the market's unpredictability and the capriciousness of protection costs in early modern Asia, he argued that the Asian market had been made up of ill-informed and poorly capitalized itinerant merchants, and none of them was able to monopolize trade in any individual market or commodity. He contended that the seventeenth-century advent of the European companies marked a 'revolution' in Asian trade. The companies, with their institutionalized lines of business and disposable forces, overcame many uncertainties and thus increasingly gained the upper hand in the market.⁵⁴ A number of scholars have since questioned the proposed vulnerability of Asian merchants, exploring various aspects of the Asian merchants' trade world in order to appreciate their commercial achievements and comprehend their setbacks. Scholars of the Asian mercantile communities in Safavid Iran, specifically the Indians and Armenians, have stressed that, despite volatile markets, Asian 'pedlars' carried on robust commerce in competition with the European 'companies'. For these scholars the family's institutional dimension is vital to understanding the activity of these mercantile societies. They argue that while expanding across the region, the communities developed profoundly intricate communication networks and legal and financial devices. These were based on familial and kinship relationships and extended family ties, to such degrees that they could financially handle unexpected developments in the market.[55]

The VOC archives are a treasure-trove of information testifying to the importance of Asian family firms' commercial activities in Safavid Iran. They show that most of the Company's local agents were members of well-established local merchant families. During the late Safavid period, besides the Rauwels and the Kiemtsjant family, the Busskens (written as Buffkens), apparently a Dutch family local to the area, were interpreters in Bandar Abbas and wine makers in Shiraz.[56] An Armenian merchant family called Sahid (Sarhad or Said?) were interpreters at Isfahan. Those who served the Dutch as wool collectors in Kirman were also from an Armenian family. This was a frequent occurrence and may not be a coincidence.

Another way of viewing at the relationship between the Company and the family firms is to see how these different institutions were compatible in terms of risk management. This can be seen in the relationship between the VOC and the Rauwels and Kiemtsjant. Keeping the brokership in the hands of one merchant family provided the VOC with a safety net for their investment. If a broker died leaving behind money owed to the Company (as was always the case), it would have been very difficult, if not entirely unrealistic, for the Company to persuade someone outside the family to take over the debt. But when the post was handed down to someone in the same family, for whom brokerage services to the Dutch was a 'family business', they would be more likely to accept the financial burden, even if reluctantly. The VOC were aware that they would be more likely to recover a debt if the broker candidates were their predecessor's heirs. At the appointment of Nata and Darmdas, the Bandar Abbas factory noted that these men were the legitimate heirs (*erfgenamen*) of the deceased brokers Toquidas and Bonidas, and in fact they had assured the Company that they would repay their predecessors' debts.[57] To protect their own financial security, Dutch officers preferred to choose the brokers from among those they had known for a long time. To substantiate the trustworthiness of Nata and Darmdas, they wrote that both of them had grown up frequenting the Company lodge.[58] Sometime later the officers endorsed Bouwendas for the same reason (*van jongs af aan 's Comp[agnie]s huys groot geworden*).[59]

What did the brokers gain in return? During this period many local personnel received a permanent, fixed salary from the VOC. The interpreters, for example, earned a monthly salary (*gagie*) and special allowance (*kostgeld*). As of 1706 the Isfahan interpreter François Sahid received a monthly salary of 112 *mahmudi*s in addition to a 45 *mahmudi*s subsidy for his service to the court.[60] The wine maker Joseph Busskens, when he was nominated as interpreter at Bandar Abbas in 1712, agreed to a similar pay scale: a stipend of 100 *mahmudi*s and an allowance of 42 *mahmudi*s.[61] However, the brokers were not on payroll. Their principal earnings were commission fees gained from trade between the Dutch and local merchants (*makelaardij*). At Bandar Abbas the brokers generally received 1 per cent of the total value of sales of the Company's merchandise, and they received different rates from the wholesalers according to the commodity.[62] The Isfahan broker likewise collected commission from the procurement of export bullion, particularly gold ducats.[63] We saw above that the income from brokerage might be insufficient for the agents to maintain their households, yet we should not ignore the possibility that they might have gained extra revenues by falsifying accounts regarding the sale or purchase value of commissioned goods. If after closing a sale, brokers at Bandar Abbas reported a total value that was lower than what they actually received, it would reduce the remuneration for their services but generate extra, hidden income. If an Isfahan broker notified the Dutch of a higher rate for gold ducats than the real market price, he would gain more brokerage fees. Ketelaar commented that if the Isfahan agents enjoyed such 'a secret brokerage' (*een stille makelaardij*), it was difficult for the Company to figure it out, because they could easily submit false account books and hide the genuine ones.[64]

The brokers were working in an uncertain commercial environment, beset with the fear of sudden and total ruin. The VOC providing a platform to safeguard their interests in times of crisis was an important reassurance. 'Protection' (*protectie/ maintenu*) from government interference was of particular importance. If a merchant died without an heir this gave the authorities an excuse to confiscate his estate, and often his resources. Kissendas died in February 1707 with no son to inherit his wealth, and the shah's merchant Mirza Murtada, who came to Bandar Abbas (see Chapter 1), claimed he had no heir and ordered the governor to confiscate his goods; they were by then in the hands of his uncles, the brokers Toquidas and Bonidas. The governor seized the brokers, along with their sons and two of their secretaries, sealed up their houses and took possession of the property. According to the governor, it was worth 15,000 *tuman*s or 637,500 guilders.[65] In this situation, the VOC represented and advocated for the brokers. They lodged strong protests in court. In Bandar Abbas they gathered evidence from various prominent people – the *shahbandar*, the English, the *qadi* (*geestelijke rechter*), etc. – to testify that Kissendas had left a widow, a daughter (who died soon afterwards) and his mother. They argued that these were 'reasonable heirs according to their laws' (*volgens haar wetten gerechtige erfgenamen*).[66] Due to this intervention, in April 1708 the court interrogated Mirza Murtada and released all the captives.[67] Even though the seized property was not returned, the Company continued lobbying for compensation for a year.[68]

The VOC would also offer their protection in commercial dispute cases. In his final report, the director of Bandar Abbas Frans Castelijn ordered that the factory should fully protect Company brokers from extortion at the hands of other merchants. Since the brokers were regarded as men of means, he pointed out that unsuccessful local merchants tended to pester them for money.[69] The brokers were surrounded by a crowd of 'jealous enemies' (*misguntige vijanden*) watching for an opportunity to pounce.[70] The brokers would treat as much of their own wealth as they could as belonging to the VOC so that it would be protected as a part of the Company's 'impregnable' assets. In August 1701 the Isfahan factors reported that the newly appointed broker Kiemtsjant, who initially intended to invest a sum of 6,000 *tuman*s with the Company, had now increased it to 16,000 *tuman*s. By doing this, they noted, he would, without a doubt, be protected under 'the Company's shadow' (*schaduw van d' Comp[agnie]*) and would not have to fear the 'crafty enterprise of the Muslim merchants' (*listige onderneming van de Moorse coopluiden*).[71]

We do not know the terms and conditions of VOC 'protection', but apparently it was applied to the entire family firm. In mid-1728, when Mirza Zahid ʿAli, the *shahbandar* of Bandar Abbas under Afghan rule, demanded a large tribute from the *Bangsalties*, the brokers Ottumsjent and Issourdas took shelter in the Dutch factory along with other members of the community, including their family, servants and dependants.[72]

Furthermore, the VOC secured royal favours for their brokers that ordinary merchants did not enjoy, such as exemption from *jizya*. At a coronation or change of regime, when all former privileges became invalid, the Company did not fail to have their agents' reconfirmed. What deserves our attention is that the *jizya* exemption was not only conferred on the brokers but also on other members in their firms. A royal edict issued in early 1730 stipulated that the brokers and their affiliates, up to seventeen in total, were exempt from the tax.[73] A Dutch memorandum from 24 August 1735 demonstrates that this particular exemption was crucial for the longevity of the Rauwels. It stated that Ottumsjent and Issourdas told the Dutch factors of a serious problem: their family was much greater than seventeen, and those who were unprotected were exposed to increased exactions from the local governors. They asked for permission to let the unlisted members leave Bandar Abbas and relocate in another of the Company's operations (*'s Comp[agnie]s district*) or in their homeland, together with Issourdas.[74]

The brokers' families were already distinguished members of merchant circles, but their association with the VOC was a significant help for maintaining their credit. When Kissendas died the Bandar Abbas factory sent a condolence gift of local neckerchiefs (*shawls*) to his family, who were observing the customary mourning. The real purpose, however, was to publicize to the general population that the Company would still back the Rauwels. Otherwise, the factors said, their loss would almost inevitably decrease the family's credibility.[75]

In Safavid Iran it was commonplace for one's superior, especially the shah, to present *khilʿa* to a subordinate to show his special favour. In the political arena, the conferment of a *khilʿa* was a public confirmation of the recipient's post and loyalty.[76] The VOC made use of this tradition to display their close association with brokers. In 1696-7, for instance, the factors at Bandar Abbas presented *khilʿa*s to Toquidas and Coridas on board the *Princeland*, a Company ship anchored in the harbour. Then they led the brokers ashore to the factory where, in the presence of many local merchants, they handed over a letter of credentials sent from the Governor General of Batavia, Willem van Outhoorn. Afterwards, crowds of people from various Asian nations came to greet the brokers and were all treated according to the local custom.[77]

Brokers as port officials

Historiography of the Indian Ocean has generated a lively debate about early modern merchant–state relations. Traditionally, historians thought that merchants in Mughal India were so prone to suffer arbitrary exploitation at the hands of the ruling elites that the country's economic development was threatened.[78] Although previous research did not dismiss the fact that the coastal ruling elites regularly sponsored maritime trade, this was perceived as a hallmark of the political elites' dominance over the mercantile sector.[79] Since the 1970s this idea has been much debated, and conclusive evidence shows that the merchants were by no means passive creatures. They could and did fight against oppression, either by boycotting trade, appealing to a higher authority or moving away.[80] M. Pearson calls attention to what he considers social segregation between maritime merchants and rulers. The ruling class were entirely land-based in terms of both revenues and ethos, and they were not especially interested in the activities of merchants, and the merchants were not interested in them. Benefiting from this mutual aloofness, the merchants maintained a certain degree of autonomy.[81] Scholars, including K. Leonard, F. Perlin, S. Subrahmanyam and C. Bayly, by contrast underline a high degree of social mobility in early modern India. They contend that as the state's commercialization developed, merchants formed an integral part of the state structure as creditors, revenue farmers and treasurers.[82]

Since the 1990s a number of substantial studies have scrutinized different aspects of the relationships between merchants and the political elite in Safavid Iran. Though working separately, these studies make a common case for there being a considerable level of social fluidity in Safavid Iran. The court made decrees or monopolized trade for certain export commodities – slaves, horses, raw silk, pearls, wine, etc. – and shahs and bureaucratic elites became actively engaged in trade, either by themselves or through proxy factors. More importantly, many merchants, specifically the Armenians, were in close contact with the government. Some, with ready cash at their disposal, served as creditors, mint masters or trading agents (*malik al-tujjar*), and others as commercial envoys or financial advisors.[83] But Floor and Matthee remind us that these cases never led to harmonious or lasting structural interdependence. Floor maintains that the ruling elites' commercial activities were purely for fiscal efficiency and consumption, and they were inclined to burden the country's population.[84] Matthee casts light on the inequality within the power distribution of the two realms, pointing out that merchants could not break into the core circles of the government; they were made up chiefly of tribes and recruited slave regiments.[85] He thinks that politics and economy were fundamentally different arenas that 'overlapped' and 'negotiated'.[86]

Available information about the relationships between the VOC's brokers and the shah and high-ranking officials also reveals negotiated merchant–state relations. A Dutch letter dated 30 November 1706 provides us with a critical clue. It relates that the second broker in Bandar Abbas, Kissendas, currently held 'the post of the town broker' (*het stadsmakelaarschap*). According to the VOC, this office belonged to the port government (*dat ambt of die bediening van de stad of de gemeente*) and was meant to help the merchants with trade and to provide each trader with a man capable of serving him as a broker.[87] No reference to this post is found in Persian literature on the Safavid administration.[88] But, things did not go well. The *shahbandar* expressed his dislike of Kissendas and claimed he should be able to appoint someone he liked. Moreover, the *shahbandar* insisted that prior to the shah conferring this office on Kissendas, Muslims (*Moor of Mohammedaan*) had always occupied it, and that he was authorized to decide whether to give it to a Muslim or let it stay in the hands of Kissendas. The VOC intervened. By acting as the mediator between these groups (*door ons tussenspreken*), the Company managed to propose a solution: Kissendas would stay in this post on the condition that he paid the *shahbandar* 30 ducats. The Dutch advised Kissendas and the other broker, Toquidas, to behave themselves, not only in their conduct with the *shahbandar* and other port officials but also with the court, to prevent further agitation.[89]

More importantly, the VOC played a crucial role acting as a mediator between Kissendas and the *shahbandar* of Bandar Abbas. In fact, in addition to being a mediator, they strongly backed their brokers' participation in the political arena. To further reflect on this point, we will look at another issue that surfaced the following year, when Kissendas died. The VOC reported that after his death the town brokership was taken over by a Banian named 'Kissiourdas'. Even though the Dutch thought this office was an honourary appointment (*aanzien*) than an income source, they decided to secure it for the Rauwels, whose status had been harmed by the issue of Kissendas's inheritance. Obtaining an imperial order, as well as the *shahbandar*'s and other officials' approval, in July 1710 the VOC successfully removed Kissiourdas and installed Toquidas's son Nata in the position. The factors wrote that this would ensure a prestigious reputation for the entire broker family living in Gulf countries.[90]

Trade skills and monetary transfer

The brokers provided the VOC with numerous commercial facilities. Brokers acted as intermediaries, linking buyers and sellers for a commission; they arranged monetary transfers, the management of factories, co-ordination of shipments, market information, etc. Brokers also arranged for the Company to give customary presents to influential state officials and local merchants.[91] Additionally, on occasions they acted as Dutch delegates to the state authorities. But this was a role beyond their usual functions; it usually fell to the interpreters, for they were known to possess negotiation skills, were familiar with local languages and had various connections to bureaucratic elites. For example, the Bandar Abbas interpreter Joseph Busskens was, according to the Dutch, not only fluent in Armenian and Persian but could also speak Turkish, Portuguese and French.[92] Although all these functions helped the VOC actively engage in commercial enterprises in Safavid Iran, here I shall focus on those more directly related to trading sugar for bullion.

The trading season in Bandar Abbas opened around October, at the start of the north-eastern monsoon and when the heat abated. Ocean-going ships came into port and merchants travelled from inland market towns, such as Lar, Shiraz, Isfahan and Kirman, to meet them. For suppliers, the key to a successful and prosperous season lay in the information they accumulated beforehand. Their business correspondents would update them on the market's current conditions so they could be sure of lucrative sales when they arrived. The brokers at Bandar Abbas were the VOC's most important informants. Not only were they familiar with the market, but they were also familiar with the population's favourite products, and they regularly advised the Company about what items should be brought the following year.[93]

In the late Safavid period the VOC's major trading partners in Bandar Abbas were rich Muslim merchants from Shiraz. At the turn of the eighteenth century, the most prominent were two Shiraz merchants, Hajji Karbalai and Hajji Yusuf. The former became a leading merchant in Iran in the late 1670s, after inheriting enormous wealth from his brother.[94] Both merchants died in 1697–8, which led to inheritance issues.[95] The next season Hajji Yusuf's heirs sent an agent to the Dutch factory, but it was another merchant from Shiraz, Hajji Nabi, who began to dominate the scene.[96] Using his nephew and business partner Hajji ʿAbd al-Jani as business agent, Hajji Nabi purchased more from the Dutch than any other merchant during the first decade of the century. Hajji ʿAbd al-Jani succeeded him and remained in this successful position until his death around 1715;[97] after that, two brothers from Shiraz, Hajji ʿAbd al-Rida and Hajji ʿAbd al-Wahhab, were the main merchants.[98] According to the Dutch, the former had traded with them since his great-grandfather's time.[99]

Matthee emphasizes that, like the Armenians and Banians, the other merchant communities conducted their business enterprises on the basis of family ties, and it is evident that while familial ties were a significant factor, local ties (e.g. acquaintances, friends, neighbors) were also important.[100] Apart from being one of the principal merchants from Shiraz, Hajji Nabi was the head of a group of merchants, comprised of his family members and fellow merchants, who aimed to monopolize the trade with the VOC. When he died in March 1711, Dutch officials reported that his heirs and close friends had rearranged their investments into one fund, with which they would continue to do business with the Company.[101] These merchants felt entitled to the trade with the VOC. In a letter to Batavia in March 1712, various Muslim merchants from Shiraz and Lar wrote that over the last few years, the Dutch officials in Bandar Abbas had broken with the 'old custom' – the Company would supply all imported goods through them. They asserted that by not notifying them of the total amount of imported merchandise, officials had embezzled the best part of it and sold it to Banian and Armenian merchants. This caused a great financial loss, as well as giving the Company a bad reputation. They requested that Batavia restore the old channel of trade by ordering the factors not to sell goods to anyone else but them or principally the Company's Banian brokers (*Baniaanse dienaars der Comp[agni]e*).[102] This episode suggests that the Muslim entrepreneurs and Bandar Abbas brokers formed one interest group.

Powerful wholesalers in the upper countries were accustomed to sending agents (*gevolmachtigde/factoor*) to Bandar Abbas to purchase imported goods. As seen in the case of Hajji Nabi and Hajji ʿAbd al-Jani, family ties were an important consideration for agents. Agents were contracted according to how much money they could spend for their clients. In 1700–1 the Dutch wrote with some disappointment that Hajji Nabi's factor sent that year was restricted to 5,000 *tumans*, implying that it was usually more.[103]

Negotiations often began when Muslim merchants' agents came to the Dutch factory. There the Rauwels (and Kiemtsjant when he was in town) acted as brokers in the sense that the word is conventionally understood: they facilitated transactions between two parties by catering to their interests. The Muslim merchants' collective attitude made them appear as 'conspirators' (*complotteerden*) against the VOC. The Dutch officials, who kept abreast (at least in their view) of all the haggling and squabbling, often complained that the merchants would bargain as a group to lower prices. The Dutch response would be to threaten to send their merchandise to Isfahan, where most of it was destined anyway.[104] In the back of their minds, however, the VOC had some sympathy for their business partners, after all they were subject to various taxes in Bandar Abbas and all along the way to the capital. They therefore aimed to trade in such a manner that the principal buyers also earned a profit despite their costly expenditure; this way they would come back to trade every year.[105]

The fact that the Dutch factors were 'present' during these talks between their brokers and the wholesalers contrasts with what happened at Surat. In his recent essay Nadri argues that, as far as the sale of VOC merchandise in Surat in the second half of the eighteenth century was concerned, the broker Mancherji Khurshedji acted as a 'merchandise-farmer'; he bought the imported goods for trade, paying the Company the agreed upon prices. The Company hardly cared about when, where or for how much he then sold these goods to other merchants.[106] In a cash-strapped country like Safavid Iran, where the risk of default was alarmingly high, the VOC became more cautious about with whom they traded their merchandise. During the reign of Sultan Husayn, large-scale trade was conducted mainly in silver coins called *mahmudi*s. In southern Iran and the Persian Gulf area, *mahmudi*s coined in the Huwayza mint circulated widely as the main trade currency.[107] Like many other local currencies, however, *mahmudi*s were chronically scarce. The Dutch were therefore obliged to sell their merchandise on credit, accepting payment by bills, though they did everything they could to receive an immediate cash payment. Around 1710 it was not unusual to allow credit over eight months to principal wholesalers. The VOC once extended Hajji ʿAbd al-Jani credit for as long as twenty months.[108] The brokers at Bandar Abbas stood surety for the buyers, and the Company debited the brokers for the outstanding money in their books.[109]

Although some Muslim merchants from Shiraz formed a strong interest group, they were not always able to control the market and faced challenges from other local merchants. The year 1716–17 gives valuable insight into this situation. In May 1717 the factors the merchant group sent that season negotiated with the VOC to buy weighed goods, especially sugar. Their proposals failed, however, because their bid was too low and they did not agree to immediate payment. On 10 July, without taking leave of the Dutch, the frustrated agents left Bandar Abbas with a group of merchants. Even though some merchants were still in town, they had no intention of trading with the Company, for they had told the agents they would not. To avoid no sales, the Dutch officials ordered Darmdas and Bouwendas to persuade the remaining merchants to come forward. Sometime later the brokers brought some Lar and Shiraz merchants to the factory, and the Company managed to sell some commodities, including sugar, to Banians in the group on three-month credit. One of the agents, Hajji Husayn, received this news while on his way to Isfahan, where he had clients. He became furious, saying that when he reached the capital he would take measures to make sure those involved paid for this. His clients later tried to obstruct the Company's trade, but were unsuccessful. They changed their minds and tried to restore their relationship with the Dutch by discharging Hajji Husayn, placing all the blame on him.[110] This incident shows that there was tremendous competition among the local merchants to trade with the VOC. The brokers also took this into account, and the Company was able to steadily import Javanese sugar into Bandar Abbas.

The VOC imported a variety of commodities from South Asia and South-East Asia, and they also exported items, such as bullion, Kirman wool and Shiraz wine. Gold specie/gold ducats were the most desirable items, as they were vital to financing the Company's intra-Asian trade.[111] At the turn of the eighteenth century, masses of gold ducats were sent to Colombo, and thence to Malabar or Coromandel according to the demand.[112] The main market for specie export was north-western Iran, centring around Isfahan, where various European coins were brought from the Mediterranean coast or Russia. Therefore, the VOC needed to transfer the proceeds of their sales to Isfahan to procure gold ducats. Brokers played a crucial role in facilitating this process.

As mentioned above, the Company usually sold their items on credit and the brokers at Bandar Abbas guaranteed the payment. No account books survive, so we have to assume that the brokers were registered as the 'buyers' of the goods in the Company's books. In any case, the Dutch kept a watchful eye on the brokers' solvency. When Darmdas and Bouwendas fell behind in their payments, Batavia ordered Bandar Abbas to collect as much unsettled money as they could and only leave the agents with enough money to subsist on.[113]

The brokers were supposed to repay the 'debt' by providing the Company with various services. They co-ordinated remittances to Isfahan and Kirman through money drafts, supplied necessities for the Bandar Abbas factory and for Dutch ships in the harbour preparing for their return voyage, and regularly sent Company presents to state officials in Gulf regions.[114]

For remittances to Isfahan, the brokers usually saw to it that the merchants who had bought goods from the Dutch on credit at Bandar Abbas wrote cheques for payment in Isfahan, so that the factory there could receive needed cash. The VOC initially directed the brokers to accept such cheques only from the principal merchants of Shiraz, those they thought solvent enough to guarantee the transfer. This helped the merchants consolidate their position when trading with the

Dutch. In 1710, however, the Company gave the brokers more leeway in this regard, for sometimes other merchants were better placed financially and could settle remittances more smoothly.[115] Apart from the solvency of the wholesalers, the brokers were required to know if they were well enough connected with the Isfahan market to transfer money. In November 1718 the Dutch expressed some annoyance about these transactions. In the previous financial year, the Bandar Abbas factory had sold some precious spices (cloves, nutmeg and cinnamon) but the Isfahan factory had not received the bills for the proceeds, because the purchasers were not regular trading partners from Lar, Shiraz or Bandar Abbas but instead came from Kirman and surrounding areas. Because they had no commercial agents in Isfahan, they could not issue the expected bills there.[116]

If a bill sent to Isfahan was not accepted for some reason, then the Bandar Abbas brokers were responsible for the outstanding money. In summer 1715 a Muslim merchant from Bandar Abbas named Agha Ma'sum (Aga Mossem) drew a bill on another Muslim merchant staying in Isfahan named Hajji Mahmud. Yet Hajji Mahmud refused to cash it for the VOC because Agha Ma'sum owed him some money. The cheque was sent back to Bandar Abbas and the factors debited the brokers for the amount overdue, because 'they always stood surety for all the unsettled money for the Company'.[117]

Isfahan was the largest market for commodities to be exported from Safavid Iran. Imported European bullion, as well as diverse local products – nuts, dried fruits, asafetida, gums, madder, etc. – were available at the market.[118] The bullion trade at Isfahan was highly competitive. While the financially pressed government often cornered the market for themselves, there were many merchants (Hindus, Armenians, Muslims and English) who regularly exported gold and silver coins to India. On top of this, Muslim pilgrims to Mecca and Karbala would collect considerable amounts of bullion from the market for their travels.[119] At the end of the seventeenth century, European gold ducats became extremely scarce in Isfahan. Therefore the VOC had to look for alternative coins, such as the 'Moorish gold ducat' (*goude Moren*), which was struck in the Ottoman Empire, and Persian silver '*abbasi*s.[120] The market, however, witnessed a remarkable increase in the inflow of silver towards the end of the Safavid period. In 1719 the Dutch noted that the merchants from upcountry had found trading in silver to be more lucrative than trading in gold, so they arrived with mainly silver coins, such as Spanish reals of eight.[121]

The Isfahan broker Kiemtsjant had the crucial task of collecting profitable coins for export for the Company. The Isfahan resident Macaré stated that without the broker, the Company could not obtain gold ducats.[122] Kiemtsjant used numerous agents and servants to complete his task. They included Madoe, Litsjeram, Wissendas, Girdil, Natta, Sjoram, Madoudas, Odoudas and Hetsjeram. The names Natta and Wissendas might refer to the Banian cleark Nagha Natta and the agent Wissendas Jedmelanie, respectively. When Kiemtsjant was out of town during the 1710s, these agents worked in his place.[123] Acquired bullion was packed up in the capital and sent by caravan to Bandar Abbas for shipment to South Asia and Batavia.

The present chapter has examined various dimensions of the relationship between the VOC and their Banian brokers from the late seventeenth century to the Afghan conquest of Isfahan. It has been argued that in Safavid Iran, both the European 'companies' and the Asian 'family firms' had to cope with rampant uncertainties while also competing with each other. A study of their relationship, however, shows that this uncertainty presented opportunities for these different commercial institutions to work together for their mutual advantage. For the VOC, keeping a brokership in the hands of one merchant family was more important than having their investments dispersed among different brokers. The brokers, apprehensive of attacks from the ruling elite and rival merchants, sought associations with the Dutch, who offered them a mechanism through which to safeguard their wealth and businesses. With the strong backing of the VOC, the Bandar Abbas brokers were able to surmount the 'boundary' between commerce *per se* and their involvement in port administration. This cooperation facilitated the smooth import of Javanese sugar into the Iranian market and the reverse flow of gold and silver coins to India.

Chapter 7

PERSISTENCE OF THE COMMERCIAL MIDDLE GROUND

The Afghan conquest of Isfahan in 1722 meant trans-regional trade was radically transformed. The central hubs (i.e. Bandar Abbas and Isfahan) were heavily damaged, but numerous alternative trade channels developed in the Persian Gulf and adjacent countries, where maritime merchants continued to trade sugar for exportable bullion and, notably, copper. While non-Dutch East India Company (*Verenigde Oostindische Compagnie* [VOC]) sugar suppliers adroitly adjusted to the new economic settings, the Company did not. Their trade steadily marginalized, they finally withdrew from the Gulf in 1766. However, the perceived Dutch downfall raises a question. How did the VOC last so long? What kept them motivated amid tough, if not unwinnable, competition. The VOC enlisted various local agents in an attempt to adjust to the new environment. In this last chapter we shall examine who these agents were, the structure of their relationships with the Company and what insights they provide about the reorganization of Gulf trade.

The Bandar Abbas agency's long struggle

After the brutal overthrow of the Safavids, Dutch sugar sales in Bandar Abbas fell substantially. The Dutch archives for the following period show a significant correlation between the decline of the Company and the decline of their business arrangements with the brokers. However, the archives also indicate that during this period, there were many other merchants who served the Dutch at Bandar Abbas and tried to revive the ailing business arrangement.

The Rauwels' bankruptcy

The Rauwel family, who served the VOC as brokers at Bandar Abbas during the Safavid period, faced a serious financial crisis after the Afghan invasion. At the end of the Safavid period, major wholesale merchants who purchased goods from the Dutch at Bandar Abbas wrote cheques payable by their business partners in Isfahan, as was customary, and these were owed to the Dutch factory in Isfahan. The Bandar Abbas brokers Ottumsjent and Issourdas guaranteed the settlement of payments. The turmoil caused by the Afghan invasion, however, resulted in the ruin of many of the rich merchants involved in these monetary transfers. Consequently, the brokers were held responsible for the accounts that were due.[1] On top of this, the brokers were hurt from the pillaging of the Baluchi nomads in south-eastern Iran, who repeatedly raided Bandar Abbas, taking full advantage of the political turmoil that engulfed the littoral in the 1720s.[2]

Earlier in the century, the VOC's brokers would improve their liquidity by selling their own commodities at Bandar Abbas, but now they could not, as most of the wholesale merchants who traded at the port previously headed to Basra.[3] In addition, Hajji ʿAbd al-Rida, one of the VOC's main trading partners, died in 1722.[4] It was not until 1730 that Hajji ʿAbd al-Wahhab, another principal wholesaler, and brother of ʿAbd al-Rida, sent the Company a letter requesting permission to restart the trading enterprise. This did not materialize, since by then his economic clout had declined, and he died soon afterwards.[5]

The VOC was alarmed by the looming bankruptcy of Ottumsjent and Issourdas and took two measures. First, they tried to hold the brokers' capital as collateral. In March 1724, the Dutch head of Bandar Abbas, Pieter 't Lam, wrote that in order to reduce the agents' debt, he had confiscated the assets at the Dutch factory they managed to save from the marauding Baluchis, and he had also searched for any cash and gold they might have hidden in their houses or elsewhere.[6] Second, the VOC tried to facilitate the brokers' own trade. As discussed earlier, the Company arranged for the brokers to transport their own sugar to Muscat and Basra. However, these attempts had an adverse effect. Trade at Muscat turned out to be detrimental to their agents, the Dutch commented, because it required heavy expenditures for transporting cargo, and it also caused serious damage to the sugar after it was housed in a hot cabin.[7] By 1727, Ottumsjent and Issourdas became so broke that they claimed to not have the means to support their big family.[8]

From the second half of the 1720s onwards, the brokers asked the VOC to release them from the enormous debt that had accrued from the lost Isfahan bills. At a meeting held at the Dutch factory on 23 August 1726 Ottumsjent and Issourdas requested permission for one of them to go to Batavia to explain their situation to the High Government and to beg for relief from being held responsible for the debt. According to the Dutch, their debt amounted to 150,598 guilders 15 stivers. The factory did not grant their request but instead asked Batavia to show special favour on this issue, saying that these men were so desperate that if adequate measures were not taken it would be almost impossible for them to continue to serve the Company.[9]

The brokers' fortunes were rapidly waning; however, some of the people who had served the Rauwel firm began to play a larger role supporting VOC commerce. Ottumsjent and Issourdas, who were still young (around twenty years old when they were appointed as co-brokers of Darmdas in 1719), received much assistance from their experienced clerks. In November 1722, the Dutch director, Jan Oets, wrote that given their age, the brokers were quite good at trade, because they were helped by their 'chief servant' (*opperste of eerste dienaar*) named 'Monsjeterdas'.

According to Oets, Monsjeterdas was trustworthy and had some experience: he had acted as the Company's broker at Basra in the past. Oets said that the factory should keep him on hand.[10] Five months later, when much of Bandar Abbas's trade was being redirected to Basra, the Bandar Abbas factory instructed the broker's Banian servant to collect information on the Basra market using his business correspondents there.[11] It is highly likely that this servant was Monsjeterdas.

Around the same time, an Armenian family who had acted as VOC wool collectors at Kirman were also in the Dutch's service at Bandar Abbas. At the turn of the eighteenth century the Company established a permanent agency in Kirman for the procurement of wool, and they hired two Armenian brothers from Julfa, named 'Martiroes' and 'Mouraet'. Both merchants died in the early 1710s and Martiroes's son, named 'Auwanees', took over the post. He remained there until his death in 1747; he died a cruel death at the hands of Nadir Shah's punitive campaign in the region.[12]

Auwanees's family served as the Company's interpreters at Bandar Abbas in the aftermath of the Afghan invasion. In March 1720, when the interpreter Joseph Busskens died, the Bandar Abbas factory wanted the Sahids – another Julfa Armenian family who had been interpreters for the Dutch at Isfahan during the late Safavid period – to take care of the port (Appendix 11). The best candidate was Elias Sahid. He had been supporting his elderly father François as second interpreter at Isfahan since around 1710,[13] but he could not leave the capital. François died in February 1721 and Elias immediately succeeded him.[14] In early 1722 the factory appointed another son of the late François named Joseph.[15] However, due to increased road insecurity he could not leave Isfahan. Therefore, in July 1723 Bandar Abbas asked Auwanees's brother 'Ghodjatoer', who lived in Kirman, to work as a provisional interpreter.[16] Ghodjatoer played a key role sustaining the Company's trade at the port. During the brokers' abrupt decline, 't Lam wrote in 1725 that he had relied on the provisional interpreter Ghodjatoer to conduct Company business. He suggested that Batavia confirm him as a broker as well, saying he was competent as both a broker and interpreter.[17]

In the later part of the decade, however, serious illness prevented Ghodjatoer from working. The factory nominated Joseph Sahid and his brother David as interpreters, asking one of them to perform the task at Bandar Abbas. Before David arrived in Bandar Abbas in July 1730, Ghodjatoer's father-in-law 'Minas' acted as a temporary interpreter.[18] The Dutch records contain no evidence that the Auwanees family served Bandar Abbas after this time, but we can infer the scope of their influence from the fact that in 1741, Auwanees used David's brother and successor Ibrahim Sahid as his business agent (*volmacht*) at the port.[19]

Declining cooperation: Nadir Shah's rule (1730–47)

The fracturing of Isfahan's bullion market and the concurrent recession experienced by the powerful wholesalers from Shiraz caused the commercial network to decline significantly. And monetary transfers from Bandar Abbas to Isfahan, and the reverse flows of gold and silver specie, depended on this market.

Although some calm was restored under the rule of Nadir Shah, the commercial situation did not improve. It was not unusual for the wholesale merchants who arrived in Bandar Abbas to bring exportable bullion and copper to exchange for imported items.

Because of the lingering instability, these merchants (mainly arriving from or via Kirman) were highly adept at changing their course of action as needed. They would only travel to the market when it appeared to be picking up, bringing their money and immediately purchasing goods (often partially on credit) so they could leave as soon as possible. This manner of trade gave foreign goods suppliers little time to determine if the merchants to whom they were selling merchandise were solvent or not. The VOC brokers stood security for these precarious deals. If a buyer turned out to be insolvent, they had to cover the loss using their own brokerage income.[20] The brokers were also responsible for collecting profitable copper coinage and copper goods.[21]

The brokers were still serving the VOC while also engaging in new methods of commerce, but their commercial clout was severely declining. In 1733, alarmed Dutch factors reported that no merchants would trust them with money, since the brokers' creditworthiness had considerably decreased.[22] Increased extortion at the hands of the local bureaucratic elite financed Nadir Shah's naval activities in the Gulf from the middle of the 1730s onwards, which added to the brokers' despondency.[23]

During the late Safavid period the VOC had given the Rauwels the brokership of Bandar Abbas along with various associated perks, most importantly 'protection'. The brokers in turn took responsibility for most of the Company's investments. In Nadir Shah's time, however, the ailing family started to dislike the old collaboration and refused to fulfill it unless the Company was willing to release them from the debt accrued from the lost Isfahan bills. When Issourdas died on 19 July 1736, the factory tried to find a successor from among his brothers, but no one came forward due to the burden of debt. The other broker, Ottumsjent, requested relief from this inheritable liability. About two months later, two of Ottumsjent's brothers, 'Koemertjent' and 'Abtjent', thirty-one and thirty years old, respectively, applied for the vacant position. The Dutch offered them the position on the condition that the merchants accepted responsibility for the debt. They insisted they would not take responsibility for any of it. After many fruitless arguments, the Dutch compromised. They appointed Koemertjent and Abtjent as co-brokers alongside Ottumsjent and then conferred them and their secretary (*secretaris*) with the customary present of neckerchiefs as a sign of the Company's favour.[24]

From then on the VOC asked many members of the Rauwel firm to share the heavy debt of the Isfahan bills. The factory kept asking Koemertjent and Abtjent to take on some of the debt, and in the end the new brokers acquiesced.[25] In April 1737 Ottumsjent left for Bombay to pick up his wife, and he died there. When he departed, the Dutch persuaded the other brokers, Koemertjent and Abtjent, another brother named 'Wisschermerdas' who was about twenty-five years of age, and their bookkeeper (*boekhouder*) 'Baboe', to take on the liability as well as all business relating to the brokership of Bandar Abbas.[26] In February 1738, at the request of Koemertjent and Abtjent, the VOC officially added Wisschermerdas, who they thought had served them well, to the brokership, thereby making it clear that he also stood security for the brokers' debt, which then amounted to 226,882 guilders 17 stivers, including a sum of 106,058 guilders 6 stivers 8 pennies for the Isfahan bills.[27]

However, the Rauwel firm became inoperative towards the end of Nadir Shah's reign. Although in 1743-4 the brokers' debt had been reduced to 169,029 guilders 11 stivers, the Dutch noted that those 'bankrupts' had not only petitioned for release from the whole obligation but also for permission to move to another Dutch factory.[28] After the death of Wisschermerdas, on 30 September 1745 Bandar Abbas convened a board that included the remaining brokers, Koemertjent, Abtjent and 'Issourdas', who was the heir of the brokers' late secretary. The Dutch factors reminded the brokers of their overdue debt, reminded Issourdas of his father's debt to the Company and demanded that they settle all accounts promptly. However, these merchants could not comply because the Persian authorities were demanding heavy tributes on them. This shocked the Company, and they added extra surety by involving another brother, 'Tackourdas', as co-broker.[29]

The flexibility of EIC brokership

During Nadir Shah's reign, the East India Company (EIC) also experienced a serious crisis with their local broker at Bandar Abbas, but their response was a marked contrast to that of the VOC. However, it dealt an additional blow to Dutch sugar trade at the port.

The EIC, like the VOC, utilized many locals to conduct business in Iran. The EIC kept one broker, one interpreter (linguist) and one Persian secretary (writer) at Bandar Abbas, and agents such as a broker, moneychanger (*sarraf*) and interpreter at Isfahan. They also posted some agents at Shiraz to obtain wine and at Kirman to obtain wool. In the early eighteenth century, the 'Banian' broker at Bandar Abbas, 'Chittorah', was a pivotal figure, providing seamless backing for the Company's trading enterprises.[30] As the EIC broker he basically acted as an intermediary, linking potential buyers of English goods – belonging officially to the Company and also to private traders – with the EIC factory and facilitating transactions on commission.[31] In addition, he offered a variety of financial services, including factory management and money transfers and exchange, while also occasionally acting as a delegate for the English in front of the port authorities.[32] After the death of Chittorah in September 1725, his son 'Kessourjee' succeeded to his position.[33] In spite of the deteriorating trading conditions in Bandar Abbas during the Afghan occupation, Kessourjee continued to mediate between the English and local wholesale merchants.[34] When no buyers were found, he traded unsold articles at agreed prices.[35] His service, though, did not last long, as he died in September 1729.[36]

The brokership was then passed on to a Banian named 'Sanchar Heridass'. This man had been involved in EIC trade, specifically Kirman wool, earlier and no doubt had completed transactions with Kessourjee.[37] It seems that he was not related to the broker family.[38] He also conducted his own trade in the growing market at Muscat, as his dinghy sailed between Bandar Abbas and Muscat, where he kept an agent.[39]

In the highly fluid commercial environment during Nadir's rule, Sanchar provided the EIC with a similar set of services as those offered by his predecessors. He even added the important function of co-ordinating shipments of copper to Bombay.[40] However, the relationship ended somewhat unexpectedly on 15 October 1739, when the broker asked for permission to resign:

> Sankhar waiting on the [EIC] agent this morning, hinted some suspicions of the Hon[ourable] Company's having given orders to discharge him from the brokership, as they had refused to let him have the last year's cloth, tho' so small a quantity and his debt to them lessened within a trifle. Complaining also of his sufferings from the government who under the distinction of being our broker, he said, and with the notion of his prodigious gettings, had taken from him at times, as he cou[ld] make appear by his books, to the amount of above four thousand tomands [*tumans*], besides obliging him to trust them great sums other ways, all which as a private merchant he sho[ul]d have been exempted from … and informed that the decline in trade of late and the little prospect he saw of its reviving whereby he might be encouraged to sit under these hardships, but on the contrary new ones approaching which his present circumstances would not allow him to submit to, with other reasons, but principally that of the Ho[nourable] Company's denying him their credit as before determined him to take our leave for his resigning, after he had collected his debts and cleaned off the remainder of what he owed the Hon[ourable] Company.[41]

Sanchar mentioned two reasons for his resignation. First, he was burdened by ceaseless extortion; the ruling elites targeted him because of his distinguished status as the EIC broker. His losses, which he claimed amounted to more than 4,000 *tumans*, made it no longer feasible for him to continue his business in Bandar Abbas, where the market had significantly declined. Second and more importantly, Sanchar had a strong suspicion that the Company might fire him from trading their merchandise.

His suspicion that the EIC might not trust him any more seems justifiable. The Bandar Abbas factory did not hesitate and allowed him to leave that same day, although they promised to keep protecting him until he recovered his investments from the port government, the English officials and others. They also allowed him to retain the status of Company broker for that purpose.[42] What is more intriguing, however, is that the English factors then suspended the brokership and took over most of Sanchar's work.[43] In October 1742 the factors wrote about the woollen goods deal they had recently made with the Persian authorities:

> This is the inconvenience of dealing with these government people, tho' unavoidable. Formerly indeed when the broker was [in good?] circumstances, they used to direct themselves to him so that [they] did not appear to the

Company, but the matter being changed [and] they nevertheless expecting to be obliged in their wants, we are applied to. But as yet we have been able to keep on tolerable terms and either by assignments on the Banians or other means secured the money, tho' we have been some time out of it. The Dutch are fair to submit to the like ... but they have been so ill-treated that they have, as some of their heads confessed, a debt outstanding of above one thousand tomands from the government.[44]

Why did the EIC stop using a broker at Bandar Abbas? One possibility is that they could not find any capable merchants in the port. But perhaps a more important factor to be considered is that from the second half of the 1730s the EIC increasingly redirected their trade from Bandar Abbas to the burgeoning market of Kirman. As discussed in Chapter 4, from the late 1730s the EIC and many associated merchants, most of them EIC officers, regularly forwarded imported goods to Kirman, including English woollen products, sugar and pepper, where they could be traded for copper ware and copper coins. As a result, a considerable part of the Bandar Abbas market for sugar was relocated to Kirman.

It is probable that the English entrusted the new venture to their representatives in Kirman. In 1695, the EIC set up a permanent trading station in Kirman before the VOC set up theirs and commissioned the Julfa Armenians to purchase Kirman wool.[45] However, during Nadir Shah's rule, the EIC deployed one English officer at a time: William Cordeux (1732–3), Nathaniel Whitwell (1733–6), Henry Savage (c. 1736–46) and Danvers Graves (1746–7).[46] Good demonstrates that the English utilized various Iranian merchants. These merchants included 'Seawax' (Diyabakhsh?), who served the Company as broker and secretary for most of this period; his son-in-law 'Espondior' (Isfandiyar?); 'Sharyar' (Shahryar?); and Mahmud, who acted as interpreter (linguist).[47] From May 1737, when the Bandar Abbas factory explicitly ordered Savage to sell the transferred woollen goods and acquire copper in return, the full-fledged Kirman agency collected copper as well as wool.[48] This went on until early in 1747, when Nadir Shah's growing financial exploitation of the region made the project ineffective, and Graves left the town. The English documentation related to Bandar Abbas in this period contains many references to Kirman caravans arriving with wool and other return goods, chiefly copper ('lump copper' and 'old copper'), though it is likely that not all the loads belonged to the English.[49] After Graves' retreat from Kirman, the EIC reactivated the local agency at Bandar Abbas. During this time the factory used three Banians, 'Chiballah', 'Parwana' and 'Keemah'.[50] Mahmud, the above-mentioned interpreter, remained in service at Kirman.[51]

It should be noted that the VOC also kept a local wool collector in Kirman and planned to develop the local agency into a permanent factory around the same time, but the plan never materialized.[52] The suspension of the EIC brokership at Bandar Abbas during Nadir Shah's reign therefore indicates that the English had a higher level of adaptability than the VOC in response to the market's relocation to Kirman. In other words, the Dutch made more efforts to shore up existing channels of trade in order to manage the precarious situation.

In the 1730s and 1740s the English explored new business frameworks for utilizing local intermediaries across the northern Indian Ocean, while the Dutch tended to foster their old networks. Nadri has pointed out that from the late 1730s, in Surat the EIC reined in their broker's power by defining and redefining his position, and by changing the nomenclature of his title from broker to *wakil* and then to *marfatia*. By contrast the VOC and their brokers deepened their interdependency over the course of the century.[53] In Bengal both Companies had long struggled to control their brokers, who were rich merchants and played a crucial role managing Company investments in export commodities. Yet the EIC abolished the office in 1741 and then engaged local merchants as *gomasta*s to procure export articles, while the VOC retained the status quo.[54] From this time on the English increasingly out-traded the Dutch in all these places – the Persian Gulf, Surat and Bengal – thus highlighting how such differences of attitude triggered markedly different results.[55]

The last effort

Thanks to a series of petitions sent to Batavia, in 1752–3 the Bandar Abbas brokers Koemertjent, Abtjent and Tackourdas were finally released from the debt for the Isfahan bills. However, their situation did not improve. Even after their debt was written off, these 'poor people' owed the Company the large sum of 97,972 guilders 10 stivers. The factory seized five houses and a garden belonging to them, but these properties turned out to have little or no value due to their condition.[56]

Although the twilight of the broker family marks irreversible decline in Bandar Abbas trade, it is intriguing to note that some countervailing forces remained. The VOC brokers' main servants were noticeably active in the marketplace. In his final report, the Dutch director Schoonderwoerd wrote that it was not the brokers but their servants who had actually handled the Company's business in Bandar Abbas during his term (1748–55).[57] Since the current brokers Abtjent and Tackourdas were raised in luxury and had not learned how to properly conduct required services, he had been able to manage his duties with the help of the brokers' secretary (*schrijver*) Issourdas. Issourdas always stood security for the Company's transactions, as he was 'rather rich' (*tamelijk gegoed*). The man had in fact died not long before the report was written, and his brother 'Duarkardas' had succeeded him.[58]

David Busskens, the son of the aforementioned Joseph Busskens, is another interesting example of this reframing of brokership. David had a vital role in the VOC enterprises in Iran after the Safavid period. In 1730–1 the Company employed him as an assistant (*assistent*), the lowest rank in the Dutch hierarchy in Persia, to help the newly appointed Isfahan head Mattheus van Leijpsigh. For this service the Company agreed to pay him 10 guilders a month on a three-year contract.[59] In 1737, when the VOC embarked on a new venture at Bushrie, they installed there David as an interpreter.[60] About three years later he was back in Isfahan as the second-in-command. After Dutch personnel withdrew from the city in 1746, he and the Isfahan interpreters looked after the properties the Company had left behind.[61]

In early 1753, when the Bandar Abbas interpreter David Sahid (on his second stint, which began in 1751) passed away, the VOC appointed David Busskens, who had conveniently arrived from Isfahan, as his successor.[62] The factory asked him to act as broker as well. Touching on the recent loss of Koemertjent, Schoonderwoerd reported that the remaining brokers were 'incapable' and 'untrustworthy', and therefore it was advisable to add David to the brokering service. As an incentive, Schoonderwoerd offered him a special privilege: the right to collect an additional 0.5 per cent commission on top of the usual 1 per cent.[63]

Nevertheless, things did not turn out as they expected. In the last days of their operation in Bandar Abbas, Dutch personnel formed the impression that the Rauwels' misery was actually instigated by the Issourdas family and David Busskens. In the last report the Dutch officials submitted to Batavia they expressed their dissatisfaction with the brokers Abtjent and Tackourdas. These men had been solvent when the former director, Schoonderwoerd, had departed at the end of 1755, but when the Dutch asked them to pay further dues a few years later, the requested payment never arrived. They felt slighted because the brokers had not been the victims of extortion, nor had they suffered bankruptcy in recent years. According to Abtjent and Tackourdas, the reason for their insolvency was that their servants Issourdas and Duarkardas, to whom they had consigned all the work, had involved David Busskens in their business, had put too much trust in him, and they had lost the money.[64] This could have been merely an excuse, but the Dutch officials were nevertheless convinced. 'It is a real pity,' they said, 'that those who formerly had such a considerable wealth have to live so miserably, and even more so because they would not be able to pay off their debt to the Company, for what we have written about the way their money has been lost from time to time is only partially reported'.[65]

In 1763, four years after the Dutch retreat, Batavia received a letter from 'Takardas' and 'Kordas', the Company's brokers at Bandar Abbas (*makelaars van de Edele Comp[agnie] in de negorij Abasi*), asking for permanent protection so that they could maintain some esteem among the local merchants. This first broker may have actually been Tackourdas.[66]

Changing role of the Isfahan broker

In August 1723, soon after the Afghan conquest, the Isfahan broker Kiemtsjant died, and his nephew Heemraadje Jedmelanie took over as broker. In the upheaval following the revolution, however, the bullion market in Isfahan crumbled, which made it impossible for the broker to procure any of the requested gold ducats.[67] Nadir Shah's re-establishment of Persian rule did not change the situation. Substantial inflows of money did not return, although the VOC occasionally collected gold and silver coins.[68]

Under these circumstances the Isfahan broker was no longer the money merchant he used to be. His main task was now limited to financial roles at the factory, such as paying workers' salaries.[69] To stress how crucial Heemraadje was for the upkeep of the Isfahan factory, Bandar Abbas reported that in order to deter the total collapse of the Isfahan factory, they had made sure to repay their debt to him, thereby motivating him to stay in their service.[70]

Over the course of the 1730s it became even more difficult for the VOC to continue the Isfahan enterprise. The highly sophisticated banking network through which Bandar Abbas had consistently supported Isfahan during the late Safavid period had virtually disappeared. In addition, the authorities' regular fiscal exploitation slowed the merchant societies in Isfahan, and one after the other they left for alternative places of trade.[71] In order to improve the situation, Bandar Abbas occasionally sent some of the imported goods they traded for cash to Isfahan by caravan. One such caravan took place in the early summer of 1737 under the supervision of the Dutch officials Joris Brand and Isaac de Crane. They were conveying goods worth 12,336 guilders 17 stivers and 8 pennies to Isfahan.[72]

In Isfahan some of these goods were traded for needed money. The rest was allocated as presents for the ruling elite, etc. The factory used Heemraadje's brother Wissendas as a substitute broker (*substituut makelaar*) for the trade, as Heemraadje had relocated to Bandar Abbas.[73] The Banians competed with other local merchants who came with goods which were purchased from the English and French. Wissendas sold various articles, including Javanese castor sugar and candy sugar, usually on credit for three or four months. He received 1 per cent of the total value from the Company.[74]

Banian connections to Basra

According to Abdullah, in the eighteenth century the Basra market was one of various mercantile societies built on networks of family, clan, tribe, birthplace and ethnicity. The Muslim merchants (Sunni and Shi'i) were the most powerful, and the Turkish Chelebi family had a prominent position among them. Among the non-Muslims, the Armenians were the richest, followed by the Jews, but during the second half of the century the Jews overtook the Armenians. These different merchant communities were involved in different trading routes: the Chelebis were mainly involved in maritime trade with India, especially Surat; the Armenians in caravan traffic with Aleppo; and the Jews in river trade with Baghdad.[75] We can add 'Indian' merchants to Abdullah's list. When he visited Basra in 1786, the Englishman Julius Griffiths saw that the population consisted of 'a mixture of Christians, Jews, Arabians, and Indians', all of them conducting commerce, and the Jews and Indians seemed to monopolize the trade of jewels and precious metals and exchanging money, while the Armenians and other Christian sects conducted general import and export.[76] In order to launch their new enterprise in Basra, the VOC aligned themselves with this 'Indian' sector.

The Company initially planned to install a Banian merchant named 'Monsje', who was in Bandar Abbas, as the Basra broker (*makelaar*). However, on 18 October 1723, when he was about to leave for Basra, he was found strangled outside the town. After months of searching, the Bandar Abbas factory found another experienced Banian named 'Moeltjent', and they sent him to Basra immediately in February 1724.[77] Little is known about Moeltjent's early career, but it is clear that he was closely associated with, if not a member of, the firm of the Isfahan broker Heemraadje. Sources show that his brother 'Sendeldas' was Heemraadje's principal agent at Isfahan.[78] Considering this association, Moeltjent came from a Sindi background. Moeltjent settled in the city of Basra with his family (six members in total) became part of the Banian society there.[79] In July 1725 port authorities arrested him on the charge that all the Banians in the city were complaining about him. As a result, the VOC were obliged to pay over 300 *tuman*s in ransom to show that Moeltjent was under their protection. However, the Dutch officers wrote with unusual annoyance that the charge was groundless, and the Banians would have paid the ransom money if the Company had not.[80] Our source materials contain few clues as to where these Banian merchants came from. 'Tollaram', a man who served the VOC as *sarraf* in 1742–3, was probably from north-west India. In April 1743 he took leave for Surat because he had recently received a considerable inheritance from a relative in Hindustan.[81]

Moeltjent undertook trade of imported Company goods. As at Bandar Abbas and Isfahan the commission was fixed at 1 per cent. Usually, the broker traded the goods for exportable gold and silver specie. The VOC directed him to hire a *sarraf* using his brokerage income to ensure this procedure would be successful.[82] Since the Company did not employ an interpreter (*tolk*) at Basra until the late 1730s, the broker would act as their delegate to the authorities alongside the Dutch personnel, some of whom were familiar with the vernacular language.[83]

Given the risk of fiscal exploitation at the hands of the port authorities and the difficulty working in unfamiliar commercial settings, one may wonder whether Moeltjent was content with his humble brokerage income. Even if he enjoyed the Company's protection, he probably was not content. The relationship between Moeltjent and the VOC came to an abrupt end in early 1735, when it was discovered that Moeltjent was embezzling Company funds. 'There was nothing ever so disheartening,' a message from Basra to Bandar Abbas declared, 'as the confession that the Company's broker Moeltjent made after receiving the news of the death of the former head Dames Heij [in Bandar Abbas on 20 December 1734]'. The broker admitted that 'he had spent the Company's cash entrusted him to settle Mr. Heij's debt [to him], and as a result became unable to effectuate the order to send it to Gamron [Bandar Abbas], while apologizing for having caused the disaster, with many lamentable and clamorous expressions'.[84]

The Basra officials seem to have felt some sympathy for Moeltjent – at least at first. The same report relates that since the establishment of the factory, Moeltjent's performance had been satisfactory. He had received and held the Company's money while also procuring specie for export according to what was available and what was ordered. He had never failed to execute his duty until this occasion. Even now, this situation had arisen unexpectedly following the death of Heij, which made it impossible for the broker to return the Company money, which he had only used temporarily.[85] The report goes on to criticize Heij severely, claiming that in spite of Moeltjent's request, Heij left for Bandar Abbas without even issuing a certificate for his debt. This reportedly totalled 2,590 *tuman*s, of which he had settled only a tiny part in Bandar Abbas.⁸⁶

These considerations, however, ultimately meant nothing to the VOC. All that mattered to them was getting back their money. The thorough investigation that ensued unearthed another interesting clue about Moeltjent's close relationship with the Heemraadje firm; namely, before his departure to Basra, Moeltjent had entered a contract with two Banians in Bandar Abbas named 'Wissendas' and 'Natta' to share all profits and losses that would occur during his brokership in Basra.⁸⁷ These Banians can be identified as Wissendas, the brother of Heemraadje, and Kiemtsjant's former clerk at Isfahan, Nagha Natta (Chapter 6).⁸⁸ Accordingly, the Company tried to sequester the guarantors' property, whatever value it had.⁸⁹ In November 1735 Moeltjent and his family were brought to Bandar Abbas, where he was subjected to further interrogations and confiscations. The Dutch held his 'friends' Wissendas and Natta responsible for the outstanding money.⁹⁰ After squeezing as much as they could out of Moeltjent, in 1739 he was sent from Bandar Abbas to Cochin so that his creditors could not run after him. He was sent with a letter to the Dutch supervisor there asking him to keep Moeltjent under strict surveillance lest he turn against the Company in the future.⁹¹ After Moeltjent's removal, the VOC asked his brother Sendeldas, who was in Isfahan, to share responsibility for the arrears, but he declined.⁹²

In the meantime, Basra used a Banian named 'Fattitjant' as a provisional broker and honoured him and his *sarraf* as subjects of the VOC by conferring *khilʿa*s on them. The Dutch officer Willem Slaars, due to his linguistic abilities, acted as interpreter.⁹³ By 1740, however, Fattitjant had also been dismissed due to misconduct, and then the post of broker was given to another Banian named 'Tjettoe'. He had been working for the Dutch factory for more than four years.⁹⁴

The Sahid family

While the Banian community was a key component of VOC trade in Basra, both facilitating and frustrating it, the Julfa Armenian Sahid family, who had been the official interpreters in Isfahan during the Safavid period, played a supporting role in Dutch trade in the early 1740s.

From the late 1670s until his death in 1721, the VOC employed the leader of the merchant house, François Sahid, as (chief) Isfahan interpreter.⁹⁵ He was a dependable go-between, and the Dutch counted on him to negotiate with the Safavid court, specifically for silk deals.⁹⁶ In return he received monthly wages and support from the Company, as well as various royal favours, such as an exemption from *jizya*.⁹⁷ As described above, the Sahid family also served as the interpreters at Bandar Abbas after the Safavid period. In July 1730 David Sahid, François's son, came down to Bandar Abbas to fulfil the function of interpreter. He had to take leave for Isfahan in November 1735 to be treated for an eye issue (*blindheid*). Bandar Abbas then called up his brother Ibrahim from Isfahan, along with the aforementioned David Busskens, who was competent in Dutch.⁹⁸

Perhaps around this time, the Sahids turned their attention to Basra. In November 1738, the VOC appointed Jacob Jan Sahid (also called Jan Jacob Sahid), the son of the Isfahan interpreter Elias, to replace Slaars as the Basra interpreter. The Dutch noted that Jacob Jan had acted as such before, and now he was to act as broker as well.[99] In February 1741 the Banian broker Tjettoe died, and the VOC found it extremely difficult to find a reliable replacement.[100] Then Jacob Jan stepped up to provide the needed skills.[101] Although the Company appointed a broker and a *sarraf* soon afterwards, since 'handling those offices was too heavy a workload' for Jacob Jan, he remained involved in managing the Company's cash.[102] Meanwhile, as interpreter Jacob Jan successfully persuaded the Basra government to reduce the Dutch tariff from 4 to 3 per cent.[103]

Because of Jacob Jan's superb performance at Basra, in 1743 the Bandar Abbas factory called him to be their interpreter. The incumbent Ibrahim, who was probably upset about his consequent dismissal, was mollified by being appointed to the vacant post of Basra interpreter.[104] In 1750 the Company made a decision to return them to their original offices, but it did not materialize. Jacob Jan returned to Basra to be interpreter there but died soon afterwards. Ibrahim, who had not yet left for Bandar Abbas, was unwilling to move again on account of 'his big family' (*zijn grote familie*) and wanted to continue his service at Basra. The VOC met his request and gave the office of Bandar Abbas interpreter to David Sahid for the second time.[105] Ibrahim remained in service in Basra until the Dutch factors deserted the city in 1753.[106]

S. Aslanian has argued that during Nadir Shah's reign, the global network of Armenian merchants underwent a critical restructuring. He contends that Nadir Shah's oppression of the Armenian society in Julfa, the centre of their business network, which culminated in devastating taxation demands at the close of his reign, led to the collapse of Julfa's once-celebrated economy. It also caused the community to disperse to other economic centres in the Mediterranean, to Iraq, to Russia and to India; places where they had strong commercial interests and thus gave new life to the network.[107] The Sahid family's commitment to the VOC enterprise at Basra, as seen above, not only supports his idea but also suggests that trading sugar for bullion was one of the stimuli for the transformation.[108]

Nagha Natta

Nagha Natta was the epitome of an eighteenth-century mobile Banian merchant. He first served Kiemtsjant at Isfahan and then moved to Bandar Abbas, Sind and then back to Bandar Abbas (Chapter 6). In order to enter the emergent market in Bushire, the VOC chose him as their Bushire broker.

When he was appointed as the Bushire broker, Natta was in residence at Bandar Abbas, but according to the Dutch he had already been trading in Bushire for two years. The Company also asked Wisschermerdas, the brother of the then Bandar Abbas broker Ottumsjent, to work jointly with Natta, but Wisschermerdas refused. David Busskens joined the project as interpreter.[109] Because of his previous contact with Bushire, it seems that Natta knew the leading Arab Madhkur family well. At least, he was more familiar to the head of the family than David Busskens. On 15 October 1737, Shaykh Madhkur returned from Shiraz and the Dutch resident Schoonderwoerd sent Natta to welcome him and to request an audience. The audience took place later that day; and Schoonderwoerd attended with David Busskens.[110]

In the northern Gulf, the Dutch prioritized sales at Basra. Bushire only occasionally received supplies according to the demand. Natta would then engage in trade there at a commission rate of 1 per cent.[111] In Bushire, too, the EIC's local agent posed a serious obstacle to Dutch trade. The agent was Agha ʿAbdi, a powerful Iranian merchant. At the close of the 1730s Agha ʿAbdi was known as the chief broker for all imported Iranian commodities. While acting as broker for Muhammad Taqi Khan, the commander of the Iranian flotilla, he schemed to take over the brokership from the Dutch. He obtained a royal order appointing him as broker for the VOC in an attempt to unseat the incumbent broker Natta.[112] By July 1743 Agha ʿAbdi also became broker for the EIC.[113] Unfortunately the English records are almost completely silent about this merchant (the EIC did not have a trading post in Bushire until 1763), but the VOC left an account of how his activities spoiled their trade. Referencing the poor sales for the period between 1 September 1745 and 31 March 1746, the Bushire factors noted that, as much as the government extortion and the commotion caused by Nadir Shah's interference in pearl fishery frustrated their business, an Armenian merchant named 'Mazok' and the English broker (*Engelse makelaar*) Agha ʿAbdi had been conducting 'illegal trade' (*morshandel*). Furthermore, the price of old copper had increased to as much as 18 *mahmudi*s per *man*.[114]

Kharg: An Armenian settlement

In early 1753 the VOC received an invitation from Mir Nasir, the Arab ruler of Bandar Rig, to come to trade at Kharg Island. Later that year they settled on the island, and in the north-eastern corner, the Company established a solid commercial base with their own fortress, *Mosselsteyn*. In 1762 the Dutch factory was manned by 186 men. Most of them were military men, including 100 soldiers and nineteen gunners.[115] On the other hand, the island was also inhabited by diverse communities, such as Arabs, Iranians, Banians, Armenians, Georgians and Africans.[116] It is possible that under the Dutch, Kharg owed much of its economic vitality to those communities, especially the Armenians.

Dutch records say that the Kharg factory used a broker, without specifying who exactly. The picture gathered from sporadic evidence is that the broker was a merchant who had close business ties with Bandar Rig. In reference to an uncollected sum of 30,024 guilders 15 stivers, in 1755 the Kharg factory wrote that this was caused by Mir Nasir's unexpected death in July 1754. Shortly before he died, they had granted his request to borrow this amount of Company goods on three-month credit. He would send them to Shiraz and thereby attract passing caravans to Bandar Rig. The factory wanted to encourage the trade and to keep on good terms with Mir Nasir, so they accepted the proposal. They thought they would have opportunities to reclaim the money that had been risked. They commented that Mir Nasir would promote trade in his port and consequently receive tolls to settle the account. Besides, the tolls that the inland merchants had to pay at Bandar Rig for the goods brought from Kharg always went into the hands of the Company's broker.[117] The broker being accountable for the toll revenue from Bandar Rig suggests that he acted as the customs master (*shahbandar*) of the port. It may be assumed that the Kharg broker was Armenian, given the fact that scores of Julfa Armenians took shelter in Bandar Rig after the Afghan invasion and founded a solid commercial base there. What is more, the VOC had several contacts among these Armenians before they came to Kharg.[118]

The Armenian community increased their presence by repeatedly incorporating Armenian merchants from the Iranian littoral, in particular from Bandar Rig. In late 1754 many inhabitants of Bandar Rig and Bushire, fearful of the approaching sounds of battle from the interior, took refuge in Kharg. According to the Dutch, this included all the Armenians from those ports. As a result, the number of Armenian citizens on the island increased to 100, including ten wealthy merchants who traded with Bengal, Coromandel and Surat.[119] Two years later the Dutch reported again that, due to the rapid decline of Bandar Rig, both the Armenian and the Iranian merchants had left; those who had some capital tried to flee to Kharg or Basra. Bandar Rig would dwindle to a fishing village within a year.[120] In 1762 the Armenian settlement consisted of 115 to 200 people. They raised enough money to build a small church there, served by two Armenians priests. The supervisor of the church, 'Auweet de Oannes', acted as the VOC interpreter at Kharg.[121]

Banian intermediary at Muscat

The significant rise of the Muscat sugar trade was key occurrence within the post-Safavid restructuring of the Gulf market. Muscat's resident merchant community mainly comprised Arabs, Indians, Iranians and Armenians. Among the richest were the Indians, especially the 'Sindis' and 'Banians'. According to C. Allen, the 'Sindis' were the first 'Banians' to settle in Muscat, and they belonged to the Hindu caste of Bhatias from Thatta in Sind.[122] When the VOC sent trial cargoes there in 1756 and 1757, the Company used the 'Banian' community there.

The Dutch voyages reflected the strong recovery of Muscat's mercantile society after Nadir Shah's invasion of Oman in the late 1730s and the 1740s. After a failed attempt in 1738, Nadir's troops took Muscat in 1742, which had negative consequences for the port's mercantile life.[123] However, the commotion seems to have generated an alternative trading venue in Barka. Lying 45 miles west of Muscat, Barka also encountered Iranian intruders but survived owing to the heroic resistance offered by the Bu Saʿid chief Ahmad b. Saʿid.[124] In mid-1747 the Multani Banian and Banksallee in Bandar Abbas sailed across the Gulf to seek refuge in Barka. The market in Barka was monetarily well equipped. Later that year the

EIC factors in Bandar Abbas, who were then in dire need of cash to maintain the factory, sent some old copper to Barka for valuation.[125]

By 1750, however, bustling activity had returned to Muscat, which was now under the Bu Saʿid regime. The town welcomed a wave of immigrants. In 1751 the EIC wrote that Banians in Kirman intended to move to Muscat.[126] By 1760, a Muslim merchant family from Hyderabad, in Sind, formed a recognized clearing house in Muscat. In October 1761 the VOC reported that they could not collect debt from their wool agent in Kirman, 'Oanes Katjeh', because of the default of Mir Hassan Beg (Mir Hassen Beek), who was the head of the '*sayyids*' (*sayds*) of the 'Memeny' family in Hyderabad (Heyderabaat). Over a long period of time, they said, many rich merchants of the Memeny family who lived in Muscat and Surat and elsewhere had annually sent large sums of money to the head of the family and his followers at home in exchange for cheques drawn against him. In recent years, however, too many cheques had been made out to him, and the merchants refused to accept them. As a result, Oanes, who was banking on one such cheque, was unable to pay his debt.[127] The EIC also mentioned the same unrest. In September of the following year, Nasir Khan, the ruler of Lar and also a creditor of the insolvent '*sayyid*' Hassan Beg (Seid Hossan Beg), ordered his brother Jaʿfar Khan, ruler of Bandar Abbas, to seize the goods belonging to some Hyderabadi merchants who had arrived from Muscat and were bound to Kirman.[128]

Nothing has been written about this particular Muslim family, but the fact that the family expanded their business network from Hyderabad seems to suggest that they belonged to the Lawatis, a renowned Shiʿi business community in Muscat, who traced their historical origins to Hyderabad. However, Allen thinks that the first Lawati migration occurred a little later. He claims that the Lawatis from Sind and the Bhatias from Kutch increasingly settled in Muscat from the 1780s and replaced the Bhatias from Sind, who had moved to other Gulf ports, such as Bahrain.[129]

The first Dutch attempt at trade there took place in January 1756, when Schoonderwoerd stopped at Muscat, with surplus goods from Bandar Abbas, on his way to Batavia, but he barely participated in the unfamiliar commercial environment.[130] What Schoonderwoerd did receive was an invitation from the governor of Sind (*raja of gouverneur van Dieuel, de hoofdplaats van Sindise Kust*) to trade in his land through a Banian resident in Muscat named Anand Ram (Annandaram). According to Schoonderwoerd, Anand Ram was the 'son of the former and old broker of the Company Natta' (*zoon van 's Comp[agnies] gewezen oude makelaar Natta*) Natta, i.e. the Bushire broker Natta, which suggests that his family had a business network that linked Bushire, Muscat and Sind.[131]

In July 1756 Batavia ordered Captain de Nijsz of *de Marienbosch* and Captain Brahé of *'t Pasgeld* to sail to Muscat with cargoes of various goods, mainly sugar. On the advice of Schoonderwoerd, who had arrived in Batavia a month earlier, the authorities also directed Brahé to set course to Sind if he did not find it feasible to trade at Muscat. As for exportable bullion and copper, the captains were authorized to accept only *keyzerdaalder*s, rupees, golden rupees, Venetian ducats and copper ware at fixed prices. Both ships left Batavia on 19 July 1756; *de Marienbosch* reached Muscat first, on 27 August 1756.[132]

Soon after his arrival de Nijsz visited the BuʿSaʿid imam Ahmad at a place called 'Bocca', which was one day away from Muscat by boat.[133] There de Nijsz used 'our Banian' who could interpret Dutch and Arabic to negotiate with the imam about trade conditions.[134] The identity of 'our Banian' was probably the broker (*makelaar*) at Muscat, 'Faram Ram'.[135] In subsequent correspondence the broker's name is spelled 'Noerotaem Anak Ram Djiendil Djoezie', who must be Narottam Ramchandar Joshi/Raoij, whom the EIC had also recruited as their broker at Muscat around this time. According to Onley, he was a Gujarati Brahmin Banian.[136] Narottam sold the imported Company goods and procured items requested for export.[137] Most of the goods were not sold until February 1757.[138] Yet the broker requested that Batavia continue to send 100 canisters of candy sugar and 2,000 canisters of castor sugar (about 0.6 million pounds in total).[139]

When Brahé reached Muscat on 19 September 1756 he decided to steer *'t Pasgeld* to Sind.[140] Following Schoonderwoerd's advice he then appointed the aforementioned Banian Anand Ram (*een Benjaanse makelaar genaamd Annamderamme*) to accompany him as broker.[141] The Dutch communicated with him in Portuguese.[142] Brahé arrived at Karachi on 8(?) November and one month later sailed up the Indus River to a market town called 'Oranga Bander', where he rented a house in which to settle. He left for Batavia in April 1757.[143] During this period Anand Ram tirelessly invited wholesale merchants to meet the Dutch party for trade. He also travelled to other trading towns, such as Thatta, to find possible buyers for the imported merchandise. He mediated deals between the Dutch and some important merchants (indigenous Banians and Afghans) for the trade of castor sugar. His commission was 2 per cent. Furthermore, he played the important role of introducing the party to members of the local ruling elite. In spite of the crucial roles that Anand Ram played, Brahé was unhappy with the quality of the broker's service. He had a strong suspicion that Anand Ram had also received payments from the local merchants to mislead the Dutch. He concluded that, if he had a good interpreter and a trustworthy broker, he could have accumulated more profits from the trade of sugar and spices.[144] All these facts confirm that while doing business in Muscat, Anand Ram was certainly an important part of the merchant world of Sind.

De Nijsz's disheartening results notwithstanding, Batavia decided to continue the Muscat project and ordered Captain Rood of *de Barbara Theodra* to sail to Muscat. They needed to get rid of the ever-growing sugar stocks, and one important consideration for Batavia must have been that they had a reliable broker in Muscat. After de Nijsz's voyage, Narottam sent presents to the Governor General of Batavia, Jacob Mossel, requesting that he reappoint him as the VOC broker for the next voyage. Mossel honoured his request and instructed him to sell the cargo of *de Barbara Theodra* at higher prices.[145]

The ship arrived at Muscat on 21 September 1757. This time the market was so active that Rood sold the whole cargo by the end of November.[146] Sugar trade was especially satisfactory (Chapter 3). Narottam was definitely a key player in this development. On 25 September, when Rood sold 800 to 1,000 canisters of castor sugar on three months' credit, the broker readily guaranteed the payment in conjunction with the governor of Muscat (*wakil*), an act to encourage the VOC to trade at Muscat.[147] Like Anand Ram in Sind, Narrotam also earned 2 per cent of the total sales.[148]

Despite the improved situation, the High Government discontinued shipping sugar to Muscat and Sind due to a serious concern that the project was prejudicial to the factories at Kharg and Surat. Even so, Narottam continued to be active in Muscat. In 1760, in reply to his request, Batavia wrote that they would not resume trade, but he could easily get what he needed for Muscat from Kharg or Cochin.[149] As the EIC broker, Narottam was expected to supply intelligence while occasionally transmitting news from the Bombay Presidency to the English settlements in the Gulf and vice versa.[150] Narottam also formed an integral part of the information network of Mancherji Khurshedji, the VOC's Parsi broker at Surat. In 1766, when the Kharg factory was conquered by Mir Muhanna, Narottam wrote about it to Nanna Bhai and Basroorji, the agents of Mancherji at Bombay, who then notified their master.[151] According to the Dutch at Cochin, Narottam sent the same news to their Jewish broker Ezechiel Rahabi.[152] Along with his father David, Ezechiel became associated with the VOC in the early eighteenth century, and until his death in October 1771, he held a dominant position in brokering Company imported goods, notably Javanese sugar.[153] These facts show that in the eighteenth century the Company brokers who sold large amounts of sugar in the Arabian Sea kept in close contact.

In 1777, Dutch private traders, backed by the High Government, resumed voyages to Muscat. The voyages continued until 1793, when Muscat became the scene of the Anglo-French war (Chapter 5). How the Dutch traders took part in the Muscat market during this phase is unknown, but it is almost certain that they also made good use of Narottam as their broker. In September 1796, to show his loyalty to the EIC, Narottam wrote to Bombay that he had given up working for the French and the Dutch, even though this would mean a considerable decrease in his income.[154] In 1798, however, the EIC discharged Narottam, accusing him of divided loyalties as well as deceiving them financially. The function of Company broker was then taken over by Vishandas, a Bhatia working for the Muscat customs house.[155]

This chapter has probed the relationships between the VOC and their local intermediaries in the Persian Gulf and its interior after the Safavid period. It has illuminated how important local agents were for the 'longevity' of the Company. Their relationships should not be overly romanticized: they went through many difficulties and uncertainties, some of which seriously jeopardized Company trade in the region, notably the bankruptcy of the Banian brokers at Bandar Abbas (the Rauwels), and the diminishing role of the Banian brokers at Isfahan (the Kiemtsjant family). However, the crisis also reveals an active supporting cast of players. At Bandar Abbas, the Dutch could rely on other business associates to carry on trade, including the family of Auwanees, a Julfa Armenian who was the Company's wool collector at Kirman.

More importantly, the VOC could leverage their associations with the Banian and Armenian communities to take part in the alternative markets of Basra, Bushire, Muscat and Sind. Their complex relationships in these places demonstrate the resilience of the local merchant communities and their role in the restructuring of the Gulf market. The case of the first Basra broker, Moeltjent, indicates the increased participation of the Banians from Bandar Abbas and Isfahan after the Afghan revolution. The treacherous Banian agency at Basra was underpinned by the participation of the Sahids, another Julfa Armenian family, who had served the Dutch at Isfahan as interpreters since the Safavid period. The former clerk of Kiemtsjant, Natta and his son Anand Ram were highly mobile merchants who helped the Company trade in Bushire, Muscat and Sind. The scene at the Kharg local agency is not very clear, but it might well have included Julfa Armenian merchants previously known to the Company. To conclude, the local merchant communities, particularly the Banians and Armenians, strove to adjust to the changing economic circumstances and this enabled the Dutch project to trade Javanese sugar for bullion in the Gulf to persist during the eighteenth century.

CONCLUSION

In September 1889, the British statesman George Nathaniel Curzon travelled to Iran. Although he only stayed for little over three months, it was long enough to convince him that the country consumed 'enormous quantities' of sugar. Before his visit, he read Chardin, but his own writings did not repeat Chardin's question concerning the origin of cane sugar. As a young, ambitious statesman, he described how the Iranian sugar market was attracting rival countries. He reported on the cut-throat competition between French and Russian sugar producers, who were each trying to dominate the market. 'Formerly sugar used to be imported from India, Java, and Mauritius; but Marseilles and Astrakhan are now the chief ports of supply'.[1]

While Curzon's report conveys a sense of the 'Great Game' that was growing in intensity across the region, the nineteenth-century shift from Asia to what we call Europe as the main sugar supplier did not, as Chaudhuri has claimed, merely indicate the arrival of Western industrial capitalism.[2] Rather, the shift was the result of a long-term development in 'demand' – the relationship between trade and consumption – which began in the seventeenth century. This study has shown that in the Persian Gulf, the eighteenth-century relationship between sugar imports and their consumption paved the way for the nineteenth-century's increased inflows of American and Russian sugar.

It is easy to highlight dreary images of Iranian society as a result of the toppling of the Safavid dynasty: the intrusion of bordering powers, repeated power struggles and the consequent fiscal exploitation of the population. However, a more nuanced and precise characterization of the aftermath of the fall of the empire would be as time when successful methods of trade emerged. I have shown that the various powers who rose after the Afghan conquest – the Durranis, the *Mamluk*s, the Qajars, the Zands and the Bu Saʿids, among others – capitalized on the political turbulence to import sugar supplies through their territories. As for Iran's political economy, Matthee argues that with the rise of the Zands, Iran's 'centre of gravity' moved south for the first time since the Buyid period (932–1062). However, even though we think of the Safavid capital, Isfahan, as the centre of Iran's political economy, sugar acted as a centrifugal force and new centres of politics and economy appeared in areas that used to be on the periphery, expanding to the east (Durranis), west (*Mamluk*s), north (Qajars) and south (Zands and Bu Saʿids).[3]

Pomeranz has stressed an uncanny resemblance between eighteenth-century European and Chinese (and Japanese to a lesser extent) urban sugar consumption; privileging the latter conveys a 'world history' that contextualizes looming Western hegemony.[4] However, this notion of parity seems an anomaly when viewed from the perspective of the Persian Gulf and the surrounding regions. The ruling elites of the post-Safavid period continued to consume sugar, forming core sites of active urban sugar consumption. However, the total volume of sugar consumed in those regions was limited in comparison to Europe and East Asia. But this makes it all the more interesting that during this century, markets in the Caspian and Iraq grew to the point that they attracted American sugar. American sugar came through Russia or the Levant, and so Gulf trade was in fact facilitating larger processes of globalization, through which economies on different bodies of water – including the Atlantic Ocean, the North Sea, the Baltic Sea, the Mediterranean, the Indian Ocean and the China Seas – became closely intertwined.

The century's tremendous mercantile efforts to maximize all possible economic gains from sugar was important for the continuation of sugar consumption. Over the years, it seems, the Dutch perception of the seventeenth century as its 'Golden Age' has created the sense that there was an eighteenth-century economic crisis in the Persian Gulf. The 'decline' of the Dutch East India Company (*Verenigde Oostindische Compagnie* [VOC]) reflected strenuous competition with other sugar suppliers, especially the English and French, for exportable gold, silver and copper. Of particular importance in this development was the rise of copper as an alternative medium for payment in trans-regional trade. Not only did these nations import Bengali, Chinese, and later Javanese, sugar from Indian ports, they also offered their sugar to local wholesale merchants at cheap prices and on long credit terms, and accepted copper for export to India.

Sugar's link with bullion and copper supported 'demand' during this time, and the local merchants who engaged in bullion and copper trade for sugar suppliers served as crucial catalysts. For the VOC, it was always vital to rely on the local merchant communities, especially Banians and Julfa Armenians, to participate in trade. Markovits ascribes the socioeconomic coherence of the Hindu merchants in Sind to personnel (men and sometimes women), credit, information and goods circulating within the network. In the case of Julfa Armenians, Aslanian adds another element: priests. On the other hand, as Aslanian asserts, due to the nature of commerce merchants, credit and goods needed to circulate widely beyond communal boundaries and connect with coexisting networks.[5] Brokering for VOC sugar in the post-Safavid Persian Gulf reflected this and provides an overview of the interplay between different merchant group networks. The VOC's Banian agencies at Bandar Abbas and Basra endured due to an active supporting cast of players who were willing to work together, including the Armenians and the Busskens, a Dutch merchant family living in the region. In the latter half of the eighteenth century, Narottam, the principal Banian broker at Muscat, was closely linked to Mancherji Khurshedji, the VOC's Parsi broker at Surat, and Ezechiel Rahabi, the VOC's Jewish broker at Cochin.

These important findings offer valuable evidence to rethink the rise of European colonial interests in the Indian Ocean in the eighteenth century. The English set up a solid base of operation in Basra as the port rapidly developed into a major hub for sugar. They gradually enhanced their influence over the region's economy, which led to the formation of their 'Informal Empire' in the nineteenth century. The Dutch, who were kicked out of the Gulf by the English, understood that their chain colonies in the southern Indian Ocean, the Cape-Ceylon-Java line, was indispensable to their enterprise in Asia. Facing an approaching threat from the English in the north, the Dutch imposed control over these places, and into Cochin, which they regarded as the location to guard Ceylon, a key site for Dutch intra-Asian traffic. Javanese sugar was one of the few goods that the Dutch could exploit and carry on trading in the western Indian Ocean since it continued to be imported to the Persian Gulf and Gujarat. Corresponding to the rise of markets in Gujarat, Sind and the Persian Gulf, the French developed cane sugar plantations on Mauritius, which were reminiscent of those in the Caribbean, using East African slave labour. Non-European actors were also surfacing on the scene. In eighteenth-century East Africa Omani Arab merchants actively participated in the slave trade in order to develop sugar production in Mauritius. In the following century, this trade also facilitated the establishment of the Bu Sa'id's power in Zanzibar by providing clove plantations on the island with regular supplies of slave labour. To understand the situation of the Gulf Arabs, it is helpful to look at the Danes. They increased their commerce by collaborating with English traders in the latter half of the century. Their colony in Tranquebar, located on the southern shore of the Coromandel Coast, became an important site at the intersection of shipping lanes passing between the Arabian Seas and the Bay of Bengal. Uncovering the extent to which the Danish settlement was frequented by Gulf Arabs, who were pursuing sugar around the Indian Ocean, is an area for future exploration. Despite the shared, entangled political, economic and social climates of Basra, Ceylon, Cochin, Mauritius, Zanzibar and Tranquebar, colonial studies have only studied them individually, as if they underwent different processes of colonization according to nationality.[6]

To conclude, our investigation of the eighteenth-century sugar trade and consumption in the Persian Gulf has provided a picture of the impressive tenacity of Indian Ocean trade and the rulers and the merchants were active, integral participants. Because of the perceived usefulness of sugar, differing stakeholder interests were routinely compared and adjusted, producing the dynamism, as well as a flexible attitude, necessary for an unceasing flow of trade. Business intermediaries were essential. Through their mediation, the Persian Gulf was the vanguard of new socio-cultural practices within the Indian Ocean economy, thus significantly accelerating eighteenth-century globalization. This continuity paved the way for further inflows of Western investments, as the arrival of European sugar increased in the following century.

NOTES

Introduction

1 J. Chardin. *Voyages du chevalier Chardin en Perse, et autres lieux de l'Orient*, ed. L. Langlès (Paris: Le Normant, 1811), vol. 3, 304.
2 S. Mintz, *Sweetness and Power: The Place of Sugar in Modern History* (London: Penguin Books, 1986). For a recent study along this line, S. Schwarts, ed., *Tropical Babylons: Sugar and the Making of the Atlantic World, 1450–1680* (Chapel Hill: The University of North Carolina Press, 2004).
3 R. Matthee, 'The Safavid Economy as Part of the World Economy,' in *Iran and the World in the Safavid Age*, eds. W. Floor and E. Herzig (London: I.B. Tauris, 2012), 33, 34, 38–9.
4 K.N. Chaudhuri, *Asia before Europe: Economy and Civilisation of the Indian Ocean from the Rise of Islam to 1750* (Cambridge: Cambridge University Press, 1990), 384–7.
5 Anon., *Tadhkirat al-mulūk: A Manual of Ṣafavid Administration (circa 1137/1725)*, trans. and ed. V. Minorsky (Cambridge: Gibb Memorial Trust, 1943), 23–4;
L. Lockhart, *The Fall of the Ṣafavī Dynasty and the Afghan Occupation of Persia* (Cambridge: Cambridge University Press, 1958).
6 R. Savory, *Iran under the Safavids* (Cambridge: Cambridge University Press, 1980), 226–54. For a revisionist view, see A.J. Newman, *Safavid Iran: Rebirth of a Persian Empire* (London: I.B. Tauris, 2006), 104–16.
7 Among others, see Ahmad Ashraf, 'Historical Obstacles to the Development of a Bourgeoisie in Iran,' *Iranian Studies* 2, no. 2 (1969): 54–79; A. Banani, 'Reflections on the Social and Economic Structure of Safavid Persia at Its Zenith,' *Iranian Studies* 11, no. 1 (1978): 83–116; M. Keyvani, *Artisans and Guild Life in the Later Safavid Period: Contributions to the Social-Economic History of Persia* (Berlin: Klaus Schwarz Verlag, 1982), 215–43. For a critical review of the debate on Safavid economic history, E. Herzig, 'The Armenian Merchants of New Julfa, Isfahan: A Study in Pre-Modern Asian Trade' (PhD diss., University of Oxford, 1991), 11–26.
8 W. Floor, *Traditional Crafts in Qajar Iran (1800–1925)* (California: Mazda Publishers, 2003); W. Floor, *History of Bread in Iran* (Washington: Mage Publishers, 2015); W. Floor and H. Javadi, *Persian Pleasures: How Iranians Relaxed through the Centuries with Food, Drink & Drugs* (Washington: Mage Publishers, 2019); R. Matthee, *The Pursuit of Pleasure: Drugs and Stimulants in Iranian History, 1500–1900* (Princeton: Princeton University Press, 2005).
9 R. Matthee, 'A Sugar Banquet for the Shah: Anglo-Dutch Competition at the Iranian Court of Šāh Sulṭān Ḥusayn (r. 1694–1722),' *Eurasian Studies* 1–2 (2006): 195–217.
10 A. Hoseini, 'Sharbat va sharbat-khana dar gudhar-i zaman [Iran's Sherbet and Sherbet Houses in Passage of Time],' *Bagh-i nazar* 10, no. 25 (2013): 57–66.
11 T. Morikawa, 'Perushia kyūtei no wain to shābetto [Wine and Sherbet at the Persian court],' in *Shoku to bunka: Jikū o koeta shokutaku kara [Food and Culture: Eating across Space and Time]*, ed. N. Hosoda (Hokkaidō: Hokkaidōdaigaku shuppankai, 2015), 65–96.

12 Floor estimates that the Iranian sugar market doubled during the Qajar period. Floor, *Traditional Crafts in Qajar Iran*, 328–75; Matthee, *The Pursuit of Pleasure*, 254–6.
13 W. Floor, *The Afghan Occupation of Safavid Persia 1721–1729* (Paris: Association pour l'avancement des études iraniennes, 1998).
14 L. Lockhart, *Nadir Shah: A Critical Study Based Mainly upon Contemporary Sources* (London: Luzac, 1938). For re-assessments of Nadir's achievements, see E.S. Tucker, *Nadir Shah's Quest for Legitimacy in Post-Safavid Iran* (Gainesville: University Press of Florida, 2006); M. Axworthy, *The Sword of Persia: Nader Shah, from Tribal Warrior to Conquering Tyrant* (London: I.B. Tauris, 2009). For the Zands and the Durranis, see J. Perry, *Karim Khan Zand: A History of Iran, 1747–1779* (Chicago: University of Chicago Press, 1979); J. Gommans, *The Rise of the Indo-Afghan Empire c. 1710–1780* (Leiden: Brill, 1995).
15 B. Slot, *The Arabs of the Gulf 1602–1784: An Alternative Approach to the Early History of the Arab Gulf States and the Arab People of the Gulf, Mainly Based on Sources of the Dutch East India Company* (Leidschendam, 1993); Sultan ibn Muhammad al-Qasimi, *Power Struggles and Trade in the Gulf 1620–1820* (Forest Row: University of Exeter Press, 1999); W. Floor, *The Persian Gulf: The Rise of the Gulf Arabs: The Politics of Trade on the Persian Littoral 1747–1792* (Washington: Mage Publishers, 2007); W. Floor, *The Hula Arabs of the Shibkuh Coast of Iran* (Washington: Mage Publishers, 2014).
16 A. Das Gupta and M. Pearson, eds., *India and Indian Ocean: 1500–1800* (Oxford: Oxford University Press, 1999, first published in 1987); K. MacPherson, *The Indian Ocean: A History of People and the Sea* (New Delhi: Oxford University Press, 2001, first published in 1993); M. Kearney, *The Indian Ocean in World History* (New York: Routledge, 2004); M. Pearson, *The Indian Ocean* (Abingdon: Routledge, 2008, first published in 2003).
17 A. Wilson, *The Persian Gulf: An Historical Sketch from the Earliest Times to the Beginning of the Twentieth Century* (Connecticut: Hyperion Press, 1928), 171–91; J. Kelly, *Britain and the Persian Gulf 1795–1800* (Oxford: Clarendon Press, 1968), 1–61; C. Allen, 'Sayyids, Shets and Sulṭāns: Politics and Trade in Masqaṭ under the Āl Bū Saʿīd' (PhD diss., University of Washington, 1978), 33–67; R. Savory, 'A.D. 600–1800,' in *The Persian Gulf States: A General Survey*, ed. A. Cottrell (Baltimore: The Johns Hopkins University Press, 1980), 33–9; J.E. Peterson, 'Britain and the Gulf: At the Periphery of Empire,' in *The Persian Gulf in History*, ed. L.G. Potter (New York: Palgrave Macmillan, 2009), 277–93. For a classical but still influential study of the British in the Gulf, see J. Lorimer, *Gazetteer of the Persian Gulf, ʿOmān, and Central Arabia*, 2 vols. (Calcutta: Office of the Superintendent Government Printing, 1908–15).
18 A. Hakima, *History of Eastern Arabia, 1750–1800: The Rise and Development of Bahrain and Kuwait* (Beirut: Khayats, 1965).
19 T. Ricks, 'Towards a Social and Economic History of Eighteenth-Century Iran,' *Iranian Studies* 6, no. 2 (1973): 110–26; T. Ricks, 'Politics and Trade in Southern Iran and the Gulf, 1745–1765' (PhD diss., Indiana University, 1975). Recently the author has published a revision of his dissertation. T. Ricks, *Notables, Merchants, and Shaykhs of Southern Iran and Its Ports: Politics and Trade of the Persian Gulf Region, AD 1728–1789* (Piscataway, NJ: Gorgias Press, 2012).
20 A. Das Gupta, 'Introduction II: The Story,' in *India and Indian Ocean: 1500–1800*, eds. A. Das Gupta and M. Pearson (Oxford: Oxford University Press, 1999, first published in 1987), 40–1; A. Das Gupta, 'India and the Indian Ocean in the Eighteenth Century,' in *India and Indian Ocean*, 133, 137–40. Floor also discusses the northward shift of Gulf trade after the Safavid period. Floor, *The Rise of the Gulf Arabs*, xvii.

21　S. Grummon, 'The Rise and Fall of the Arab Shaykhdom of Būshire: 1750–1850' (PhD diss., Johns Hopkins University, 1985).
22　T. Abdullah, *Merchants, Mamluks, and Murder: The Political Economy of Trade in Eighteenth-Century Basra* (Albany: State University of New York Press, 2001).
23　H. Fattah, *The Politics of Regional Trade in Iraq, Arabia, and the Gulf 1745–1900* (Albany: State University of New York Press, 1997).
24　P. Risso, *Oman & Muscat: An Early Modern History* (New York: St. Martin's Press, 1986).
25　Among others, see S. Dale, *Indian Merchants and Eurasian Trade, 1600–1750* (Cambridge: Cambridge University, 1994); M. Alam, 'Trade, State Policy and Regional Change: Aspects of Mughal-Uzbek Commercial Relations, c. 1550–1750,' *Journal of the Economic and Social History of the Orient* 37, no. 3 (1994): 202–27; Gommans, *The Rise of the Indo-Afghan Empire*; S. Levi, *The Indian Diaspora in Central Asia and Its Trade, 1550–1900* (Leiden: Brill, 2002).
26　Gommans, *The Rise of the Indo-Afghan Empire*, 35–8.
27　R. Barendse, *The Western Indian Ocean in the Eighteenth Century*, vol. 1 of *Arabian Seas 1700–1763* (Leiden: Brill, 2009), 299, 301–2, 312–14.
28　For a critical overview of this argument, see B. Bhattacharya, G. Dharampal-Frick, and J. Gommans, 'Spatial and Temporal Continuities of Merchant Networks in South Asia and the Indian Ocean,' *Journal of the Economic and Social History of the Orient* 50, no. 2–3 (2007): 99–103. The revisionist scholars, though, have taken little heed of their Iranian counterparts. See L. Blussé and F. Gaastra, eds., *On the Eighteenth Century as a Category of Asian History* (Aldershot: Ashgate, 1998).
29　W. Floor, *The Economy of Safavid Persia* (Wiesbaden: Reichert Verlag, 2000), 126–33; G. Nadri, 'The Dutch Intra-Asian Trade in Sugar in the Eighteenth Century,' *International Journal of Maritime History* 20, no. 1 (2008): 63–96.
30　Floor, *The Rise of the Gulf Arabs*, 200.
31　O. Prakash, *European Commercial Enterprise in Pre-Colonial India*, part 5 of *Indian States and the Transition to Colonialism*, vol. 2 of *The New Cambridge History of India* (Cambridge: Cambridge University Press, 1998), 250.
32　Nadri and Risso note that the Arabs of Bahrain also engaged in the sugar trade in the Arabian Sea, Bay of Bengal and the Malay Archipelago. Nadri, 'The Dutch Intra-Asian Trade,' 77; Risso, *Oman and Muscat*, 80–1, 195–6, 198.
33　W. Floor, *The Persian Gulf, Dutch-Omani Relations: A Commercial & Political History 1651–1806* (Washington: Mage Publishers, 2014), 161–70.
34　Floor, *Traditional Crafts in Qajar Iran*, 332–44.
35　S. Mintz, *Sweetness and Power*, 151–8.
36　S. Mintz, *Sweetness and Power*, 166–71.
37　S. Mintz, 'Introduction,' in *Sugarlandia Revisited: Sugar and Colonialism in Asia and the Americas, 1800 to 1940*, eds. U. Bosma, J. Giusti-Cordero, and G.R. Knight (New York: Berghahn Books, 2007), 1–4. For recent studies, see E. Abbott, *Sugar: A Bittersweet History* (Toronto: Penguin Canada, 2008); M. Aronson and M. Budhos, *Sugar Changed the World: A Story of Magic, Spice, Slavery, Freedom, and Science* (Boston: Clarion Books, 2010); A.F. Smith, *Sugar: A Global History* (London: Reaktion Books, 2015); U. Bosma, *The World of Sugar: How the Sweet Stuff Transformed Our Politics, Health, and Environment over 2,000 Years* (Cambridge: The Belknap Press of Harvard University Press, 2023).

38 E. Wallerstein, *The Modern World-System*, 4 vols. (Berkeley: University of California Press, 2011).
39 J. de Vries, 'The Industrial Revolution and the Industrious Revolution,' *The Journal of Economic History* 54, no. 2 (1994): 249–70; J. de Vries, *The Industrious Revolution: Consumer Behavior and the Household Economy, 1650 to the Present* (Cambridge: Cambridge University Press, 2008).
40 E. Stols, 'The Expansion of the Sugar Market in Western Europe,' in *Tropical Babylons: Sugar and the Making of the Atlantic World, 1450–1680*, ed. S. Schwarts (Chapel Hill: The University of North Carolina Press, 2004), 237–88.
41 M. Berg, *Luxury and Pleasure in Eighteenth-Century Britain* (Oxford: Oxford University Press, 2008). An important American project 'Culture and Consumption in the Seventeenth and Eighteenth Centuries', active between 1989 and 1991, resulted in the publication of three pioneering volumes on this subject: J. Brewer and R. Porter, eds., *Consumption and the World of Goods* (London: Routledge, 1993); J. Brewer and S. Staves, eds., *Early Modern Conceptions of Property* (London: Routledge, 1995); J. Brewer and A. Bermingham, eds., *The Consumption of Culture, 1600–1800: Image, Object, Text* (London: Routledge, 1995).
42 Similar debates have come up on other luxury and exotic items such as Indian cotton textiles and Chinese porcelains. G. Riello and T. Roy, eds., *How India Clothed the World: The World of South Asian Textiles, 1500–1850* (Leiden: Brill, 2009); F. Trentmann, ed., *The Oxford Handbook of the History of Consumption* (Oxford: Oxford University Press, 2013); A. Gerritsen and G. Riello, *The Global Lives of Things: The Material Culture of Connections in the Early Modern World* (Abingdon: Routledge, 2016); P. Machado, S. Fee, and G. Campbell, eds., *Textile Trades, Consumer Cultures, and the Material Worlds of the Indian Ocean: An Ocean of Cloth* (Cham: Palgrave Macmillan, 2018).
43 T. Sato, *Sugar in the Social Life of Medieval Islam* (Leiden: Brill, 2015), 15–17.
44 C. Daniels, *Agro-Industries and Forestry: Sugarcane Technology*, part 3 of *Biology and Biological Technology*, vol. 6 of *Science and Civilization in China* (Cambridge: Cambridge University Press, 1996).
45 G. Souza, 'Hinterlands, Commodity Chains, and Circuits,' 15–47. For the concept of 'commodity chains' and its implications, see S. Topik, C. Marichal, and Z. Frank, eds., *From Silver to Cocaine: Latin American Commodity Chains and the Building of the World Economy, 1500–2000* (Durham: Duke University Press, 2006). Chinese sugar exports also stimulated cultural interactions between China and Japan. A. Matsuura, 'The Import of Chinese Sugar in the Nagasaki Junk Trade and Its Impact,' in *Copper in the Early Modern Sino-Japanese Trade*, ed. K. Nagase-Reimer (Leiden: Brill, 2016), 157–74.
46 G. Xu, 'From the Atlantic to the Manchu: Taiwan Sugar and the Early Modern World, 1630s–1720s,' *Journal of World History* 33, no. 2 (2022): 265–99.
47 K. Pomeranz, *The Great Divergence: China, Europe, and the Making of the Modern World Economy* (Oxford: Princeton University Press, 2009), 114–65.
48 K. Yao, *Satō no tōtta michi: kashi kara mita sekaishi [Sugar Road: World History Seen through Sweets]* (Fukuoka: Gen shobō, 2011). The Japanese consumption of cane sugar in sweetmeats began to develop in the sixteenth century. The Portuguese played an important role: Not only did they supply sugar from China, but they also introduced European confectionaries to Japan. Recently, M. Oka has explored similar dietary encounters in Thailand and India (Goa). M. Oka, 'Nanbanbōeki no bunkateki haikei [A Cultural Background of the Nanban Trade],' in *Nanbanbōeki to kasutera [The Nanban Trade and Kasutera]* (Nagasaki: Fukusaya, 2016), 65–99.

49 K. Sugihara, *Ajiakanbōeki no keisei to kōzō [Patterns and Development of Intra-Asian Trade]* (Kyoto: Mineruva shobō, 1996); K. Sugihara, *Sekaishi no naka no Higashiajia no kiseki [The East Asian Miracle in Global History]* (Aichi: Nagoyadaigaku shuppankai, 2020). See also T. Hamashita and H. Kawakatsu, eds., *Ajiakōekiken to Nihon kōgyōka: 1500–1900 [Intra-Asian Trade and Japanese Industrialization: 1500–1900]* (Tokyo: Riburopōto, 1991).

50 Sugihara, *Ajiakanbōeki no keisei to kōzō*, 18–19, 29–30, 70, 72–3, 77, 84, 119. Cf. G.R. Knight, *Commodities and Colonialism: The Story of Big Sugar in Indonesia, 1880–1942* (Leiden: Brill, 2013), 17–51, appendix 2; U. Bosma, *The Sugar Plantation in India and Indonesia: Industrial Production, 1770–2010* (New York: Cambridge University Press, 2013), 164–210.

51 K. Hirai, *Satō no teikoku: Nihon shokuminchi to Ajia shijō [Empire of Sugar: External Forces of Change in the Economy of Japanese Colonies]* (Tokyo: Tōkyōdaigaku shuppankai, 2017).

52 Sato, *Sugar in the Social Life*, 48–50.

53 Ibid., 166–9.

54 Ibid., 173.

55 Ibid., 75–7.

56 Floor, *The Economy of Safavid Persia*, 126.

57 Floor, *The Economy of Safavid Persia*, 184–95; E. Jacobs, *Merchant in Asia: The Trade of the Dutch East India Company during the Eighteenth Century* (Leiden: CNWS Publications, 2006), 98–9, 248; R. Matthee, W. Floor, and P. Clawson, *The Monetary History of Iran from the Safavids and the Qajars* (New York: I.B. Tauris, 2013), 139–76. Japan stopped exporting bullion in the eighteenth century, and from 1763 onwards, it imported gold and silver. R. Shimada, *The Intra-Asian Trade in Japanese Copper by the Dutch East India Company during the Eighteenth Century* (Leiden: Brill, 2006), 61–4.

58 Jacobs, *Merchant in Asia*, 116-21; G. Nadri, *Eighteenth-Century Gujarat: The Dynamics of Its Political Economy, 1750–1800* (Leiden: Brill, 2009), 122.

59 G. Souza, 'Ballast Goods: Chinese Maritime Trade in Zinc and Sugar in the Seventeenth and Eighteenth Centuries,' in *Emporia, Commodities and Entrepreneurs in Asian Maritime Trade, c. 1400–1750*, ed. R. Ptak and D. Rothermund (Stuttgart: Franz Steiner Verlag, 1991), 307–12.

60 K.N. Chaudhuri, *The Trading World of Asia and the English East India Company, 1660–1760* (Cambridge: Cambridge University Press, 1978), 70–1; G. Sood, '"Correspondence is Equal to Half a Meeting": The Composition and Comprehension of Letters in Eighteenth-Century Islamic Eurasia,' *Journal of the Economic and Social History of the Orient* 50, no. 2–3 (2007): 172–214.

61 He revised J. van Leur's 'peddling trade'. J. van Leur, *Indonesian Trade and Society: Essays in Asian Social and Economic History* (The Hague: W. van Hoeve Publishers, 1967), 133; N. Steensgaard, *The Asian Trade Revolution of the Seventeenth Century: The East India Companies and the Decline of the Caravan Trade* (Chicago: The University of Chicago Press, 1974). As Steensgaard admits, the caravan traffic to the Levant remained considerable, particularly in Iranian raw silk. Cf. R. Matthee, *The Politics of Trade in Safavid Iran: Silk for Silver, 1600–1730* (Cambridge: Cambridge University Press, 1999).

62 Dale, *Indian Merchants and Eurasian Trade*, 112–27; Levi, *The Indian Diaspora in Central Asia*, 180–222; Herzig, 'The Armenian Merchants of New Julfa,' 153–272; I. McCabe, *The Shah's Silk for Europe's Silver: The Eurasian Trade of the Julfa Armenians in Safavid Iran and India (1530–1750)* (Atlanta: Scholars Press, 1999),

199–239; S. Aslanian, *From the Indian Ocean to the Mediterranean: The Global Trade Networks of Armenian Merchants from New Julfa* (Berkeley: University of California Press, 2011), 86–201.
63 Herzig, 'The Armenian Merchants of New Julfa,' 198–9, 210–12. For the relationship between the Julfa Armenians and the EIC during the Safavid period, see R. Ferrier, 'The Armenians and the East India Company in Persia in the Seventeenth and Early Eighteenth Centuries,' *The Economic History Review* 26, no. 1 (1973): 38–62. V. Baladouni and M. Makepeace, *Armenian Merchants of the Seventeenth and Early Eighteenth Centuries: English East India Company Sources* (Philadelphia: American Philosophical Society, 1998).
64 Floor, *The Economy of Safavid Persia*, 123.
65 Among many early works, see W. Moreland, *From Akbar to Aurangzeb: A Study in Indian Economic History* (London: Macmillan, 1923).
66 M. Pearson, 'India and the Indian Ocean in the Sixteenth Century,' in *India and the Indian Ocean*, 71–93; A. Das Gupta, *Indian Merchants and the Decline of Surat c. 1700–1750* (New Delhi: Manohar Publishers, 1994, first published in 1979); K. Leonard, 'The "Great Firm" Theory of the Decline of the Mughal Empire,' *Comparative Studies in Society and History* 21, no. 2 (1979): 151–67; S. Subrahmanyam and C. Bayly, 'Portfolio Capitalists and the Political Economy of Early Modern India,' *The Indian Economic and Social History Review* 25, no. 4 (1988): 401–24.
67 R. Matthee, 'Politics and Trade in Late Safavid Iran: Commercial Crisis and Government Reaction under Shah Solayman (1666–1694)' (PhD diss., University of California Los Angeles, 1991); R. Matthee, *The Politics of Trade in Safavid Iran*; R. Matthee, 'Merchants in Safavid Iran: Participants and Perceptions,' *Journal of Early Modern History* 4, no. 3 (2000): 254–63; R. Klein, 'Trade in the Safavid Port City Bandar Abbas and the Persian Gulf (ca. 1600–1680): A Study of Selected Aspects' (PhD diss., University of London, 1993–4), 67–115; Floor, *The Economy of Safavid Persia*, 27–64; W. Floor, *A Political and Economic History of Five Port Cities 1500–1730* (Washington: Mage Publishers, 2006), 237–322, 429–77.
68 Matthee, *The Politics of Trade in Safavid Iran*, 7–9, 63, 73–4, 89.
69 Floor, *A Political and Economic History*, 312.
70 Matthee, 'Merchants in Safavid Iran,' 246–8.
71 A. Qaisar, 'The Role of Brokers in Medieval India,' *The Indian Historical Review* 1, no. 2 (1974): 224–5.
72 Dale, *Indian Merchants and Eurasian Trade*, 55–64.
73 Floor, *The Economy of Safavid Persia*, 21, 24.
74 J. Onley, 'Indian Communities in the Persian Gulf, c. 1500–1947,' in *The Persian Gulf in Modern Times: People, Ports and History*, ed. L.G. Potter (New York: Palgrave Macmillan, 2014), 240–3.
75 M. Haneda, 'Les compagnies des Indes orientales et les interprètes de Bandar ʿAbbās,' *Eurasian Studies* 1–2 (2006): 175–93.
76 P. Good, *The East India Company in Persia: Trade and Cultural Exchange in the Eighteenth Century* (London: I.B. Tauris, 2022), 73–95, 127–51.
77 W. Floor, 'The Persian Economy in the Eighteenth Century: A Dismal Record,' in *Crisis, Collapse, Militarism and Civil War*, ed. M. Axworthy (Oxford: Oxford University Press, 2018), 125–50.
78 For a vivid illustration of this point, see S. Subrahmanyam, *Three Ways to Be Alien: Travails & Encounters in the Early Modern World* (Waltham: Brandeis University Press, 2011).

79 L. Bes, *The Heirs of Vijayanagara: Court Politics in Early Modern South India* (Leiden: Leiden University Press, 2022); M. Chaiklin, *Cultural Commerce and Dutch Commercial Culture: The Influence of European Material Culture on Japan, 1700–1850* (Leiden: CNWS, 2003); M. Laver, *The Dutch East India Company in Early Modern Japan: Gift Giving and Diplomacy* (London: Bloomsbury Academic, 2020); G. van Meersbergen, *Ethnography and Encounter: The Dutch and English in Seventeenth-Century South Asia* (Leiden: Brill, 2022); B. Ruangsilp, *Dutch East India Company Merchants at the Court of Ayutthaya: Dutch Perceptions of the Thai Kingdom, c. 1604–1765* (Leiden: Brill, 2007); N. Um, *Shipped but Not Sold: Material Culture and the Social Protocols of Trade during Yemen's Age of Coffee* (Honolulu: University of Hawai'i Press, 2017); C. Viallé, '"To Capture Their Favor": On Gift-Giving by the VOC,' in *Mediating Netherlandish Art and Material Culture in Asia*, ed. Th.D. Kaufmann and M. North (Amsterdam: Amsterdam University Press, 2014), 291–320; M. Vink, *Encounters on the Opposite Coast: The Dutch East India Company and the Nayaka State of Madurai in the Seventeenth Century* (Leiden: Brill, 2015). See also Z. Biedermann, A. Gerritsen, and G. Riello, eds., *Global Gifts: The Material Culture of Diplomacy in Early Modern Eurasia* (Cambridge: Cambridge University Press, 2018).
80 Das Gupta, 'India and the Indian Ocean,' 139.

Chapter 1

1 K.N. Chaudhuri, *Trade and Civilisation in the Indian Ocean: An Economic History from the Rise of Islam to 1750* (Cambridge: Cambridge University Press, 1985), 16–17; K.N. Chaudhuri, *Asia before Europe: Economy and Civilisation of the Indian Ocean from the Rise of Islam to 1750* (Cambridge: Cambridge University Press, 1990), 159, 180–1.
2 As of 1670, the EIC's share in the customs revenue of Bandar Abbas was fixed at 1,000 *tuman*s per year. W. Floor, *A Political and Economic History of Five Port Cities 1500–1730* (Washington: Mage Publishers, 2006), 312–14. According to Khalifa, the English continued to receive their share of customs after the Safavid period. K.K. al-Khalifa, 'Commerce and Conflict: The English East India Company Factories in the Gulf, 1700–47' (PhD diss., University of Essex, 1988), 19–20, 99, 100.
3 Floor, *A Political and Economic History*, 250–3.
4 As with the EIC in Bandar Abbas, the Portuguese were entitled to a 50 per cent share in the customs revenue of Bandar Kong. Floor, *A Political and Economic History*, 429–36.
5 W. Floor, *The Economy of Safavid Persia* (Wiesbaden: Reichert Verlag, 2000), 441–2; R. Klein, 'Trade in the Safavid Port City Bandar Abbas and the Persian Gulf (ca. 1600–1680): A Study of Selected Aspects' (PhD diss., University of London, 1993–94), 114.
6 Floor, *A Political and Economic History*, 436–8; Klein, 'Trade in the Safavid Port City,' 110.
7 Floor, *The Economy of Safavid Persia*, 27–64; Floor, *A Political and Economic History*, 281–2.
8 Floor, *A Political and Economic History*, 439–41; Klein, 'Trade in the Safavid Port City,' 109–10.

9 Floor, *A Political and Economic History*, 291–3, 296–304; Klein, 'Trade in the Safavid Port City,' 111–14.
10 R. Matthee, *Persia in Crisis: Safavid Decline and the Fall of Isfahan* (London: I.B. Tauris, 2012), 227–35.
11 Anon., *Tadhkirat al-mulūk: A Manual of Ṣafavid Administration (circa 1137/1725)*, trans. and ed. V. Minorsky (Cambridge: Gibb Memorial Trust, 1943), 23–4; L. Lockhart, *The Fall of the Ṣafavī Dynasty and the Afghan Occupation of Persia* (Cambridge: Cambridge University Press, 1958).
12 S. Mintz, *Sweetness and Power: The Place of Sugar in Modern History* (London: Penguin Books, 1986); J. de Vries, *The Industrious Revolution: Consumer Behavior and the Household Economy, 1650 to the Present* (Cambridge: Cambridge University Press, 2008).
13 A.J. Newman, *Safavid Iran: Rebirth of a Persian Empire* (London: I.B. Tauris, 2006), 114–15.
14 Matthee, *Persia in Crisis*, xxi–xxx.
15 Ibid., 6.
16 Floor, *The Economy of Safavid Persia*, 64, 197; R. Matthee, 'The Safavid Economy as Part of the World Economy,' in *Iran and the World in the Safavid Age*, ed. W. Floor and E. Herzig (London: I.B. Tauris, 2012), 31–47; Matthee, *Persia in Crisis*, 4–8.
17 W. Floor, *The Persian Gulf: Links with the Hinterland: Bushehr, Borazjan, Kazerun, Banu Ka'b, & Bandar Abbas* (Washington: Mage Publishers, 2011), 251–93.
18 J. Fryer, *A New Account of East-India and Persia, in VIII Letters: Being Nine Years Travels, Begun 1672 and Finished 1681* (London: R.R. for Ri. Chiswell, 1698), 293, 405.
19 J. Chardin, *Voyages du chevalier Chardin en Perse, et autres lieux de l'Orient*, ed. L. Langlès (Paris: Le Normant, 1811), vol. 4, 44–5.
20 R. Matthee, 'A Sugar Banquet for the Shah: Anglo-Dutch Competition at the Iranian Court of Šāh Sulṭān Ḥusayn (r. 1694–1722),' *Eurasian Studies*, 1–2 (2006): 195–217.
21 Nationaal Archief, Den Haag (NL-HaNA), Verenigde Oostindische Compagnie (VOC), nummer toegang 1.04.02, inventarisnummer 1100, diary, J. Smidt, fol. 301r-v.
22 Shiraz, for instance, produced preserves with grapes and vinegar. J. de Thévenot, *Suite du Voyage de Levant* (Paris: Charles Angot, 1674), 243–4. For the ways of extracting sugar from grapes and dates, G.A. Olivier, *Voyage dans l'Empire Othoman, l'Égypte et la Perse* (Paris: H. Agasse, 1801–7), vol. 5, 283; J. Taylor, *Travels from England to India, in the Year 1789 by Way of the Tyrol, Venice, Scandaroon, Aleppo, and over the Great Desert to Bussora* (London: S. Low, 1799), vol. 2, 211, 220.
23 At the banquet, coffee was served to Della Valle because he could not drink wine. P. Della Valle, *Der voortreffelyke reizen van de deurluchtige reiziger, Pietro Della Valle, edelman van Romen*, trans. J. Glazemaker (Amsterdam: A. Wolfgang and J. Rieuwertsz., 1664), vol. 2, 81–4.
24 A. Olearius, *Vermehrte newe Beschreibung der muscowitischen und persischen Reyse* (Tübingen: Max Niemeyer Verlag, 1971), 425.
25 R. Klein, 'Trade in the Safavid Port City,' 393.
26 C. de Bruyn, *Reizen over Moskovië door Persië en Indië* (Amsterdam: Rudolph en Gerard Wetstein, Joannes Oosterwyk, Hendrik van de Gaete, 1714), 176.
27 Fryer, *A New Account of East-India*, 398.
28 Klein, 'Trade in the Safavid Port City,' 404.

29 'eine Schüssel mit Zuckermandeln, worunter sich roter und weißer Zucker befand'. E. Kaempfer, *Die Reisetagebücher Engelbert Kaempfers*, ed. K. Meier-Lemgo (Wiesbaden: Franz Steiner Verlag, 1968), 45.
30 De Bruyn, *Reizen over Moskovië*, 131.
31 R. Matthee, 'Politics and Trade in Late Safavid Iran: Commercial Crisis and Government Reaction under Shah Solayman (1666–1694)' (PhD diss., University of California Los Angeles, 1991), 394–5.
32 At that time, the sugar used in the caliph's kitchen was produced in the alluvial plain of Mesopotamia and southern Iran. T. Sato, *Sugar in the Social Life of Medieval Islam* (Leiden: Brill, 2015), 18–22, 142–7.
33 Klein, 'Trade in the Safavid Port City,' 393; W.Ph. Coolhaas, ed., *Generale missiven van Gouverneurs-Generaal en Raden aan Heren XVII der Verenigde Oostindische Compagnie* (The Hague: Martinus Nijhoff, 1964), vol. 2, 39.
34 Floor, *A Political and Economic History*, 497–597; R. Matthee, 'Boom and Bust: The Port of Basra in the Sixteenth and Seventeenth Centuries,' in *The Persian Gulf in History*, ed. L. Potter (New York: Palgrave Macmillan, 2009), 105–27.
35 For the development of Muscat trade, see C. Allen, 'Sayyids, Shets and Sulṭāns: Politics and Trade in Masqaṭ under the Āl Bū Saʿīd' (PhD diss., University of Washington, 1978), 7–32; Klein, 'Trade in the Safavid Port City,' 121–33; W. Floor, *The Persian Gulf, Dutch-Omani Relations: A Commercial & Political History 1651–1806* (Washington: Mage Publishers, 2014), 127.
36 Floor, *A Political and Economic History*, 351–5. For the concept and structures of the imamate of Oman, see J.C. Wilkinson, *The Imamate Tradition of Oman* (Cambridge: Cambridge University Press, 1987).
37 Floor, *Dutch-Omani Relations*, 120–7.
38 Ibid., 191; NL-HaNA, VOC, 1.04.02, inv.nr. 1304, report, Georg Wilmson, 20 February 1674, fol. 487r.
39 Klein, 'Trade in the Safavid Port City,' 392.
40 Chardin, *Voyages*, vol. 4, 22.
41 J. Hanway, *An Historical Account of the British Trade over the Caspian Sea with a Journal of Travels from London Through Russia into Persia, and Back Again Through Russia, Germany, and Holland* (Dublin: William Smith and Richard James, 1754), vol. 1, 144–5.
42 Lockhart, *The Fall of the Ṣafavī Dynasty*, 8–11.
43 The Sarhads, a powerful Armenian family, entertained Chardin in Julfa before his departure for Bandar Abbas. Chardin, *Voyages*, vol. 8, 178–90. The VOC's Banian brokers at Bandar Abbas entertained de Bruyn with a 'sugar banquet' (*suikerbanket*) treat in a village close to the port. De Bruyn, *Reizen over Moskovië*, 405.
44 R. du Mans, *Estat de la Perse en 1660* (Paris: Ernest Leroux, 1890), 216.
45 H. Walcher and Habibollah Zanjani, 'Isfahan iii. Population,' *Encyclopædia Iranica*, last modified 30 March 2012.
46 R. Matthee, *The Pursuit of Pleasure: Drugs and Stimulants in Iranian History, 1500–1900* (Princeton: Princeton University Press, 2005), 256. A.K.S. Lambton notes that tea and sugar were the only luxuries available to the peasant. A. Lambton, *Landlord and Peasant in Persia: A Study of Land Tenure and Land Revenue Administration* (London: Oxford University Press, 1953), 389.
47 Anon., *Tadhkirat al-mulūk*, 68–9 (English translation), 52 (manuscript).
48 E. Kaempfer, *Am Hofe des persischen Grosskönings (1684–85): Das erste Buch der Amoenitates exoticae*, trans. W. Hintz (Leipzig: K.F. Koehler Verlag, 1940), 118;

E. Kaempfer, *Amoenitatum exoticarum politico-physico-medicarum fasciculi V: quibus continentur variae relationes, observationes et descriptiones rerum Persicarum et ulterioris Asiae* (Lemgoviae: Typis & impensis Henrici Wilhelmi Meyeri, 1712), 121–2.
49 NL-HaNA, VOC, 1.04.02, inv.nr. 2448, diary, J. Brand and I. de Crane, Bandar Abbas to Isfahan, pp. 1559–60.
50 Floor, *The Economy of Safavid Persia*, 126; Sato, *Sugar in the Social Life*, 18–22.
51 Portuguese Hormuz imported sugar from Goa, and some of it might have been travelled on to Iranian cities. J. Aubin, 'Le royaume d'Ormuz au début du XVIe siècle,' *Mare Luso-Indicum* 2 (1973): 166–8.
52 Klein, 'Trade in the Safavid Port City,' 377.
53 Floor, *The Economy of Safavid Persia*, 127–8, 131.
54 O. Prakash, *The Dutch East India Company and the Economy of Bengal, 1630–1720* (Delhi: Oxford University Press, 1988), 173.
55 Klein, 'Trade in the Safavid Port City,' 376–82.
56 Floor, *The Economy of Safavid Persia*, 131.
57 Klein, 'Trade in the Safavid Port City,' 406.
58 Klein, 'Trade in the Safavid Port City,' 408–9.
59 W. Floor, 'Sugar,' *Encyclopædia Iranica*, last modified 20 July 2009.
60 NL-HaNA, VOC, 1.04.02, inv.nr. 1559, letter from Bandar Abbas to Batavia, 2 August 1693, fols. 715v–6r.
61 NL-HaNA, VOC, 1.04.02, inv.nr. 1603, letter from Bandar Abbas to Batavia, 1 July 1699, fol. 1863r.
62 NL-HaNA, VOC, 1.04.02, inv.nr. 1571, letter from Bandar Abbas to Batavia, 24 June 1695, pp. 105–7.
63 NL-HaNA, VOC, 1.04.02, inv.nr. 1564, letter from Bandar Abbas to Batavia, 15 May 1696, fols. 1772r–v.
64 The VOC's financial year began on 1 September and ended on 31 August the following year.
65 NL-HaNA, VOC, 1.04.02, inv.nr. 1763, annual sales statement, Bandar Abbas, 1706–7, pp. 336–41; VOC, 1.04.02, inv.nr. 1753, annual sales statement, 1707–8, Bandar Abbas, fols. 280v–3r. For the wholesale prices of those varieties during 1646–88, see Klein, 'Trade in the Safavid Port City,' 396–400.
66 NL-HaNA, VOC, 1.04.02, inv.nr. 1564, letter from Bandar Abbas to The Netherlands, 14 June 1696, fol. 1755v.
67 NL-HaNA, VOC, 1.04.02, inv.nr. 1747 1, letter from Bandar Abbas to The Netherlands, 31 July 1706, pp. 71, 74, 77, 79–80; VOC, 1.04.02, inv.nr. 1747 1, annual sales statement, Bandar Abbas, 1705–6, pp. 372–4.
68 NL-HaNA, VOC, 1.04.02, inv.nr. 1559, letter from Bandar Abbas to Batavia, 20 March 1694, fols. 834v–5r.
69 NL-HaNA, VOC, 1.04.02, inv.nr. 1667, letter from Bandar Abbas to Batavia, 30 April 1702, pp. 437–8, 443–4.
70 NL-HaNA, VOC, 1.04.02, inv.nr. 1897, instruction from J.J. Ketelaar to Bandar Abbas, 8 March 1717, p. 171.
71 Klein, 'Trade in the Safavid Port City,' 409.
72 NL-HaNA, VOC, 1.04.02, inv.nr. 1559, letter from Bandar Abbas to Batavia, 20 March 1694, fols. 833r–4r, 838r.
73 For the commercialization of China's sugar production, see S. Mazumdar, *Sugar and Society in China: Peasants, Technology, and the World Market* (Cambridge: Harvard

University Asia Center, 1998); G. Souza, 'Hinterlands, Commodity Chains, and Circuits in Early Modern Asian History,' in *Hinterlands and Commodities: Place, Space and the Political Economic Development of Asia over the Long Eighteenth Century*, eds. T. Mizushima, G. Souza, and D. Flynn (Leiden: Brill, 2013), 20–32.

74 NL-HaNA, VOC, 1.04.02, inv.nr. 1732, letter from Bandar Abbas to Batavia, 31 January 1706, pp. 306–7.
75 NL-HaNA, VOC, 1.04.02, inv.nr. 1732, letter from Bandar Abbas to Batavia, 15 April 1706, p. 474.
76 Ibid., 476–7.
77 NL-HaNA, VOC, 1.04.02, inv.nr. 1732, shipping list, Bandar Abbas, 19 July 1705–15 April 1706, p. 593; VOC, 1.04.02, inv.nr. 1747 1, shipping list, Bandar Abbas, 13 April 1706–30 November 1706, pp. 375–7.
78 Sato, *Sugar in the Social Life*, 91–103.
79 T. Morikawa, 'Perushia kyūtei no wain to shābetto [Wine and Sherbet at the Persian court],' in *Shoku to bunka: Jikū o koeta shokutaku kara [Food and Culture: Eating across Space and Time]*, ed. N. Hosoda (Hokkaidō: Hokkaidōdaigaku shuppankai, 2015), 82–3, 92.
80 Chardin, *Voyages*, vol. 3, 190–1; vol. 4, 44.
81 Ibid., vol. 4, 65.
82 Du Mans, *Estat de la Perse*, 110–11.
83 A. Hoseini, 'Sharbat va sharbat-khana dar gudhar-i zaman [Iran's Sherbet and Sherbet Houses in Passage of Time],' *Bagh-i nazar* 10, no. 25 (2013): 64–6.
84 Morikawa, 'Perushia kyūtei,' 88–9, 91–2.
85 Chardin, *Voyages*, vol. 4, 26–30, 46–7. For similar observations, du Mans, *Estat de la Perse*, 110–11; Fryer, *A New Account of East-India*, 405.
86 Thévenot, *Suite du Voyage de Levant*, 180; Fryer, *A New Account of East-India*, 293.
87 Chardin, *Voyages*, vol. 4, 42, 44.
88 Fryer, *A New Account of East-India*, 343–4.
89 Klein, 'Trade in the Safavid Port City,' 402–3.
90 Kaempfer, *Am Hofe des persischen Grosskönings*, 218–22.
91 NL-HaNA, VOC, 1.04.02, inv.nr. 2554, description of the rise of Nadir Shah, 31 May 1741, fols. 2265v–6r.
92 Morikawa, 'Perushia kyūtei,' 93–4.
93 Della Valle, *Der voortreffelyke reizen*, vol. 3, 177.
94 R. Matthee, 'Gift-Giving iv: The Safavid Period,' *Encyclopædia Iranica*, last modified 9 February 2012.
95 C. Speelman, *Journaal der reis van den gezant der O.I. Compagnie Joan Cunaeus naar Perzië in 1651-1652*, ed. A. Hotz (Amsterdam: Johannes Müller, 1908), 152.
96 NL-HaNA, VOC, 1.04.02, inv.nr. 1901, diary, J.J. Ketelaar, fols. 981v–2r.
97 Klein, 'Trade in the Safavid Port City,' 404–5.
98 Fryer, *A New Account of East-India*, 239.
99 NL-HaNA, VOC, 1.04.02, inv.nr. 1747 1, edict from Sultan Husayn to Mirza Sayyid Murtada, 6 October 1706, pp. 378–80. For Mirza Murtada, see W. Floor, *The Economy of Safavid Persia*, 58.
100 NL-HaNA, VOC, 1.04.02, inv.nr. 1747 1, letter from Bandar Abbas to Batavia, 30 November 1706, pp. 49–51. Mirza Murtada left Isfahan on 28 November 1706 and arrived at Bandar Abbas on 2 April 1707. VOC, 1.04.02, inv.nr. 1747 1, letter from Bandar Abbas to Batavia, 4 April 1707, p. 430.

101 W. Floor, 'Dutch Relations with the Persian Gulf,' in *The Persian Gulf in History*, ed. L.G. Potter (New York: Palgrave Macmillan, 2009), 240–5; F.W. Stapel, ed., *Corpus diplomaticum* (The Hague: Martinus Nijhoff, 1935), vol. 4, 116–19.
102 R. Matthee, *The Politics of Trade in Safavid Iran: Silk for Silver, 1600–1730* (Cambridge: Cambridge University Press, 1999), 208–9.
103 Stapel, ed., *Corpus diplomaticum*, vol. 4, 153–4.
104 Ibid., 209–12.
105 NL-HaNA, VOC, 1.04.02, inv.nr. 1763, letter from Bandar Abbas to Batavia, 21 December 1707, p. 117; Matthee, *The Politics of Trade in Safavid Iran*, 245.
106 Stapel, ed., *Corpus diplomaticum*, vol. 4, 212.
107 Floor, 'Dutch Relations with the Persian Gulf,' 246–7.
108 NL-HaNA, VOC, 1.04.02, inv.nr. 1886, report from W. Backer Jacobsz to Batavia, 24 March 1716, pp. 20–1; VOC, 1.04.02, inv.nr. 1886, letter from Bandar Abbas to Batavia, 15 February 1716, pp. 69–70.
109 NL-HaNA, VOC, 1.04.02, inv.nr. 1913, report from J.J. Ketelaar at Bandar Abbas to Batavia, 31 March 1718, pp. 473–5; Floor, 'Dutch Relations with the Persian Gulf,' 247–8.
110 S. Subrahmanyam and C. Bayly, 'Portfolio Capitalists and the Political Economy of Early Modern India,' *The Indian Economic and Social History Review* 25, no. 4 (1988): 401–24.
111 '[De VOC] voorshrevene schenkagiegoederen voor haar verkregene vrijheden sonder uitstel sullen hebben te leveren.' Stapel, ed., *Corpus diplomaticum*, vol. 4, 495–500.

Chapter 2

1 W. Floor, *The Persian Gulf: The Rise of the Gulf Arabs: The Politics of Trade on the Persian Littoral 1747–1792* (Washington: Mage Publishers, 2007); W. Floor, 'The Persian Economy in the Eighteenth Century: A Dismal Record,' in *Crisis, Collapse, Militarism and Civil War*, ed. M. Axworthy (Oxford: Oxford University Press, 2018), 125–50.
2 T. Abdullah, *Merchants, Mamluks, and Murder: The Political Economy of Trade in Eighteenth-century Basra* (Albany: State University of New York Press, 2001); R. Barendse, *The Western Indian Ocean in the Eighteenth Century*, vol. 1 of *Arabian Seas 1700–1763* (Leiden: Brill, 2009); H. Fattah, *The Politics of Regional Trade in Iraq, Arabia, and the Gulf 1745–1900* (Albany: State University of New York Press, 1997); J. Gommans, *The Rise of the Indo-Afghan Empire c. 1710–80* (Leiden: Brill, 1995); S. Grummon, 'The Rise and Fall of the Arab Shaykhdom of Būshire: 1750–1850' (PhD diss., Johns Hopkins University, 1985); A. Hakima, *History of Eastern Arabia, 1750–1800: The Rise and Development of Bahrain and Kuwait* (Beirut: Khayats, 1965); T. Ricks, *Notables, Merchants, and Shaykhs of Southern Iran and its Ports: Politics and Trade of the Persian Gulf Region, AD 1728–1789* (Piscataway: Gorgias Press, 2012); P. Risso, *Oman & Muscat: An Early Modern History* (New York: St. Martin's Press, 1986).
3 W. Floor, *The Afghan Occupation of Safavid Persia 1721–1729* (Paris: Association pour l'avancement des études iraniennes, 1998), 152.
4 Ibid., 158–9.
5 British Library (BL), India Office Records (IOR) G/29/5, 14 February 1730.
6 J. Spilman, *A Journey Through Russia into Persia by Two English Gentlemen, Who Went in the Year 1739, from Petersburg* (London: R. Dodsley, 1742), 56.

7   NL-HaNA, VOC, 1.04.02, inv.nr. 2766, letter from Bandar Abbas to Batavia, 10 May 1750, p. 218.
8   He noted that some neighbouring cities, such as Kashan, Qum and Tehran, were also damaged. L.-F. Comte de Ferrières-Sauveboeuf, *Mémoires historiques, politiques et géographiques des voyages faits en Turquie, en Perse et en Arabie depuis 1782 jusqu'en 1789* (Paris, Buisson: 1790), vol. 2, 37, 39, 41, 42, 43, 76.
9   G.A. Olivier, *Voyage dans l'Empire Othoman, l'Égypte et la Perse* (Paris: H. Agasse, 1801–7), vol. 5, 19–20.
10 Ibid., vol. 5, 322–3.
11 Ibid., vol. 5, 131–2.
12 W. Floor, *Traditional Crafts in Qajar Iran (1800–1925)* (California: Mazda Publishers, 2003), 330–2; S. Mahdavi, 'Qajar Dynasty xiv: Qajar Cuisine,' *Encyclopædia Iranica*, last modified 19 March 2015.
13 NL-HaNA, VOC, 1.04.02, inv.nr. 2042, letter from Bandar Abbas to The Netherlands, 16 June 1727, fol. 3945r.
14 NL-HaNA, VOC, 1.04.02, inv.nr. 2824, letter from J. van Schoonderwoerd at Bandar Abbas to Batavia, 28 April 1753, pp. 38–9; VOC, 1.04.02, inv.nr. 2968, letter from the ship *Nieuw Nieuwerkerk* to Batavia, 1 May 1759, pp. 9–10.
15 NL-HaNA, VOC, 1.04.02, inv.nr. 2448, diary, J. Brand and I. de Crane, Bandar Abbas to Isfahan, pp. 1561–5. According to the VOC, most of the caravan leaders (*qafiladars*) who guided the Dutch party from Bandar Abbas to Isfahan lived in Sirjan. Ibid., p. 1550.
16 Ibid., pp. 1545, 1547–8, 1561.
17 P. Good, *The East India Company in Persia: Trade and Cultural Exchange in the Eighteenth Century* (London: I.B. Tauris, 2022), xv–xvi.
18 BL, IOR G/29/14, 20 July 1762.
19 BL, IOR G/29/13, 9 February 1761.
20 NL-HaNA, VOC, 1.04.02, inv.nr. 2968, letter from the ship *Nieuw Nieuwerkerk* to Batavia, 1 May 1759, p. 18.
21 R. Barendse, *The Western Indian Ocean in the Eighteenth Century*, vol. 1 of *Arabian Seas 1700–1763* (Leiden: Brill, 2009), 301–2.
22 G. Nadri, 'The Dutch Intra-Asian Trade in Sugar in the Eighteenth Century,' *International Journal of Maritime History* 20, no. 1 (2008): 93–5.
23 Ibid., 'The Dutch Intra-Asian Trade,' 83; G. Nadri, *Eighteenth-Century Gujarat: The Dynamics of Its Political Economy, 1750–1800* (Leiden: Brill, 2009), 114–15.
24 A. Hove, *Tours for Scientific and Economical Research, Made in Guzerat, Kattiawar, and the Conkuns, in 1787–88* (Bombay: Bombay Education Society's Press, 1855), 92, 99, 100.
25 Nadri, *Eighteenth-Century Gujarat*, 115–16.
26 W. Floor, *The Dutch East India Company (VOC) and Diewel-Sind (Pakistan) in the 17th and 18th Centuries (Based on Original Dutch Records)* (Karachi: University of Karachi Institute of Central and West Asian Studies, 1993–94), 43–9.
27 'zonder dewelk [poedersuiker] het die natie onmogelijk is te leven'. NL-HaNA, VOC, 1.04.02, inv.nr. 2937, report, W. Brahé and N. Mahué, 8 May 1757, p. 18.
28 Ibid., pp. 10–11, 25–6.
29 Ibid., pp. 30–1.
30 BL, IOR P/414/51, report on the commerce of Arabia and Persia, S. Manesty and H. Jones, 15 August 1790, pp. 125–6.
31 M. Axworthy, ed., *Crisis, Collapse, Militarism and Civil War* (Oxford: Oxford University Press, 2018).

32 E. Ceylan, 'Baghdad, 1500–1932,' *Encyclopaedia of Islam, THREE*; F. Zachs, 'Ahmed Paşa,' *Encyclopaedia of Islam, THREE*.
33 NL-HaNA, VOC, 1.04.02, inv.nr. 2448, letter from Isfahan to Bandar Abbas, received on 3 September 1737, pp. 1384–5.
34 Abdullah, *Merchants, Mamluks, and Murder*, 11–13, 29–37.
35 C. Niebuhr, *Reize naar Arabië en andere omliggende landen*, trans. S.J. Baalde and J. van Schoonhoven (Amsterdam: S.J. Baalde, 1776–80), vol. 2, 92, 301–2.
36 J. Griffiths, *Travels in Europe, Asia Minor and Arabia* (London: T. Cadell and W. Davies, 1805), 389.
37 E. Eldem, *French Trade in Istanbul in the Eighteenth Century* (Leiden: Brill, 1999), 68–70.
38 E. Ives, *A Voyage from England to India, in the year MDCCLIV* (London: printed for Edward and Charles Dilly, 1773), 327.
39 Olivier, *Voyage dans l'Empire Othoman*, vol. 4, 433, 439.
40 For the early history of Bushire, see Floor, *The Rise of the Gulf Arabs*, 224–35.
41 BL, IOR G/29/5, 30 January 1729, 5 April 1729.
42 Floor, *The Rise of the Gulf Arabs*, 7–21, 224–47; L. Lockhart, 'Nādir Shāh's Campaigns in Oman, 1737–1744,' *Bulletin of the School of Oriental and African Studies* 8, no. 1 (1935): 151–71.
43 Grummon, 'The Rise and Fall of the Arab Shaykhdom,' 61–73; Ricks, *Notables, Merchants, and Shaykhs*, 120 (table 3).
44 NL-HaNA, VOC, 1.04.02, inv.nr. 2885 1, letter from Kharg to Batavia, 27 September 1755, p. 7.
45 W. Kleiss, *Karawanenbauten in Iran* (Berlin: Reimer, 1999), vol. 4, 68–9 (Qavamabad), 80–3 (Robat Dovom), 121–2 (Mudkhun), 143–4 (Čeki).
46 Risso, *Oman & Muscat*, 57–62.
47 W. Francklin, *Observations Made on a Tour from Bengal to Persia, in the Years 1786-7* (London: T. Cadell, 1790), 74–5.
48 On the popularity of grape and manna in Shiraz, see Olivier, *Voyage dans l'Empire Othoman*, vol. 5, 282–3; E.-T. Hamy, *Voyage d'André Michaux en Syrie et en Perse (1782–85) d'après son journal et sa correspondance* (Geneva: Société générale d'imprimerie, 1911), 31.
49 S. Waring, *A Tour to Sheeraz by the Route of Kazroon and Feerozabad* (London: T. Cadell and W. Davies, 1807), 117.
50 S.G. Gmelin, *Travels through Northern Persia 1770–1774*, trans. W. Floor (Washington: Mage Publishers, 2007), 90. However, the lower classes could not afford sugar, and they used coagulated grape juice called '*shira*' instead. G. Forster, *A Journey from Bengal to England: Through the Northern Part of India, Kashmire, Afghanistan, and Persia, and into Russia, by the Caspian-Sea* (London: R. Faulder, 1798), vol. 2, 184.
51 Ibid., 216–17. For sugar-producing areas in Mazandaran, see Gmelin, *Travels through Northern Persia*, 241.
52 Gmelin, *Travels through Northern Persia*, 253–4.
53 Ibid., 245.
54 BL, IOR R/15/1/1, account of the raw silk received from a 'Coja Sarkees', undated, fols. 67r–9r.
55 Kahan, *The Plow, the Hammer and the Knout*, 210.
56 Gmelin, *Travels through Northern Persia*, 40, 223.
57 Forster, *A Journey from Bengal*, vol. 2, 213.
58 I will deal with this subject in Chapters 4, 6 and 7.

59 A. Das Gupta, *Malabar in Asian Trade 1740–1800* (London: Cambridge University Press, 1967), 90–3.
60 Lockhart, 'Nādir Shāh's Campaigns in Oman,' 167–70; P. Risso, *Oman & Muscat*, 39–42.
61 W. Floor, *The Persian Gulf, Dutch-Omani Relations: A Commercial & Political History 1651–1806* (Washington: Mage Publishers, 2014), 141–70.
62 BL, IOR P/414/51, report on the commerce of Arabia and Persia, Manesty and Jones, Basra, 15 August 1790, p. 84.
63 For example, NL-HaNA, VOC, 1.04.02, inv.nr. 2448, list of presents submitted to Nadir Shah, etc. at Isfahan, 27 June 1737, p. 1683.
64 NL-HaNA, VOC, 1.04.02, inv.nr. 2448, diary, J. van Schoonderwoerd, Bushire, pp. 1538–9.
65 Ibid., p. 2527.
66 J. Hanway, *An Historical Account of the British Trade over the Caspian Sea with a Journal of Travels from London through Russia into Persia, and back again through Russia, Germany, and Holland* (Dublin: William Smith and Richard James, 1754), vol. 1, 144–5.
67 Francklin, *Observations*, 156–7. In his recent essay, Assef Ashraf also discusses the crucial roles that the custom of gift-giving played in the state-formation of the Qajars from the late eighteenth to the early nineteenth century. Assef Ashraf, 'The Politics and Gift Exchange in Early Qajar Iran, 1785–1834,' *Comparative Studies in Society and History* 58, no. 2 (2016): 550–76.
68 NL-HaNA, VOC, 1.04.02, inv.nr. 2448, diary, Brand and de Crane, Bandar Abbas to Isfahan, pp. 1557, 1559–60, 1564, 1566.
69 Francklin, *Observations*, 109–10, 120–2.
70 P.H. Bruce, *Memoirs of Peter Henry Bruce, Esq. A Military Officer, in the Services of Prussia, Russia, and Great Britain* (Dublin: J. and R. Byrn, 1783), 322–3.
71 Spilman, *A Journey through Russia*, 16–18.
72 Hanway, *An Historical Account of the British Trade*, vol. 1, 250–2.
73 Olivier, *Voyage dans l'Empire Othoman*, vol. 5, 288–9.
74 A. Parsons, *Travels in Asia and Africa Including a Journey From Scanderoon to Aleppo, and over the Desert to Bagdad and Bussora, a Voyage from Bussora to Bombay, and along the Western Coast of India, a Voyage from Bombay to Mocha and Suez in the Red Sea, and a Journey from Suez to Cairo and Rosetta, in Egypt* (London: Longman, Hurst, Rees and Orme, 1808), 128–30.
75 Ibid., 131.
76 Ibid., 133. Iman al-Attar provides valuable insight into the urban and material life of Baghdad in the eighteenth century. Iman al-Attar, 'Textual Representations of the Socio-Urban History of Baghdad: Critical Approaches to the Historiography of Baghdad in the 18th and 19th Centuries' (PhD diss., University of Tasmania, 2014).
77 Parsons, *Travels in Asia and Africa*, 140.
78 Niebuhr, *Reize naar Arabië*, vol. 2, 40, 345.
79 S. Eversfield, *A Journal, Kept on a Journey from Bassora to Bagdad over the Little Desert, to Aleppo, Cyprus, Rhodes, Zante, Corfu, and Otranto, in Italy, in the Year 1779* (Horsham: Arthur Lee, 1784), 44, 48, 51.
80 Ferrières-Sauveboeuf, *Mémoires historiques*, vol. 2, 82–3.
81 Olivier, *Voyage dans l'Empire Othoman*, vol. 4, 269, 272–3, 277–8.

82 Ibid., 313, 324–5. The migration theory might also be applicable to Khurasan and the Caspian. R. Barendse, *Kings, Gangsters and Companies*, vol. 2 of *Arabian Seas 1700–1763* (Leiden: Brill, 2009), 790–1, 806–7.
83 Ives, *A Voyage from England*, 259, 260, 262.
84 Ibid., 259.
85 This Frenchman probably belonged to the Hermet family who worked for the EIC as interpreters (linguists) in Isfahan from 1730 onwards. It is difficult to identify him, but he might be Jacques Charles Hermet, whom we know at least served as such in 1750. Ives, *A Voyage from England*, 237; BL, IOR G/29/7, 1 November 1750.
86 Ives, *A Voyage from England*, 260–2.
87 Parsons, *Travels in Asia and Africa*, 146.
88 NL-HaNA, VOC, 1.04.02, inv.nr. 9091, diary, Basra, p. 460.
89 J. Otter, *Voyage en Turquie et en Perse avec une relation des expéditions de Tahmas Kouli-khan* (Paris: Freres Guerin, 1748), vol. 2, 251–2, 263–4.
90 R. Kazemi, 'Tobacco, Eurasian Trade, and the Early Modern Iranian Economy,' *Iranian Studies* 49, no. 4 (2016): 613–33; G. Sood, *India and the Islamic Heartlands: An Eighteenth-century World of Circulation and Exchange* (Cambridge: Cambridge University Press, 2016). Concerning eighteenth-century India, Barendse also suggests a shift in the pattern of demand from courts to what he calls 'the middling sort' of the population, saying that these people began to boost consumption in urban arenas. Barendse, *Kings, Gangsters and Companies*, 838–46.

Chapter 3

1 G. Nadri, 'The Dutch Intra-Asian Trade in Sugar in the Eighteenth Century,' *International Journal of Maritime History* 20, no. 1 (2008): 63–96.
2 W. Floor, *The Afghan Occupation of Safavid Persia 1721–1729* (Paris: Association pour l'avancement des études iraniennes, 1998), 8–9, 12–14; W. Floor, *The Rise and Fall of Nader Shah: Dutch East India Company Reports, 1730–47* (Washington: Mage Publishers, 2009), xiii–xvi; W. Floor, 'Dutch Relations with the Persian Gulf,' in *The Persian Gulf in History*, ed. L.G. Potter (New York: Palgrave Macmillan, 2009), 236–7.
3 For quantitative data on Dutch exports of bullion from Safavid Iran, see W. Floor, *The Economy of Safavid Persia* (Wiesbaden: Reichert Verlag, 2000), 194–5.
4 Ibid., 127–31.
5 O. Prakash, *The Dutch East India Company and the Economy of Bengal, 1630–1720* (Delhi: Oxford University Press, 1988), 175.
6 Ibid., 176. For the development of sugar production in Batavia during the VOC period, see L. Blussé, *Strange Company: Chinese Settlers, Mestizo Women and the Dutch in VOC Batavia* (Dordrecht: Foris Publications, 1988), 73–96; E. Jacobs, *Merchant in Asia: The Trade of the Dutch East India Company during the Eighteenth Century* (Leiden: CNWS Publications, 2006), 247–59; A. Ota, *Changes of Regime and Social Dynamics in West Java: Society, State and Outer World of Banten 1750–1830* (Leiden: Brill, 2006), 132–42; G. Xu, 'The "Perfect Map" of Widow Hiamtse: A Micro-Spatial History of Sugar Plantations in Early Modern Southeast Asia,' *International Review of Social History* 67, no. 1 (2022): 97–126.
7 Prakash, *The Dutch East India Company*, 176.

8 Nadri, 'The Dutch Intra-Asian Trade,' 71.
9 Ota, *Changes of Regime*, 243.
10 Nationaal Archief, Den Haag (NL-HaNA), Verenigde Oostindische Compagnie (VOC), nummer toegang 1.04.02, inventarisnummer 2593, letter from Bandar Abbas to Batavia, 31 October 1742, fol. 1669r.
11 W. Floor, *The Persian Gulf: The Rise of the Gulf Arabs: The Politics of Trade on the Persian Littoral 1747–1792* (Washington: Mage Publishers, 2007), 54, 62–3.
12 For instance, NL-HaNA, VOC, 1.04.02, inv.nr. 2448, letter from Bandar Abbas to Batavia, 30 April 1738, p. 1927.
13 NL-HaNA, VOC, 1.04.02, inv.nr. 2476, annual sales statement, Isfahan, 1737–8, pp. 1390–1; VOC, 1.04.02, inv.nr. 2610 2, annual sales statement, Isfahan, 1741–2, pp. 62–3. See also Chart 2.1.
14 Floor, *The Rise of the Gulf Arabs*, 252.
15 NL-HaNA, VOC, 1.04.02, inv.nr. 2787, letter from Basra to Batavia, 10 August 1750, pp. 6–8.
16 NL-HaNA, VOC, 1.04.02, inv.nr. 2863, sales statement, Bandar Rig, undated, p. 46.
17 NL-HaNA, VOC, 1.04.02, inv.nr. 2303, letter from Basra to The Netherlands, 30 April 1734, fol. 5413r.
18 NL-HaNA, VOC, 1.04.02, inv.nr. 2323, final report (*memorie van overgave*) from D. Heij to G. Gutchi, Basra, 25 May 1734, pp. 1412–13.
19 NL-HaNA, VOC, 1.04.02, inv.nr. 2448, letter from Bandar Abbas to Batavia, 31 December 1737, p. 164.
20 NL-HaNA, VOC, 1.04.02, inv.nr. 2824, letter from Basra to Batavia, 11 January 1753, pp. 10–11.
21 Floor, *The Rise of the Gulf Arabs*, 252; NL-HaNA, VOC, 1.04.02, inv.nr. 2824, letter from J. van der Hulst at Bushire to Batavia, 25 March 1753, p. 78.
22 Floor, *The Rise of the Gulf Arabs*, 200.
23 Ibid., 208.
24 NL-HaNA, VOC, 1.04.02, inv.nr. 2885 1, sales statement, January 1756, p. 53.
25 NL-HaNA, VOC, 1.04.02, inv.nr. 2885 1, letter from J. van Schoonderwoerd at Muscat to Batavia, 27 January 1756, pp. 52–4. According to Floor, 'the Mocha monsoon' refers to the coffee traders who sailed from Mocha to Basra in July to sell their coffee and buy dates and other return goods. These traders often stopped at Muscat for trade on their way back to Mocha. Floor, *The Rise of the Gulf Arabs*, 209.
26 Ibid., 210–12.
27 W. Floor, *The Dutch East India Company (VOC) and Diewel-Sind (Pakistan) in the 17th and 18th Centuries (Based on Original Dutch Records)* (Karachi: University of Karachi Institute of Central and West Asian Studies, 1993–4), 58.
28 NL-HaNA, VOC, 1.04.02, inv.nr. 2937, report, W. Brahé and N. Mahué, 8 May 1757, pp. 7–15.
29 NL-HaNA, VOC, 1.04.02, inv.nr. 2937, sales statement, Sind, 1756–7, pp. 44–5.
30 NA VOC2937, report, Brahé and Mahué, pp. 47, 48, 60–1.
31 NL-HaNA, VOC, 1.04.02, inv.nr. 2937, report, S. Rood, 8 March 1758, pp. 77–8.
32 NL-HaNA, VOC, 1.04.02, inv.nr. 2937, sales statement, Muscat, 21 September 1757–7 December 1757, p. 85.
33 NL-HaNA, VOC, 1.04.02, inv.nr. 2937, report, Rood, 8 March 1758, p. 86.
34 NL-HaNA, VOC, 1.04.02, inv.nr. 2937, letter from Kharg to Batavia, 26 October 1757, p. 19.

35 During the 1750s, the Surat factory also explored the prospect of sugar trade at Kutch. They established a subordinate factory in Mandvi, the main port city in the Gulf of Kutch, providing it with merchandise, including Javanese sugar, ivory, lead, iron and some spices. G. Nadri, 'Exploring the Gulf of Kachh: Regional Economy and Trade in the Eighteenth Century,' *Journal of the Economic and Social History of the Orient*, no. 51 (2008): 460–86.
36 NL-HaNA, VOC, 1.04.02, inv.nr. 3156, letter from Kharg to Batavia, 30 September 1764, pp. 21–2. For a brief note on the shipwreck of *Amstelveen*, see W. Floor, *The Persian Gulf, Dutch-Omani Relations: A Commercial & Political History 1651–1806* (Washington: Mage Publishers, 2014), 217–23 (Annex 4).
37 Floor, *The Rise of the Gulf Arabs*, 200, 204–6.
38 A. Das Gupta, *Malabar in Asian Trade 1740–1800* (London: Cambridge University Press, 1967), 91–102.
39 Jacobs, *Merchant in Asia*, 256; Nadri, 'The Dutch Intra-Asian Trade,' 84–5.
40 C. Nierstrasz, *In the Shadow of the Company: The Dutch East India Company and Its Servants in the Period of its Decline* (Leiden: Brill, 2012), 80–3.
41 For example, see Das Gupta, *Malabar in Asian Trade*, 100–1.
42 Ibid., 98–9.
43 NL-HaNA, VOC, 1.04.02, inv.nr. 3027 1, letter from Kharg to Batavia, 15 October 1760, p. 8.
44 NL-HaNA, VOC, 1.04.02, inv.nr. 3027 1, letter from Kharg to Batavia, 1 October 1760, pp. 2–3.
45 NL-HaNA, VOC, 1.04.02, inv.nr. 3027 1, letter from Kharg to Batavia, 30 November 1760, pp. 16–17.
46 Floor, *The Rise of the Gulf Arabs*, 157–62, 172–3.

Chapter 4

1 R. Klein, 'Trade in the Safavid Port City Bandar Abbas and the Persian Gulf (ca. 1600–1680): A Study of Selected Aspects' (PhD diss., University of London, 1993–4), 380–2.
2 O. Prakash, *The Dutch East India Company and the Economy of Bengal, 1630–1720* (Delhi: Oxford University Press, 1988), 175–6.
3 R. Barendse, *The Arabian Seas: The Indian Ocean World of the Seventeenth Century* (New York: M.E. Sharpe, 2002), 447.
4 Klein, 'Trade in the Safavid Port City,' 381.
5 Prakash, *The Dutch East India Company*, 176; W. Floor, *The Economy of Safavid Persia* (Wiesbaden: Reichert Verlag, 2000), 132.
6 For instance, British Library (BL), IOR G/29/15, list of the arrival and departure of shipping, Bandar Abbas, 14 October 1726–24 March 1727, fols. 247r–v.
7 Klein, 'Trade in the Safavid Port City,' 408.
8 Nationaal Archief, Den Haag (NL-HaNA), Verenigde Oostindische Compagnie (VOC), nummer toegang 1.04.02, inventarisnummer 1768, shipping list, Bandar Abbas, 1 November 1708–23 December 1709, fol. 1884v.
9 NL-HaNA, VOC, 1.04.02, inv.nr. 1667, shipping list, Bandar Abbas, 28 February 1701–27 January 1702, p. 250.

10 NL-HaNA, VOC, 1.04.02, inv.nr. 1598 1, shipping list, Bandar Abbas, 1 November 1696–31 March 1697, p. 72. Besides the English, Muslim traders exported Bengali sugar to Surat throughout the eighteenth century. NL-HaNA, VOC, 1.04.02, inv.nr. 8736, shipping list, Hugli, 20 October 1704–15 April 1705, pp. 92–7.
11 Many English and Muslim vessels from Surat brought conserves to Bandar Abbas in the late Safavid period. NL-HaNA, VOC, 1.04.02, inv.nr. 1650, shipping list, Bandar Abbas, 10 June 1700–11 December 1700, p. 30; VOC, 1.04.02, inv.nr. 1611 2, shipping list, Bandar Abbas, 5 April 1698–28 July 1698, p. 70.
12 NL-HaNA, VOC, 1.04.02, inv.nr. 1732, shipping list, Bandar Abbas, 19 July 1705–15 April 1706, pp. 592–3; VOC, 1.04.02, inv.nr. 1747 1, shipping list, Bandar Abbas, 13 April 1706–30 November 1706, pp. 375–7.
13 NL-HaNA, VOC, 1.04.02, inv.nr. 8081, shipping list, Bandar Abbas, 11 December 1710–23 May 1712, p. 102; VOC, 1.04.02, inv.nr. 2034 2, instruction from P. 't Lam to B. Lispensier, Bandar Abbas, 15 June 1725, p. 344.
14 NL-HaNA, VOC, 1.04.02, inv.nr. 1747 1, shipping list, Bandar Abbas, 13 April 1706–30 November 1706, p. 375.
15 See Appendix 2.
16 NL-HaNA, VOC, 1.04.02, inv.nr. 1559, letter from Bandar Abbas to Batavia, 2 August 1693, fols. 711v–12v. For English privileges in Safavid Iran, see R.W. Ferrier, 'The Terms and Conditions under which English Trade Was Transacted with Ṣafavid Persia,' *Bulletin of the School of Oriental and African Studies* 49, no. 1 (1986): 48–66; P. Good, 'The East India Company's Farmān, 1622–1747,' *Iranian Studies* 52, no. 1–2 (2019): 181–97.
17 NL-HaNA, VOC, 1.04.02, inv.nr. 1582, final report from A. Verdonk to A. Berganje, Bandar Abbas, 15 May 1696, p. 164.
18 NL-HaNA, VOC, 1.04.02, inv.nr. 1779, shipping list, Bandar Abbas, 21 December 1707–12 January 1709, p. 321.
19 NL-HaNA, VOC, 1.04.02, inv.nr. 1685, shipping list, Bandar Abbas, 20 May 1704–31 July 1705, p. 2572.
20 NL-HaNA, VOC, 1.04.02, inv.nr. 1763, shipping list, Bandar Abbas, 30 November 1706–21 December 1707, p. 346; VOC, 1.04.02, inv.nr. 1829, shipping list, Bandar Abbas, 11 December 1710–23 May 1712, pp. 187–8; VOC, 1.04.02, inv.nr. 1802, shipping list, Bandar Abbas, 7 June 1710–17 July 1711, fol. 2204v.
21 NL-HaNA, VOC, 1.04.02, inv.nr. 1779, shipping list, Bandar Abbas, 21 December 1707–12 January 1709, p. 324.
22 NL-HaNA, VOC, 1.04.02, inv.nr. 1626 1, shipping list, Bandar Abbas, 2 September 1698–22 March 1699, p. 104.
23 NL-HaNA, VOC, 1.04.02, inv.nr. 1598 1, shipping list, Bandar Abbas, 1 November 1696–31 March 1697, p. 72; VOC, 1.04.02, inv.nr. 1802, shipping list, Bandar Abbas, 7 June 1710–17 July 1711, fol. 2204r.
24 NL-HaNA, VOC, 1.04.02, inv.nr. 1694, shipping list, Bandar Abbas, 14 December 1703–24 May 1704, pp. 346–7.
25 NL-HaNA, VOC, 1.04.02, inv.nr. 1660, list of foreign vessels present at Surat, 30 June 1701, fol. 964v; A. Das Gupta, *Indian Merchants and the Decline of Surat, c. 1700–1750* (New Delhi: Manohar Publishers, 1994, first published in 1979), 104.
26 NL-HaNA, VOC, 1.04.02, inv.nr. 1714, list of arrival of non-VOC vessels, Surat, 29 June 1705, p. 42.
27 NL-HaNA, VOC, 1.04.02, inv.nr. 1870, shipping list, Bandar Abbas, 30 September 1714–13 April 1715, p. 651.

28 NL-HaNA, VOC, 1.04.02, inv.nr. 9056, pass book, Surat, 2 May 1711–16 April 1712, pp. 145–6.
29 NL-HaNA, VOC, 1.04.02, inv.nr. 1913, pass book, Surat, 28 January 1717–23 December 1717, pp. 80–1; VOC, 1.04.02, inv.nr. 1947, pass book, Surat, 9 March 1719–2 March 1720, pp. 202–3.
30 NL-HaNA, VOC, 1.04.02, inv.nr. 1598 1, shipping list, Bandar Abbas, 1 November 1696–31 March 1697, p. 72; VOC, 1.04.02, inv.nr. 8367, shipping list, Bandar Abbas, 10 June 1700–11 December 1700, p. 53; VOC, 1.04.02, inv.nr. 1732, shipping list, Bandar Abbas, 19 July 1705–15 April 1706, p. 590; VOC, 1.04.02, inv.nr. 1886, shipping list, Bandar Abbas, 13 April 1715–15 February 1716, p. 401; VOC, 1.04.02, inv.nr. 1870, shipping list, Bandar Abbas, 30 September 1714–13 April 1715, pp. 650–1.
31 NL-HaNA, VOC, 1.04.02, inv.nr. 1614, letter from Bandar Abbas to Batavia, 31 May 1700, fol. 1131r.
32 For instance, NL-HaNA, VOC, 1.04.02, inv.nr. 1714 1, list of freight goods for Surat loaded into the ship *Kauw*, Bandar Abbas, 30 November 1704, pp. 150–61.
33 On this occasion, freight fees were charged at a rate of 1.5 per cent per value of the commodity. NL-HaNA, VOC, 1.04.02, inv.nr. 1737, list of freight goods for Tuticorin loaded into the ship *de Lek*, Bandar Abbas, 18 July 1705, fols. 114r–15r.
34 NL-HaNA, VOC, 1.04.02, inv.nr. 1779, letter from Bandar Abbas to The Netherlands, 31 August 1708, pp. 61–3.
35 NL-HaNA, VOC, 1.04.02, inv.nr. 1571, letter from Bandar Abbas to The Netherlands, 23 July 1694, pp. 52–3.
36 NL-HaNA, VOC, 1.04.02, inv.nr. 1763, letter from Bandar Abbas to Batavia, 21 September 1707, pp. 112–13; VOC, 1.04.02, inv.nr. 1732, letter from Bandar Abbas to Batavia, 31 January 1706, p. 274.
37 NL-HaNA, VOC, 1.04.02, inv.nr. 1559, letter from Bandar Abbas to Batavia, 20 March 1694, fols. 838r–v.
38 NL-HaNA, VOC, 1.04.02, inv.nr. 1667, separate letter from M. Wichelman at Bandar Abbas to Batavia, 27 January 1702, pp. 375–6.
39 NL-HaNA, VOC, 1.04.02, inv.nr. 1582, letter from Bandar Abbas to The Netherlands, 19 July 1695, p. 34.
40 NL-HaNA, VOC, 1.04.02, inv.nr. 1843, letter from Bandar Abbas to Batavia, 22 June 1713, p. 305.
41 R. Matthee, 'Boom and Bust: The Port of Basra in the Sixteenth and Seventeenth Centuries,' in *The Persian Gulf in History*, ed. L. G. Potter (New York: Palgrave Macmillan, 2009), 116–20.
42 NL-HaNA, VOC, 1.04.02, inv.nr. 1714 1, letter from Bandar Abbas to Batavia, 6 April 1705, p. 201.
43 NL-HaNA, VOC, 1.04.02, inv.nr. 1904, letter from Bandar Abbas to Batavia, 7 November 1718, fols. 2372v–3r.
44 NL-HaNA, VOC, 1.04.02, inv.nr. 2105, letter from Bandar Abbas to Batavia, 1 April 1728, pp. 232–3.
45 G. Nadri, 'The Dutch Intra-Asian Trade in Sugar in the Eighteenth Century,' *International Journal of Maritime History* 20, no.1 (2008): 75–8, 91–2.
46 NL-HaNA, VOC, 1.04.02, inv.nr. 1870 1, letter from Bandar Abbas to Batavia, 27 September 1714, pp. 23–4.
47 NL-HaNA, VOC, 1.04.02, inv.nr. 1886, letter from Bandar Abbas to Batavia, 15 February 1716, p. 40.
48 BL, IOR G/29/3, 12 December 1726.

49 BL, IOR G/29/4, 29 April 1727. For the EIC's relations with Basidu, see B. Slot, *The Arabs of the Gulf 1602–1784: An Alternative Approach to the Early History of the Arab Gulf States and the Arab People of the Gulf, Mainly Based on Sources of the Dutch East India Company* (Leidschendam, 1993), 259–63.
50 NL-HaNA, VOC, 1.04.02, inv.nr. 2055 1, letter from Bandar Abbas to The Netherlands, 15 December 1725, pp. 17, 31–2.
51 J.C. Wilkinson, *Water and Tribal Settlement in South-East Arabia: A Study of the Aflāj of Oman* (Oxford: Clarendon Press, 1977), 211.
52 W. Floor, *The Persian Gulf, Dutch-Omani Relations: A Commercial & Political History 1651–1806* (Washington: Mage Publishers, 2014), 100–1.
53 NL-HaNA, VOC, 1.04.02, inv.nr. 2006, letter from Bandar Abbas to The Netherlands, 20 June 1724, fol. 2985r.
54 NL-HaNA, VOC, 1.04.02, inv.nr. 2034 2, instruction from 't Lam to Lispensier, Bandar Abbas, 15 June 1725, p. 345.
55 NL-HaNA, VOC, 1.04.02, inv.nr. 2168, letter from Bandar Abbas to Batavia, 13 April 1730, p. 48.
56 NL-HaNA, VOC, 1.04.02, inv.nr. 2034 2, instruction from 't Lam to Lispensier, Bandar Abbas, 15 June 1725, pp. 341, 344.
57 NL-HaNA, VOC, 1.04.02, inv.nr. 2034 2, letter from B. Lispensier at Muscat to Bandar Abbas, 10 July 1725 pp. 329–30; VOC, 1.04.02, inv.nr. 2034 2, letter from B. Lispensier at Muscat to Bandar Abbas, 27 July 1725, pp. 331–3; VOC, 1.04.02, inv.nr. 2034 2, report from B. Lispensier to Bandar Abbas, 11 Augustus 1725, pp. 350–4.
58 NL-HaNA, VOC, 1.04.02, inv.nr. 1999, letter from Bandar Abbas to Batavia, 15 November 1722, p. 48.
59 NL-HaNA, VOC, 1.04.02, inv.nr. 2105, letter from Bandar Abbas to Batavia, 1 April 1728, pp. 232–4.
60 NL-HaNA, VOC, 1.04.02, inv.nr. 2042, letter from Bandar Abbas to The Netherlands, 16 June 1727, fol. 3945r.
61 NL-HaNA, VOC, 1.04.02, inv.nr. 2079, letter from Bandar Abbas to Batavia, 10 January 1727, pp. 15–16.
62 NL-HaNA, VOC, 1.04.02, inv.nr. 2091, letter from Bandar Abbas to The Netherlands, 15 August 1728, fol. 4899r.
63 BL, IOR G/29/5, 30 January 1729. The EIC followed the Julian calendar until September 1752.
64 Ibid., 6 February 1729.
65 Ibid., 3 February 1729, 5 April 1729, inserted report from W. May to Bandar Abbas dated 6 April 1729.
66 Ibid., 7 February 1729. During the first half of the eighteenth century, high-ranking EIC officers in Bombay and Surat also regularly engaged in private ventures through their relationships with EIC factors in Bandar Abbas and Basra. T. Davies, 'British Private Trade Network in the Arabian Seas, *c.*1680–*c.*1760' (PhD diss., University of Warwick, 2012), 179–87.
67 NL-HaNA, VOC, 1.04.02, inv.nr. 2323, letter from Bandar Abbas to Batavia, 23 September 1734, pp. 161–3.
68 K.K. al-Khalifa, 'Commerce and Conflict: The English East India Company Factories in the Gulf, 1700–47' (PhD diss., University of Essex, 1988), 32–4.
69 NL-HaNA, VOC, 1.04.02, inv.nr. 2416, letter from Bandar Abbas to Batavia, 10 December 1736, pp. 149, 152.

70 Ibid., pp. 81–2. Interestingly, the EIC viewed the French as being more popular with the government of Bandar Abbas, since unlike the English and the Dutch, the French paid customs duties at the port. BL, IOR G/29/6, 6 March 1740.
71 NL-HaNA, VOC, 1.04.02, inv.nr. 2357, letter from Bandar Abbas to Batavia, 24 August 1735, p. 34.
72 NL-HaNA, VOC, 1.04.02, inv.nr. 2416, letter from Bandar Abbas to Batavia, 10 December 1736, p. 152. According to an existing Dutch *rendement*, in the year 1736–7, the Company sold castor sugar at 3 2/5 *mahmudis* per *man*, 0.1 *mahmudi* cheaper than the above-mentioned price. NL-HaNA, VOC, 1.04.02, inv.nr. 2448, annual sales statement, Bandar Abbas, 1736–7, pp. 1664–5.
73 NL-HaNA, VOC, 1.04.02, inv.nr. 2477, letter from Bandar Abbas to Batavia, 14 May 1739, p. 73.
74 NL-HaNA, VOC, 1.04.02, inv.nr. 1947, letter from Bandar Abbas to The Netherlands, 25 May 1719, p. 62.
75 NL-HaNA, VOC, 1.04.02, inv.nr. 2254, letter from Bandar Abbas to Batavia, 19 July 1732, p. 412.
76 NL-HaNA, VOC, 1.04.02, inv.nr. 2357 1, letter from Bandar Abbas to Batavia, 24 August 1735, pp. 438–9. For the EIC's 'coloring' practices, see W. Floor, *A Political and Economic History of Five Port Cities 1500–1730* (Washington: Mage Publishers, 2006), 315; P. Good, *The East India Company in Persia: Trade and Cultural Exchange in the Eighteenth Century* (London: I.B. Tauris, 2022), 90–2.
77 NL-HaNA, VOC, 1.04.02, inv.nr. 2390, letter from Bandar Abbas to Batavia, 19 March 1736, pp. 18–19.
78 NL-HaNA, VOC, 1.04.02, inv.nr. 2368, letter from Bandar Abbas to The Netherlands, 18 May 1737, fol. 3782v.
79 NL-HaNA, VOC, 1.04.02, inv.nr. 2416, letter from Bandar Abbas to Batavia, 10 December 1736, pp. 149–50.
80 NL-HaNA, VOC, 1.04.02, inv.nr. 2448, letter from Bandar Abbas to Batavia, 31 December 1737, p. 65.
81 NL-HaNA, VOC, 1.04.02, inv.nr. 2885 2, final report from J. van Schoonderwoerd to G. Aansorg, Bandar Abbas, 28 November 1755, p. 17.
82 Matthee, Floor, and Clawson, *The Monetary History of Iran from the Safavids and the Qajars*, 140, 146–50.
83 NL-HaNA, VOC, 1.04.02, inv.nr. 2203, letter from Bandar Abbas to Batavia, 15 May 1731, p. 23.
84 Matthee, Floor, and Clawson, *The Monetary History of Iran*, 154.
85 NL-HaNA, VOC, 1.04.02, inv.nr. 2323, letter from Bandar Abbas to The Netherlands, 6 February 1734, p. 687.
86 Iran imported Japanese copper until the late seventeenth century, when the exploitation of the copper mines in Kirman caused the discontinuation of copper imports. Much copper was also produced in the north-eastern provinces of Iran, such as Sabzavar and Mashhad. Matthee, Floor, and Clawson, *The Monetary History of Iran*, 49.
87 NL-HaNA, VOC, 1.04.02, inv.nr. 2323, letter from Bandar Abbas to The Netherlands, 6 February 1734, pp. 687–8; VOC, 1.04.02, inv.nr. 2323, letter from Bandar Abbas to Batavia, 23 September 1734, p. 164.
88 NL-HaNA, VOC, 1.04.02, inv.nr. 2254, letter from Bandar Abbas to Batavia, 19 July 1732, pp. 303–4; Matthee, Floor, and Clawson, *The Monetary History of Iran*, 164–5 (table 5.6).

89 NL-HaNA, VOC, 1.04.02, inv.nr. 2448, letter from Bandar Abbas to Batavia, 30 April 1738, pp. 1803–5; Matthee, Floor, and Clawson, *The Monetary History of Iran*, 156–7.
90 NL-HaNA, VOC, 1.04.02, inv.nr. 2416, letter from Bandar Abbas to Batavia, 10 December 1736, pp. 209–10.
91 NL-HaNA, VOC, 1.04.02, inv.nr. 2448, letter from Bandar Abbas to Batavia, 30 April 1738, pp. 1803–4.
92 Good, *The East India Company in Persia*, 85–6.
93 BL, IOR G/29/5, 5 January 1737.
94 Ibid., 7 February 1737, 29 April 1737, 30 April 1737.
95 NL-HaNA, VOC, 1.04.02, inv.nr. 2416, letter from Bandar Abbas to Batavia, 10 December 1736, p. 83.
96 Ibid., p. 150.
97 NL-HaNA, VOC, 1.04.02, inv.nr. 2417, letter from Bandar Abbas to Batavia, 4 April 1737, p. 3520.
98 W. Floor, *The Persian Gulf: The Rise of the Gulf Arabs: The Politics of Trade on the Persian Littoral 1747–1792* (Washington: Mage Publishers, 2007), 39–40, 93–4.
99 T. Ricks, *Notables, Merchants, and Shaykhs of Southern Iran and Its Ports: Politics and Trade of the Persian Gulf Region, AD 1728–1789* (Piscataway: Gorgias Press, 2012), 71–3, 110–13, 156–60, 204–20.
100 NL-HaNA, VOC, 1.04.02, inv.nr. 2610 1, letter from Bandar Abbas to Batavia, 31 October 1742, pp. 100–1.
101 NL-HaNA, VOC, 1.04.02, inv.nr. 2610 2, letter from Bandar Abbas to Batavia, 29 June 1743, pp. 74–5.
102 Nationaal Archief, Den Haag, Hoge Regering van Batavia, nummer toegang 1.04.17, inventarisnummer 846, report on sugar trade at Surat, 1 March 1766, Article 34.
103 NL-HaNA, VOC, 1.04.02, inv.nr. 2610 1, letter from Bandar Abbas to Batavia, 31 October 1742, p. 56.
104 NL-HaNA, VOC, 1.04.02, inv.nr. 2610 2, letter from Bandar Abbas to Batavia, 29 June 1743, p. 41.
105 Ibid., pp. 80–1.
106 NL-HaNA, VOC, 1.04.02, inv.nr. 2610 1, letter from Bandar Abbas to Batavia, 31 October 1742, pp. 55–6.
107 NL-HaNA, VOC, 1.04.02, inv.nr. 2705, letter from Bandar Abbas to Batavia, 31 July 1746, p. 47.
108 BL, IOR G/29/7, 30 April 1747.
109 Ibid., 2 November 1747, 10 November 1747.
110 NL-HaNA, VOC, 1.04.02, inv.nr. 2710, letter from Bandar Abbas to The Netherlands, 10 October 1748, fols. 1317r–v. In order to re-establish the Company's trade in Iran, the Dutch factors suggested that the Company set up a new factory in Kirman to sell spices and other items. Ibid., fols. 1318r–v.
111 BL, IOR G/29/7, 24 February 1752, inserted letter from Bandar Abbas to Bombay under the same date.
112 BL, IOR G/29/7, 13 May 1748.
113 Ibid., 17 March 1749 (from Kirman with Mashhad merchants), 17 September 1750 (from Lar).
114 Ibid., 30 April 1752.
115 NL-HaNA, VOC, 1.04.02, inv.nr. 2863, shipping list, Bandar Abbas, 1 September 1753–20 December 1754, p. 65; VOC, 1.04.02, inv.nr. 2968, shipping list, Bandar Abbas, 21 November 1757–4 February 1759, pp. 27–8.

116 NL-HaNA, VOC, 1.04.02, inv.nr. 2863, letter from Bandar Abbas to Batavia, 20 December 1754, p. 62; BL, IOR G/29/8, 3 December 1754, 4 December 1754, 12 December 1754.
117 BL, IOR G/29/10, 15 April 1757, inserted letter from Bandar Abbas to London under the same date.
118 NL-HaNA, VOC, 1.04.02, inv.nr. 2885 2, final report from Schoonderwoerd to Aansorg, Bandar Abbas, 28 November 1755, pp. 18–19.
119 NL-HaNA, VOC, 1.04.02, inv.nr. 2824, letter from J. van Schoonderwoerd at Bandar Abbas to Batavia, 28 April 1753, p. 40.
120 NL-HaNA, VOC, 1.04.02, inv.nr. 2885 3, letter from Bandar Abbas to Batavia, 8 September 1756, p. 5.
121 NL-HaNA, VOC, 1.04.02, inv.nr. 2885 2, final report from Schoonderwoerd to Aansorg, Bandar Abbas, 28 November 1755, p. 19.
122 *Realia: register op de generale resolutiën van het Kasteel Batavia, 1632–1805*, ed. Bataviaasch Genootschap van Kunsten en Wetenschappen (Leiden: Gualth Kolff, 1882–6), vol. 3, 262; NL-HaNA, VOC, 1.04.02, inv.nr. 781: Kopie-resoluties te Batavia, 31 August 1751, pp. 567–9.
123 NL-HaNA, VOC, 1.04.02, inv.nr. 2843, letter from Bandar Abbas to Batavia, 10 October 1753, pp. 55–6.
124 NL-HaNA, VOC, 1.04.02, inv.nr. 2863, letter from J. van Schoonderwoerd at Bandar Abbas to Batavia, 20 December 1754, p. 31. For the Dutch's private trade in the Persian Gulf, see B. Slot, 'At the Backdoor of the Levant: Anglo-Dutch Competition in the Persian Gulf, 1623–1766,' in *Friends and Rivals in the East: Studies in Anglo-Dutch Relations in the Levant from the Seventeenth to the Early Nineteenth Century*, eds. A. Hamilton, A. de Groot, and M. van de Boogert (Leiden: Brill, 2000), 121; W. Floor and M.H. Faghfoory, *The First Dutch-Persian Commercial Conflict: The Attack on Qeshm Island, 1645* (Costa Mesa: Mazda Publishers, 2004), 205–9.
125 NL-HaNA, VOC, 1.04.02, inv.nr. 2968 2, letter from the ship *Nieuw Nieuwerkerk* to Batavia, 1 May 1759, p. 18.
126 NL-HaNA, VOC, 1.04.02, inv.nr. 2937, letter from Bandar Abbas to Batavia, 24 September 1757, p. 4; VOC, 1.04.02, inv.nr. 2968 2, letter from the ship *Nieuw Nieuwerkerk* to Batavia, 1 May 1759, pp. 8–10.
127 BL, IOR G/29/13, 11 February 1761, inserted letter from Bandar Abbas to London under the same date. On the other hand, the EIC factors thought that, if the port government was in proper hands, Bandar Abbas would be the best place in the Gulf from which to supply woollen goods for a large part of the interior markets, particularly those at Kirman, Yazd, Astrabad (Istraband), Khurasan, and those of the Afghans and the Uzbeks. BL, IOR G/29/14, 24 December 1761.

Chapter 5

1 T. Abdullah, *Merchants, Mamluks, and Murder: The Political Economy of Trade in Eighteenth-Century Basra* (Albany: State University of New York Press, 2001), 49–50.
2 Nationaal Archief, Den Haag (NL-HaNA), Verenigde Oostindische Compagnie (VOC), nummer toegang 1.04.02, inventarisnummer 2091, letter from Basra to The Netherlands, 1 November 1728, fols. 4923r–v, 4925r.

3 NL-HaNA, VOC, 1.04.02, inv.nr. 2253, letter from Bandar Abbas to Batavia, 15 May 1731, pp. 14–15; K.K. al-Khalifa, 'Commerce and Conflict: The English East India Company Factories in the Gulf, 1700–47' (PhD diss., University of Essex, 1988), 247.
4 NL-HaNA, VOC, 1.04.02, inv.nr. 2034, diary, Basra, 6 April 1725, 15 April 1725, pp. 235, 236.
5 Ibid., 22 May 1725, p. 246.
6 Khalifa, 'Commerce and Conflict,' 96–7, 180–1.
7 T. Davies, 'British Private Trade Network in the Arabian Seas, c. 1680–c. 1760' (PhD diss., University of Warwick, 2012), 182.
8 NL-HaNA, VOC, 1.04.02, inv.nr. 9099, diary, Basra, 10 August 1725, p. 25.
9 Ibid., 14 August 1725, p. 26.
10 NL-HaNA, VOC, 1.04.02, inv.nr. 9059, pass book, Surat, 12 August 1724–4 May 1725, pp. 152–3.
11 NL-HaNA, VOC, 1.04.02, inv.nr. 2091, letter from Basra to The Netherlands, 22 July 1729, inserted shipping list, Basra, 1 November 1728–22 July 1729, fols. 4967r-v; VOC, 1.04.02, inv.nr. 9090, diary, Basra, 27 May 1729, 11 July 1729, pp. 433, 444.
12 NL-HaNA, VOC, 1.04.02, inv.nr. 2016 2, letter from Bandar Abbas to Batavia, 25 August 1724, p. 6; VOC, 1.04.02, inv.nr. 2091, letter from Basra to The Netherlands, 22 July 1729, fol. 4967r.
13 NL-HaNA, VOC, 1.04.02, inv.nr. 2610 1, letter from Bandar Abbas to Batavia, 31 October 1742, pp. 137–8; Khalifa, 'Commerce and Conflict,' 62; B. Slot, *The Arabs of the Gulf 1602–1784: An Alternative Approach to the Early History of the Arab Gulf States and the Arab People of the Gulf, Mainly Based on Sources of the Dutch East India Company* (Leidschendam, 1993), 288–9; Abdullah, *Merchants, Mamluks, and Murder*, 42–3.
14 NL-HaNA, VOC, 1.04.02, inv.nr. 2055 2, letter from Basra to The Netherlands, 19 April 1726, p. 70.
15 NL-HaNA, VOC, 1.04.02, inv.nr. 2323, final report from D. Heij to G. Gutchi, Basra, 25 May 1734, p. 1415.
16 NL-HaNA, VOC, 1.04.02, inv.nr. 2023, letter from Basra to The Netherlands, 22 January 1726, fol. 3349v.
17 NL-HaNA, VOC, 1.04.02, inv.nr. 2091, letter from Basra to The Netherlands, 22 July 1729, fol. 4967v.
18 Ibid., inserted shipping list, Basra, 1 November 1728–22 July 1729, fol. 4967r.
19 NL-HaNA, VOC, 1.04.02, inv.nr. 2546, letter from Bandar Abbas to Batavia, 31 March 1741, pp. 68–9.
20 R. Barendse, *Men and Merchandise*, vol. 3 of *Arabian Seas 1700–1763* (Leiden: Brill, 2009), 970–1.
21 Abdullah, *Merchants, Mamluks, and Murder*, 75–6.
22 G.A. Olivier, *Voyage dans l'Empire Othoman, l'Égypte et la Perse* (Paris: H. Agasse, 1801–7), vol. 1, 252; vol. 4, 273. Some of the copper sent to Basra was meant for Iran. Sultan ibn Muhammad al-Qasimi, *Power Struggles and Trade in the Gulf 1620–1820* (Forest Row: University of Exeter Press, 1999), 173–4.
23 Abdullah, *Merchants, Mamluks, and Murder*, 48–9.
24 NL-HaNA, VOC, 1.04.02, inv.nr. 2303, letter from Basra to The Netherlands, 30 April 1734, inserted shipping list, Basra, 1 January 1733–30 April 1734, fol. 5415r.
25 See Appendix 4.
26 NL-HaNA, VOC, 1.04.02, inv.nr. 2357 1, extract of letter from Basra to Bandar Abbas, 25 May 1735, inserted shipping list, Basra, 1 May 1734–25 May 1735, pp. 1317–19.

27 NL-HaNA, VOC, 1.04.02, inv.nr. 2416, letter from Basra to Batavia, 28 June 1736, pp. 10–12.
28 A. Das Gupta, *Malabar in Asian Trade 1740–1800* (London: Cambridge University Press, 1967), 98–9; G. Nadri, *Eighteenth-Century Gujarat: The Dynamics of Its Political Economy, 1750–1800* (Leiden: Brill, 2009), 114–15; G. Souza, 'Ballast Goods: Chinese Maritime Trade in Zinc and Sugar in the Seventeenth and Eighteenth Centuries,' in *Emporia, Commodities and Entrepreneurs in Asian Maritime Trade, c. 1400–1750*, eds. R. Ptak and D. Rothermund (Stuttgart: Franz Steiner Verlag, 1991), 311–13.
29 NL-HaNA, VOC, 1.04.02, inv.nr. 3164, report on sugar trade, Nagapattinam, 12 October 1766, fols. 601v–2r.
30 NL-HaNA, VOC, 1.04.02, inv.nr. 2546, letter from Basra to Bandar Abbas, 31 October 1740, p. 1009.
31 NL-HaNA, VOC, 1.04.02, inv.nr. 2416, letter from Basra to Batavia, 28 June 1736, pp. 21–3.
32 When the merchants arrived, the VOC sold goods, including candy sugar. NL-HaNA, VOC, 1.04.02, inv.nr. 2511, letter from Basra to Bandar Abbas, 31 January 1740, pp. 1026–8.
33 NL-HaNA, VOC, 1.04.02, inv.nr. 2426, letter from Basra to Bandar Abbas, 30 September 1738, fols. 3608v–9r.
34 NL-HaNA, VOC, 1.04.02, inv.nr. 2448, letter from Isfahan to Bandar Abbas, received on 3 September 1737, pp. 1384–5.
35 NL-HaNA, VOC, 1.04.02, inv.nr. 2824, report on Basra and Bushire, T. von Kniphausen on the ship *het Fortuin*, 15 February 1753, pp. 63–4.
36 NL-HaNA, VOC, 1.04.02, inv.nr. 2417, letter from Bandar Abbas to Batavia, 4 April 1737, pp. 3543–5.
37 NL-HaNA, VOC, 1.04.02, inv.nr. 2426, letter from Basra to Bandar Abbas, 30 September 1738, fols. 3607r–v.
38 NL-HaNA, VOC, 1.04.02, inv.nr. 2476, annual sales statement, Basra, 1737–8, pp. 1384–5.
39 NL-HaNA, VOC, 1.04.02, inv.nr. 2034 1, letter from Bandar Abbas to Batavia, 15 May 1725, pp. 30–1.
40 NL-HaNA, VOC, 1.04.02, inv.nr. 2546, letter from Basra to Bandar Abbas, 31 October 1740, pp. 1009–10.
41 Abdullah, *Merchants, Mamluks, and Murder*, 91.
42 Davies, 'British Private Trade Network,' 184–7, 210–17.
43 P.J. Marshall, 'Private British Trade in the Indian Ocean before 1800,' in *India and Indian Ocean: 1500–1800*, eds. A. Das Gupta and M. Pearson (Oxford: Oxford University Press, 1999, first published in 1987), 276–300.
44 NL-HaNA, VOC, 1.04.02, inv.nr. 2448, letter from Bandar Abbas to Batavia, 31 December 1737, pp. 133–4.
45 R. Shimada, *The Intra-Asian Trade in Japanese Copper by the Dutch East India Company during the Eighteenth Century* (Leiden: Brill, 2006), 86–128; Nadri, *Eighteenth-Century Gujarat*, 103–11.
46 NL-HaNA, VOC, 1.04.02, inv.nr. 2546, letter from Bandar Abbas to Batavia, 31 March 1741, p. 68.
47 Abdullah, *Merchants, Mamluks, and Murder*, 49.
48 W. Floor, *The Persian Gulf: The Rise of the Gulf Arabs: The Politics of Trade on the Persian Littoral 1747–1792* (Washington: Mage Publishers, 2007), 247. An illustrative example is the Portuguese ship *Santa Catharina*, which arrived from Bengal with various goods, including textiles for the Armenians in Bengal, in late 1747. After

delivering its cargo and acquiring silver, the ship sailed for Bengal in February 1748. When *Santa Catharina* passed by Nagapattinam, however, it was captured by the English, who thought the ship belonged to the French, with whom they were at war. The English confiscated the whole shipload, which included a collection of documents written in Arabic, Persian and Ottoman Turkish. For this valuable historical source and its analysis, see G. Sood, *India and the Islamic Heartlands: An Eighteenth-Century World of Circulation and Exchange* (Cambridge: Cambridge University Press, 2016).
49 Floor, *The Rise of the Gulf Arabs*, 96–8.
50 NL-HaNA, VOC, 1.04.02, inv.nr. 2766, letter from Basra to Batavia, 30 June 1749, pp. 50–1.
51 Ibid., pp. 18–19.
52 NL-HaNA, VOC, 1.04.02, inv.nr. 2766, letter from Bandar Abbas to Batavia, 25 December 1749, pp. 86–7.
53 NL-HaNA, VOC, 1.04.02, inv.nr. 2766, letter from Basra to Batavia, 30 March 1750, pp. 97–8.
54 NL-HaNA, VOC, 1.04.02, inv.nr. 2804, letter from Basra to Batavia, 11 January 1752, p. 11.
55 NL-HaNA, VOC, 1.04.02, inv.nr. 2804, letter from Basra to Batavia, 24 August 1752, pp. 35–6. Davies points out increased consulage duties collected at Bandar Abbas and Basra after 1750. Davies 'British Private Trade Network,' 181–4.
56 The silver brought to Basra might have come from Russia through Iran, considering there was a growth of trade between Iran and Russia in the first half of the 1750s. W. Floor, 'The Persian Economy in the Eighteenth Century: A Dismal Record,' in *Crisis, Collapse, Militarism and Civil War*, ed. M. Axworthy (Oxford: Oxford University Press, 2018), 143–4.
57 NL-HaNA, VOC, 1.04.02, inv.nr. 2804, letter from Basra to Batavia, 24 August 1752, pp. 38–9.
58 Bottomry is a contract by which the owner of a ship provides his or her ship as collateral for a loan to run a voyage.
59 NL-HaNA, VOC, 1.04.02, inv.nr. 2804, letter from Basra to Batavia, 24 August 1752, p. 37. The Dutch factors were particularly interested in Bahrain pearls. Later in 1754, the VOC had short-lived plan to take over Bahrain and control its lucrative pearling activities. There is no doubt some officials conducted private trade in this commodity. Floor, *The Rise of the Gulf Arabs*, 321–31 (Appendix I); S. Martin, 'Was the VOC Funding Mozart? The Diaries of Wilhelm Buschman on Kharg Island,' *Journal of the Royal Asiatic Society* 33, no. 2 (2023): 489–511. See also R. Carter, 'The History and Prehistory of Pearling in the Persian Gulf,' *Journal of the Economic and Social History of the Orient* 48, no. 2 (2005): 139–209.
60 NL-HaNA, VOC, 1.04.02, inv.nr. 2804, letter from Basra to Batavia, 11 January 1752, p. 11.
61 NL-HaNA, VOC, 1.04.02, inv.nr. 2787, letter from Basra to Batavia, 10 August 1750, p. 5.
62 NL-HaNA, VOC, 1.04.02, inv.nr. 2787, letter from Basra to Batavia, 7 February 1751, p. 23.
63 T. Ricks, *Notables, Merchants, and Shaykhs of Southern Iran and Its Ports: Politics and Trade of the Persian Gulf Region, AD 1728–1789* (Piscataway: Gorgias Press, 2012), 121–32.
64 NL-HaNA, VOC, 1.04.02, inv.nr. 2804, letter from Basra to Batavia, 11 January 1752, pp. 11–12.

65 NL-HaNA, VOC, 1.04.02, inv.nr. 2824, report on Basra and Bushire, von Kniphausen on the ship *het Fortuin*, 15 February 1753, pp. 63–4. Four years later, in 1757, the merchants embarked on a desert trip from Basra to Aleppo after buying a special pass from Sulayman Pasha. Anon., 'Overlandreis van Indië naar Europa, in 1757,' *Kronijk van het Historisch Genootschap gevestigd te Utrecht* 16 (1860): 124–5. For details on the desert routes, see C.P. Grant, *The Syrian Desert: Caravans, Travel and Exploration* (London: A. & C. Black, 1937).
66 A. Hakima, *History of Eastern Arabia, 1750–1800: The Rise and Development of Bahrain and Kuwait* (Beirut: Khayats, 1965), 71–3.
67 British Library (BL), India Office Records (IOR) G/29/5, 5 April 1729, inserted report from W. May to Bandar Abbas dated 6 April 1729.
68 S. Grummon, 'The Rise and Fall of the Arab Shaykhdom of Būshire: 1750–1850' (PhD diss., Johns Hopkins University, 1985), 242–64. Toward the end of the 1730s the chief merchant was Shaykh Muhammad Rida Shushtari, a *nisba* suggesting he could have a Shushtar origin. Floor, *The Rise of the Gulf Arabs*, 238.
69 Floor, *The Rise of the Gulf Arabs*, 239; Grummon, 'The Rise and Fall of the Arab Shaykhdom,' 246–8.
70 Floor, *The Rise of the Gulf Arabs*, 237–47.
71 NL-HaNA, VOC, 1.04.02, inv.nr. 2448, diary, J. van Schoonderwoerd, Bushire, 18 Augustus 1737–10 April 1738, pp. 1522, 1523, 1527, 1529, 1531, 1534, 1536, 1540, 1541, 2521, 2523, 2527, 2528, 2530, 2532, 2536, 2538, 2539.
72 See Appendix 3.
73 NL-HaNA, VOC, 1.04.02, inv.nr. 2610 2, letter from Bandar Abbas to Batavia, 29 June 1743, p. 120. Some of silver coins brought into Bushire were also re-exported to Basra, where they could fetch better prices. Matthee, Floor, and Clawson, *The Monetary History of Iran from the Safavids and the Qajars*, 154.
74 NL-HaNA, VOC, 1.04.02, inv.nr. 2610 2, letter from Bandar Abbas to Batavia, 29 June 1743, pp. 120–1.
75 Floor, *The Rise of the Gulf Arabs*, 237–8.
76 NL-HaNA, VOC, 1.04.02, inv.nr. 2511, letter from Bushire to Bandar Abbas, 5 April 1740, p. 1095.
77 NL-HaNA, VOC, 1.04.02, inv.nr. 2546, letter from Bandar Abbas to Batavia, 31 March 1741, pp. 101–2. For the copper trade at Bushire, see Matthee, Floor and, Clawson, *The Monetary History of Iran*, 156, 162.
78 He argued the same for the Isfahan factory. NL-HaNA, VOC, 1.04.02, inv.nr. 2584, final report from C. Koenad to S. Clement, 22 January 1742, p. 1793.
79 NL-HaNA, VOC, 1.04.02, inv.nr. 2824, report on Basra and Bushire, von Kniphausen on the ship *het Fortuin*, 15 February 1753, pp. 62–3.
80 It is unclear if Mir Nasir ceded the entirety of Kharg to the VOC, although the High Government of Batavia was convinced of their ownership. Floor, *The Rise of the Gulf Arabs*, 112–13, 252–4. In 1752, Mir Nasir also extended an invitation to the EIC to Bandar Rig. For the EIC's contact with Bandar Rig, see Abdul Amir Amin, *British Interests in the Persian Gulf* (Leiden: Brill, 1967), 35–9.
81 NL-HaNA, VOC, 1.04.02, inv.nr. 2824, report on Basra and Bushire, von Kniphausen on the ship *het Fortuin*, 15 February 1753, p. 66.
82 Ibid., p. 67.
83 Slot, *The Arabs of the Gulf*, 15; D.T. Potts, 'Kharg Island ii: History and Archeology,' *Encyclopædia Iranica*, last modified 20 July 2004.

84 Floor, *The Rise of the Gulf Arabs*, 116; NL-HaNA, VOC, 1.04.02, inv.nr. 2864, letter from Kharg to Batavia, 31 May 1755, pp. 47–8.
85 Floor, *The Rise of the Gulf Arabs*, 106–8.
86 See Chapter 3.
87 NL-HaNA, VOC, 1.04.02, inv.nr. 2804, letter from Basra to Batavia, 11 January 1752, pp. 12–13.
88 NL-HaNA, VOC, 1.04.02, inv.nr. 2824, translation of a letter from five Armenians of Bandar Rig to Basra, 20 February 1753, pp. 78–80.
89 NL-HaNA, VOC, 1.04.02, inv.nr. 2864, letter from Kharg to Batavia, 27 February 1755, p. 38.
90 NL-HaNA, VOC, 1.04.02, inv.nr. 2864, letter from Kharg to Batavia, 31 May 1755, pp. 51–2.
91 NL-HaNA, VOC, 1.04.02, inv.nr. 2885 1, letter from Kharg to Batavia, 27 September 1755, pp. 6–7.
92 NL-HaNA, VOC, 1.04.02, inv.nr. 2885 3, letter from Kharg to Batavia, 5 August 1756, pp. 22–4.
93 BL, IOR G/29/14, 24 December 1761, inserted letter from Bandar Abbas to Bombay under the same date.
94 Abdullah, *Merchants, Mamluks, and Murder*, 93–5.
95 NL-HaNA, VOC, 1.04.02, inv.nr. 2937, letter from Kharg to Batavia, 26 October 1757, pp. 18–19.
96 NL-HaNA, VOC, 1.04.02, inv.nr. 2885 3, letter from Kharg to Batavia, 5 August 1756, p. 8.
97 NL-HaNA, VOC, 1.04.02, inv.nr. 2909, shipping list, Kharg, 8 December 1755–20 July 1756, pp. 1–8; VOC, 1.04.02, inv.nr. 2937, shipping list, Kharg, 11 July 1756–4 August 1757, pp. 29–32.
98 NL-HaNA, VOC, 1.04.02, inv.nr. 3156, letter from W.J. Buschman at Kharg to Batavia, 30 September 1764, pp. 22–3.
99 Floor, *The Rise of the Gulf Arabs*, xvii, 317–19.
100 J. Lorimer, *Gazetteer of the Persian Gulf, 'Omān, and Central Arabia*, 2 vols. (Calcutta: Office of the Superintendent Government Printing, 1908–15). Qasimi also supports the idea of an overall catastrophe in the eighteenth century, but he does not ascribe it to 'Arab piracy' but to the political commotion in the Iranian littoral. Qasimi, *Power Struggles and Trade*, xi, xxxiii–xxxiv, 190–2. Cf. Sultan ibn Muhammad al-Qasimi, *The Myth of Arab Piracy* (London: Croom Helm, 1986).
101 Grummon, 'The Rise and Fall of the Arab Shaykhdom,' 89–90.
102 Ricks, *Notables, Merchants, and Shaykhs*, 182–3.
103 Abdullah, *Merchants, Mamluks, and Murder*, 50–1.
104 NL-HaNA, VOC, 1.04.02, inv.nr. 3027 2, letter from Kharg to Batavia, 22 June 1761, pp. 4–5.
105 NL-HaNA, VOC, 1.04.02, inv.nr. 3123, letter from W. J. Buschman at Kharg to Batavia, 8 May 1763, p. 5.
106 NL-HaNA, VOC, 1.04.02, inv.nr. 3123, letter from W. J. Buschman at Kharg to Batavia, 5 October 1763, p. 19.
107 NL-HaNA, VOC, 1.04.02, inv.nr. 3123, letter from Buschman at Kharg to Batavia, 8 May 1763, pp. 8–9.
108 Grummon, 'The Rise and Fall of the Arab Shaykhdom,' 91–3.

109 Qasimi, *Power Struggles and Trade*, 100; NL-HaNA, VOC, 1.04.02, inv.nr. 3156, letter from Buschman at Kharg to Batavia, 30 September 1764, p. 36.
110 Floor, *The Rise of the Gulf Arabs*, 262–5.
111 NL-HaNA, VOC, 1.04.02, inv.nr. 3123, letter from Buschman at Kharg to Batavia, 8 May 1763, p. 7.
112 NL-HaNA, VOC, 1.04.02, inv.nr. 3156, letter from Buschman at Kharg to Batavia, 30 September 1764, p. 27.
113 NL-HaNA, VOC, 1.04.02, inv.nr. 3156, shipping list, Kharg, 1763–4, pp. 55–60.
114 NL-HaNA, VOC, 1.04.02, inv.nr. 3156, letter from Buschman at Kharg to Batavia, 30 September 1764, pp. 28–30; VOC, 1.04.02, inv.nr. 3156, annual sales statement, Kharg, 1763–4, pp. 18–19.
115 NL-HaNA, VOC, 1.04.02, inv.nr. 3156, letter from Buschman at Kharg to Batavia, 30 September 1764, p. 27.
116 Qasimi, *Power Struggles and Trade*, 105, 110.
117 Abdullah, *Merchants, Mamluks, and Murder*, 48 (figure 2.1).
118 Ibid., 50–4. Abdullah also argues that English shipping to Basra significantly increased between 1763 and 1774. Ibid., 60–3 (figure 3.3).
119 Qasimi, *Power Struggles and Trade*, 149–54.
120 Abdullah, *Merchants, Mamluks, and Murder*, 54–6.
121 P. Risso, *Oman & Muscat: An Early Modern History* (New York: St. Martin's Press, 1986), 76–7.
122 BL, IOR P/414/51, report on the trade of Persia and Arabia, S. Manesty and H. Jones, Basra, 15 August 1790, pp. 80–1, 91, 96–7.
123 Ibid., p. 120.
124 Ibid., p. 78.
125 Ibid., p. 84.
126 Ibid., pp. 82–3. The tariff disparity between Basra and Muscat might have favoured the latter. According to the English officers, Basra imposed duties on the import of 'fine goods' and 'gross goods' from sea and Baghdad: 7½ per cent and 8½ per cent respectively. It also imposed a 'similar rate' on the export of goods to Aleppo and 5½ per cent on the maritime export of all sorts of goods. Muscat by contrast collected a 6½ per cent duty on all imports and provisions. Ibid., pp. 84, 93.
127 Ibid., p. 84.
128 Ibid., pp. 83, 123.
129 Ibid., p. 82.
130 Ibid., pp. 83–4.
131 Ibid., pp. 125–6.
132 Ibid., p. 123.
133 Ibid., pp. 86–8.
134 Risso, *Oman & Muscat*, 195–6, 198; W. Floor, *The Persian Gulf, Dutch–Omani Relations: A Commercial & Political History 1651–1806* (Washington: Mage Publishers, 2014), 167–9. B. Slot points out the possibility of regular Omani shipping to Danish settlements in south India during the last half of the eighteenth century. Slot, *The Arabs of the Gulf*, 58.
135 J.A. Saldanha, *The Persian Gulf Précis* (Gerrards Cross: Archive Editions, 1986), vol. 1, 445 (Appendix H: Report on trade between Persia and India, J. Malcolm, Bushire, 26 February 1800).

Chapter 6

1. N. Steensgaard, *The Asian Trade Revolution of the Seventeenth Century: The East India Companies and the Decline of the Caravan Trade* (Chicago: The University of Chicago Press, 1974).
2. For instance, E. Herzig, 'The Armenian Merchants of New Julfa, Isfahan: A Study in Pre-Modern Asian Trade' (PhD diss., University of Oxford, 1991), 198-9, 210-12; W. Floor, *The Economy of Safavid Persia* (Wiesbaden: Reichert Verlag, 2000), 123.
3. When the VOC utilized the Basra market, they used a broker and an interpreter there, too. Nationaal Archief, Den Haag (NL-HaNA), Verenigde Oostindische Compagnie (VOC), nummer toegang 1.04.02, inventarisnummer 1747 2, letter from Bandar Abbas to Batavia, 22 August 1707, p. 37.
4. NL-HaNA, VOC, 1.04.02, inv.nr. 1779, final report from F. Castelijn to W. Backer Jacobsz, Bandar Abbas, 1 May 1709, p. 434.
5. H. Dunlop, ed., *Bronnen tot de geschiedenis der Oostindische Compagnie in Perzië* (The Hague: Martinus Nijhoff, 1930), 460, 643.
6. C. Speelman, *Journaal der reis van den gezant der O.I. Compagnie Joan Cunaeus naar Perzië in 1651-1652*, ed. A. Hotz (Amsterdam: Johannes Müller, 1908), 332.
7. NL-HaNA, VOC, 1.04.02, inv.nr. 1667, letter from Bandar Abbas to Batavia, 27 January 1702, pp. 36-7.
8. NL-HaNA, VOC, 1.04.02, inv.nr. 1802, letter from Bandar Abbas to The Netherlands, 22 October 1712, fols. 2165r-v; VOC, 1.04.02, inv.nr. 1747 1, letter from Bandar Abbas to Batavia, 4 April 1707, pp. 412-14.
9. The word Banian stems from the Sanskrit *vaṇik*, which means a merchant or trader.
10. H. Yule and A. Burnell, *Hobson-Jobson: A Glossary of Colloquial Anglo-Indian Words and Phrases, and of Kindred Terms, Etymological, Historical, Geographical and Discursive* (Hertfordshire: Wordsworth Editions Ltd, 1996, first published in 1886), 63-4.
11. R. Matthee, 'Merchants in Safavid Iran: Participants and Perceptions,' *Journal of Early Modern History* 4, no. 3 (2000): 246-7.
12. A. Qaisar, 'The Role of Brokers in Medieval India,' *The Indian Historical Review* 1, no. 2 (1974): 224-5.
13. S. Dale, *Indian Merchants and Eurasian Trade, 1600-1750* (Cambridge: Cambridge University, 1994), 55-64.
14. Floor, *The Economy of Safavid Persia*, 21, 24; W. Floor, *The Persian Gulf, Dutch-Omani Relations: A Commercial & Political History 1651-1806* (Washington: Mage Publishers, 2014), 148.
15. J. Onley, 'Indian Communities in the Persian Gulf, c. 1500-1947,' in *The Persian Gulf in Modern Times: People, Ports and History*, ed. L.G. Potter (New York: Palgrave Macmillan, 2014), 240-3.
16. NL-HaNA, VOC, 1.04.02, inv.nr. 1913, secret letter from J.J. Ketelaar at Bandar Abbas to Batavia, 1 April 1718, p. 450.
17. By the word '*Khatris*', the Dutch might mean Indian merchants, specifically those who rendered brokering services. NL-HaNA, VOC, 1.04.02, inv.nr. 1802, letter from Isfahan to some merchants at Bandar Abbas, 3-4 December 1712, fols. 2258v-9r.
18. NL-HaNA, VOC, 1.04.02, inv.nr. 1559, letter from Bandar Abbas to Batavia, 2 August 1693, fols. 721r-2r.
19. British Library (BL), India Office Records (IOR) G/29/7, 30 April 1747.

20 Yule and Burnell, *Hobson-Jobson*, 61–2.
21 H. Fischer-Tiné, *Shyamji Krishnavarma: Sanskrit, Sociology and Anti-Imperialism* (New Delhi: Routlege, 2014), 3.
22 R. Enthoven, *The Tribes and Castes of Bombay* (Delhi: Cosmo Publications, 1975, first published in 1920), 113.
23 NL-HaNA, VOC, 1.04.02, inv.nr. 1650, letter from Bandar Abbas to Batavia, 11 December 1700, pp. 11–12.
24 C. Markovits, *The Global World of Indian Merchants, 1750–1947: Traders of Sind from Bukhara to Panama* (Cambridge: Cambridge University Press, 2000), 4–5, 24–31.
25 Ibid., 265–76.
26 NL-HaNA, VOC, 1.04.02, inv.nr. 2417, letter from Bandar Abbas to Batavia, 4 April 1737, pp. 3540–1; VOC, 1.04.02, inv.nr. 2448, letter from Bandar Abbas to Batavia, 31 December 1737, p. 151.
27 BL, IOR G/29/7, 30 April 1747.
28 NL-HaNA, VOC, 1.04.02, inv.nr. 1802, letter from Bandar Abbas to The Netherlands, 22 October 1712, fol. 2165r.
29 NL-HaNA, VOC, 1.04.02, inv.nr. 1843 1, letter from Bandar Abbas to Batavia, 22 June 1713, pp. 291–2.
30 NL-HaNA, VOC, 1.04.02, inv.nr. 1928, letter from Bandar Abbas to Batavia, 30 January 1719, p. 141.
31 NL-HaNA, VOC, 1.04.02, inv.nr. 1829, letter from Bandar Abbas to Batavia, 23 May 1712, pp. 66–7.
32 NL-HaNA, VOC, 1.04.02, inv.nr. 1897, instruction from J.J. Ketelaar to Bandar Abbas, 8 March 1717, pp. 175–9.
33 NL-HaNA, VOC, 1.04.02, inv.nr. 1947, letter from Bandar Abbas to The Netherlands, 25 May 1719, pp. 69–70.
34 NL-HaNA, VOC, 1.04.02, inv.nr. 1928, letter from Bandar Abbas to Batavia, 20 March 1719, pp. 269–70.
35 NL-HaNA, VOC, 1.04.02, inv.nr. 1964, letter from Bandar Abbas to Batavia, 5 April 1721, pp. 360–1.
36 NL-HaNA, VOC, 1.04.02, inv.nr. 1667, letter from Isfahan to Bandar Abbas, 6 August 1701, pp. 349–50; VOC, 1.04.02, inv.nr. 2016 1, letter from Bandar Abbas to Batavia, 1 November 1723, pp. 29–30.
37 NL-HaNA, VOC, 1.04.02, inv.nr. 1785, letter from Bandar Abbas to Batavia, 12 December 1710, fol. 482v.
38 NL-HaNA, VOC, 1.04.02, inv.nr. 1812, letter from Bandar Abbas to Batavia, 26 February 1711, p. 24.
39 NL-HaNA, VOC, 1.04.02, inv.nr. 2016 1, letter from Bandar Abbas to Batavia, 1 November 1723, pp. 29–30.
40 Natta '*tegenwoordig wederom in loco zich onthouden hebbende bij des eerste nazaat Heemraeds Jedmelanie*'. The report also notes that Natta was hated by entire Kiemtsjant family and encountered trouble due to their accusations. NL-HaNA, VOC, 1.04.02, inv.nr. 2368, letter from Bandar Abbas to The Netherlands, 18 May 1737, fol. 3783v. Cf. VOC, 1.04.02, inv.nr. 2448, resolution, Bandar Abbas, 30 April 1737, pp. 289–302; Ibid., 26 May 1737, pp. 364–8.
41 Matthee, 'Merchants in Safavid Iran,' 247. For the Persian classification of merchants in Safavid Iran, see M. Keyvani, *Artisans and Guild Life in the Later Safavid Period: Contributions to the Social-economic History* (Berlin: Klaus Schwarz Verlag, 1982), 215–58.

42 Dale, *Indian Merchants and Eurasian Trade*, 72–3; Matthee, 'Merchants in Safavid Iran,' 247–8; Floor, *The Economy of Safavid Persia*, 25.
43 NL-HaNA, VOC, 1.04.02, inv.nr. 2034 2, instruction from P. 't Lam to B. Lispensier, Bandar Abbas, 15 June 1725, pp. 341, 343–4.
44 It seems that this attempt failed. In 1728, the Bandar Abbas factory sequestered the brokers' sugar and zinc into the Company's treasury. NL-HaNA, VOC, 1.04.02, inv.nr. 2023, letter from Basra to The Netherlands, 22 January 1726, fol. 3349r; VOC, 1.04.02, inv.nr. 2105, letter from Bandar Abbas to Batavia, 1 April 1728, p. 273.
45 NL-HaNA, VOC, 1.04.02, inv.nr. 1667, letter from Isfahan to Bandar Abbas, 6 August 1701, pp. 349–51.
46 NL-HaNA, VOC, 1.04.02, inv.nr. 1582, final report from A. Verdonk to A. Berganje, Bandar Abbas, 15 May 1696, p. 158.
47 W. Floor, 'Dutch Relations with the Persian Gulf,' in *The Persian Gulf in History*, ed. L.G. Potter (New York: Palgrave Macmillan, 2009), 247. See also Chapter 1.
48 NL-HaNA, VOC, 1.04.02, inv.nr. 1843 1, letter from Bandar Abbas to Batavia, 15 March 1713, pp. 20, 21.
49 NL-HaNA, VOC, 1.04.02, inv.nr. 1818, letter from the suburb of Isfahan to The Netherlands, 12 January 1713, fols. 391v–4v.
50 Much in the same vein, Ketelaar admonished the Isfahan interpreter François Sahid. NL-HaNA, VOC, 1.04.02, inv.nr. 1913, report from J.J. Ketelaar at Bandar Abbas to Batavia, 31 March 1718, pp. 486–7.
51 See Chapter 4.
52 For instance, NL-HaNA, VOC, 1.04.02, inv.nr. 1694, shipping list, Bandar Abbas, 14 December 1703–24 May 1704, pp. 347–8 ('Abd al-Shaykh); VOC, 1.04.02, inv.nr. 1746, shipping list, Surat, 12 February 1706–25 March 1707, p. 263 ('Ali b. Sultan). For Persian and Arab merchants in Surat in the late Safavid period, see A. Das Gupta, *Indian Merchants and the Decline of Surat, c. 1700–1750* (New Delhi: Manohar Publishers, 1994, first published in 1979), 75–6.
53 G. Nadri, 'The Maritime Merchants of Surat: A Long-Term Perspective,' *Journal of the Economic and Social History of the Orient* 50, no. 2–3 (2007): 241, 247–8; G. Nadri, 'Commercial World of Mancherji Khurshedji and the Dutch East India Company: A Study of Mutual Relationships,' *Modern Asian Studies* 41, no. 2 (2007): 329–30. There has been a long debate on the origin of the word 'Banians' and their status in eighteenth-century Surat. Among others, see L. Subramanian, 'The Eighteenth-Century Social Order in Surat: A Reply and an Excursus on the Riots of 1788 and 1795,' *Modern Asian Studies* 25, no. 2 (1991): 321–65.
54 N. Steensgaard, *The Asian Trade Revolution*.
55 Dale, *Indian Merchants and Eurasian Trade*, 112–27; S. Levi, *The Indian Diaspora in Central Asia and Its Trade, 1550–1900* (Leiden: Brill, 2002), 180–222; E. Herzig, 'The Armenian Merchants of New Julfa,' 153–272; I. McCabe, *The Shah's Silk for Europe's Silver: The Eurasian Trade of the Julfa Armenians in Safavid Iran and India (1530–1750)* (Atlanta: Scholars Press, 1999), 199–239; S. Aslanian, *From the Indian Ocean to the Mediterranean: The Global Trade Networks of Armenian Merchants from New Julfa* (Berkeley: University of California Press, 2011), 86–201.
56 This family had settled in Iran by the middle of the seventeenth century, if not earlier. Speelman mentioned a Dutchman named Huybert Busskens who served the Safavid shah as a diamond cutter (*diamantslijper*). Huybert Busskens was buried in the Armenian graveyard in Julfa. Speelman, *Journaal der reis*, 133; W. Floor, 'Dutch-Persian Relations,' *Encylopædia Iranica*, updated 27 February 2013; G. Schwartz 'Terms of Reception: Europeans and Persians and Each Other's Art,' in *Mediating*

Netherlandish Art and Material Culture in Asia, ed. Th.D. Kaufmann and M. North (Amsterdam: Amsterdam University Press, 2014), 61.

57 NL-HaNA, VOC, 1.04.02, inv.nr. 1802, letter from Bandar Abbas to The Netherlands, 22 October 1712, fols. 2165r–v.

58 Nata and Darmdas '*onder het dagelijks frequenteren van 's Comp[agnie]s huis tot die jaren gekomen*'. Ibid., fol. 2165r.

59 NL-HaNA, VOC, 1.04.02, inv.nr. 1843 1, letter from Bandar Abbas to Batavia, 22 June 1713, pp. 291–2.

60 NL-HaNA, VOC, 1.04.02, inv.nr. 1732, letter from Bandar Abbas to Batavia, 31 January 1706, pp. 302–4.

61 Seven years later, however, Busskens requested that his salary be adjusted to 130 *mahmudi*s, the amount the former interpreter and his forefather Marcus Varijn enjoyed, which the Company granted. NL-HaNA, VOC, 1.04.02, inv.nr. 1829, letter from Bandar Abbas to Batavia, 23 May 1712, p. 63; VOC, 1.04.02, inv.nr. 1947, letter from Bandar Abbas to Batavia, 25 November 1719, p. 9.

62 NL-HaNA, VOC, 1.04.02, inv.nr. 1999, final report from J. Oets to J. de Croeze, Bandar Abbas, 15 November 1722, p 269.

63 NL-HaNA, VOC, 1.04.02, inv.nr. 1913, report from Ketelaar at Bandar Abbas to Batavia, 31 March 1718, pp. 503–4.

64 Ibid.

65 NL-HaNA, VOC, 1.04.02, inv.nr. 1737, edict from Sultan Husayn to the governor of Bandar Abbas, etc., March 1708, fols. 24r–v; VOC, 1.04.02, inv.nr. 1763, letter from Bandar Abbas to Batavia, 1 April 1708, p. 421.

66 NL-HaNA, VOC, 1.04.02, inv.nr. 1737, edict from Sultan Husayn to the governor of Bandar Abbas, etc., March 1708, fol. 24r; VOC, 1.04.02, inv.nr. 1763, letter from Bandar Abbas to The Netherlands, 15 March 1708, p. 439; VOC, 1.04.02, inv.nr. 1763, letter from Bandar Abbas to Batavia, 1 April 1708, p. 424.

67 Ibid., p. 425; VOC, 1.04.02, inv.nr. 1779, letter from Bandar Abbas to The Netherlands, 31 August 1708, p. 69.

68 NL-HaNA, VOC, 1.04.02, inv.nr. 1779, letter from Bandar Abbas to The Netherlands, 6 March 1709, pp. 486–7.

69 NL-HaNA, VOC, 1.04.02, inv.nr. 1779, final report from Castelijn to Backer Jacobsz, Bandar Abbas, 1 May 1709, p. 437.

70 NL-HaNA, VOC, 1.04.02, inv.nr. 1897, instruction from Ketelaar to Bandar Abbas, 8 March 1717, p. 178.

71 NL-HaNA, VOC, 1.04.02, inv.nr. 1667, letter from Isfahan to Batavia, 21 August 1701, p. 279.

72 W. Floor, *The Afghan Occupation of Safavid Persia 1721–1729* (Paris: Association pour l'avancement des études iraniennes, 1998), 324–31.

73 F.W. Stapel, ed., *Corpus diplomaticum* (The Hague: Martinus Nijhoff, 1935), vol. 5, 82 (Article 6).

74 NL-HaNA, VOC, 1.04.02, inv.nr. 2357 1, letter from Bandar Abbas to Batavia, 24 August 1735, pp. 383–6.

75 NL-HaNA, VOC, 1.04.02, inv.nr. 1747 1, letter from Bandar Abbas to Batavia, 4 April 1707, pp. 412–13.

76 W. Floor, 'Ḵelʿat,' *Encylopædia Iranica*, last modified 15 June 2017.

77 NL-HaNA, VOC, 1.04.02, inv.nr. 1598 1, letter from Bandar Abbas to Batavia, 31 March 1697, pp. 59–60. The EIC also did the same practice. P. Good, *The East India Company in Persia: Trade and Cultural Exchange in the Eighteenth Century* (London: I.B. Tauris, 2022), 147–9.

78 W. Moreland, *From Akbar to Aurangzeb: A Study in Indian Economic History* (London: Macmillan, 1923); I. Habib, 'Potentialities of Capitalistic Development in the Economy of Mughal India,' *The Journal of Economic History* 29, no.1 (1969): 32–78.
79 J. van Leur, *Indonesian Trade and Society: Essays in Asian Social and Economic History* (The Hague: W. van Hoeve Publishers, 1967).
80 Among others, see Das Gupta, *Indian Merchants and the Decline of Surat*.
81 M. Pearson, 'India and the Indian Ocean in the Sixteenth Century,' in *India and Indian Ocean: 1500–1800*, eds. A. Das Gupta and M. Pearson (Oxford: Oxford University Press, 1999, first published in 1987), 71–93.
82 K. Leonard, 'The "Great Firm" Theory of the Decline of the Mughal Empire,' *Comparative Studies in Society and History* 21, no. 2 (1979): 151–67; F. Perlin, 'The Precolonial Indian State in History and Epistemology: A Reconstruction of Social Formation in the Western Deccan from the Fifteenth to the Early Nineteenth Century,' in *The Study of the State*, eds. H. Claessen and P. Skalnik (The Hague: Mouton Publishers, 1981), 275–302; S. Subrahmanyam and C. Bayly, 'Portfolio Capitalists and the Political Economy of Early Modern India,' *The Indian Economic and Social History Review* 25, no. 4 (1988): 401–24.
83 R. Matthee, 'Politics and Trade in Late Safavid Iran: Commercial Crisis and Government Reaction under Shah Solayman (1666–1694)' (PhD diss., University of California Los Angeles, 1991); R. Matthee, *The Politics of Trade in Safavid Iran: Silk for Silver, 1600–1730* (Cambridge: Cambridge University Press, 1999); R. Matthee, 'Merchants in Safavid Iran'; R. Klein, 'Trade in the Safavid Port City Bandar Abbas and the Persian Gulf (ca. 1600–1680): A Study of Selected Aspects' (PhD diss., University of London, 1993–4), 67–115; Floor, *The Economy of Safavid Persia*, 27–64; W. Floor, *A Political and Economic History of Five Port Cities 1500–1730* (Washington: Mage Publishers, 2006), 237–322, 429–77.
84 He also notes that Safavid Iran's economy was mainly agrarian. Floor, *The Economy of Safavid Persia*, 27, 56; Floor, *A Political and Economic History*, 312. Cf. M. Pearson, 'Merchants and States,' in *The Political Economy of Merchant Empires*, ed. J. Tracy (Cambridge: Cambridge University Press, 1991), 100.
85 Matthee, 'Merchants in Safavid Iran,' 260.
86 Matthee, *The Politics of Trade in Safavid Iran*, 7–9, 63, 73–4, 89.
87 NL-HaNA, VOC, 1.04.02, inv.nr. 1747 1, letter from Bandar Abbas to Batavia, 30 November 1706, p. 34.
88 Anon., *Tadhkirat al-mulūk: A Manual of Ṣafavid Administration (circa 1137/1725)*, trans. and ed. V. Minorsky (Cambridge: Gibb Memorial Trust, 1943); Mirza Muhammad Rafiʿa Ansari, *Dastūr al-Molūk: A Complete Edition of the Safavid Manual of Administration*, ed. N. Kondo (Tokyo: Research Institute for Languages and Cultures of Asia and Africa, 2018); Mirza Muhammad Rafiʿa Ansari, *Mīrzā Rafīʿāʾs Dastūr al-Mulūk: A Manual of Later Ṣafavid Administration*, trans. M. Marcinkowski (Kuala Lumpur: International Institute of Islamic Thought and Civilization, 2002). There was a 'town broker' in Basra. The officer inspected the general trade and collected a 7 per mille duty on sales by private traders. Qaisar notes that there were state-appointed brokers at commercial centres in India as well. BL, IOR G/29/19, letter from Basra to London, 22 February 1736, fol. 31r; Qaisar, 'The Role of Brokers in Medieval India,' 226. For a comparative study of brokers in the Indian Ocean, see M. Pearson, 'Brokers in Western Indian Port Cities Their Role in Serving Foreign Merchants,' *Modern Asian Studies* 22, no. 3 (1988): 455–72.
89 NL-HaNA, VOC, 1.04.02, inv.nr. 1747 1, letter from Bandar Abbas to Batavia, 30 November 1706, pp. 34–6.

90 NL-HaNA, VOC, 1.04.02, inv.nr. 1798 2, letter from Bandar Abbas to Batavia, 1 August 1710, p. 9.
91 NL-HaNA, VOC, 1.04.02, inv.nr. 1802, letter from Bandar Abbas to The Netherlands, 22 October 1712, fol. 2164v. For the practice of gift-giving in Bandar Abbas, see Floor, *A Political and Economic History*, 306–9. For formalities of gift exchange in Islamic history, see L. Komaroff, ed., *Gifts of the Sultan: The Arts of Giving at the Islamic Courts* (New Haven: Yale University Press, 2011).
92 NL-HaNA, VOC, 1.04.02, inv.nr. 1829, letter from Bandar Abbas to Batavia, 23 May 1712, p. 63.
93 NL-HaNA, VOC, 1.04.02, inv.nr. 1694, letter from Bandar Abbas to Batavia, 20 August 1703, p. 22 (chintz); for the country's sugar taste preference, see Chapter 1.
94 Klein, 'Trade in the Safavid Port City,' 103.
95 NL-HaNA, VOC, 1.04.02, inv.nr. 1611 1, letter from Bandar Abbas to Batavia, 31 March 1698, p. 89.
96 NL-HaNA, VOC, 1.04.02, inv.nr. 1603, letter from Bandar Abbas to Batavia, 1 July 1699, fols. 1862r-v; Matthee, 'Merchants in Safavid Iran,' 254.
97 NL-HaNA, VOC, 1.04.02, inv.nr. 1848, letter from Bandar Abbas to Batavia, 13 April 1715, fol. 2352v.
98 NL-HaNA, VOC, 1.04.02, inv.nr. 1999, final report from Oets to de Croeze, Bandar Abbas, 15 November 1722, p. 260.
99 NL-HaNA, VOC, 1.04.02, inv.nr. 1897, letter from various Shiraz merchants including Hajji 'Abd al-Rida to J.J. Ketelaar, received on 6 December 1716, p. 347. Hajji Abd al-Wahhab was based on Isfahan. VOC, 1.04.02, inv.nr. 1856, letter from Bandar Abbas to The Netherlands, 23 April 1714, p. 133.
100 Matthee, 'Merchants in Safavid Iran,' 253–4.
101 NL-HaNA, VOC, 1.04.02, inv.nr. 1829, letter from Bandar Abbas to The Netherlands, 17 July 1711, pp. 116–17, 126.
102 NL-HaNA, VOC, 1.04.02, inv.nr. 1818, petition from various merchants from Shiraz and Lar to Batavia, March 1712, fols. 285r–8r. Ketelaar denied the asserted corruption. VOC, 1.04.02, inv.nr. 1913, report from Ketelaar at Bandar Abbas to Batavia, 31 March 1718, pp. 483–5.
103 NL-HaNA, VOC, 1.04.02, inv.nr. 1667, letter from Bandar Abbas to Batavia, 27 January 1702, pp. 5, 15.
104 NL-HaNA, VOC, 1.04.02, inv.nr. 1559, letter from Bandar Abbas to Batavia, 2 August 1693, fols. 749v–50r.
105 NL-HaNA, VOC, 1.04.02, inv.nr. 1779, final report from Castelijn to Backer Jacobsz, Bandar Abbas, 1 May 1709, pp. 424–5.
106 Nadri, 'Commercial World of Mancherji Khurshedji,' 321–6.
107 Floor, *The Economy of Safavid Persia*, 84; R. Matthee, *Persia in Crisis: Safavid Decline and the Fall of Isfahan* (London: I.B. Tauris, 2012), 94.
108 NL-HaNA, VOC, 1.04.02, inv.nr. 1829, letter from Bandar Abbas to Batavia, 23 May 1712, p. 26.
109 NL-HaNA, VOC, 1.04.02, inv.nr. 1582, final report from Verdonk to Berganje, Bandar Abbas, 15 May 1696, pp. 157–8.
110 NL-HaNA, VOC, 1.04.02, inv.nr. 1913, letter from Bandar Abbas to Batavia, 31 December 1717, pp. 3–9, 14–17.
111 E. Jacobs, *Merchant in Asia: The Trade of the Dutch East India Company during the Eighteenth Century* (Leiden: CNWS Publications, 2006), 158–64.

112 NL-HaNA, VOC, 1.04.02, inv.nr. 1582, final report from Verdonk to Berganje, Bandar Abbas, 15 May 1696, p. 165. For the critical position of Ceylon in the VOC's intra-Asian trade, see Jacobs, *Merchant in Asia*, 43–6.
113 NL-HaNA, VOC, 1.04.02, inv.nr. 1897, instruction from Ketelaar to Bandar Abbas, 8 March 1717, pp. 175–7.
114 NL-HaNA, VOC, 1.04.02, inv.nr. 1904, letter from Bandar Abbas to Batavia, 7 November 1718, fols. 2357r–v; VOC, 1.04.02, inv.nr. 1913, letter from Bandar Abbas to Batavia, 30 May 1718, p. 262.
115 NL-HaNA, VOC, 1.04.02, inv.nr. 1798 1, letter from Bandar Abbas to Batavia, 1 June 1710, pp. 400–2.
116 The Kirman merchants, though, brought gold specie with them. NL-HaNA, VOC, 1.04.02, inv.nr. 1904, letter from Bandar Abbas to Batavia, 7 November 1718, fols. 2367v–8r.
117 '*zij in alle gevallen voor 's Comp[agnie]s uitstaande penn[ingen] haar als borgen interponeren*'. NL-HaNA, VOC, 1.04.02, inv.nr. 1897, letter from Bandar Abbas to Batavia, 30 November 1716, pp. 7–8.
118 According to the Dutch, the Armenian and Muslim merchants actively exported those items to Surat. NL-HaNA, VOC, 1.04.02, inv.nr. 1650, letter from Bandar Abbas to Batavia, 11 December 1700, p. 3 (Armenians); VOC, 1.04.02, inv.nr. 1614, letter from Bandar Abbas to Batavia, 31 May 1700, fol. 1131r (Muslims).
119 R. Matthee, W. Floor, and P. Clawson, *The Monetary History of Iran from the Safavids and the Qajars* (New York: I.B. Tauris, 2013), 58–62.
120 Ibid., 71–7; NL-HaNA, VOC, 1.04.02, inv.nr. 1812, letter from Bandar Abbas to Batavia, 26 February 1711, pp. 27–8.
121 NL-HaNA, VOC, 1.04.02, inv.nr. 1928, letter from Bandar Abbas to Batavia, 30 January 1719, p. 150.
122 NL-HaNA, VOC, 1.04.02, inv.nr. 1768, postscript from P. Macaré at Isfahan to Batavia, sent on 15 October 1710, fol. 2054r.
123 NL-HaNA, VOC, 1.04.02, inv.nr. 1785, report on ducat trade in Isfahan, 7 August 1711, fol. 432r; VOC, 1.04.02, inv.nr. 1818, letter from the suburb of Isfahan to The Netherlands, 12 January 1713, fols. 391v–3r.

Chapter 7

1 Nationaal Archief, Den Haag (NL-HaNA), Verenigde Oostindische Compagnie (VOC), nummer toegang 1.04.02, inventarisnummer 2168, letter from Bandar Abbas to Batavia, 13 April 1730, p. 48.
2 NL-HaNA, VOC, 1.04.02, inv.nr. 2016 2, separate letter from P. 't Lam at Bandar Abbas to Batavia, 25 August 1724, p. 48.
3 NL-HaNA, VOC, 1.04.02, inv.nr. 1999, letter from Bandar Abbas to Batavia, 30 April 1723, pp. 419–21.
4 NL-HaNA, VOC, 1.04.02, inv.nr. 1999, final report from J. Oets to J. de Croeze, Bandar Abbas, 15 November 1722, p. 260.
5 NL-HaNA, VOC, 1.04.02, inv.nr. 2253, letter from Bandar Abbas to Batavia, 15 May 1731, pp. 121–3; VOC, 1.04.02, inv.nr. 2254, letter from Bandar Abbas to Batavia, 19 July 1732, p. 595; VOC, 1.04.02, inv.nr. 2322 1, letter from Bandar Abbas to Batavia, 30 September 1733, fol. 108v. Cf. W. Floor, *The Rise and Fall of Nader Shah: Dutch East India Company Reports, 1730–47* (Washington: Mage Publishers, 2009), 220–1.

6   NL-HaNA, VOC, 1.04.02, inv.nr. 2016 1, separate letter from P. 't Lam at Bandar Abbas to Batavia, 31 March 1724, pp. 121–2.
7   NL-HaNA, VOC, 1.04.02, inv.nr. 2034 2, letter from Bandar Abbas to Batavia, 20 September 1725, pp. 38–9.
8   NL-HaNA, VOC, 1.04.02, inv.nr. 2042, letter from Bandar Abbas to The Netherlands, 16 June 1727, fol. 3946v.
9   NL-HaNA, VOC, 1.04.02, inv.nr. 2055 2, letter from Bandar Abbas to Batavia, 10 September 1726, pp. 9–11.
10 NL-HaNA, VOC, 1.04.02, inv.nr. 1999, final report from Oets to de Croeze, Bandar Abbas, 15 November 1722, p. 269.
11 NL-HaNA, VOC, 1.04.02, inv.nr. 1999, letter from Bandar Abbas to Batavia, 30 April 1723, p. 421.
12 R. Matthee, 'The East India Company Trade in Kerman Wool, 1658–1730,' in *Études safavides*, ed. J. Calmard (Paris and Tehran: Institut français de recherche en Iran, 1993), 366, 377, 378; NL-HaNA, VOC, 1.04.02, inv.nr. 1779, final report from F. Castelijn to W. Backer Jacobsz, Bandar Abbas, 1 May 1709, p. 409.
13 NL-HaNA, VOC, 1.04.02, inv.nr. 1798 1, letter from Bandar Abbas to Batavia, 1 June 1710, p. 405.
14 Meanwhile, Bandar Abbas used a Persian secretary named Mulla Muhammad Shah as a provisional interpreter, and after his death an Armenian named 'Aphlataer'. NL-HaNA, VOC, 1.04.02, inv.nr. 1964, letter from Bandar Abbas to Batavia, 15 February 1721, pp. 70–1; VOC, 1.04.02, inv.nr. 1964, letter from Bandar Abbas to Batavia, 5 April 1721, pp. 359–60.
15 NL-HaNA, VOC, 1.04.02, inv.nr. 1999, final report from Oets to de Croeze, Bandar Abbas, 15 November 1722, pp. 295–6.
16 NL-HaNA, VOC, 1.04.02, inv.nr. 2016 1, letter from Bandar Abbas to Batavia, 1 November 1723, pp. 28–9.
17 NL-HaNA, VOC, 1.04.02, inv.nr. 2034 1, letter from Bandar Abbas to Batavia, 15 May 1725, pp. 12–13, 18.
18 NL-HaNA, VOC, 1.04.02, inv.nr. 2168, letter from Bandar Abbas to Batavia, 13 April 1730, pp. 79–80; VOC, 1.04.02, inv.nr. 2253, letter from Bandar Abbas to Batavia, 15 May 1731, pp. 111–12.
19 NL-HaNA, VOC, 1.04.02, inv.nr. 2511, letter from Bandar Abbas to Batavia, 31 July 1741, p. 138.
20 NL-HaNA, VOC, 1.04.02, inv.nr. 2584, final report from C. Koenad to S. Clement, 22 January 1742, pp. 1845–8.
21 NL-HaNA, VOC, 1.04.02, inv.nr. 2448, letter from Bandar Abbas to Batavia, 30 April 1738, pp. 1804–5.
22 NL-HaNA, VOC, 1.04.02, inv.nr. 2322 1, letter from Bandar Abbas to Batavia, 30 September 1733, fols. 108v–9r.
23 Floor, *The Rise and Fall of Nader Shah*, 226–31.
24 NL-HaNA, VOC, 1.04.02, inv.nr. 2416, letter from Bandar Abbas to Batavia, 10 December 1736, pp. 248–52.
25 NL-HaNA, VOC, 1.04.02, inv.nr. 2417, letter from Bandar Abbas to Batavia, 4 April 1737, pp. 3339–40.
26 Ibid., p. 3541.
27 NL-HaNA, VOC, 1.04.02, inv.nr. 2448, letter from Bandar Abbas to Batavia, 30 April 1738, pp. 1831–2.

28 NL-HaNA, VOC, 1.04.02, inv.nr. 2655, letter from Bandar Abbas to Batavia, 10 January 1745, p. 66.
29 NL-HaNA, VOC, 1.04.02, inv.nr. 2705, letter from Bandar Abbas to Batavia, 31 July 1746, pp. 53-5.
30 Similar to the VOC brokers, he lived with male and female family members in the port. He left three daughters behind when he died. British Library (BL), India Office Records (IOR) G/29/5, 27 April 1730. As for the Banians in EIC service, also see P. Good, *The East India Company in Persia: Trade and Cultural Exchange in the Eighteenth Century* (London: I.B. Tauris, 2022), 142-6.
31 C. Lockyer, *An Account of the Trade in India* (London: Samuel Crouch, 1711), 225-6.
32 BL, IOR G/29/2, 6 November 1708 (paying monthly expenses), 24 August 1709 (collecting the EIC's share of customs revenues of Bandar Abbas), 20 February 1710 (arranging bills for Kirman), 23 June 1710 (negotiating with the port government); Lockyer, *An Account of the Trade in India*, 226-7 (exchanging coins).
33 BL, IOR G/29/18, letter from Basra to London, 22 December 1725, fol. 42v.
34 BL, IOR G/29/5, 6 February 1729.
35 BL, IOR G/29/3, 9 January 1727.
36 BL, IOR G/29/5, 12 September 1729.
37 When Kessourjee was young, Sanchar acted as the EIC broker at Bandar Abbas. In 1727, the EIC called him broker. BL, IOR G/29/4, 5 July 1727; IOR G/29/5, 20 May 1729 (his accounts with the Company's secretary and Kirman wool merchant called 'Cossum'); IOR G/29/16, letter from Bandar Abbas to London, 2 April 1731, fol. 87r.
38 Sanchar also established a business colony-cum-home in Bandar Abbas. BL, IOR G/29/5, 7 January 1737 (his son's wedding).
39 Ibid., 30 August 1736; G/29/6, 13 November 1740.
40 Ibid., 15 May 1738.
41 Ibid., 4 October 1739.
42 Ibid., 4 October 1739, 14 December 1740.
43 Sanchar occasionally helped with the Company's woollen goods trade until around mid-1742. Ibid., 28 April 1742 (his last brokerage service).
44 Ibid., 20 October 1742.
45 Matthee, 'The East India Company Trade in Kerman Wool,' 365.
46 BL, IOR G/29/5, 28 January 1732, 23 March 1732, 21 April 1733, 22 April 1733, 6 September 1736, 1 January 1737; IOR G/29/6, 7 July 1746, IOR G/29/7, 23 March 1747.
47 Good, *The East India Company in Persia*, 147-8. I assume that 'Seawax', 'Espondior' and 'Sharyar' might be Zoroastrians, while Mahmud was a Muslim.
48 BL, IOR G/29/5, 30 April 1737.
49 For instance, BL, IOR G/29/6, 24 September 1737, 13 January 1738, 3 December 1739, 22 September 1743, 16 September 1745; IOR G/29/7, 24 September 1746, 10 January 1747. Nadir Shah also sent from Kirman to Bandar Abbas a large caravan loaded with copper, asafetida, etc. for export to India. Ibid., 18 February 1747.
50 Ibid., 13 September 1750 (Chiballah), 23 June 1752 (Parwana and Keemah). Parwana died by July 1761. IOR G/29/13, 25 June 1761.
51 BL, IOR G/29/8, 13 August 1754; 20 October 1754.
52 NL-HaNA, VOC, 1.04.02, inv.nr. 2710, letter from Bandar Abbas to The Netherlands, 10 October 1748, fols. 1318r-v.
53 G. Nadri, 'Commercial World of Mancherji Khurshedji and the Dutch East India Company: A Study of Mutual Relationships,' *Modern Asian Studies* 41, no. 2

(2007): 342. Cf. A. Das Gupta, 'The Broker at Mughal Surat, c. 1740,' *Revista de cultura* 13–14 (1991): 173–80.
54 S. Chaudhury, *From Prosperity to Decline: Eighteenth Century Bengal* (New Delhi: Manohar Publishers, 1995), 47–65, 93–108.
55 A number of scholars have scrutinized the role of local intermediaries in the eighteenth-century development of British power in India. Among others, see L. Subramanian, *Indigenous Capital and Imperial Expansion: Bombay, Surat, and the West Coast* (Delhi: Oxford University Press, 1996); S. Neild-Basu, 'The Dubashes of Madras,' *Modern Asian Studies* 18, no. 1 (1984): 1–31; P.J. Marshall, 'Masters and Banians in Eighteenth-Century Calcutta,' in *The Age of Partnership: Europeans in Asia Before Dominion*, eds. B. Kling and M. Pearson (Honolulu: University Press of Hawai'i, 1979), 191–213. For the case of the nineteenth-century Persian Gulf, see J. Onley, *The Arabian Frontier of the British Raj: Merchants, Rulers, and the British in the Nineteenth-Century Gulf* (Oxford: Oxford University Press, 2007).
56 NL-HaNA, VOC, 1.04.02, inv.nr. 2843, letter from J. van Schoonderwoerd at Bandar Abbas to Batavia, 1 October 1753, p. 18; VOC, 1.04.02, inv.nr. 2885 2, final report from J. van Schoonderwoerd to D. Aansorg, 28 November 1755, p. 15.
57 The VOC temporarily withdrew from Bandar Abbas in 1751.
58 NL-HaNA, VOC, 1.04.02, inv.nr. 2885 2, final report from Schoonderwoerd to Aansorg, 28 November 1755, p. 25.
59 NL-HaNA, VOC, 1.04.02, inv.nr. 2253, letter from Bandar Abbas to Batavia, 15 May 1731, pp. 118–19.
60 NL-HaNA, VOC, 1.04.02, inv.nr. 2448, resolution, Bandar Abbas, 21 June 1737, p. 443.
61 NL-HaNA, VOC, 1.04.02, inv.nr. 2584, letter from Bushire to Bandar Abbas, pp. 1544–5; Floor, *The Rise and Fall of Nader Shah*, 88, 99, 175.
62 In his second term, David Sahid's work was hindered due to his age and obesity (*zwaarlijvigheid*). NL-HaNA, VOC, 1.04.02, inv.nr. 2787, letter from J. van Schoonderwoerd at Bandar Abbas to Batavia, 17 February 1751, p. 41; VOC, 1.04.02, inv.nr. 2824, letter from J. van Schoonderwoerd at Bandar Abbas to Batavia, 8 February 1753, pp. 22–3.
63 Ibid., p. 23.
64 NL-HaNA, VOC, 1.04.02, inv.nr. 2968, letter from the ship *Nieuw Nieuwerkerk* to Batavia, 1 May 1759, pp. 6–7.
65 '*de wijs op welk zij het van tijd tot tijd zijn kwijtgemaakt vooral gedeeltelijk is terneder gesteld*'. Ibid., p. 20.
66 NL-HaNA, VOC, 1.04.02, inv.nr. 3092 1, translation of a Persian letter from Takardas and Kordas to Batavia, received on 1 March 1763, pp. 57–8.
67 NL-HaNA, VOC, 1.04.02, inv.nr. 2253, final report from N. Schorer to M. van Leijpsigh, Isfahan, 1 October 1730, pp. 660–1.
68 NL-HaNA, VOC, 1.04.02, inv.nr. 2390, letter from Bandar Abbas to Batavia, 19 March 1736, p. 13.
69 NL-HaNA, VOC, 1.04.02, inv.nr. 2254, letter from Bandar Abbas to Batavia, 19 July 1732, pp. 451–2; VOC, 1.04.02, inv.nr. 2356, letter from Bandar Abbas to Batavia, 9 November 1734, p. 30.
70 NL-HaNA, VOC, 1.04.02, inv.nr. 2322 1, letter from Bandar Abbas to Batavia, 30 September 1733, fol. 51r.
71 For a detailed description of the city during Nadir Shah's time, see Floor, *The Rise and Fall of Nader Shah*, 1–99.

72 NL-HaNA, VOC, 1.04.02, inv.nr. 2448, letter from Bandar Abbas to Isfahan, 7 May 1737, pp. 1199–200.
73 NL-HaNA, VOC, 1.04.02, inv.nr. 2610 1, letter from Bandar Abbas to Batavia, 31 October 1742, pp. 182–3.
74 NL-HaNA, VOC, 1.04.02, inv.nr. 2448, price list, Isfahan, 6 August 1737, pp. 1580–3; VOC, 1.04.02, inv.nr. 2610 2, annual sales statement, Isfahan, 1741–2, pp. 62–3.
75 T. Abdullah, *Merchants, Mamluks, and Murder: The Political Economy of Trade in Eighteenth-Century Basra* (Albany: State University of New York Press, 2001), 83–98. Sood emphasizes the value of family, especially the father–son relationship, in this commercial environment. G. Sood, *India and the Islamic Heartlands: An Eighteenth-Century World of Circulation and Exchange* (Cambridge: Cambridge University Press, 2016), 79–94.
76 J. Griffiths, *Travels in Europe, Asia Minor and Arabia* (London: T. Cadell and W. Davies, 1805), 390.
77 NL-HaNA, VOC, 1.04.02, inv.nr. 2016 1, letter from Bandar Abbas to Batavia, 31 March 1724, p. 70.
78 NL-HaNA, VOC, 1.04.02, inv.nr. 2357 1, resolution, Bandar Abbas, 21 March 1735, pp. 683–4; VOC, 1.04.02, inv.nr. 2511, letter from Isfahan to Bandar Abbas, 4 July 1740, pp. 944–5.
79 NL-HaNA, VOC, 1.04.02, inv.nr. 2476, resolution, Bandar Abbas, 16 February 1739, p. 502.
80 NL-HaNA, VOC, 1.04.02, inv.nr. 2023, extract letter from Basra, 8 October 1725, fols. 3342v–3r.
81 NL-HaNA, VOC, 1.04.02, inv.nr. 2610 1, letter from Bandar Abbas to Batavia, 31 October 1742, p. 133; VOC, 1.04.02, inv.nr. 2610 2, letter from Bandar Abbas to Batavia, 29 June 1743, pp. 202–3. Sood suggests that a merchant named 'Manbūr', who acted as a broker (*dallal*) in Basra in the late 1740s, was a '*baniyā*' from Gujarat. Sood, *India and the Islamic Heartlands*, 112.
82 NL-HaNA, VOC, 1.04.02, inv.nr. 2006, instruction from P. 't Lam to L. de Cleen and J. de Villiers, Bandar Abbas, 29 February 1724, fol. 3002r.
83 Bandar Abbas sent bookkeeper Dames Heij to Basra due to his proficiency in Persian. Ibid., fol. 3001r.
84 NL-HaNA, VOC, 1.04.02, inv.nr. 2357 2, charge against Moeltjent from G. Gutchi at Basra to Batavia, 25 May 1735, p. 88.
85 Ibid., pp. 88–9.
86 Ibid., pp. 89–92. Cf. NL-HaNA, VOC, 1.04.02, inv.nr. 2357 2, Moeltjent's confession, Basra, undated, pp. 98–9.
87 NL-HaNA, VOC, 1.04.02, inv.nr. 2357 2, charge against Moeltjent from G. Gutchi at Basra to Batavia, 25 May 1735, p. 93.
88 In a Dutch resolution, Natta (Nacha Natta Coetjek) was called a son-in-law of Moeltjent. NL-HaNA, VOC, 1.04.02, inv.nr. 2416, resolution, Bandar Abbas, 6 July 1736, pp. 1198–9.
89 NL-HaNA, VOC, 1.04.02, inv.nr. 2357 2, report on the goods confiscated from Wissendas and Natta, Bandar Abbas, 19 April 1735, pp. 82–3.
90 NL-HaNA, VOC, 1.04.02, inv.nr. 2417, separate letter from Bandar Abbas to Batavia, 30 November 1736, pp. 3451–5.
91 NL-HaNA, VOC, 1.04.02, inv.nr. 2476, resolution, Bandar Abbas, 16 February 1739, pp. 501–3.
92 NL-HaNA, VOC, 1.04.02, inv.nr. 2511, letter from Isfahan to Bandar Abbas, 4 July 1740, pp. 944–6.

93 The VOC described Fattitjant as 'a bad man and not capable enough to stay away from bankruptcy' (*een slim en buiten vermogen van respondentie voor bankroeten*). NL-HaNA, VOC, 1.04.02, inv.nr. 2448, letter from Basra to Bandar Abbas, 1 November 1737, pp. 1075–6.
94 NL-HaNA, VOC, 1.04.02, inv.nr. 2511, letter from Basra to Bandar Abbas, 31 January 1740, pp. 1016–18.
95 NL-HaNA, VOC, 1.04.02, inv.nr. 1732, letter from Bandar Abbas to Batavia, 31 January 1706, pp. 302–4.
96 NL-HaNA, VOC, 1.04.02, inv.nr. 1694, letter from Bandar Abbas to The Netherlands, 20 May 1704, p. 288.
97 F.W. Stapel, ed., *Corpus diplomaticum* (The Hague: Martinus Nijhoff, 1935), vol. 5, 82 (Article 9). Later in 1730, the Company secured an additional right for François's offspring: a thirty-year contract for the right to collect brokerage for trade in textiles (*lijwaten*), weighed goods and asafetida, as well as [goods] on Muslim ships, at Bandar Abbas. Ibid., 81 (Article 2); NL-HaNA, VOC, 1.04.02, inv.nr. 2254, order by Muhammad ʿAli Khan, October 1731, pp. 1414–17.
98 NL-HaNA, VOC, 1.04.02, inv.nr. 2390, letter from Bandar Abbas to Batavia, 19 March 1736, pp. 14–15. About six years later, David acted as the substitute for his brother and Isfahan interpreter Elias. Floor, *The Rise and Fall of Nader Shah*, 95–7, 98–9.
99 NL-HaNA, VOC, 1.04.02, inv.nr. 2476, resolution, Bandar Abbas, 28 November 1738, pp. 381–2. He received a monthly salary of 80 *mahmudi*s. VOC, 1.04.02, inv.nr. 2511, specification of monthly expenses, Basra, March 1740, p. 1222.
100 NL-HaNA, VOC, 1.04.02, inv.nr. 2583, letter from Basra to Bandar Abbas, 31 March 1741, pp. 1017–19.
101 NL-HaNA, VOC, 1.04.02, inv.nr. 2583, letter from Basra to Bandar Abbas, 10 August 1741, p. 1085.
102 NL-HaNA, VOC, 1.04.02, inv.nr. 2610 1, letter from Bandar Abbas to Batavia, 31 October 1742, p. 133.
103 Ibid., pp. 137–8. See also Chapter 5.
104 NL-HaNA, VOC, 1.04.02, inv.nr. 2610 2, letter from Bandar Abbas to Batavia, 29 June 1743, pp. 199–200; VOC, 1.04.02, inv.nr. 2680, letter from Bandar Abbas to Batavia, 10 August 1745, pp. 166–7.
105 NL-HaNA, VOC, 1.04.02, inv.nr. 2787, letter from Basra to Batavia, 10 August 1751, p. 9.
106 NL-HaNA, VOC, 1.04.02, inv.nr. 3064, letter from Kharg to Batavia, 30 September 1761, p. 16.
107 Aslanian has developed Herzig's argument. E. Herzig, 'The Armenian Merchants of New Julfa, Isfahan: A Study in Pre-modern Asian Trade' (PhD diss., University of Oxford, 1991), 102–9; S. Aslanian, *From the Indian Ocean to the Mediterranean: The Global Trade Networks of Armenian Merchants from New Julfa* (Berkeley: University of California Press, 2011), 202–14. Good has pointed out the Anglo-Armenian cooperation behind the relocation of Julfa Armenians to India in the eighteenth century. Good, *The East India Company in Persia*, 134–5.
108 The nature of the Dutch's local agency at Basra would be more accurately understood if we studied their English counterpart further. For an overview, see Onley, *The Arabian Frontier of the British Raj*, 229 (Appendix 3).
109 NL-HaNA, VOC, 1.04.02, inv.nr. 2448, resolution, Bandar Abbas, 21 June 1737, p. 443, pp. 445–6; Ibid., 3 July 1737, p. 460.

110 NL-HaNA, VOC, 1.04.02, inv.nr. 2448, diary, J. van Schoonderwoerd, Bushire, pp. 1528, 1530.
111 NL-HaNA, VOC, 1.04.02, inv.nr. 2476, annual sales statement, Bushire, 1737–8, pp. 1388–9.
112 W. Floor, *The Persian Gulf: The Rise of the Gulf Arabs: The Politics of Trade on the Persian Littoral 1747–1792* (Washington: Mage Publishers, 2007), 242–4.
113 BL, IOR G/29/6, 9 July 1743.
114 NL-HaNA, VOC, 1.04.02, inv.nr. 2705, letter from Bandar Abbas to Batavia, 31 July 1746, p. 89.
115 Floor, *The Rise of the Gulf Arabs*, 147.
116 For the population of Kharg in the Dutch period, see Floor, *The Rise of the Gulf Arabs*, 121–9.
117 In Bandar Rig, 'd'E[dele] Comp[agni]e door de op Bender Riek van de inlandse kooplieden voor d'ons afgekochte goederen te betalende tollen (die altijd in handen van onze makelaar komen) gelegentheid genoeg heeft, aan haar guarant te komen'. NL-HaNA, VOC, 1.04.02, inv.nr. 2864, letter from Kharg to Batavia, 31 May 1755, pp. 51–2.
118 See Chapters 3 and 5. It is interesting to note that in 1748, an Armenian called 'Coja Melleck' held the post of *shahbandar* at Bushire. BL, IOR G/29/7, 14 September 1748; Floor, *The Rise of the Gulf Arabs*, 248.
119 These refugees also included Banian and Iranian merchants. NL-HaNA, VOC, 1.04.02, inv.nr. 2864, letter from Kharg to Batavia, 1 November 1754, pp. 18–19; Floor, *The Rise of the Gulf Arabs*, 119.
120 NL-HaNA, VOC, 1.04.02, inv.nr. 2885 3, letter from Kharg to Batavia, 5 August 1756, pp. 20–2.
121 NL-HaNA, VOC, 1.04.02, inv.nr. 3092 1, letter from Kharg to Batavia, 19 October 1762, p. 37.
122 C. Allen, 'The Indian Merchant Community of Masqat,' *Bulletin of the School of Oriental and African Studies* 44, no. 1 (1981): 40–1; R. Klein, 'Trade in the Safavid Port City Bandar Abbas and the Persian Gulf (ca. 1600–1680): A Study of Selected Aspects' (PhD diss., University of London, 1993–94), 132–3; W. Floor, *The Persian Gulf, Dutch-Omani Relations: A Commercial & Political History 1651–1806* (Washington: Mage Publishers, 2014), 103–7, 118–20.
123 L. Lockhart, 'Nādir Shāh's Campaigns in 'Oman, 1737–1744,' *Bulletin of the School of Oriental and African Studies* 8, no. 1 (1935): 163–4, 167. Sood, *India and the Islamic Heartlands*, 184.
124 Lockhart, 'Nādir Shāh's Campaigns in 'Oman,' 167–70; P. Risso, *Oman & Muscat: An Early Modern History* (New York: St. Martin's Press, 1986), 39–42.
125 BL, IOR G/29/7, 30 November 1747.
126 Ibid., 24 December 1750. The Banians were also leaving for India at the time. Ibid., 6 February 1751.
127 NL-HaNA, VOC, 1.04.02, inv.nr. 3064, letter from Kharg to Batavia, 1 October 1761, pp. 30–1.
128 BL, IOR G/29/14, 2 September 1762.
129 Allen, 'The Indian Merchant Community of Masqat,' 41–53; L. Louër, *Transnational Shia Politics: Religious and Political Networks in the Gulf* (New York: Columbia University Press, 2008), 146–9. Hyderabadi merchants also constituted an integral

part of the merchant society of Bandar Abbas during Nadir's time. Floor, *The Rise and Fall of Nader Shah*, 229.
130 See Chapter 3.
131 NL-HaNA, VOC, 1.04.02, inv.nr. 2885 1, letter from J. van Schoonderwoerd at Muscat to Batavia, 27 January 1756, p. 56.
132 Floor, *The Rise of the Gulf Arabs*, 210.
133 Floor suggests that Bocca refers to Dikkah near Matrah. Ibid., 210–11.
134 NL-HaNA, VOC, 1.04.02, inv.nr. 2909, report, C. de Nijsz, 6 May 1757, pp. 8–9.
135 Ibid., p. 12.
136 NL-HaNA, VOC, 1.04.02, inv.nr. 2937, letter from Noerotaem Anak Ram Djiendil Djoezie to Batavia, received on 8 March 1758, pp. 107–9; Onley, *The Arabian Frontier of the British Raj*, 84; BL, IOR G/29/11, 16 September 1757.
137 NL-HaNA, VOC, 1.04.02, inv.nr. 2909, letter from Faram Ram (Narottam) to Batavia, received on 20 April 1757, pp. 4–5.
138 Floor, *The Rise of the Gulf Arabs*, 212.
139 NL-HaNA, VOC, 1.04.02, inv.nr. 2909, report, de Nijsz, 6 May 1757, pp. 12–13.
140 Floor, *The Rise of the Gulf Arabs*, 212.
141 When Brahé arrived at Muscat, Anand Ram was in Bandar Abbas. NL-HaNA, VOC, 1.04.02, inv.nr. 2937, report, W. Brahé and N. Mahué, 8 May 1757, pp. 6–7.
142 Ibid., pp. 9–10.
143 W. Floor, *The Dutch East India Company (VOC) and Diewel-Sind (Pakistan) in the 17th and 18th Centuries (Based on Original Dutch Records)* (Karachi: University of Karachi Institute of Central and West Asian Studies, 1993–4), 52–3, 58–60.
144 Ibid., 58–68, 79.
145 NL-HaNA, VOC, 1.04.02, inv.nr. 1011 2, letter from J. Mossel to Faram Ram (Narottam), 25 July 1757, pp. 209–11.
146 Floor, *The Rise of the Gulf Arabs*, 212, 215.
147 Ibid., 213.
148 NL-HaNA, VOC, 1.04.02, inv.nr. 2937, sales statement, Muscat, 21 September 1757–7 December 1757, p. 85.
149 NL-HaNA, VOC, 1.04.02, inv.nr. 1014 1, letter from J. Mossel to Narottam, 13 August 1760, pp. 519–20. In 1761, Kharg also wrote a letter to Narottam instructing him to help the wool agent Oanes Katjeh, who was then in Muscat, to collect the debt from the Memeny family and then transfer the money to Kharg. VOC, 1.04.02, inv.nr. 3064, letter from Kharg to Batavia, 30 September 1761, pp. 24–5.
150 He received a monthly salary of 100 rupees. Onley, *The Arabian Frontier of the British Raj*, 84–5.
151 Nadri, 'Commercial World of Mancherji Khurshedji,' 331–2.
152 A. Das Gupta, *Malabar in Asian Trade 1740–1800* (London: Cambridge University Press, 1967), 178.
153 For the Rahabi family at Dutch Cochin, see W.J. Fischel, 'Cochin in Jewish History: Prolegomena to a History of the Jews in India,' *Proceedings of the American Academy for Jewish Research* 30 (1962): 37–59; W.J. Fischel, 'The Rotenburg Family in Dutch Cochin of the Eighteenth Century,' *Studia Rosenthaliana* 1, no. 2 (1967): 32–44; Das Gupta, *Malabar in Asian Trade*, 103–36.
154 Risso, *Oman & Muscat*, 145–6.
155 Narottan died in that year. Ibid., 49; Onley, *The Arabian Frontier of the British Raj*, 84–5.

Conclusion

1. G.N. Curzon, *Persia and the Persian Question* (London: Longmans, Greens and Co., 1892), vol. 2, 288, 496, 560.
2. K.N. Chaudhuri, *Asia Before Europe: Economy and Civilisation of the Indian Ocean from the Rise of Islam to 1750* (Cambridge: Cambridge University Press, 1990), 384–7.
3. R. Matthee, 'Historiographical Reflections on the Eighteenth Century in Iranian History: Decline and Insularity, Imperial Dreams, or Regional Specificity?' in *Crisis, Collapse, Militarism and Civil War*, ed. M. Axworthy (Oxford: Oxford University Press, 2018), 35.
4. K. Pomeranz, *The Great Divergence: China, Europe, and the Making of the Modern World Economy* (Oxford: Princeton University Press, 2009), 114–65.
5. S. Aslanian, *From the Indian Ocean to the Mediterranean: The Global Trade Networks of Armenian Merchants from New Julfa* (Berkeley: University of California Press, 2011), 13.
6. For basic studies, see J. Kelly, *Britain and the Persian Gulf 1795–1800* (Oxford: Clarendon Press, 1968); A. Singh, *Fort Cochin in Kerala: The Social Condition of a Dutch Community in an Indian Milieu* (Leiden: Brill, 2010); A. Schrikker, *Dutch and British Colonial Intervention in Sri Lanka, 1780–1815: Expansion and Reform* (Leiden: Brill, 2007); A. North-Coombes, *A History of Sugar Production in Mauritius* (Floréal: Mauritius Printing Specialists, 1993); A. Sheriff, *Slaves, Spices & Ivory in Zanzibar: Integration of an East African Commercial Empire into the World Economy, 1770–1873* (James Currey, 1987); O. Feldbæk, *India Trade under the Danish Flag 1772–1808: European Enterprise and Anglo-Indian Remittance and Trade* (Lund: Studentlitteratur, 1969); E. Fihl, ed., *The Governor's Residence in Tranquebar: The House and the Daily Life of Its People, 1770–1845* (Copenhagen: Museum Tusculanum Press, 2017).

BIBLIOGRAPHY

1. Archival sources

The Netherlands

Nationaal Archief, The Hague:

Archief van de Verenigde Oost-Indische Compagnie (VOC)

Heren Zeventien en Kamer Amsterdam

INGEKOMEN STUKKEN UIT INDIË

Kopie-resoluties van gouverneur-generaal en raden
VOC781

Kopie-uitgaande stukken van gouverneur-generaal en raden
VOC1011, 1014

Overgekomen brieven en papieren
VOC1100, 1304, 1559, 1564, 1571, 1582, 1598, 1603, 1611, 1614, 1626, 1639, 1650, 1652, 1660, 1667, 1679, 1685, 1694, 1714, 1732, 1737, 1746, 1747, 1753, 1763, 1768, 1779, 1785, 1798, 1802, 1812, 1818, 1829, 1834, 1843, 1848, 1856, 1870, 1886, 1897, 1901, 1904, 1913, 1928, 1947, 1964, 1999, 2006, 2016, 2023, 2034, 2042, 2055, 2079, 2091, 2105, 2168, 2203, 2253, 2254, 2303, 2322, 2323, 2356, 2357, 2368, 2390, 2416, 2417, 2426, 2448, 2476, 2477, 2510, 2511, 2546, 2554, 2583, 2584, 2593, 2610, 2680, 2655, 2705, 2710, 2766, 2787, 2804, 2824, 2843, 2863, 2864, 2885, 2909, 2937, 2968, 3027, 3064, 3092, 3123, 3156, 3164, 3184

Kamer Zeeland

INGEKOMEN STUKKEN UIT GOUVERNEUR-GENERAAL EN RADEN

Kopie-missiven en -rapporten ingekomen uit Bengalen
VOC8736

Kopie-missiven en -rapporten ingekomen uit Surat
VOC9056, 9059

Kopie-missiven en -rapporten ingekomen uit Perzië
VOC8081, 8367, 9054, 9090, 9091

Kopie-missiven en -rapporten ingekomen uit Basra
VOC9099

Archief van de Hoge Regering van Batavia (HRB)
HRB846

England

British Library, London:

India Office Records (IOR)

East India Company Factory Records (IOR G)

    Factory Records: Persia and the Persian Gulf
        IOR G/29/2, G/29/3, G/29/4, G/29/5, G/29/6, G/29/7, G/29/8, G/29/10, G/29/11, G/29/13, G/29/14, G/29/15, G/29/16, G/29/18, G/29/19

Records of the British Residency and Agencies in the Persian Gulf (IOR R/15)

    Political Residency, Bushire
        IOR R/15/1/1

Proceedings and Consultations of the Government of India and of its Presidencies and Provinces (IOR P)

    Bombay
        IOR P/414/51

2. Published primary sources and reference works

Anon. *Tadhkirat al-mulūk: A Manual of Safavid Administration (circa 1137/1725)*. Translated and edited by V. Minorsky. Cambridge: Gibb Memorial Trust, 1943.

Anon. 'Overlandreis van Indië naar Europa, in 1757.' *Kronijk van het Historisch Genootschap gevestigd te Utrecht* 16 (1860): 124–8.

[Bronnen]. *Bronnen tot de geschiedenis der Oostindische Compagnie in Perzië*. Edited by H. Dunlop. The Hague: Martinus Nijhoff, 1930.

Bruce, P.H. *Memoirs of Peter Henry Bruce, Esq. A Military Officer, in the Services of Prussia, Russia, and Great Britain*. Dublin: J. and R. Byrn, 1783.

Bruyn, C. de. *Reizen over Moskovië door Persië en Indië*. Amsterdam: Rudolph en Gerard Wetstein, Joannes Oosterwyk, Hendrik van de Gaete, 1714.

Chardin, J. *Voyages du chevalier Chardin en Perse, et autres lieux de l'Orient*. Edited by L. Langlès, 10 vols. Paris: Le Normant, 1811.

[Corpus diplomaticum]. *Corpus diplomaticum Neerlando-Indicum: verzameling van politieke contracten en verdere verdragen door de Nederlanders in het Oosten gesloten, van privilegebrieven aan hen verleend, enz*. 6 vols. Vols. 1–2, edited by J.E. Heeres; Vols. 3–6, edited by F.W. Stapel. The Hague: Martinus Nijhoff, 1907–55.

Curzon, G.N. *Persia and the Persian Question*. 2 vols. London: Longmans, Greens and Co., 1892.

Della Valle, P. *Der voortreffelyke reizen van de deurluchtige reiziger, Pietro Della Valle, edelman van Romen*. Translated by J. Glazemaker, 6 vols. Amsterdam: A. Wolfgang and J. Rieuwertsz, 1664–5.

Du Mans, R. *Estat de la Perse en 1660*. Paris: Ernest Leroux, 1890.

Enthoven, R. *The Tribes and Castes of Bombay*. Delhi: Cosmo Publications, 1975 (first published in 1920).

Eversfield, S. *A Journal, Kept on a Journey from Bassora to Bagdad over the Little Desert, to Aleppo, Cyprus, Rhodes, Zante, Corfu, and Otranto, in Italy, in the Year 1779*. Horsham: Arthur Lee, 1784.
Ferrières-Sauveboeuf, L.-F. Comte de. *Mémoires historiques, politiques et géographiques des voyages faits en Turquie, en Perse et en Arabie depuis 1782 jusqu'en 1789*. 2 vols. Paris: Buisson, 1790.
Forster, G. *A Journey from Bengal to England: Through the Northern Part of India, Kashmire, Afghanistan, and Persia, and into Russia, by the Caspian-Sea*. 2 vols. London: R. Faulder, 1798.
Francklin, W. *Observations Made on a Tour from Bengal to Persia, in the Years 1786–7*. London: T. Cadell, 1790.
Fryer, J. *A New Account of East-India and Persia, in VIII Letters: Being Nine Years Travels, Begun 1672 and Finished 1681*. London: R.R. for Ri. Chiswell, 1698.
[*Generale missiven*]. *Generale missiven van Gouverneurs-Generaal en Raden aan Heren XVII der Verenigde Oostindische Compagnie*. 14 vols. Vols. 1–8, edited by W.Ph. Coolhaas; Vol. 9, edited by J. van Goor; Vols. 10–12, edited by J.E. Schooneveld-Oosterling; Vols. 13–14, edited by H.K. s'Jacob. The Hague: Martinus Nijhoff, 1960–2017.
Gmelin, S.G. *Travels through Northern Persia 1770–1774*. Translated by W. Floor. Washington: Mage Publishers, 2007.
Griffiths, J. *Travels in Europe, Asia Minor and Arabia*. London: T. Cadell and W. Davies, 1805.
Hamy, E.-T. *Voyage d'André Michaux en Syrie et en Perse (1782–85) d'après son journal et sa correspondance*. Geneva: Société générale d'imprimerie, 1911.
Hanway, J. *An Historical Account of the British Trade over the Caspian Sea with a Journal of Travels from London through Russia into Persia, and Back Again Through Russia, Germany, and Holland*. 2 vols. Dublin: William Smith and Richard James, 1754.
Hove, A. *Tours for Scientific and Economical Research, Made in Guzerat, Kattiawar, and the Conkuns, in 1787–88*. Bombay: Bombay Education Society's Press, 1855.
Ives, E. *A Voyage from England to India, in the Year MDCCLIV*. London: printed for Edward and Charles Dilly, 1773.
Kaempfer, E. *Amoenitatum exoticarum politico-physico-medicarum fasciculi V: quibus continentur variae relationes, observationes et descriptiones rerum Persicarum et ulterioris Asiae*. Lemgoviae: Typis & impensis Henrici Wilhelmi Meyeri, 1712.
Kaempfer, E. *Am Hofe des persischen Grosskönings (1684–85): Das erste Buch der Amoenitates exoticae*. Translated by W. Hintz. Leipzig: K.F. Koehler Verlag, 1940.
Kaempfer, E. *Die Reisetagebücher Engelbert Kaempfers*. Edited by K. Meier-Lemgo. Wiesbaden: Franz Steiner Verlag, 1968.
Lockyer, C. *An Account of the Trade in India*. London: Samuel Crouch, 1711.
Lorimer, J. *Gazetteer of the Persian Gulf, 'Omān, and Central Arabia*. 2 vols. Calcutta: Office of the Superintendent Government Printing, 1908–15.
Mirza Muhammad Rafi'a Ansari. *Mīrzā Rafī'ā's Dastūr al-Mulūk: A Manual of Later Safavid Administration*. Translated by M. Marcinkowski. Kuala Lumpur: International Institute of Islamic Thought and Civilization, 2002.
Mirza Muhammad Rafi'a Ansari. *Dastūr al-Molūk: A Complete Edition of the Safavid Manual of Administration*. Edited by N. Kondo. Tokyo: Research Institute for Languages and Cultures of Asia and Africa, 2018.
Niebuhr, C. *Reize naar Arabië en andere omliggende landen*. Translated by S.J. Baalde and J. van Schoonhoven, 2 vols. Amsterdam: S.J. Baalde, 1776–80.

Olearius, A. *Vermehrte newe Beschreibung der muscowitischen und persischen Reyse*. Tübingen: Max Niemeyer Verlag, 1971.

Olivier, G.A. *Voyage dans l'Empire Othoman, l'Égypte et la Perse*. 6 vols. Paris: H. Agasse, 1801–7.

Otter, J. *Voyage en Turquie et en Perse avec une relation des expéditions de Tahmas Koulikhan*. 2 vols. Paris: Freres Guerin, 1748.

Parsons, A. *Travels in Asia and Africa including a Journey from Scanderoon to Aleppo, and over the Desert to Bagdad and Bussora, a Voyage from Bussora to Bombay, and along the Western Coast of India, a Voyage from Bombay to Mocha and Suez in the Red Sea, and a Journey from Suez to Cairo and Rosetta, in Egypt*. London: Longman, Hurst, Rees and Orme, 1808.

[*Realia*]. *Realia: register op de generale resolutiën van het Kasteel Batavia, 1632–1805*. Edited by Bataviaasch Genootschap van Kunsten en Wetenschappen, 3 vols. Leiden: Gualth Kolff, 1882–6.

Saldanha, J.A. *The Persian Gulf Précis*. 8 vols. Gerrards Cross: Archive Editions, 1986.

Speelman, C. *Journaal der reis van den gezant der O.I. Compagnie Joan Cunaeus naar Perzië in 1651–1652*. Edited by A. Hotz. Amsterdam: Johannes Müller, 1908.

Spilman, J. *A Journey through Russia into Persia by Two English Gentlemen, Who Went in the Year 1739, from Petersburg*. London: R. Dodsley, 1742.

Taylor, J. *Travels from England to India, in the Year 1789 by Way of the Tyrol, Venice, Scandaroon, Aleppo, and over the Great Desert to Bussora*. 2 vols. London: S. Low, 1799.

Thévenot, J. de. *Suite du Voyage de Levant*. Paris: Charles Angot, 1674.

Waring, S. *A Tour to Sheeraz by the Route of Kazroon and Feerozabad*. London: T. Cadell and W. Davies, 1807.

Yule, H., and A. Burnell. *Hobson-Jobson: A Glossary of Colloquial Anglo-Indian Words and Phrases, and of Kindred Terms, Etymological, Historical, Geographical and Discursive*. Hertfordshire: Wordsworth Editions Ltd, 1996 (first published in 1886).

3. Secondary sources

Abbott, E. *Sugar: A Bittersweet History*. Toronto: Penguin Canada, 2008.

Abdullah, T. *Merchants, Mamluks, and Murder: The Political Economy of Trade in Eighteenth-Century Basra*. Albany: State University of New York Press, 2001.

Alam, M. 'Trade, State Policy and Regional Change: Aspects of Mughal-Uzbek Commercial Relations, c. 1550–1750.' *Journal of the Economic and Social History of the Orient* 37, no. 3 (1994): 202–27.

Allen, C. 'Sayyids, Shets and Sultāns: Politics and Trade in Masqat under the Āl Bū Saʿīd.' PhD diss., University of Washington, 1978.

Allen, C. 'The Indian Merchant Community of Masqat.' *Bulletin of the School of Oriental and African Studies* 44, no. 1 (1981): 39–53.

Amin, Abdul Amir. *British Interests in the Persian Gulf*. Leiden: Brill, 1967.

Aronson, M., and M. Budhos. *Sugar Changed the World: A Story of Magic, Spice, Slavery, Freedom, and Science*. Boston: Clarion Books, 2010.

Ashraf, Ahmad. 'Historical Obstacles to the Development of a Bourgeoisie in Iran.' *Iranian Studies* 2, no. 2 (1969): 54–79.

Ashraf, Assef. 'The Politics and Gift Exchange in Early Qajar Iran, 1785–1834.' *Comparative Studies in Society and History* 58, no. 2 (2016): 550–76.

Aslanian, S. *From the Indian Ocean to the Mediterranean: The Global Trade Networks of Armenian Merchants from New Julfa*. Berkeley: University of California Press, 2011.

Attar, Iman al-. 'Textual Representations of the Socio-Urban History of Baghdad: Critical Approaches to the Historiography of Baghdad in the 18th and 19th Centuries.' PhD diss., University of Tasmania, 2014.

Axworthy, M. *The Sword of Persia: Nader Shah, from Tribal Warrior to Conquering Tyrant*. London: I.B. Tauris, 2009.

Aubin, J. 'Le royaume d'Ormuz au début du XVIᵉ siècle.' *Mare Luso-Indicum* 2 (1973): 77–179.

Baladouni, V., and M. Makepeace. *Armenian Merchants of the Seventeenth and Early Eighteenth Centuries: English East India Company Sources* (Philadelphia: American Philosophical Society, 1998).

Banani, A. 'Reflections on the Social and Economic Structure of Safavid Persia at Its Zenith.' *Iranian Studies* 11, no. 1 (1978): 83–116.

Barendse, R. *The Arabian Seas: The Indian Ocean World of the Seventeenth Century*. New York: M.E. Sharpe, 2002.

Barendse, R. *Arabian Seas 1700–1763*. 4 vols. Leiden: Brill, 2009.

Berg, M. *Luxury and Pleasure in Eighteenth-Century Britain*. Oxford: Oxford University Press, 2008.

Bes, L. *The Heirs of Vijayanagara: Court Politics in Early Modern South India*. Leiden: Leiden University Press, 2022.

Bhattacharya, B., G. Dharampal-Frick, and J. Gommans, 'Spatial and Temporal Continuities of Merchant Networks in South Asia and the Indian Ocean.' *Journal of the Economic and Social History of the Orient* 50, no. 2–3 (2007): 91–105.

Biedermann, Z., A. Gerritsen, and G. Riello, eds. *Global Gifts: The Material Culture of Diplomacy in Early Modern Eurasia*. Cambridge: Cambridge University Press, 2018.

Blussé, L. *Strange Company: Chinese Settlers, Mestizo Women and the Dutch in VOC Batavia*. Dordrecht: Foris Publications, 1988.

Blussé, L., and F. Gaastra, eds. *On the Eighteenth Century as a Category of Asian History*. Aldershot: Ashgate, 1998.

Bosma, U. *The Sugar Plantation in India and Indonesia: Industrial Production, 1770–2010*. New York: Cambridge University Press, 2013.

Bosma, U. *The World of Sugar: How the Sweet Stuff Transformed Our Politics, Health, and Environment over 2,000 Years*. Cambridge: The Belknap Press of Harvard University Press, 2023.

Brewer, J., and A. Bermingham, eds. *The Consumption of Culture, 1600–1800: Image, Object, Text*. London: Routledge, 1995.

Brewer, J., and R. Porter, eds. *Consumption and the World of Goods*. London: Routledge, 1993.

Brewer, J., and S. Staves, eds. *Early Modern Conceptions of Property*. London: Routledge, 1995.

Carter, R. 'The History and Prehistory of Pearling in the Persian Gulf.' *Journal of the Economic and Social History of the Orient* 48, no. 2 (2005): 139–209.

Ceylan, E. 'Baghdad, 1500–1932.' *Encyclopaedia of Islam*, THREE.

Chaiklin, M. *Cultural Commerce and Dutch Commercial Culture: The Influence of European Material Culture on Japan, 1700–1850*. Leiden: CNWS, 2003.

Chaudhuri, K.N. *The Trading World of Asia and the English East India Company, 1660–1760*. Cambridge: Cambridge University Press, 1978.

Chaudhuri, K.N. *Trade and Civilisation in the Indian Ocean: An Economic History from the Rise of Islam to 1750*. Cambridge: Cambridge University Press, 1985.
Chaudhuri, K.N. *Asia before Europe: Economy and Civilisation of the Indian Ocean from the Rise of Islam to 1750*. Cambridge: Cambridge University Press, 1990.
Chaudhury, S. *From Prosperity to Decline: Eighteenth Century Bengal*. New Delhi: Manohar Publishers, 1995.
Dale, S. *Indian Merchants and Eurasian Trade, 1600–1750*. Cambridge: Cambridge University, 1994.
Daniels, C. *Agro-Industries and Forestry: Sugarcane Technology*, part 3 of *Biology and Biological Technology*, vol. 6 of *Science and Civilization in China*. Cambridge: Cambridge University Press, 1996.
Das Gupta, A. *Malabar in Asian Trade 1740–1800*. London: Cambridge University Press, 1967.
Das Gupta, A. 'The Broker at Mughal Surat, c. 1740.' *Revista de cultura* 13–14 (1991): 173–80.
Das Gupta, A. *Indian Merchants and the Decline of Surat c. 1700–1750*. New Delhi: Manohar Publishers, 1994 (first published in 1979).
Das Gupta, A. 'Introduction II: The Story.' In *India and Indian Ocean: 1500–1800*, edited by A. Das Gupta and M. Pearson, 25–45. Oxford: Oxford University Press, 1999 (first published in 1987).
Das Gupta, A. 'India and the Indian Ocean in the Eighteenth Century.' In *India and Indian Ocean: 1500–1800*, edited by A. Das Gupta and M. Pearson, 131–61. Oxford: Oxford University Press, 1999 (first published in 1987).
Das Gupta, A., and M. Pearson, eds. *India and Indian Ocean: 1500–1800*. Oxford: Oxford University Press, 1999 (first published in 1987).
Davies, T. 'British Private Trade Network in the Arabian Seas, c. 1680–c. 1760.' PhD diss., University of Warwick, 2012.
Eldem, E. *French Trade in Istanbul in the Eighteenth Century*. Leiden: Brill, 1999.
Fattah, H. *The Politics of Regional Trade in Iraq, Arabia, and the Gulf 1745–1900*. Albany: State University of New York Press, 1997.
Feldbæk, O. *India Trade under the Danish Flag 1772–1808: European Enterprise and Anglo-Indian Remittance and Trade*. Lund: Studentlitteratur, 1969.
Ferrier, R. 'The Armenians and the East India Company in Persia in the Seventeenth and Early Eighteenth Centuries.' *The Economic History Review* 26, no. 1 (1973): 38–62.
Ferrier, R. 'The Terms and Conditions under which English Trade Was Transacted with Ṣafavid Persia.' *Bulletin of the School of Oriental and African Studies* 49, no. 1 (1986): 48–66.
Fihl, E., ed. *The Governor's Residence in Tranquebar: The House and the Daily Life of Its People, 1770–1845*. Copenhagen: Museum Tusculanum Press, 2017.
Fischel, W.J. 'Cochin in Jewish History: Prolegomena to a History of the Jews in India.' *Proceedings of the American Academy for Jewish Research* 30 (1962): 37–59.
Fischel, W.J. 'The Rotenburg Family in Dutch Cochin of the Eighteenth Century.' *Studia Rosenthaliana* 1, no. 2 (1967): 32–44.
Fischer-Tiné, H. *Shyamji Krishnavarma: Sanskrit, Sociology and Anti-Imperialism*. New Delhi: Routledge, 2014.
Floor, W. *The Dutch East India Company (VOC) and Diewel-Sind (Pakistan) in the 17th and 18th Centuries (Based on Original Dutch Records)*. Karachi: University of Karachi Institute of Central and West Asian Studies, 1993–4.

Floor, W. *The Afghan Occupation of Safavid Persia 1721–1729*. Paris: Association pour l'avancement des études iraniennes, 1998.
Floor, W. *The Economy of Safavid Persia*. Wiesbaden: Reichert Verlag, 2000.
Floor, W. *Traditional Crafts in Qajar Iran (1800–1925)*. California: Mazda Publishers, 2003.
Floor, W. *A Political and Economic History of Five Port Cities 1500–1730*. Washington: Mage Publishers, 2006.
Floor, W. *The Persian Gulf: The Rise of the Gulf Arabs: The Politics of Trade on the Persian Littoral 1747–1792*. Washington: Mage Publishers, 2007.
Floor, W. *The Rise and Fall of Nader Shah: Dutch East India Company Reports, 1730–47*. Washington: Mage Publishers, 2009.
Floor, W. 'Dutch Relations with the Persian Gulf.' In *The Persian Gulf in History*, edited by L.G. Potter, 235–59. New York: Palgrave Macmillan, 2009.
Floor, W. 'Sugar.' *Encyclopædia Iranica*. Last modified 20 July 2009.
Floor, W. The Persian Gulf: Links with the Hinterland: *Bushehr, Borazjan, Kazerun, Banu Ka'b & Bandar Abbas*. Washington: Mage Publishers, 2011.
Floor, W. 'Dutch-Persian Relations.' *Encyclopædia Iranica*. Last modified 27 February 2013.
Floor, W. *The Persian Gulf, Dutch-Omani Relations: A Commercial & Political History 1651–1806*. Washington: Mage Publishers, 2014.
Floor, W. *The Hula Arabs of the Shibkuh Coast of Iran*. Washington: Mage Publishers, 2014.
Floor, W. *History of Bread in Iran*. Washington: Mage Publishers, 2015.
Floor, W. 'Ḵelʿat.' *Encyclopædia Iranica*. Last modified 15 June 2017.
Floor, W. 'The Persian Economy in the Eighteenth Century: A Dismal Record.' In *Crisis, Collapse, Militarism and Civil War*, edited by M. Axworthy, 125–50. Oxford: Oxford University Presss, 2018.
Floor, W., and M.H. Faghfoory, *The First Dutch-Persian Commercial Conflict: The Attack on Qeshm Island, 1645*. Costa Mesa: Mazda Publishers, 2004.
Floor, W., and H. Javadi, *Persian Pleasures: How Iranians Relaxed through the Centuries with Food, Drink & Drugs*. Washington: Mage Publishers, 2019.
Gerritsen, A., and G. Riello, *The Global Lives of Things: The Material Culture of Connections in the Early Modern World*. Abingdon: Routledge, 2016.
Gommans, J. *The Rise of the Indo-Afghan Empire c. 1710–1780*. Leiden: Brill, 1995.
Good, P. 'The East India Company's Farmān, 1622-1747.' *Iranian Studies* 52, no. 1–2 (2019): 181–97.
Good, P. *The East India Company in Persia: Trade and Cultural Exchange in the Eighteenth Century*. London: I.B. Tauris, 2022.
Grant, C.P. *The Syrian Desert: Caravans, Travel and Exploration*. London: A. & C. Black, 1937.
Grummon, S. 'The Rise and Fall of the Arab Shaykhdom of Būshire: 1750–1850.' PhD diss., Johns Hopkins University, 1985.
Habib, I. 'Potentialities of Capitalistic Development in the Economy of Mughal India.' *The Journal of Economic History* 29, no. 1 (1969): 32–78.
Hakima, A. *History of Eastern Arabia, 1750–1800: The Rise and Development of Bahrain and Kuwait*. Beirut: Khayats, 1965.
Hamashita, T., and H. Kawakatsu, eds. *Ajiakōekiken to Nihon kōgyōka: 1500–1900 [Intra-Asian Trade and Japanese Industrialization: 1500–1900]*. Tokyo: Riburopōto, 1991.
Haneda, M. 'Les compagnies des Indes orientales et les interprètes de Bandar ʿAbbās.' *Eurasian Studies* 1–2 (2006): 175–93.

Herzig, E. 'The Armenian Merchants of New Julfa, Isfahan: A Study in Pre-Modern Asian Trade.' PhD diss., University of Oxford, 1991.
Hirai, K. *Satō no teikoku: Nihon shokuminchi to Ajia shijō [Empire of Sugar: External Forces of Change in the Economy of Japanese Colonies]*. Tokyo: Tōkyōdaigaku shuppankai, 2017.
Hoseini, A. 'Sharbat va sharbat-khana dar gudhar-i zaman [Iran's Sherbet and Sherbet Houses in Passage of Time].' *Bagh-i nazar* 10, no. 25 (2013): 57–66.
Jacobs, E. *Merchant in Asia: The Trade of the Dutch East India Company during the Eighteenth Century*. Leiden: CNWS Publications, 2006.
Kahan, A. *The Plow, the Hammer and the Knout: An Economic History of Eighteenth-Century Russia*. Chicago: University of Chicago Press, 1985.
Kelly, J. *Britain and the Persian Gulf 1795–1800*. Oxford: Clarendon Press, 1968.
Keyvani, M. *Artisans and Guild Life in the Later Safavid Period: Contributions to the Social-Economic History of Persia*. Berlin: Klaus Schwarz Verlag, 1982.
Khalifa, K.K. al-. 'Commerce and Conflict: The English East India Company Factories in the Gulf, 1700–47.' PhD diss., University of Essex, 1988.
Klein, R. 'Trade in the Safavid Port City Bandar Abbas and the Persian Gulf (ca. 1600–1680): A Study of Selected Aspects.' PhD diss., University of London, 1993–4.
Kleiss, W. *Karawanenbauten in Iran*. 6 vols. Berlin: Reimer, 1996–2001.
Knight, G.R. *Commodities and Colonialism: The Story of Big Sugar in Indonesia, 1880–1942*. Leiden: Brill, 2013.
Lambton, A.K.S. *Landlord and Peasant in Persia: A Study of Land Tenure and Land Revenue Administration*. London: Oxford University Press, 1953.
Laver, M. *The Dutch East India Company in Early Modern Japan: Gift Giving and Diplomacy*. London: Bloomsbury Academic, 2020.
Leonard, K. 'The "Great Firm" Theory of the Decline of the Mughal Empire.' *Comparative Studies in Society and History* 21, no. 2 (1979): 151–67.
Leur, J. van. *Indonesian Trade and Society: Essays in Asian Social and Economic History*. The Hague: W. van Hoeve Publishers, 1967.
Levi, S. *The Indian Diaspora in Central Asia and Its Trade, 1550–1900*. Leiden: Brill, 2002.
Lockhart, L. 'Nādir Shāh's Campaigns in ʿOman, 1737–1744.' *Bulletin of the School of Oriental and African Studies* 8, no. 1 (1935): 157–71.
Lockhart, L. *Nadir Shah: A Critical Study Based Mainly upon Contemporary Sources*. London: Luzac, 1938.
Lockhart, L. *The Fall of the Ṣafavī Dynasty and the Afghan Occupation of Persia*. Cambridge: Cambridge University Press, 1958.
Louër, L. *Transnational Shia Politics: Religious and Political Networks in the Gulf*. New York: Columbia University Press, 2008.
Kazemi, R. 'Tobacco, Eurasian Trade, and the Early Modern Iranian Economy.' *Iranian Studies* 49, no. 4 (2016): 613–33.
Kearney, M. *The Indian Ocean in World History*. New York: Routledge, 2004.
Komaroff, F., ed. *Gifts of the Sultan: The Arts of Giving at the Islamic Courts*. New Haven: Yale University Press, 2011.
Machado, P., S. Fee, and G. Campbell, eds. *Textile Trades, Consumer Cultures, and the Material Worlds of the Indian Ocean: An Ocean of Cloth*. Cham: Palgrave Macmillan, 2018.
MacPherson, K. *The Indian Ocean: A History of People and the Sea*. New Delhi: Oxford University Press, 2001 (first published in 1993).

Mahdavi, S. 'Qajar Dynasty xiv: Qajar Cuisine.' *Encyclopædia Iranica*. Last modified 19 March 2015.
Markovits, C. *The Global World of Indian Merchants, 1750–1947: Traders of Sind from Bukhara to Panama*. Cambridge: Cambridge University Press, 2000.
Marshall, P.J. 'Masters and Banians in Eighteenth-Century Calcutta.' In *The Age of Partnership: Europeans in Asia before Dominion*, edited by B. Kling and M. Pearson, 191–213. Honolulu: University Press of Hawai'i, 1979.
Marshall, P.J. 'Private British Trade in the Indian Ocean before 1800.' In *India and Indian Ocean: 1500–1800*, edited by A. Das Gupta and M. Pearson, 276–300. Oxford: Oxford University Press, 1999 (first published in 1987).
Martin, S. 'Was the VOC Funding Mozart? The Diaries of Wilhelm Buschman on Kharg Island.' *Journal of the Royal Asiatic Society* 33, no. 2 (2023): 489–511.
Matsuura, A. 'The Import of Chinese Sugar in the Nagasaki Junk Trade and Its Impact.' In *Copper in the Early Modern Sino-Japanese Trade* Copper, edited by K. Nagase-Reimer, 157–74. Leiden: Brill, 2016.
Matthee, R. 'Politics and Trade in Late Safavid Iran: Commercial Crisis and Government Reaction under Shah Solayman (1666–1694).' PhD diss., University of California Los Angeles, 1991.
Matthee, R. 'The East India Company Trade in Kerman Wool, 1658–1730.' In *Études safavides*, edited by J. Calmard, 343–83. Paris and Tehran: Institut français de recherche en Iran, 1993.
Matthee, R. *The Politics of Trade in Safavid Iran: Silk for Silver, 1600–1730*. Cambridge: Cambridge University Press, 1999.
Matthee, R. 'Merchants in Safavid Iran: Participants and Perceptions.' *Journal of Early Modern History* 4, no. 3 (2000): 254–63.
Matthee, R. *The Pursuit of Pleasure: Drugs and Stimulants in Iranian History, 1500–1900*. Princeton: Princeton University Press, 2005.
Matthee, R. 'A Sugar Banquet for the Shah: Anglo-Dutch Competition at the Iranian Court of Šāh Sultān Ḥusayn (r. 1694–1722).' *Eurasian Studies* 1–2 (2006): 195–217.
Matthee, R. 'Boom and Bust: The Port of Basra in the Sixteenth and Seventeenth Centuries.' In *The Persian Gulf in History*, edited by L. G. Potter, 105–27. New York: Palgrave Macmillan, 2009.
Matthee, R. *Persia in Crisis: Safavid Decline and the Fall of Isfahan*. London: I.B. Tauris, 2012.
Matthee, R. 'The Safavid Economy as Part of the World Economy.' In *Iran and the World in the Safavid Age*, edited by W. Floor and E. Herzig, 31–47. London: I.B. Tauris, 2012.
Matthee, R. 'Gift-Giving iv: In the Safavid Period.' *Encyclopædia Iranica*. Last modified 9 February 2012.
Matthee, R. 'Historiographical Reflections on the Eighteenth Century in Iranian History: Decline and Insularity, Imperial Dreams, or Regional Specificity?' In *Crisis, Collapse, Militarism and Civil War*, edited by M. Axworthy, 21–41. Oxford: Oxford University Press, 2018.
Matthee, R., W. Floor, and P. Clawson. *The Monetary History of Iran from the Safavids and the Qajars*. New York: I.B. Tauris, 2013.
Mazumdar, S. *Sugar and Society in China: Peasants, Technology, and the World Market*. Cambridge: Harvard University Asia Center, 1998.
McCabe, I. *The Shah's Silk for Europe's Silver: The Eurasian Trade of the Julfa Armenians in Safavid Iran and India (1530–1750)*. Atlanta: Scholars Press, 1999.

Meersbergen, G. van. *Ethnography and Encounter: The Dutch and English in Seventeenth-Century South Asia*. Leiden: Brill, 2022.

Mintz, S. *Sweetness and Power: The Place of Sugar in Modern History*. London: Penguin Books, 1986.

Mintz, S. 'Introduction.' In *Sugarlandia Revisited: Sugar and Colonialism in Asia and the Americas, 1800 to 1940*, edited by U. Bosma, J. Giusti-Cordero, and G.R. Knight, 1–4. New York: Berghahn Books, 2007.

Moreland, W. *From Akbar to Aurangzeb: A Study in Indian Economic History*. London: Macmillan, 1923.

Morikawa, T. 'Perushia kyūtei no wain to shābetto [Wine and Sherbet at the Persian court].' In *Shoku to bunka: Jikū o koeta shokutaku kara [Food and Culture: Eating across Space and Time]*, edited by N. Hosoda, 65–96. Hokkaidō: Hokkaidōdaigaku shuppankai, 2015.

Nadri, G. 'Commercial World of Mancherji Khurshedji and the Dutch East India Company: A Study of Mutual Relationships.' *Modern Asian Studies* 41, no. 2 (2007): 315–42.

Nadri, G. 'The Maritime Merchants of Surat: A Long-Term Perspective.' *Journal of the Economic and Social History of the Orient* 50, no. 2–3 (2007): 235–58.

Nadri, G. 'The Dutch Intra-Asian Trade in Sugar in the Eighteenth Century.' *International Journal of Maritime History* 20, no. 1 (2008): 63–96.

Nadri, G. 'Exploring the Gulf of Kachh: Regional Economy and Trade in the Eighteenth Century.' *Journal of the Economic and Social History of the Orient*, no. 51 (2008): 460–86.

Nadri, G. *Eighteenth-Century Gujarat: The Dynamics of Its Political Economy, 1750–1800*. Leiden: Brill, 2009.

Neild-Basu, S. 'The Dubashes of Madras.' *Modern Asian Studies* 18, no. 1 (1984): 1–31.

Newman, A.J. *Safavid Iran: Rebirth of a Persian Empire*. London: I.B. Tauris, 2006.

Nierstrasz, C. *In the Shadow of the Company: The Dutch East India Company and Its Servants in the Period of Its Decline*. Leiden: Brill, 2012.

North-Coombes, A. *A History of Sugar Production in Mauritius*. Floréal: Mauritius Printing Specialists, 1993.

Oka, M. 'Nanbanbōeki no bunkateki haikei [A Cultural Background of the Nanban Trade].' In *Nanbanbōeki to kasutera [The Nanban Trade and Kasutera]*, 65–99. Nagasaki: Fukusaya, 2016.

Onley, J. *The Arabian Frontier of the British Raj: Merchants, Rulers, and the British in the Nineteenth-Century Gulf*. Oxford: Oxford University Press, 2007.

Onley, J. 'Indian Communities in the Persian Gulf, c. 1500–1947.' In *The Persian Gulf in Modern Times: People, Ports and History*, edited by L.G. Potter, 231–66. New York: Palgrave Macmillan, 2014.

Ota, A. *Changes of Regime and Social Dynamics in West Java: Society, State and Outer World of Banten 1750–1830*. Leiden: Brill, 2006.

Paris, R. *De 1600 à 1789. Le Levant*, vol. 5 of *Histoire du commerce de Marseille*. Paris: Librairie Plon, 1957.

Pearson, M. 'Brokers in Western Indian Port Cities Their Role in Serving Foreign Merchants.' *Modern Asian Studies* 22, no. 3 (1988): 455–72.

Pearson, M. 'Merchants and States.' In *The Political Economy of Merchant Empires*, edited by J. Tracy, 41–116. Cambridge: Cambridge University Press, 1991.

Pearson, M. 'India and the Indian Ocean in the Sixteenth Century.' In *India and Indian Ocean: 1500–1800*, edited by A. Das Gupta and M. Pearson, 71–93. Oxford: Oxford University Press, 1999 (first published in 1987).

Pearson, M. *The Indian Ocean*. Abingdon: Routledge, 2008 (first published in 2003).
Perlin, F. 'The Precolonial Indian State in History and Epistemology: A Reconstruction of Social Formation in the Western Deccan from the Fifteenth to the Early Nineteenth Century.' In *The Study of the State*, edited by H. Claessen and P. Skalnik, 275–302. The Hague: Mouton Publishers, 1981.
Perry, J. *Karim Khan Zand: A History of Iran, 1747–1779*. Chicago: University of Chicago Press, 1979.
Peterson, J.E. 'Britain and the Gulf: At the Periphery of Empire.' In *The Persian Gulf in History*, edited by L.G. Potter, 277–93. New York: Palgrave Macmillan, 2009.
Pomeranz, K. *The Great Divergence: China, Europe, and the Making of the Modern World Economy*. Oxford: Princeton University Press, 2009.
Potts, D.T. 'Kharg Island ii: History and Archeology.' *Encyclopædia Iranica*. Last modified 20 July 2004.
Prakash, O. *The Dutch East India Company and the Economy of Bengal, 1630–1720*. Delhi: Oxford University Press, 1988.
Prakash, O. *European Commercial Enterprise in Pre-Colonial India*, part 5 of *Indian States and the Transition to Colonialism*, vol. 2 of *The New Cambridge History of India*. Cambridge: Cambridge University Press, 1998.
Qaisar, A. 'The Role of Brokers in Medieval India.' *The Indian Historical Review* 1, no. 2 (1974): 220–46.
Qasimi, Sultan ibn Muhammad al-. *The Myth of Arab Piracy*. London: Croom Helm, 1986.
Qasimi, Sultan ibn Muhammad al-. *Power Struggles and Trade in the Gulf 1620–1820*. Forest Row: University of Exeter Press, 1999.
Ricks, T. 'Towards a Social and Economic History of Eighteenth-Century Iran.' *Iranian Studies* 6, no. 2 (1973): 110–26.
Ricks, T. 'Politics and Trade in Southern Iran and the Gulf, 1745–1765.' PhD diss., Indiana University, 1975.
Ricks, T. *Notables, Merchants, and Shaykhs of Southern Iran and Its Ports: Politics and Trade of the Persian Gulf Region, AD 1728–1789*. Piscataway: Gorgias Press, 2012.
Riello, G., and T. Roy, eds. *How India Clothed the World: The World of South Asian Textiles, 1500–1850*. Leiden: Brill, 2009.
Risso, P. *Oman & Muscat: An Early Modern History*. New York: St. Martin's Press, 1986.
Ruangsilp, B. *Dutch East India Company Merchants at the Court of Ayutthaya: Dutch Perceptions of the Thai Kingdom, c. 1604–1765*. Leiden: Brill, 2007.
Sato, T. *Sugar in the Social Life of Medieval Islam*. Leiden: Brill, 2015.
Savory, R. *Iran under the Safavids*. Cambridge: Cambridge University Press, 1980.
Savory, R. 'A.D. 600–1800.' In *The Persian Gulf States: A General Survey*, edited by A. Cottrell, 14–40. Baltimore: The Johns Hopkins University Press, 1980.
Schrikker, A. *Dutch and British Colonial Intervention in Sri Lanka, 1780–1815: Expansion and Reform*. Leiden: Brill, 2007.
Schwarts, S., ed. *Tropical Babylons: Sugar and the Making of the Atlantic World, 1450–1680*. Chapel Hill: The University of North Carolina Press, 2004.
Schwartz, G. 'Terms of Reception: Europeans and Persians and Each Other's Art.' In *Mediating Netherlandish Art and Material Culture in Asia*, edited by Th.D. Kaufmann and M. North, 25–65. Amsterdam: Amsterdam University Press, 2014.
Sheriff, A. *Slaves, Spices & Ivory in Zanzibar: Integration of an East African Commercial Empire into the World Economy, 1770–1873*. James Currey, 1987.
Shimada, R. *The Intra-Asian Trade in Japanese Copper by the Dutch East India Company during the Eighteenth Century*. Leiden: Brill, 2006.

Singh, A. *Fort Cochin in Kerala: The Social Condition of a Dutch Community in an Indian Milieu.* Leiden: Brill, 2010.
Slot, B. *The Arabs of the Gulf 1602–1784: An Alternative Approach to the Early History of the Arab Gulf States and the Arab People of the Gulf, Mainly Based on Sources of the Dutch East India Company.* Leidschendam, 1993.
Slot, B. 'At the Backdoor of the Levant: Anglo-Dutch Competition in the Persian Gulf, 1623–1766.' In *Friends and Rivals in the East: Studies in Anglo-Dutch Relations in the Levant from the Seventeenth to the Early Nineteenth Century,* edited by A. Hamilton, A. de Groot, and M. van de Boogert, 117–33. Leiden: Brill, 2000.
Smith, A.F. *Sugar: A Global History.* London: Reaktion Books, 2015.
Steensgaard, N. *The Asian Trade Revolution of the Seventeenth Century: The East India Companies and the Decline of the Caravan Trade.* Chicago: The University of Chicago Press, 1974.
Stols, E. 'The Expansion of the Sugar Market in Western Europe.' In *Tropical Babylons: Sugar and the Making of the Atlantic World, 1450–1680,* edited by S. Schwarts, 237–88. Chapel Hill: The University of North Carolina Press, 2004.
Sood, G. '"Correspondence is Equal to Half a Meeting": The Composition and Comprehension of Letters in Eighteenth-Century Islamic Eurasia.' *Journal of the Economic and Social History of the Orient* 50, no. 2–3 (2007): 172–214.
Sood, G. *India and the Islamic Heartlands: An Eighteenth-Century World of Circulation and Exchange.* Cambridge: Cambridge University Press, 2016.
Souza, G. 'Ballast Goods: Chinese Maritime Trade in Zinc and Sugar in the Seventeenth and Eighteenth Centuries.' In *Emporia, Commodities and Entrepreneurs in Asian Maritime Trade, c. 1400–1750,* edited by R. Ptak and D. Rothermund, 291–315. Stuttgart: Franz Steiner Verlag, 1991.
Souza, G. 'Hinterlands, Commodity Chains, and Circuits in Early Modern Asian History.' In *Hinterlands and Commodities: Place, Space and the Political Economic Development of Asia over the Long Eighteenth Century,* edited by T. Mizushima, G. Souza, and D. Flynn, 15–47. Leiden: Brill, 2013.
Subramanian, L. 'The Eighteenth-Century Social Order in Surat: A Reply and an Excursus on the Riots of 1788 and 1795.' *Modern Asian Studies* 25, no. 2 (1991): 321–65.
Subramanian, L. *Indigenous Capital and Imperial Expansion: Bombay, Surat, and the West Coast.* Delhi: Oxford University Press, 1996.
Subrahmanyam, S. *Three Ways to Be Alien: Travails & Encounters in the Early Modern World.* Waltham: Brandeis University Press, 2011.
Subrahmanyam, S., and C. Bayly. 'Portfolio Capitalists and the Political Economy of Early Modern India.' *The Indian Economic and Social History Review* 25, no. 4 (1988): 401–24.
Sugihara, K. *Ajiakanbōeki no keisei to kōzō [Patterns and Development of Intra-Asian Trade].* Kyoto: Mineruva shobō, 1996.
Sugihara, K. *Sekaishi no naka no Higashiajia no kiseki [The East Asian Miracle in Global History].* Aichi: Nagoyadaigaku shuppankai, 2020.
Topik, S., C. Marichal, and Z. Frank, eds. *From Silver to Cocaine: Latin American Commodity Chains and the Building of the World Economy, 1500–2000.* Durham: Duke University Press, 2006.
Trentmann, T., ed. *The Oxford Handbook of the History of Consumption.* Oxford: Oxford University Press, 2013.
Tucker, E.S. *Nadir Shah's Quest for Legitimacy in Post-Safavid Iran.* Gainesville: University Press of Florida, 2006.

Um, N. *Shipped but Not Sold: Material Culture and the Social Protocols of Trade during Yemen's Age of Coffee*. Honolulu: University of Hawai'i Press, 2017.
Viallé, C. '"To Capture Their Favor": On Gift-Giving by the VOC.' In *Mediating Netherlandish Art and Material Culture in Asia*, edited by Th.D. Kaufmann and M. North, 291–320. Amsterdam: Amsterdam University Press, 2014.
Vink, M. *Encounters on the Opposite Coast: The Dutch East India Company and the Nayaka State of Madurai in the Seventeenth Century*. Leiden: Brill, 2015.
Vries, J. de. 'The Industrial Revolution and the Industrious Revolution.' *The Journal of Economic History* 54, no. 2 (1994): 249–70.
Vries, J. de. *The Industrious Revolution: Consumer Behavior and the Household Economy, 1650 to the Present*. Cambridge: Cambridge University Press, 2008.
Walcher, W., and Habibollah Zanjani, 'Isfahan iii. Population.' *Encyclopædia Iranica*. Last modified 30 March 2012.
Wallerstein, E. *The Modern World-System*. 4 vols. Berkeley: University of California Press, 2011.
Wilkinson, J.C. *The Imamate Tradition of Oman*. Cambridge: Cambridge University Press, 1987.
Wilkinson, J.C. *Water and Tribal Settlement in South-East Arabia: A Study of the Aflāj of Oman*. Oxford: Clarendon Press, 1977.
Wilson, A. *The Persian Gulf: An Historical Sketch from the Earliest Times to the Beginning of the Twentieth Century*. Connecticut: Hyperion Press, 1928.
Xu, G. 'From the Atlantic to the Manchu: Taiwan Sugar and the Early Modern World, 1630s–1720s.' *Journal of World History* 33 no. 2 (2022): 265–99.
Xu, G. 'The "Perfect Map" of Widow Hiamtse: A Micro-Spatial History of Sugar Plantations in Early Modern Southeast Asia.' *International Review of Social History* 67, no. 1 (2022): 97–126.
Yao, K. *Satō no tōtta michi: kashi kara mita sekaishi [Sugar Road: World History Seen through Sweets]*. Fukuoka: Gen shobō, 2011.
Zachs, F. 'Ahmed Paşa.' *Encyclopaedia of Islam, THREE*.

APPENDICES

Appendix 1: Sugar prices at the Isfahan market, 1737–41
(mahmudis *per* man-i shahi)

Year	Javanese castor sugar	Javanese candy sugar	Bengali castor sugar called *caluppie*
April 1737	13¼	15½	
June 1737	13¼	15½	
July 1737	11¼	13½	
August 1737	11¼	13½	8½
October 1737	10¼	13½	8¼
December 1738	11	15	
June 1739	11	15	
12 August 1739	16½	18½	
18 August 1739	11½	12⅗	
March 1740	18	21	
April 1740	16½	20	
July 1740	16½	21	
June 1741	18½	25	
August 1741	17	27	
October 1741	17	27	
November 1741	17	27	

Sources: NL-HaNA, VOC2448, pp. 1576–86, 1589–92; VOC2476, pp. 1396–8; VOC2510, pp. 1472–7; VOC2511, pp. 1429–40; VOC2584, pp. 2444–9, 2453–7.

Appendix 2: Sales of sugar by the VOC at Bandar Abbas, 1701–56 (Dutch pounds and guilders)

Year	Castor sugar (pounds)	Invoice value (guilders)	Sale value (guilders)	Profit (%)	Candy sugar (pounds)	Invoice value (guilders)	Sale value (guilders)	Profit (%)	Total invoice value (guilders)	Total sale value (guilders)
1701–2	935,250	84,317	195,019	131	0		0			1,032,389
1702–3	1,303,181	99,484	323,080	224.7	165,047	24,912	49,562	98.9	24,912	995,036
1703–4	1,724,236	127,398	464,107	264.3	406,302	61,933	129,509	109	61,933	1,331,067
1704–5	1,871,135	139,018	397,616	186	336,737	50,602	107,335	112	50,602	1,222,708
1705–6	1,871,135	139,018	397,616	186	336,736	50,602	107,335	112	50,602	1,222,708
1706–7	1,562,469	141,570	298,213	110.6	67,435	11,378	21,495	89	11,378	1,362,191
1707–8	1,160,713	117,991	212,085	72	106,242	16,718	33,112	87	16,718	1,511,840
1708–9	1,297,434	124,048	241,241	94.5	225,794	38,692	70,372	81.9	38,692	1,294,171
1709–10	1,630,142	138,430	288,671	108.5	543,719	78,548	154,054	96	78,548	1,475,822
1710–11	1,076,561	80,291	190,641	137.4	382,536	54,659	113,804	108.2	54,659	980,354
1711–12	588,347	44,642	114,603	136.7	286,890	41,205	85,350	107	41,205	
1712–13	755,450	56,408	149,831	165.4	411,721	60,409	122,487	102.7	60,409	914,512
1713–14	640,095	640,095	131,486	172.5	179,807	25,076	52,259	106	25,076	806,696
1714–15	817,104	60,517	173,635	186	240,250	34,150	69,773	104	34,150	1,195,012
1715–16	1,575,808	117,307	351,602	198.2	50,351	7,091	16,049	126.2	7,091	1,149,675
1716–17	1,350,321	99,215	310,855	213	54,060	7,499	22,976	206.4	7,499	867,909
1717–18	1,283,047	94,227	304,456	223	288,980	41,032	120,770	193.9	41,032	938,580
1718–19	1,057,393	80,733	262,145	224.4	287,021	40,236	111,019	177.9	40,236	1,335,549
1719–20	1,157,799	85,057	266,535	213.4	313,653	45,109	99,977	121.6	45,109	1,259,000

Continued

Year	Castor sugar (pounds)	Invoice value (guilders)	Sale value (guilders)	Profit (%)	Candy sugar (pounds)	Invoice value (guilders)	Sale value (guilders)	Profit (%)	Total invoice value (guilders)	Total sale value (guilders)
1720-1	940,616	92,110	193,211	109	145,871	26,562	46,469	75	26,562	1,222,644
1721-2	866,662				148,934					
1722-3										
1723-4										
1724-5	57,065	5,285	11,116	110.3	5,973	1,077	2,539	136	1,077	54,430
1725-6	139,801	12,940	28,534	1206	61,937	10,471	26,333	151.5	10,471	122,426
1726-7	75,041	6,944	15,946	129.6	69,047	12,173	31,790	161	12,173	117,428
1727-8	522	51	91	77.2	29,954	4,858	10,650	180.5	4,858	159,879
1728-9	385,458	60,524	52,387	13.2	82,983	13,856	28,586	106.2	13,856	398,561
1729-30	0		0		0		0			153,461
1730-1										
1731-2	98,393	8,701	18,836	116.5	91,366	15,269	27,486	80	15,269	287,846
1732-3	161,914	14,995	35,425	136.2	33,431	5,320	11,429	114.9	5,320	263,535
1733-4	41,781	3,880	7,998	106	6,655	1,059	2,184	106.2	1,059	291,112
1734-5	331,686	29,630	63,498	114.5	120,696	19,205	39,610	106.2	19,205	432,261
1735-6										
1736-7	129,434	10,205	24,179	136	39,530	6,295	10,595	68.3	6,295	227,749
1737-8										
1738-9	189,713	16,238	35,281	117	69,146	11,002	18,531	68	11,002	175,838
1739-40	293,323	25,145	57,749		51,435	6,590	14,320		6,590	161,589

Year	Castor sugar (pounds)	Invoice value (guilders)	Sale value (guilders)	Profit (%)	Candy sugar (pounds)	Invoice value (guilders)	Sale value (guilders)	Profit (%)	Total invoice value (guilders)	Total sale value (guilders)
1740–1								90.2		196,642
1741–2	0		0		2,183	351	672	91	351	156,696
1742–3	0		0		0		0			75,481
1743–4	9,878	908	1,760	94	14,286	2,242	3,712	65.5	2,242	131,021
1744–5	140,311	12,311	25,483	107	45,182	6,562	11,593	82	6,562	138,119
1745–6	125,551	10,719	24,859	131	34,896	5,013	10,364	106.5	5,013	37,073
1746–7	9,879	932	2,557	131	654	88	307	106	88	59,506
1747–8	0		0		0		0			234,439
1748–9	134,244	12,517	29,483	135	41,857	5,601	16,631	198	5,601	169,691
1749–50	125,244	10,948	35,131	221	0		0			89,551
1750–1	0		0		0		0			
1751–2										
1752–3	113,427	9,271	26,514	186	6,002	943	3,217	241	943	135,098
1753–4	173,433	15,034	36,486	142	64,468	9,182	21,097	129	9,182	165,549
1754–5	170,327	15,034	34,065	113	25,671	3,584	7,701	114.7	3,584	192,766
1755–6	189,171	17,702	35,943	103	105,094	14,451	30,290	109.5	14,451	188,056
1756–7	549,700	48,227	87,846	82	176,425	24,430	43,899	80	24,430	208,667

Note: Data for 1722–3, 1723–4, 1730–1, 1735–6, 1737–8, 1740–1, and 1751–2 are not available. For the years 1704–5 and 1705–6, the VOC made one sales statement (NL-HaNA, VOC1747 1, pp. 373–4).

Source: G. Nadri, 'The Dutch Intra-Asian Trade in Sugar in the Eighteenth Century', *International Journal of Maritime History* 20, no. 1 (2008): 87–90.

Appendix 3: Sales of sugar by the VOC at Bushire, 1737–48 (Dutch pounds and guilders)

Year	Castor sugar (pounds)	Invoice value (guilders)	Sale value (guilders)	Profit (%)	Candy sugar (pounds)	Invoice value (guilders)	Sale value (guilders)	Profit (%)	Total invoice value (guilders)	Total sale value (guilders)
1737–8	18,896	1,504	4,412	193	32,768	5,215	11,438	119	11,577	32,456
1738–9	27,607	2,364	6,195	193	30,402	4,837	10,612	119	15,453	49,523
1739–40										
1740–1	11,683	1,001	2,767	176	775	123	270	119	20,719	46,878
1741–2	0				0				13,574	35,599
1742–3	0				0				15,321	49,933
1743–4										
1744–5										
1745–6	34,934	3,107	7,685	147	19,268	3,001	6,325	111	13,023	35,646
1746–7	26,722	2,382	5,890	147	4,000	626	1,320	111	4,548	12,780
1747–8	47,086	4,421	10,523	138	20,061	2,922	7,154	145	14,982	45,430
1748–9	19,301	1,826	4,606	152	17,547	2,387	6,948	191	11,701	28,252

Note: Data for 1739–40, 1743–4 and 1744–5 are not available.

Sources: NL-HaNA, VOC2476, pp. 1388–9 (1737–8); VOC2510, pp. 146–7 (1738–9); VOC2584, pp. 2474–5 (1740–1); VOC2610, pp. 64–5 (1741–2); VOC2610, pp. 72–3 (1 September 1742–28 February 1743); VOC2710, fols. 1419v–20r (1745–6); VOC2710, fols. 1422v–3r (1746–7); VOC2766, pp. 24–5 (1 February 1748–31 August 1748); VOC2766, pp. 26–7 (1 September 1748–28 February 1749).

Appendix 4: Sales of sugar by the VOC at Basra, 1723–51 (Dutch pounds and guilders)

Year	Castor sugar (pounds)	Invoice value (guilders)	Sale value (guilders)	Profit (%)	Candy sugar (pounds)	Invoice value (guilders)	Sale value (guilders)	Profit (%)	Total invoice value (guilders)	Total sale value (guilders)
1723-4	55,445	5,146	13,196	157	22,452	4,048	11,355	180	53,876	118,893
1724-5	0				0				19,204	41,510
1725-6	146,949	13,638	32,475	138	38,396	6,923	17,623	155	34,414	83,302
1726-7	55,740	6,038	12,096	100	27,987	5,505	13,325	142	53,212	108,402
1727-8	66,256	7,109	15,565	119	92,476	17,832	43,625	145	51,126	104,358
1728-9	33,570	2,465	4,258	72	0				22,428	36,431
1729-30	66,129	10,416	10,506	1	13,408	2,155	3,787	75	13,417	16,493
1730-1	70,250	11,066	10,497	-5	0				47,725	55,774
1731-2	0				0				25,611	27,282
1732-3										
1733-4	85,638	7,704	15,040	95	1,325	210	481	128	74,827	101,873
1734-5	0				12,500	1,989	4,542	128	36,765	46,542
1735-6	15,000	1,148	2,725	137	19,925	3,170	7,240	128	74,285	104,000
1736-7	112,625	8,625	19,136	122	0				110,752	168,733
1737-8	40,650	3,088	6,943	124	0				31,834	47,473
1738-9	174,577	14,329	24,590	71	0				41,719	83,217

Continued

Year	Castor sugar (pounds)	Invoice value (guilders)	Sale value (guilders)	Profit (%)	Candy sugar (pounds)	Invoice value (guilders)	Sale value (guilders)	Profit (%)	Total invoice value (guilders)	Total sale value (guilders)
1739–40	108,410	9,293	19,045	109	24,546	3,940	3,904	86	80,592	127,196
1740–1	0				0				45,137	54,514
1741–2	0				0				52,749	60,848
1742–3	0				0				38,322	82,110
1743–4	15,083	1,375	3,041	121	22,898	3,594	7,122	98	12,293	75,481
1744–5										
1745–6	87,834	8,286	17,707	113	17,973	2,718	5,590	105	43,654	103,775
1746–7	49,327	4,583	5,731	64	8,605	1,257	2,542	102	50,742	101,509
1747–8	271,004	23,689	52,447	121	106,855	14,572	30,691	110	209,504	406,134
1748–9	0				0				53,344	86,262
1749–50	191,304	15,922	46,074	121	74,738	10,245	25,385	110	108,065	250,556
1750–1	85,266	6,957	17,693	154	94,493	13,416	27,702	106	56,322	139,681
1751–2	58,114	5,121	11,695	128	82,088	12,043	23,280	93	164,826	275,820

Note: Data for 1732–3 and 1744–5 are not available.

Sources: Nadri, 'The Dutch Intra-Asian Trade,' 88–90 (1723–4, 1739–40, 1743–4); NL-HaNA, VOC2023, fol. 3352r (1724–5); VOC2042, fol. 3979v–80r (1725–6); VOC2042, fol. 3992 (1726–7); VOC2091, fols. 4927v–8r (1727–8); VOC2168, pp. 52–3 (1728–9); VOC2253, pp. 40–1 (1729–30); VOC2254, pp. 398–9 (1731–2); VOC2322 2, pp. 248–9 (1731–2); VOC2357, 1 pp. 986–7 (1733–4); VOC2416, pp. 128–9 (1734–5); VOC2416, pp. 274–5 (1735–6); VOC2448, pp. 130–1 (1736–7); VOC2476, pp. 1384–5 (1737–8); VOC2510, pp. 52–3 (1738–9); VOC2584, pp. 2473–4 (1 September 1740–28 February 1741); VOC2610, pp. 60–1 (1741–2); VOC2610, pp. 70–1 (31 August 1742–28 February 1743); VOC2710, fols. 1418v–19r (1745–6); VOC2710, fols. 1421v–2r (1746–7); VOC2766, pp. 20–1 (1747–8); VOC2766, pp. 22–3 (1748–9); VOC2787, pp. 12–13 (1 January 1750–31 August 1750); VOC2804, pp. 6–7 (1750–1); VOC2824, pp. 6–9 (1751–2).

Appendix 5: Sales of sugar by the VOC at Kharg, 1753–64 (Dutch pounds and guilders)

Year	Castor sugar (pounds)	Invoice value (guilders)	Sale value (guilders)	Profit (%)	Candy sugar (pounds)	Invoice value (guilders)	Sale value (guilders)	Profit (%)	Total invoice value (guilders)	Total sale value (guilders)
1753–4	12,869	1,137	3,024	165.8	13,646	1,870	4,442	137.5	18,752	44,065
1754–5										
1755–6										
1756–7										
1757–8										
1758–9										
1759–60	918,445	73,612	142,358	93	196,540	27,660	40,703	47	296,387	566,974
1760–1	771,000	67,669	127,215	88	615,027	91,330	132,001	44	249,660	501,881
1761–2	694,375	60,823	124,987	105	0	0	0		106,320	284,090
1762–3	1,035,507	90,868	192,829	113	45,171	7,520	11,563	52	132,903	358,438
1763–4	667,666	51,651	112,949	119	28,000	4,299	6,496	51	74,686	181,254
1764–5	243,380	18,892	38,940	106	95,717	15,358	22,206	44	70,630	176,370

Note: Data for 1754–5, 1755–6, 1756–7, 1757–8 and 1758–9 are not available.

Sources: Nadri, 'The Dutch Intra-Asian Trade,' 90 (1753–4); NL-HaNA, VOC3027, pp. 10–11 (1759–60); VOC3064, pp. 6–7 (1760–1); VOC3092, p. 8 (1761–2); VOC3156, pp. 6–7 (1762–3); VOC3156, pp. 18–19 (1763–4); VOC3184, pp. 38–9 (1764–5).

Appendix 6: Non-VOC sugar suppliers to Bandar Abbas, 1694–1715 (number)

Year	Sugar suppliers	Others
1694–5	2	2
1695–6	0	2
1696–7	2	10
1697–8	4	7
1698–9	5	16
1699–1700	8	9
1700–1	4	5
1701–2	2	9
1702–3	5	7
1703–4	3	8
1704–5	8	3
1705–6	6	3
1706–7	5	9
1707–8	3	8
1708–9	3	17
1709–10	4	7
1710–11	6	12
1711–12	8	5
1712–13	6	8
1713–14	5	7
1714–15	4	4
1715–16	1	4

Note: Sugar suppliers shown in the figure include those who conveyed cargoes of conserves.

Sources: NL-HaNA, VOC1582, pp. 179–81; VOC9054, pp. 188–90 (28 June 1695–31 October 1695); VOC1598 1, pp. 71–3 (1 November 1696–31 March 1697); VOC1598 1, pp. 90–2 (1 April 1697–8 June 1697); VOC1598 2, pp. 26–8 (8 June 1697–31 August 1697); VOC1611 1, p. 49 (1 September 1697–8 January 1698); VOC1611 1, pp. 106–7 (1 February 1698–26 March 1698); VOC1611 2, pp. 69–72 (5 April 1698–28 July 1698); VOC1626 1, pp. 103–8 (2 September 1698–22 March 1699); VOC1626 2, pp. 30–4 (26 March 1699–1 July 1699); VOC1639, pp. 23–7 (15 September 1699–31 May 1700); VOC1650, pp. 29–30; VOC8367, pp. 51–3 (10 June 1700–11 December 1700); VOC1652, fols. 1013r–v (1 January 1703–23 July 1703); VOC1667, pp. 248–52 (28 February 1701–27 January 1702); VOC1667, pp. 484–6 (27 January 1702–30 April 1702); VOC1679, pp. 136–8 (1 May 1702–30 September 1702); VOC1679, pp. 249–50 (19 November 1702–29 March 1703); VOC1685, p. 2572 (20 May 1704–31 July 1705); VOC1694, pp. 109–11 (28 March 1703–20 August 1703); VOC1694, pp. 346–8 (14 December 1703–24 May 1704); VOC1714 1, pp. 343–4 (31 May 1704–31 March 1705); VOC1714 1, pp. 382–4 (1 April 1705–18 July 1705); VOC1732, pp. 590–3 (19 July 1705–15 April 1706); VOC1747 1, pp. 375–7 (13 April 1706–30 November 1706); VOC1763, pp. 342–8 (30 November 1706–21 December 1707); VOC1768, fols. 1884r–v (1 November 1708–23 December 1709); VOC1779, pp. 318–27 (21 December 1707–12 January 1709); VOC1785, fols. 421r–v (7 June 1710–17 July 1711); VOC1798 1, pp. 154–60 (15 January 1709–9 March 1710); VOC1798 1, pp. 464–6 (9 March 1710–31 May 1710); VOC1802, fols. 2114r–15v (7 June 1710–17 July 1711); VOC1802, fols. 2204r–5v (9 March 1712–22 October 1712); VOC1812, pp. 245–9 (18 May 1710–11 December 1710); VOC1829, pp. 178–91; VOC8081, pp. 94–103 (11 December 1710–23 May 1712); VOC1834, fols. 2669r–71r (22 October 1712–23 April 1714); VOC1843 1, pp. 278–81 (18 May 1712–15 March 1713); VOC1843 2, pp. 197–201 (10 March 1713–23 June 1713); VOC1856, pp. 1146–53 (22 March 1713–23 May 1714); VOC1870, p. 335 (15 June 1714–25 September 1714); VOC1870, pp. 650–2 (30 September 1714–13 April 1715); VOC1886, pp. 401–4 (13 April 1715–15 February 1716).

Appendix 7: Registrations of arrivals at Bandar Abbas, 1694–1715 (number)

Nationality	English	EIC	English private	Muslim	Local	Portuguese	Arab	Danish	Danish company	French	French company	Armenian	Unknown
Sugar suppliers	65	0	4	14	1	0	0	5	1	2	0	1	1
Others	58	8	1	62	8	7	6	0	0	2	1	0	9

Appendix 8: Origins of English arrivals at Bandar Abbas, 1694–1715 (number)

Origin	Europe/England	Basra	Kong	Surat	Bombay	Calicut	Madras	Bengal	Batavia	China	Accident	Unknown
Sugar suppliers	0	1	0	8	5	1	2	46	1	5	0	0
Others	2	5	4	17	25	2	1	8	0	0	1	2

Appendix 9: Origins of Muslim arrivals at Bandar Abbas, 1694–1715 (number)

Origin	Mocha	Basra	Kong	Kishm Island	Ghogha	Patan	Bharuch	Surat	Goa	Bombay	Mangalore	Bengal	Unknown
Sugar suppliers	0	0	0	0	0	0	0	12	0	0	0	2	0
Others	2	1	14	2	1	2	4	27	2	1	2	1	3

Sources: See Appendix 6.

Appendix 10: Family tree of the Rauwels

```
                                    Rauwel
                                      ┆
        ┌─────────────────────────────┼─────────────────────────────┐
     Toquidas                      Coridas                       Bonidas
   d. June 1712                 d. January 1702               d. October 1712
        │                            │                             │
        │                        Kissendas              ┌──────────┼──────────┐
        │                     d. February 1707       Darmdas   Bouwendas  Bilbilderdas
        │                                          d. April 1721 d. March 1719
        │
   ┌────┴────┬──────────┬──────────┬──────────┬──────────┬──────────┐
Ottumsjent Issourdas Koemertjent Abtjent Wisschermerdas Tackourdas
 d. 1737   d. July 1736  d. c. 1753          d. 1745
   │
  Nata
d. April 1713
```

Appendix 11: Family tree of the Sahids

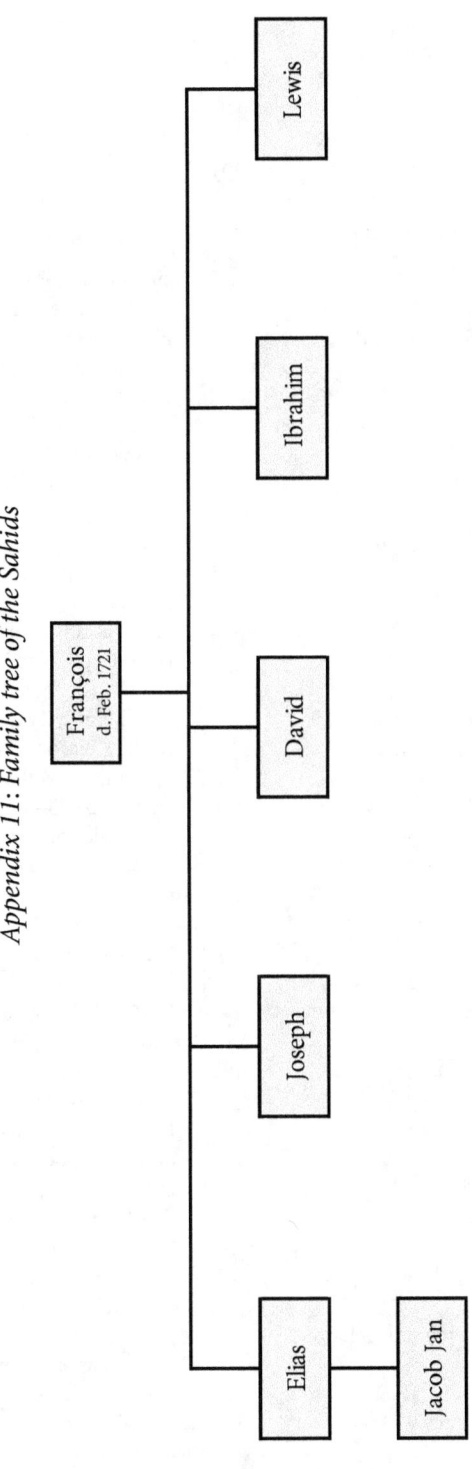

INDEX

Bold page numbers indicate tables, *italic* numbers indicate figures.

'Abbas I, reign of 18
'Abbas II, reign of 19
Abdullah, T. 4, 41, 91, 94, 105, 108, 138
'Adil Shah 36
Afghan invasion of Iran, impact of 35–6, 77–9
agents. *see* brokers, local
Agha 'Abdi 142
Agha Muhammad Khan Qajar 36
agricultural land 20–1
Ahmad b. Sa'id 43, 46, 143
Ahmad Pasha 41
'Ali Agha 50
Allen, C. 143
Arab Muslims, history of sugar and 9–11
  see also Muslim merchants
Armenians 101
  Basra factories 41
  bullion exports by 75–6
  interpreters, merchants as 13–14
  Julfa, as merchants in Iran 12, 143
  on Kharg Island 142–3
  merchants 138
  Nadir Shah's oppression of 141
  relocation to Julfa 18
  VOC wool collectors 131
Aslanian, S. 141, 150
Auwanees 131, 147

Baghdad 49–50
Bahrain as free port 5
Baluchi tribesmen 19
Bandar Abbas 4, 11
  1740s 85
  1750s–60s 87–8
  authorities and merchants, relations between 13
  bullion 85
  business intermediaries 13
  copper trade 85
  customs administration 19
  decline of, reasons for 86–7
  EIC brokers at 133–5
  English arrivals **219**
  establishment 18
  ethnic groups in 19
  Kirman and Yazd, route to from 38–9
  as major node of trans-regional trade 19
  non-VOC suppliers to **218**
  Rauwel family as local merchants 112–15
  registrations of arrivals **219**
  rival suppliers to VOC 69–76, *72*, *73*, *74*
  Sahid family 141
  trading season 124
  uprising by Muhammad Taqi Khan Shirazi 85–6
  VOC sales of sugar at 53–7, *54*, *55*, *56*, *60*, *61*, *62*, *63*, **211–13**
Bandar Deylam 102, 103
Bandar Ganaveh 103
Bandar Kong 19, 76
Bandar Rig 103
  VOC sales of sugar at 58, *60*, *62*, *63*
Bangsalties 86, 113
Banians
  Bangsalties 113
  Basra connections 138–40
  bullion exports by 75–6
  as business intermediaries 13
  EIC brokers at Bandar Abbas 133–5
  Hindu 112–13
  Kiemtsjant family 115–16
  Muscat intermediaries 143–6
  painting by Cornelis de Bruyn *xv*
  use and application of term 112–13
Barendse, R. 5, 39, 70, 93
Barka 143–4
barter 96

Basidu 77–8
Basra 4
  1720s 91–3
  1730s 94–5
  1740s onwards 97–9
  Banian connections 138–40
  bullion trade in 78–9, 93, 97–8
  cash payment, VOC's insistence on 96
  decline of 108
  departure of VOC, shipping to after 107–8
  efficiency of trade at, concerns over 98–9
  English traders 92, 94, 96, 97
  freight to Surat, VOC and 98
  French traders 92–3, 94, 96, 97
  interior markets 98
  Kharg, sugar shipments from 103
  Madras and Surat, imports from 94–5
  Moeltjent as broker 139–40, 147
  non-VOC shipping and trade at 92–9
  political turmoil 97
  purchasers of sugar at 95
  re-export of goods from 98–9
  re-structuring of sugar market 41–2
  rival suppliers to VOC 76–7
  Sahid family 141
  siege and occupation 1775–8 43, 108
  sugar trade through 23–4
  tariff disparity with Muscat 181 n.126
  urban life 49
  VOC sales of sugar at 58–62, *59, 60, 61, 62, 63*, **215–16**
Bengali sugar 25–7, 28
Berg, M. 7
brokers, local
  Armenians on Kharg Island 142–3
  Auwanees family 131
  Banian intermediaries at Muscat 143–6
  bullion, trading sugar for 124–7
  changing role of Isfahan brokers 137–8
  competitive relationship with VOC 111
  decline of network 131–3
  families of, VOC and 119–21
  flexibility of EIC's brokership 133–6
  Hindu Banians 112–13
  as individual merchants 116–18
  as informants to the VOC 124
  Kiemtsjant family 115–17, 137
  Nagha Natta 141–2

  overseas trade, commitment to 117–18
  as port officials 122–3
  Rauwel family 112–15, 116, 117, 129–31, 132–3, 136
  reframing of brokership 136–7
  trade skills 123–7
  variety of used by VOC 111
  as vital for VOC 150
Bruce, Peter Henry 48
Bruyn, Cornelis de *xv*, 23
bullion 108, 144–5
  Afghan invasion of Iran, impact of 78–9, 137
  Bandar Abbas 85
  Basra trade 93, 97–8
  Bushire trade 100
  Kiemtsjant family and exports of 117
  rival suppliers to VOC 75–6, 82–3
  sugar traded for 11–12
  as supporting demand for sugar 150
  trading sugar for, brokers and 124–7
bureaucratic elites, relations with merchants 13
Buschman, Wilhelm Johannes 104, 106, 107
Bushire 4, 106
  bullion trade 100
  copper trade 100
  Madhkur family 99
  Nagha Natta as broker 141–2
  re-structuring of sugar market 42–3
  secondary importance of 99–100
  stagnation of 108
  trade in 99
  uncertainties of 1740s 101
  VOC sales of sugar at 57–8, *58, 60, 62, 63*, **214**
business intermediaries at Bandar Abbas 13
  see also brokers, local
Busskens, David 136–7

caravan trade 5
Caspian coast and provinces
  consumption of sugar and 48
  re-structuring of sugar market 44–5
Chardin, Jean 1, 29
Chaudhuri, K.N. 2, 3, 17, 33, 149
China
  Chinese sugar 28–9
  copper, sugar traded for 11

demand for sugar 7–9
  sugar industry 8
  trans-regional flow of sugar from 8
circulation society 114
class, lower, sugar consumption by 25
Clawson, P. 82
colonialism, European, rise of 151
commercial production of sugar in China 8
commodity chains 8
competition, declining prices and 29
competitors of VOC. *see* rival suppliers to VOC
conserves 21–2, 29, 30, 50–1
consumption of sugar
  Bushire 42–3
  Caspian coast 48
  China and Japan 7–9
  domestic servants 24
  England and Europe 6–7
  ethnic groups 24
  European courts 20
  festivals 30
  gift-giving of sugar 30–1, 46
  Gujarat 39–40
  hospitality 47, 48, 50
  Iranian context 17–25
  Iraq 41–2
  Isfahan 36–8
  Kirman 47
  maximization of gains from 150
  post-Safavid period 149–50
  Qajar court 38
  Safavid court 22–3
  servants of rulers 46–7
  Shiraz 43–4, 47–8
  Sind 40
  social lives and 49
  special occasions 47–8
  sugar banquets 21–2
  Surat 39–40
  Tehran 38
  tributes of sugar 30–1
  urban areas 47
  war and 46–51
  women 24
copper 51, 108
  Bandar Abbas 85
  Basra trade 93, 96–7
  Bushire trade 100

English traders 83
  rival suppliers to VOC 82–3
  sugar traded for 11
  as supporting demand for sugar 150
Cowan, Robert 96
credit 81–2, 96, 125
cultivation of sugarcane, origin of 7–8
Cunaeus, Joan 31
Curzon, George Nathaniel 149

Dale, S. 13, 112
Daniels, C. 8
Danish traders 151
Das Gupta, A. 4, 16, 66
Davies, T. 96
Della Valle, Pietro 22, 30–1
demand for sugar
  China and Japan 7–9
  England and Europe 6–7
  see also consumption of sugar
development of sugar markets
  China and Japan 7–9
  England 6–7
  Europe 6–7
  see also consumption of sugar
diet, Iranian 21, 30, 33, 48
diplomatic practices, silk/sugar trade and 32–3
domestic servants, consumption of sugar and 24, 46–7
Du Mans, Raphaël 29
Durrani dynasty 36
Dutch East India Company (*Verenigde Oostindische Compagnie* (VOC))
  Afghan invasion of Iran, impact of 78
  Afghan siege of Isfahan 108
  Bandar Abbas, establishment of 18
  Bandar Abbas, sales of sugar at 54, 54–7, 55, 56, 60, 61, 62, 63
  Bandar Rig, sales of sugar at 58, 60, 62, 63
  Banian connections to Basra 138–40
  bankruptcy of Rauwel family 130–1
  Basra, sales of sugar at 58–62, 59, 60, 61, 62, 63, **215–16**
  Bengali sugar imports 25–6
  bullion, sugar traded for 11–12
  Bushire, sales of sugar at 57–8, 58, **214**
  cash payment, insistance on 96

commercial disputes, VOC protection in 120–1
competition, declining prices and 29
competition between merchants for trade with 125–6
conflicts between ruling elites and 104–7
departure of, sugar shipping and trading after 107–10
diplomatic practices, silk/sugar trade and 32–3
downfall of 5–6
families of brokers and 119–21
government interference, VOC protection from 120
Isfahan, sales of sugar at 57
Kharg Island 41, 63, 101–7, **217**
local merchants, relations with 12
Malabar market 65–6
merchant/state relations and 122–3
Muscat, sales of sugar at 63–5
Muscat trading station 24
Muslim merchants 124–5
Nagha Natta 141–2
post-Safavid period 5–6
re-entry to market 41
royal favours secured by VOC 121
Sind, sales of sugar at 64
sources of information from 14–15
staffing 53–4
varieties of sugar imported 25–9
see also brokers, local; rival suppliers to VOC

East India Company (EIC)
after Safavids decline 3
Bandar Abbas, establishment of 18
at Basra 96
English private traders and 70
flexibility of brokership 133–6
Iran commerce, downturn in 80
local merchants, relations with 12
Muscat, imports to 46
re-entry to market 41
resilience of 79–80
as rival to VOC 71, 73
on Sind 40
woollen manufacturing 106
economy, sugar trade's influence on 21

Elton, John 48
England, development of sugar market in 6–7
English shipping/private traders
at Basra 92, 94, 96, 97
Chinese sugar exports to India 94
conflicts between ruling elites and 106–7
copper 83
flooding of market by 104
Iran commerce, downturn in 80
resilience of 79–80
as rival suppliers to VOC 73–4, 85
as suppliers 6
as VOC rivals 69–70
see also East India Company (EIC)
ethnic groups, sugar consumption and 24, 33
Eurasia, early modern land commerce 5
Europe, development of sugar market in 6–7
European colonialism, rise of 151
European courts, consumption of sugar at 20
Eversfield, Samuel 49

family firms of brokers/merchants
commercial disputes, VOC protection in 120–1
government interference, VOC protection from 120
Kiemtsjant family 115–17, 119, 137
Madhkur family 43, 99
Rauwel family 112–15, 116, 117, 119, 121, 129–31, 132–3, 136, *221*
risk management by VOC 119
royal favours secured for by VOC 121
Sahid family 140–1, *221*
salaries/commissions from VOC 119–20
VOC and 119–21
Fattah, H. 5
Ferrières-Sauveboeuf, L.-F. de 37, 49
festivals, consumption of sugar at 30
Floor, W. 3, 6, 11, 12, 13, 14, 26, 35, 65, 78, 82, 84, 104, 105, 112–13, 122
Forster, George 45
Francklin, William 43–4, 47
free ports 5

French shipping and traders
   at Basra 92–3, 94, 96, 97
   cane sugar plantations 151
   flooding of market by 104
   imports to the Levant **42**
   as rival suppliers to VOC 81, 85
fruit
   abundance of 21–2
   diet centred on 21, 30
Fryer, John 21, 23, 30, 31

Garmsir (hot country) 21
*Ghulam*s (royal slaves) 18
gift-giving of sugar 30–1, 46
gluttony as concern 24–5
Gmelin, Samuel Gottlieb 45
gold 51, 54, 78–9, 82, 85, 137
   sugar traded for 11–12
   see also bullion
Gommans, J. 5
Good, P. 14, 84, 135
government interference, VOC protection from 120
governors of ports and provinces, rewards offered by sugar 31
Griffiths, Julius 41, 138
Grummon, S. 4, 105
Gujarat 39–40

Hakima, A. 3–4
Haneda, M. 13–14
Hanway, Jonas 24, 46–7, 48
harems, royal 18
Hercules, Edward 107
Herzig, E. 12
al-Hilla 49
Hindu Banians 112–13
Hoogkamer, Jacob 32
Hoseini, A. 2, 29–30
hospitality, consumption of sugar and 47, 48, 50

Imam Quli Khan 18, 19, 30, 41
India
   business intermediaries, Indians as 13
   merchants in Safavid Iran 12
   merchant/state relationship 5
   as supplier 6
Indian Ocean maps *xiv*, *xvi*

industrious revolution 7
interpreters 131
   Armenian merchants as 13–14
   skills of 123
Iran
   Chardin's visit to 1
   as major sugar importer during Safavid period 2
   reasons for high demand for sugar 2
   Western supplies of sugar in nineteenth century 2–3
   see also Safavid period in Iran; individual ports
Iraq
   consumption of sugar 41–2, 49–50
   as trading site 40–1
Isfahan
   Afghan conquest of and power struggle following 35–6
   Afghan siege 108
   bullion exports 127
   as distribution centre 23
   Kiemtsjant family as local brokers 115–16
   population size 24
   price of sugar 37, **38**
   prices of sugar at market **210**
   sugar consumption in 36–8
   VOC sales of sugar at 57
Islamic civilization, history of sugar and 9–11
   see also Muslim merchants
Isma'il's reign 17
Ives, Edward 42, 50

Jacobs, E. 66
Japan
   demand for sugar 7–9
   sweet culture in northern Kyushu 8–9
Java
   Dutch industrial production in 9
   Javanese sugar imports to Iran in seventeenth century 5–6, 26–8
Jewish merchants 138

Kaempfer, Engelbert 23, 25
Karim Khan Zand 36, 43, 108
Kazemi, R. 51
Kern, H. 112

Ketelaar, Joan Josua 31, 114, 117, 120
Kharg Island
    Armenians on 142–3
    destruction of factory 66
    VOC factory 101–7
    VOC sales of sugar at 63–4, 65, *65*, 66, **217**
Khurasan 39, 40
Kiemtsjant family 115–17, 119, 137
king's merchants, role expected of 31
Kirman 79
    1740s–60s 84–5
    consumption of sugar 47
    EIC brokers at 135
    Muscat-Minab trade 89
    rival suppliers to VOC 83–4
    route to from Bandar Abbas 38–9
    wool trade 79
Klein, R. 13, 25, 28
Kniphausen, Tido von 98, 99, 101–2
Kong. *see* Bandar Kong
Kuwait as free port 5

Lispensier, Bartholomeus 78
local officials, rewards offered by sugar 31
Lockhart, L. 19–20

Madhkur family 43, 99
Madhkurs 4
Malabar market 65–6
Malcolm, John 109
Mamluk rulers 4, 41
Manila sugar 28
maps
    Indian Ocean *xiv*, *xvi*
    Persian Gulf *xvii*
Markovits, C. 114, 150
Matthee, R. 2, 13, 20, 82, 112, 122, 124, 149
May, William 80, 99
medicine, sugar and 29
merchants
    king's merchants, role expected of 31
    see also local merchants
military elites, relations with merchants 13
Minab 39
    Muscat-Minab trade 88–9
Minorsky, V. 19–20

Mintz, S. 1, 6, 7, 11, 20
Mir Muhanna 105, 106
Mir Nasir 102
Mocha
    Kharg, sugar shipments from 103–4
    rival suppliers to VOC 77, 78
modernity, sugar and 6–11
Moeltjent 139–40, 147
Morikawa, T. 2
Mosul 49
Muhammad Muhsin 2
Multani merchants 13, 86, 112–13
Muscat 5
    Banian intermediaries at 143–6
    departure of VOC, shipping to after 108–9
    Dutch private sectors 88
    Muscat-Minab trade 88–9
    re-structuring of sugar market 45–6
    rival suppliers to VOC 76, 78
    sugar 26
    sugar trade through 24
    tariff disparity with Basra 181 n.126
Muslim merchants 124–5, 138, 143–6
Muslim ships as rival suppliers to VOC 74, 74–5
Muslim sugar industry, history of sugar and 9–11

Nadir Shah 30, 36, 39, 41, 43, 46, 49, 84, 87, 97, 98, 99, 105, 131–2, 133, 137, 141, 142, 143
Nadri, G. 40, 53, 125, 136
Nagha Natta 141–2
Newman, A.J. 20
Niebuhr, Carsten 41, 49

Olearius, Adam 22
Olivier, Guillaume-Antoine 38, 42, 48, 49, 93
Oman, civil war in 78
Omani merchants as suppliers 6
Omani sugar 26
Onley, J. 13, 113
Otter, Jean 50–1
overland trade routes to Afghanistan 5

Parsons, Abraham 49
Pearson, M. 122

Perkins, Justin 38
Persian Gulf map *xvii*
political elite/merchant relations 13
Pomeranz, K. 8, 150
port officials, local merchants/brokers as 122–3
Portuguese traders, Chinese sugar exports to India 94
precious metals
    sugar traded for 11–12
    see also bullion
public baths (*hammam*s) 30

Qaisar, A. 13, 112
Qajar court's sugar consumption 38

Rauwel family 116, 117, 119, 121
    bankruptcy 129–31
    as brokers 112–15
    decline of local networks 132–3
    family tree *221*
    release from debt 136
recipes for using sugar 23
religious groups, sugar consumption and 33
re-structuring of sugar market
    Basra 41–2
    Bushire 42–3
    Caspian provinces 44–5
    French imports **42**
    Gujarat 39–40
    Iraq 40–1
    Isfahan 36–8
    Muscat 45–6
    Shiraz 43–4
    Sind 40
    Surat 39–40
    Tehran 38
Ricks, T. 4, 35, 84, 98, 104, 105
Risso, P. 5
rival suppliers to VOC
    1750s–60s 87–9
    Afghan conquest of Iran, impact of 77–9
    Basidu 77–8
    Basra 76–7, 92–9
    bullion 75–6, 82–3
    Bushire 99–101
    change in patterns of competition in 1730s 80–4
    continuing trade after VOC departure 107–10
    copper 82–3
    credit 81–2
    departing ships, cargo carried by 75
    Dutch private sectors 88
    English shipping/private traders 69–70, 71, *72*, *73*, 73–4, 77, 85
    flexibility of the Gulf market 76–7
    French shipping and trade 81, 85
    identities of ship owners 75
    Kirman market 83–4
    Kong 76
    late Safavid period 69–76, *72*, *73*, *74*
    measures taken by VOC 81–4
    Mocha 77, 78
    Muscat 76, 78
    Muscat-Minab trade 88–9
    Muslim ships *74*, 74–5
    price adjustments by VOC 81
    records at VOC 70–1
    relocation in 1740s 84–7
    total sugar import 71
rulers and merchants, relations with 12–13
    see also local merchants
Russia 45

Safavid period in Iran
    bullion and copper, sugar traded for 11–12
    consumption of sugar after 51
    court's consumption of sugar 22–3, 31, 32–3
    fall of the Safavids 35, 149–50
    instability at end of 3
    Isma'il's reign 17
    major sugar imports during 2
    paintings of Banian men *xv*
    reasons for high demand for sugar 2
    Safavids' origin 17
    Safi's reign 19
    Sulayman's reign 19
    Tahmasb's reign 17–18
    tensions with Ya'rubi Imamate/Baluchi tribesmen 19

Western supplies of sugar in
    nineteenth century 2–3
  see also Sultan Husayn
Safi's reign 19
Sahid family
  family tree *221*
  VOC employment of 140–1
Sato, T. 9, 10–11
scholarship on sugar history
  demand for sugar 6–11
  eighteenth century 3–5
  fall of the Safavids 35
  Marxist 2
  narrow focus of majority 1
  reasons for high demand for sugar 2
Schoonderwoerd, Jacob van 46, 63–4, 99, 136, 137, 144
servants of rulers as consumers of sugar 46–7
Shah Quli Khan Zangana 33
sherbet 2, 25, 26, 29–30, 50–1
Shiraz
  consumption of sugar 47–8
  re-structuring of sugar market 43–4
Shushtar 98
silk trade
  diplomatic practices 32–3
  exports 18, 21
  Safavid involvement in 13
silver 11–12, 51, 54, 78–9, 82, 85, 137
  see also bullion
Sind 40, 144–6
Smidt, Jan 21–2, 31
social lives, consumption of sugar and 49
Sood, G. 51
sources of information
  anecdotal descriptions 15, 17
  multi-layered interactions between countries 15
  VOC as 14–15
Souza, G. 8, 94
special occasions, consumption of sugar at 47–8
Spilman, James 37
state/merchant relations 12–13, 122–3
  see also local merchants
Steensgaard, N. 12, 111, 118
Stols, E. 7

sugar banquets 21–2, 27, 30, 31
sugarcane cultivation, origin of 7–8
sugar consumption. *see* consumption of sugar
sugar trade, diplomatic practices and 32–3
Sugihara, K. 9
Sulayman Pasha 41, 97
Sulayman's reign 19
Sultan Husayn 117
  Bandar Abbas and Kong 19
  degeneration of the state and 2, 19–20
  diplomatic practices, silk/sugar trade and 32–3
  king's merchants, role expected of 31
  *mahmudi*s (silver coin), use of for trade 125
suppliers of sugar to Iran
  other than VOC 6
  see also Dutch East India Company; East India Company; rival suppliers to VOC
Surat 39–40, 74, 118

Tahmasb Quli Khan 30, 81, 83
  see also Nadir Shah
Tahmasb's reign 17–18, 35–6
Taiwan 9, 26
Tehran, sugar consumption in 38
Thévenot, Jean de 30
Timur Shah 36
trade imbalance with Indian subcontinent 21
transcontinental routes, Persian Gulf sea-lanes and 5
transliteration xi
tributes of sugar 30–1, 46

varieties of sugar
  Bengali sugar 25–7, 28
  Chinese sugar 28–9
  Manila sugar 28
  Omani sugar 26
  sugar market and 25–6
  Taiwanese sugar 26
  taste, consumption and 33

trade in 25–9
VOC. *see* Dutch East India Company
Vries, J. de 7, 20

Wallerstein, E. 7
war, consumption of sugar and 46–51
Waring, Scott 44
Waters, Thomas 79
western supplies of sugar in nineteenth
    century 2–3
Wilmson, Georg 24
women, consumption of sugar and 24

wool 79, 106

Xu, G. 8

Yao, K. 8
Yazd
    consumption of sugar 47
    route to from Bandar Abbas
        38–9
Ya'rubi Imamate 19, 24

al-Zubara as free port 5

www.ingramcontent.com/pod-product-compliance
Lightning Source LLC
Chambersburg PA
CBHW071826300426
44116CB00009B/1454